The monastic life has always been a central part of the Christian experience, and a unique experiment in community life. Yet despite the desire of those who entered the religious life to turn their backs on the world, monastic houses remained very much a part of it. This book explores the development of monasticism in Britain from the last half-century of Anglo-Saxon England to the year 1300. It investigates how the monastic order was affected by the Norman settlement in the years after 1066, traces the impact on Britain of new European interpretations of monasticism, and details Britain's response to the challenge of providing for the needs of religious women. It also examines the constant tensions between the monastic ideal and the demands made on religious communities by the world, by their founders and patrons, by kings, and by the secular church, and explores the vital role of the religious orders in the economy. This is the first general book on monastic history to cover England, Wales and Scotland, and the first general textbook to explore the interdependence of religious communities and the wider secular world.

Cambridge Medieval Textbooks

MONASTIC AND RELIGIOUS ORDERS IN BRITAIN 1000–1300

Cambridge Medieval Textbooks

This is a series of specially commissioned textbooks for teachers and students, designed to complement the monograph series Cambridge Studies in Medieval Life and Thought by providing introductions to a range of topics in medieval history. This series combines both chronological and thematic approaches, and will deal with British and European topics. All volumes in the series will be published in hard covers and in paperback.

For a list of titles in the series, see end of book.

MONASTIC AND RELIGIOUS ORDERS IN BRITAIN 1000–1300

JANET BURTON

St David's University College,
Lampeter

CAMBRIDGE
UNIVERSITY PRESS

Published by the Press Syndicate of the University of Cambridge
The Pitt Building, Trumpington Street, Cambridge CB2 IRP
40 West 20th Street, New York, NY 10011–4211, USA
10 Stamford Road, Oakleigh, Melbourne 3166, Australia

First published 1994

Printed in Great Britain at the University Press, Cambridge

A catalogue record for this book is available from the British Library

Library of Congress cataloguing in publication data
Burton, Janet E.
Monastic and religious orders in Britain 1000–1300 / Janet E. Burton
p.   cm. – (Cambridge medieval textbooks)
Includes bibliographical references.
ISBN 0 521 37441 3. – ISBN 0 521 37797 8 (pbk.)
1. Monasticism and religious orders – Great Britain – History –
Middle Ages, 600–1500. 2. Great Britain – Church history –
Medieval period, 1066–1485. I. Title. II. Series.
BX2592.B86 1994
271'.00941'09021–dc20   93–3469   CIP

ISBN 0 521 37441 3 hardback
ISBN 0 521 37797 8 paperback

WD

CONTENTS

ILLUSTRATIONS

FIGURES

MAPS

PREFACE

From the beginnings of the Christian era, men and women have always sought the perfect way to serve their God in obedience to the commandments laid down by Christ himself. Their efforts have led to many forms of religious life and service, both within the world as layfolk or as churchmen, and withdrawn from it, as members of religious communities devoted in different ways to the service of God. The word 'monk' itself derives from the Greek *monos*, meaning one, alone, and has always described those who sought the solitary life, as hermits in the desert, in the European countryside, or enclosed in cells adjoining the walls of parish churches and elsewhere. But the term 'monasticism' as we most frequently use it refers – somewhat paradoxically – to religious life within communities. As such, monasticism has been, and continues to be, a central part of the Christian experience, a unique experiment in community life.

This book explores the ways in which men and women's ideals of how best they might achieve this goal of perfect communal life altered and developed over a period of roughly three hundred years. The scope, geographically, is England, Wales and Scotland. However, the approach taken in the first two chapters of this work is chronological, in that they survey the state of monastic life in the sixty years before the Norman Conquest of England, and analyse how religious institutions developed in the forty years or so thereafter. Some of these changes were the direct results of conquest and the implantation of a foreign ruling élite in England, including the more gradual Norman infiltration north into Scotland and west into Wales; some were part of a more complex

European development. The next four chapters are essentially about experiment, an account of how, in the eleventh and twelfth centuries, Britain became receptive to new forms of monastic life which grew out of the debate about the nature of primitive monasticism; out of dissatisfaction with contemporary practice; out of pressure, notably from women, for more appropriate modifications of existing monastic rules; and out of the new fervour for poverty and evangelism inspired by the teachings of two remarkable men, St Francis and St Dominic. I have attempted, in all these chapters, to characterize the observances and distinctiveness of each religious group, and briefly to describe the European context, before isolating their contribution to British monasticism. For it must be remembered that of all the new forms of monastic observance which were born in Christendom during the eleventh and twelfth centuries, only one, the order of St Gilbert of Sempringham, originated in Britain.

These early chapters are therefore primarily concerned with how men and women interpreted their role as members of religious communities. In chapters 7–9, I have described in more detail how their lives within the cloister were organized: the buildings which made up the monastic complex; the daily timetable, the internal government of the house and the maintenance of discipline; intellectual pursuits followed by some at least of the religious orders, their attitudes to learning and education, their writing of history and saints' lives, and their contributions to theological debate. Yet monasticism is not just about forms of Christian service, the daily round of prayer and contemplation by those who lived within the cloister, or, in the case of the friars, a more evangelical mission. More often than not monasteries and nunneries were established by lay men and lay women, founded on lands given by the pious, and sustained by property and revenue provided by kings and queens, barons and countesses, members of knightly families, archbishops and bishops. These founders and patrons, no less than monks and nuns, played a vital role in the spread of monasticism. By their giving – and withholding – of benefactions, and by their expectations, they too did much to determine the way monasticism spread and developed. Religious houses were also corporations which owned land, administered estates and enjoyed rights and privileges which needed ratifying and defending. The daily life of the religious was not always confined to the cloister, but brought them into contact with the outside world, in court, estate and manor house, as statesmen, managers and litigants. Chapter 10 is therefore concerned with the relationship between religious houses and their founders, patrons and benefactors, and their place in the wider community. Accordingly here an attempt is made to investigate a number of crucial questions: how did patrons view their monasteries, what did they expect from them, and how did they view their duties and responsibilities? No previous general treatment of monasticism has looked in detail at the role of the local laity and their relationship, as patrons and benefactors, to the monastic houses. Finally, the book turns to economic issues, and examines the sources of revenue enjoyed by religious houses, how they administered their financial affairs, and their involvement in commercial activities.

The religious orders were thus, in all sorts of ways, a vital force in medieval society. The explosion of monasticism in the period covered by this book has never been – and perhaps cannot be – fully explained. The fierce competition engendered by the search among the religious themselves for the ideal form of religious life undoubtedly contributed to the great number of experiments which the era witnessed. Not all manifestations of religious fervour sought their outlet in a community which was, to all intents and purposes, enclosed and withdrawn from the world. Others, most notably the crusading movement which burst forth on the European scene from the late eleventh century, could not have contrasted more greatly. However, for at least a century and a half after the Norman Conquest, until the coming of the friars, who succeeded in fusing the concept of monastic life with a sense of evangelical mission, the various forms of monastic observance were still held by many to offer the highest form of Christian life.

It is a great pleasure to acknowledge my debt to those who have helped me in the writing of this book. Professor Barrie Dobson of the University of Cambridge, who a number of years ago supervised my D.Phil. thesis at the University of York, has been characteristically unstinting with his help and encouragement, as he has on so many other occasions. Dr David Smith of the Borthwick Institute, University of York and Dr Brian Golding of the University of Southampton have also given generously of their time to read this book in draft, have made helpful suggestions and have enabled me to eradicate errors from the text. Professor Peter Fergusson of Wellesley College, Boston, was kind enough to read and comment on chapter 7. I have benefited much from their encouragement and expertise, and I am grateful to them all. I would also like to acknowledge the assistance of Dyfed County Council in granting me leave of absence from my post in order to complete the writing of the book. However, my chief debt, as always, is to my husband, who has cast a kindly but critical eye over my work, and has been ready and willing to discuss (or hear me talk about) the religious orders of medieval Britain.

I

BEFORE THE NORMANS

___ • ___

Monasticism reached Anglo-Saxon England with the mission sent by Pope Gregory the Great from Rome in 597 to begin the conversion of the Anglo-Saxons. Its leader was a monk, Augustine, and the base which he established for his activities was a monastery dedicated to St Peter and St Paul (later St Augustine's) in Canterbury. Thus monasticism was an important and integral part of Christianity from its earliest days in England, and as Augustine's mission advanced further into the Anglo-Saxon kingdoms, other monasteries were sponsored by kings and queens who embraced the new religion. The daily routine at the Canterbury house and at others which the conversion spawned would have been that with which Augustine was familiar from the religious houses of Rome; and among the monastic observances of the time the Rule of Benedict of Nursia (c. 480–550), written for the monastery of Monte Cassino, probably after 535, was beginning to gain currency. But although it is likely that Benedict's Rule was used in the Roman monasteries and in others influenced by them,[1] it was only one of several available, and it was some time before it emerged as the basis of monastic observance throughout the West. It is more appropriate, therefore, to think of religious houses in early Anglo-Saxon England following a pattern of existence shaped both by Benedict's rule and by local customs. Abbots like Benedict Biscop of Monkwearmouth–Jarrow in Northumbria, who travelled on many occasions to Rome, had the opportunity, as his biographer tells us, to observe and bring back the customs followed in many European religious houses. Contacts with Rome and the continent

I

were reinforced, not just by the visits of Anglo-Saxons like Benedict Biscop and Wilfrid, bishop of Hexham and founder of monasteries at Hexham and Ripon, but also by the appointment of foreign bishops to the English church. These were not confined to the Roman missionaries who accompanied Augustine, but included later churchmen, like Theodore, a monk of Tarsus in Cilicia (Asia Minor), appointed to be archbishop of Canterbury by Pope Vitalian in 667; Theodore was accompanied on his journey to England by Hadrian, an African-born monk of a monastery near Naples, who came to be abbot of the Canterbury house. Clearly Anglo-Saxon monasticism was not isolated, but very much in touch with European culture.

In the seventh century Roman influence was accordingly one factor which shaped monastic life in Anglo-Saxon England. But influence, particularly in the West and North, infiltrated from another direction, the Celtic lands. From the Scottish island-monastery of Iona, founded by the Irish saint Columba, came the mission of Aidan in the 630s, invited into Northumbria by its king, Oswald. Aidan and his monks brought with them a monasticism quite different from the Roman, and distinguished by its physical layout of separate cells within an enclosure, its asceticism and penitential practices. Celtic monasticism spread outwards from the monastery which Aidan established on Lindisfarne; and Cuthbert, who became its prior in 664, perpetuated the Irish ascetic and eremitical traditions, retiring from time to time to live as a hermit on Farne Island. Much of what we know of monasticism in the eighth century – an era which later monks looked back on as a golden age – derived from the writings of one man, Bede (d. 735), who had spent his life from the age of seven in one of the northern monasteries, Jarrow. Towards the end of his life Bede wrote an ecclesiastical history of the English people, the purpose of which was to demonstrate the working out of God's designs in the conversion of the Anglo-Saxons to Christianity. Almost incidentally, he tells us much about the life of his people, both secular and religious. It is from Bede's *Ecclesiastical history of the English people* and from his *Lives of the abbots* that we know so much of the celebrated centres of monastic life in the seventh and eighth century, of his own house of Jarrow and its sister abbey of Monkwearmouth, and of the double house of male and female religious at Whitby presided over by the royal princess, Abbess Hilda. The meeting of the two traditions – the Roman, with its emphasis on cenobitism, communal religious life, one of the hallmarks of the Rule of St Benedict, and the Celtic, with its features derived from the eremiticism of the East – in the monasteries of northern England have bequeathed a particularly rich legacy from their material culture in the form of illuminated manuscripts and other treasures.[2]

Many sources attest to the dynamic state of monasticism in this its first golden age, but by the late eighth century it had deteriorated. And by the ninth a combination of external forces – the Vikings who raided the east coast from the 790s onwards – and internal decline had apparently wiped out the monasteries of England so completely that Asser, the biographer of King Alfred of Wessex (871–99), could remark on the complete absence of monastic life. Although this was probably exaggerated, there can be little doubt that Anglo-Saxon monasticism was in a moribund state.[3] Alfred made an attempt to inject new life into religion and learning, and founded two religious houses, Shaftesbury for women, which prospered, and Athelney for men, which did not. The sponsorship of a wholesale revival of monastic life was left to one of Alfred's successors in Wessex and the first king of England, Edgar (959–73). The 'tenth-century monastic revival' was a remarkable product of co-operation between a king and three monks: Dunstan, abbot of Glastonbury and later archbishop of Canterbury, Æthelwold, abbot of Abingdon, who was appointed bishop of Winchester, and Oswald, who rose to be bishop of Worcester. All three were familiar with the reformed monasteries of Europe, such as Ghent and Fleury, on which the authority of Benedict's Rule had by now been stamped as supreme, and so were able to bring to England a wealth of experience based on their observations of the practices of European monastic movements of the period. By the time of Edgar's death over thirty monasteries and nunneries had been founded or restored. Three groups of houses emerged, based on the centres of the three reformers: the spokes of the monastic wheels now emanated from Dunstan's revived monastery at Glastonbury, Æthelwold's strongholds of Abingdon and Winchester, and Ramsey, to which Oswald's community of Westbury on Trym near Bristol transferred in 969. Some of these new houses were for women;[4] most were male foundations; some, notably Winchester, replaced secular clerks (that is, those who did not live according to a rule) with monks. All were dependent for their very existence on royal support.

The aim of the reformers was to rekindle monastic life, and beyond this – in line with continental aspirations – to enforce a strict observance of the Rule of St Benedict and to make sure that lay patrons and founders did not exercise undue influence in monastic affairs. This they attempted to achieve through the *Regularis Concordia*,[5] a code of law devised by Æthelwold and promulgated at Winchester around 970, which selected regulations from both continental and native sources to establish a basis for religious observance in all houses. That basis was the Rule of St Benedict, augmented by practices, particularly liturgical ones, from the continent.[6] A peculiarly English feature, however, was the bond which the *Regularis Concordia* established between the religious houses and the king, who was proclaimed to be the protector of all monasteries; the queen had a similar responsibility towards the nunneries. For both, special prayers were said in all religious houses each day. It was the achievement of Edgar and the three bishops to cover England, or rather central Wessex, Mercia and the Danelaw,[7] with a network of religious houses, free from dependency on the nobles and loyal to the king, in territory both traditionally a royal stronghold and rewon from the Danes. The monastic revival thus gave to the king not only a series of religious houses whose occupants would pray for his soul, but powerful ecclesiastical support for his unique position as monarch. As on the continent, the foundation of monastic houses was at this period a royal prerogative. The rewards of patronage were great: the Anglo-Saxon kings, like the rulers of the Carolingian empire of a slightly earlier period, cultivated monasteries to provide a religious and cultural base for their political authority. Edgar, like the emperor Louis the Pious (814–40), gave powerful backing to the creation of a network of religious houses, enjoying liturgical if not constitutional unity, and radiating royal authority. There was indeed a strong political dimension to monastic reform.

THE RELIGIOUS HOUSES BETWEEN C. 1000 AND 1066: LOCATION[8]

The monastic revival was thus in many ways dependent on a small number of individuals who provided both the impetus for reform and a personal bond among the houses. The deaths of Edgar (975), Æthelwold (984), Dunstan (988) and Oswald (992) not only signalled the end of the revival but were followed by two threats to the newly established order: an attempt by certain nobles to reclaim lands which had been granted to religious houses; and the renewal of Danish invasions which led to a period of political instability during which a number of monasteries, such as Tavistock, were attacked and damaged. Yet the foundations which had been laid by the tenth-century reform proved strong enough to withstand both kinds of assault, and most houses survived to the Conquest and beyond. By 1000 the reform had produced a loose network of some forty independent monasteries and nunneries, all south of the Trent. A number lay in Wessex, the power base of the kings of England: Tavistock and Exeter in Devon; Bath, Glastonbury, Athelney and Muchelney in Somerset; the cathedral community of Sherborne, and within its own diocese the monasteries of Milton Abbas and Cerne and the nunneries of Shaftesbury and Wareham; in the diocese of Ramsbury lay Malmesbury, Abingdon and Cholsey and the nunnery of Wilton. The city of Winchester boasted three houses, the Old Minster (the cathedral), New Minster (later Hyde Abbey) and Nunnaminster, and within the diocese were also Chertsey and the female houses of Romsey and Wherwell. The successors of King Alfred had merged with Wessex the ancient kingdom of Mercia, and here were to be found monastic communities at Worcester (the cathedral), Evesham, Pershore, Tewkesbury, Winchcombe, Deerhurst and Berkeley (for women). Over in the south-east of England there were Canterbury's two foundations, the cathedral church (Christ Church), where a clerical community was replaced by a monastic one early in the eleventh century,[9] and St Augustine's. Westminster and the nunnery of Barking lay in the diocese of London, and St Albans within that of Dorchester. Finally, in an area over which political control had been regained from the Danes was an important group of houses comprising Crowland, Thorney, Peterborough, Ely, Ramsey and St Neots.

Neither of King Edgar's two sons, Edward the Martyr (d. 978 or 979) and Æthelred the Unready (d. 1016), was able to provide the monasteries and nunneries of England with strong royal protection, but after the death of Æthelred these once again found an effective royal patron. King Cnut (1016–35) had political reasons for seeking the support of the church: he was king by conquest, and to strengthen, even legitimize his position by gaining sanction as a protector of the monastic order, he gave lands to the Old Minster at Winchester, Bury St Edmunds and Sherborne, and helped to secure benefactions for Canterbury, Abingdon, Evesham and New Minster (Winchester). Tradition says that he founded St Benet Holme (1019) and Bury St Edmunds (1020), and he is also associated with a small nunnery at Ramsey, but firm evidence is lacking.[10] Later members of the royal family also offered material support to the monastic life: Edward the Confessor restored and rebuilt Westminster, and his queen, Edith, contributed towards the rebuilding of the nunnery of Wilton. However – and this is a development that can be discerned on the continent as well as in England – founders were not now exclusively royal. As wealth and political power fragmented and filtered downwards from the king, the foundation of a religious house came within the aspirations of the aristocracy. And so we encounter houses like Burton on Trent, the most northerly of the late Anglo-Saxon houses, founded in 1002 by the thegn Wulfric Spot, Eynsham near Oxford, established in 1005 by the ealdorman Æthelmar, and Coventry, founded in 1045 by Leofric of Mercia and his wife.[11] The geographical distribution of monastic houses in late Anglo-Saxon England was uneven: there were clusters in the central-southern area of the country, in East Anglia and the West Midlands around Worcester, but no house west of Tavistock. Most striking, however, was the complete absence of religious houses in the north of England. The strength of the monastic order in the Anglo-Saxon kingdom coincided with those areas in which royal power and authority were a reality.

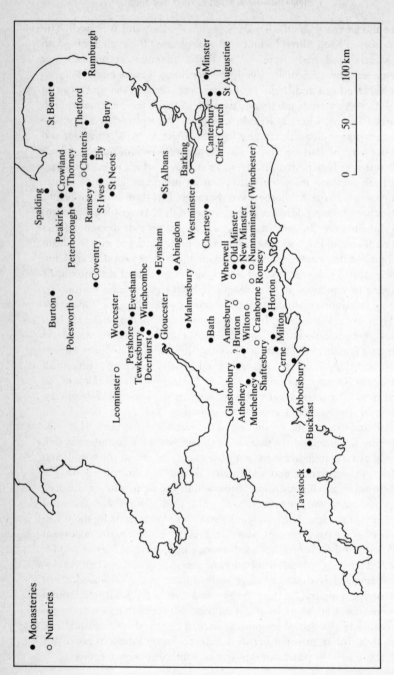

Map 1 Religious houses in late Anglo-Saxon England

Monasteries ●
Nunneries ○

0   50   100 km

St Benet
Peakirk ● Crowland
Spalding ● Peterborough ● Thorney ● Rumburgh
Thetford
Chatteris ○ ● Bury
Ramsey ● Ely
St Ives ● St Neots
St Albans ●
Coventry ●
Barking ○
Eynsham ● Westminster ●
Abingdon ● Minster ● St Augustine
Burton ● Malmesbury ● Canterbury—Christ Church
Polesworth ○ Chertsey ●
Worcester ● Wherwell ○
Pershore ● Evesham ● Old Minster ○
Leominster ○ Tewkesbury ● Winchcombe ● New Minster ○ Nunnaminster (Winchester)
Deerhurst ● Amesbury ● Romsey ○
Gloucester ● Bruton ? Wilton ○
Bath ● Cranborne ○
Glastonbury ● Horton ●
Athelney ● Shaftesbury ● Cerne ● Milton ●
Muchelney ●
Abbotsbury ●
Buckfast ●
Tavistock ●

THE STATE OF MONASTIC LIFE

Writers of the eleventh century looked back on the religious life of the Anglo-Saxon past and perceived these two golden ages, the age of Bede[12] and the tenth-century revival, against which to measure their own achievements. That they should seem to fall short is hardly surprising, nor is it surprising that the years after the revival, an era when there were few new foundations or leaders of note, should be seen as unexciting. One modern writer has called it 'the monastic world at its most ordinary',[13] while others have gone further and seen the last sixty years or so of Anglo-Saxon monasticism as a period of stagnation, even decline. Their view has largely derived from writers of the late eleventh and early twelfth century, especially Eadmer, monk of Canterbury and biographer of Archbishop Anselm, William of Malmesbury, and Orderic Vitalis, the Shropshire-born monk of the Norman monastery of St Evroul, who considered the period just before the Norman Conquest as a hiatus between the tenth-century reform and the changes brought in the wake of Norman settlement, and had little good to say of the English church in the late Anglo-Saxon period. William of Malmesbury spoke generally of English monks who 'mocked the rule of their order with fine vestments and with the use of every kind of food' and claimed that the Normans 'revived the rule of religion which had there grown lifeless',[14] while Eadmer directed his criticism at the monks of Canterbury, who lived in luxury and excess, and treated the boys in the monastic school badly.

Recent scholarship has done much to correct the bias of the rather scanty historical sources for the period and to rescue eleventh-century monasticism from the condemnation of post-Conquest historians. But how healthy was monasticism in the last years of the Old English state? By what yardsticks may we assess it? Documentary evidence for this period is scarce, and what we have is not of the sort to enable us to comment on the spiritual state of the religious houses and their occupants. Even the size of monastic communities is difficult to estimate, although most were modest compared with later expectations for a major house – on the eve of the Norman Conquest there were probably only six houses with over forty monks.[15] If negative evidence may be admitted, then we can say that apart from the criticisms just cited there is little evidence to suggest laxity. So our investigations must pursue other questions. Did the monastic order receive the support of lay men and women, as expressed in their benefactions? Can we say if religious houses seemed, to those who supported them, to be fulfilling their function? Further, is there any evidence for scholarly and literary activity, for patronage of the arts, or for new church building? What follows will examine these issues.

LANDS, WEALTH AND ECONOMY

Medieval culture recognized that society was divided into three orders (*ordines*): those who fought (*bellatores*), those who worked (*laboratores*) and those who prayed (*oratores*); not surprisingly monastic writers placed the *oratores* at the top of the hierarchy. This classification reminds us that prayer was not seen as a private activity, but had a social purpose as well. Monks and nuns were as essential for the functioning of society as those who worked and those who fought; they were spiritual equivalents of earthly soldiers, who fought against the unseen enemies and the powers of evil. Corporate prayer was the backbone of the monastic timetable, and although manual work was a part of the daily routine prescribed by St Benedict as an activity to be undertaken between public and private devotions, its function was spiritual, to induce humility and banish boredom; it was not intended to make a religious house economically self-supporting. It follows that religious communities needed to be sustained by the gifts and the work of others. The other two orders of society provided material sustenance in return for spiritual services. And so, when a house was founded, it was provided with a site on which to erect its buildings and lands to yield food or revenue. From time to time these endowments could be increased. Monasteries and nunneries quickly became land-owning corporations – sometimes wealthy ones – a status which was in no way perceived as being incompatible with the personal poverty to which individual monks and nuns were wedded. Quite how wealthy religious houses became was determined by a number of factors. Foremost was the importance and wealth of the patron – could he or she be generous, and be likely to inspire others to be the same? The patronage of the royal family was even more important, for it brought not only wealth but also the kind of prestige which in turn generated more attention. The queen was the special protector of seven wealthy nunneries, and three-quarters of the estates of Shaftesbury and a substantial portion of those of Wilton were provided by the royal house.[16] A monastery or nunnery which possessed relics could hope to attract endowments both from local people and pilgrims from further afield; Queen Edith's alleged attempts to secure relics for the nunnery of Wilton, which she had rebuilt in the 1060s, is evidence of their importance.[17] Finally the managerial ability of abbots could be a significant factor in the territorial expansion of a monastery's estates.

We have an indication of the wealth which the support of their founders and benefactors had brought to the late Old English monasteries and nunneries in Domesday Book, that great enquiry commissioned by William I twenty years after the Conquest. Some changes took place in the amount of property controlled by individual houses between 1066 and 1086; a number lost lands, and few attracted the patronage of the Normans in this period.[18] However, Domesday Book does give us a good idea of their relative wealth on the eve of the Conquest. It shows us some forty-five houses which were in existence in the late Anglo-Saxon period. We can tabulate their values thus:[19]

Yearly value £500–£900	*Yearly value £200–£500*
Glastonbury	Abingdon
Ely	New Minster, Winchester
Christ Church, Canterbury	Ramsey
Bury St Edmunds	Peterborough
St Augustine's Canterbury	St Albans
St Swithun's (Old Minster), Winchester	Wilton (nunnery)
Westminster	Shaftesbury (nunnery)
Yearly value £100–£200	*Yearly value under £100*
Chertsey	Twenty-five houses,
Malmesbury	including five nunneries
Barking (nunnery)	
Cerne	
Coventry	
Romsey (nunnery)	
Evesham	

Roughly one-sixth of the landed wealth of England south of the Humber (amounting to about £11,000) was in the hands of the monastic order. Studies of the records of individual houses have contributed to our understanding of the territorial extent and expansion of monastic lands in the period between the late tenth century and the Domesday Survey, and enable us to suggest whether this wealth was the result of initial endowment, or whether religious houses enjoyed continued popularity among benefactors in the years between 1000 and 1066. As is to be expected, there is wide divergence. Some houses failed to expand their territorial holdings in the period after their foundation, and even lost lands between 1000 and 1066; the richly endowed west-country house of Tavistock, for example, failed to retain some of its estates. In contrast, analysis of the Peterborough records has identified three periods of growth: an initial period of rapid expansion; years of slower consolidation; and finally a geographical extension in the years 1025–66, when the benefactions of the family of Abbot Brand spread the abbey estates north into Lincolnshire.[20] At another East Anglian house, Ely, the first territorial expansion coincided roughly with the death of the abbey's founder, Bishop

Æthelwold, in 984. But between then and c. 1020 the monks consolidated their holdings by securing grants from local landowners. Despite their apparent inability to attract endowments between 1020 and 1066, Ely was a rich house, and by 1086 its estates included property in 116 villages spread over six counties.[21] Ramsey enjoyed a period of expansion in the eleventh century, stimulated by the abbey school and the generosity of three monks who went on to be bishops of Dorchester, especially Æthelric (1016–34).[22] Thorney was dependent mainly on its initial endowment, while Crowland, by acquiring aristocratic patronage, extended its estates.[23] The general pattern which emerges is that the monasteries founded during the revival enjoyed a brief period of rapid expansion during the lifetimes of the leaders of the movement, but that the consolidation of estates continued into at least the first quarter of the eleventh century if not longer. For one abbey, Westminster, the high point of its existence was the years between 1042 and 1066, when King Edward the Confessor rebuilt and endowed it, furnishing it to be suitable for a royal mausoleum. Edward's generosity to Westminster had the effect of dispersing the abbey estates over fifteen counties,[24] and this was in contrast to houses like St Augustine's, Canterbury, whose endowments were provided mostly by local men and therefore lay within the county of Kent.[25]

The extent and amount of a monastery's property determined how it would be managed. Ely, with an annual value in 1086 of over £760 and second only in wealth to Glastonbury, controlled estates spread over six counties and more than a hundred villages, which presented considerable logistical problems, especially in the transport of food yielded by these lands to the abbey for consumption there. Between 1029 and 1035 Abbot Leofsige obtained permission from King Cnut to introduce a new system of administration. There was now to be a system of food rents: a proportion of abbey lands (thirty-three manors) was divided into units which each produced one week's supply of food for the abbey. The other manors, which were not required to function as food farms, yielded money derived from the sale of excess produce. Ely, then, relied on a number of sources of revenue: the food farm from thirty-three manors and a money farm from the rest; free tenants paying a money rent; the profits of jurisdiction (see below), and the sale of excess animals and wool.[26] Similar management presumably operated at other large houses, like Westminster, Abingdon, Peterborough, Ramsey and Bury, but the details may have varied greatly. If a religious house had more land than it required for its own immediate needs, it could lease it in order to obtain money or services, and indeed this could become a method of acquiring yet more land: houses like Ramsey Abbey, for example, devised leases called *precaria remuneratoria* under which a lessee held property for life from the abbey, under the guarantee that on his or her death not only would the leased land revert to the abbey, but all the lessee's other lands as well. The abbey received no annual rent, but was assured of future acquisitions.[27] A particularly well-developed form of land-lease existed at Worcester, where the reorganization of estates to include leased or 'loan' land can be traced back to the days of Bishop Oswald (961–92). The term of the lease was generally three lives, and in return for the land the lessees provided service. The disadvantage for the church was that the third generation might refuse to give up the property; the cartulary containing copies of the deeds and leases of the priory compiled by Hemming under the administration of Wulfstan bears witness to this problem.[28] All this indicates a more complex management of estates as religious houses grew richer and became more embedded in the agrarian and seignorial framework of society.

The revenues which derived from the possession of land were required for the maintenance of the monastic community, to feed and clothe its members, and to provide them with the material means to perform their task of corporate prayer for the welfare of humankind, and an architectural setting worthy of the service of the Lord. The wealth which the monastic order – the poor in Christ – controlled was therefore not seen as a contradiction in terms. The Rule of St Benedict was quite clear: personal poverty is required from the monks, but this is distinct from corporate possessions. The principle of the Rule, that all land and property belonged to the house and not to an individual, seems to have been maintained, and the evidence from Abingdon to which both Knowles and Barlow pointed, suggesting that monks were allowed to hold private property,[29] seems to represent a lingering local custom that a man had a say in the way his entry grant – the gift which he offered to the monastery when he was accepted as a novice – was used, not a general or a 'peculiarly English practice' of private ownership of property within a religious house. Indeed, some religious houses guarded against the notion that the lands which had been held by a man in his secular life remained his after his conversion. At Ramsey one charter makes it clear that, although a family had given land to the abbey to provide money to clothe their son when he became a monk there, that son had no right to administer the land, and was moreover enjoined to obey the abbot and brethren in all things, and to be humble and devout.[30]

MONASTERIES AND THE GOVERNMENT OF THE REALM

The holding of land brought with it obligations to contribute towards the good order of the kingdom. Most of the property held by religious houses was 'bookland', a term which denotes that title to possession of land was enshrined in writing, rather than dependent on oral testimony. The general services owed by any holder of bookland, whether lay or ecclesiastical, were the *trinoda necessitas*, a threefold obligation under which landowners had to contribute to the defence of the country by providing men for the fyrd, or army, to help with the building and repair of fortifications, and with the construction and renovation of bridges. On a general level, then, religious houses were, like any landowner, a part of the system of defence and communication.

Late Anglo-Saxon England was administered through shires and hundreds, although by the eleventh century this system was not complete over all the country. The shire court was in general the forum through which the king's will was made known to the people; however, for local matters it was the hundred court that was important. Normally the court was administered on behalf of the king by a hundred reeve. From the tenth century onwards, however, it became common for kings to appoint abbots, rather than thegns, as the governors of many hundreds. Edgar and his successors saw the advantages for royal authority in delegating hundredal rights to churchmen, rather than laymen who might use them as a basis for private power. There are a number of striking examples. Worcester was granted jurisdiction over the triple hundred known as the Oswald-low, and here the bishop exercised governmental and military powers. Alongside this tendency to appoint abbots as governors of hundreds another trend can be detected. Where a landowner held extensive estates, he might be granted franchisal powers, and exemption from the usual hundredal jurisdiction. In other words, he was allowed by the king to hold his own court and hear cases which pertained to tenants on his estates; by the end of the Anglo-Saxon period these franchisal courts were beginning to merge with, and become indistinguishable from, hundredal ones. This process affected both laymen and ecclesiastical landowners, like Peterborough Abbey, which came to have jurisdiction over the 'Soke of Peterborough', a large area in Cambridgeshire and Northamptonshire. Bury St Edmunds governed eight and a half hundreds in Suffolk, and Ely five and a half hundreds in Wicklaw in Suffolk and two in Ely. Other powers and freedoms could be granted by the king: with its eight and a half hundreds, Bury St Edmunds received exemption from taxation and the right to mint coins. Monastic houses by the late Anglo-Saxon period had become an integral part of royal government in many localities.

Monasteries also had a role to play in government from the centre as well as in the localities,[31] for it was from among his abbots and monks that the king might draw his administrators and advisers. Admittedly, no monarch between Edgar and William I had that close working relationship with their churchmen that those two kings enjoyed, and the monasteries of the period 1000–66 produced no monk-statesmen of the calibre of Dunstan or Lanfranc, archbishop of Canterbury (1070–89). Nevertheless we may isolate occasions when abbots were figures in national as well as local government. Ælfwine, abbot of Ramsey, attended the papal council of Reims in 1049 and then journeyed on to Rome as a member of a royal delegation. Leofric of Peterborough acted as an agent of the king, as did Æthelwig of Evesham – a function he was to continue after the Conquest. It is especially important to remember that monasteries were not only centres of worship, but centres of literacy. Certainly in the tenth century, and into the eleventh, monasteries provided the king with scribes, men who could keep the royal records. A twelfth-century tradition at Ely suggests that the monasteries of St Augustine's, Ely and Glastonbury took it in turn to supply the king with chancellors in the persons of their abbots. This lacks contemporary witness, and may enshrine a later tradition, but that the king turned to the monasteries of his realm for advisers and scribes is certain.[32] This role may have declined by the immediate pre-Conquest period, when the shadowy evidence appears to point to the emergence of a more professional 'civil service' of clerics who were not necessarily monks.

Religious houses were therefore tied by loyalty to the royal house both as landowners and as agents of local government. This relationship, reinforced by the obligations imposed by the *Regularis Concordia*, that monks and nuns pray for the king and queen as special patrons of all monasteries and nunneries, had the effect (in theory) of freeing religious houses from the control of nobles, and making them royal *Eigenkloster*, that is, the property of kings and queens. Links between the royal family and the religious houses of their realm were emphasized when members of that family entered a monastery or nunnery, or ruled over it, and connections of this nature can be seen in both male and female houses. From the early days of Anglo-Saxon monasticism, royal princesses had entered the religious life, and ended, not unexpectedly, in charge of houses. Abbess Hilda of Whitby, of whom mention has already been made, was a member of the royal house of Northumbria, and was succeeded by her niece, Ælfled, and Ælfled's mother. The evidence suggests that in the late Saxon period, too, abbesses were drawn from the royal family, stressing the links between the royal founders and patrons and the religious houses of their kingdom, women such as St Wulfthryth, concubine of King Edgar, and abbess of Wilton (c. 965–1000) and her daughter St Edith, abbess of Barking (before 984) and Winchester (Nunnaminster). In the reign of Edward the Confessor Wherwell was ruled by the granddaughter of its founder, Queen Ælfthryth.

As patron of all the monasteries of his kingdom, the king now had the right to have a voice in abbatial elections. The Rule of St Benedict laid down that the head of a monastery should be elected by the monks from among their number. With pragmatism, the *Regularis Concordia* added that royal guidance should be taken. When a vacancy occurred, the monks or nuns applied to the king for permission to elect a superior, and afterwards for confirmation of their choice. Sometimes it suited the king to abide by the decision of the community; on other occasions he judged it necessary or expedient for his own interests to intervene to put in his own candidate. Abingdon went to a royal nominee, the king's goldsmith Spearhafoc, in c. 1047, and in 1051 when the monks of Canterbury tried to elect a candidate of their own choice, Edward the Confessor intervened to put in the Norman Robert of Jumièges. Here Edward was trying to stamp his authority on the Canterbury monks whose patron, Earl Godwine – after the king the most powerful man in England – was in political decline. Royal patronage could lead to some anomalies, as when the king granted to Leofric, who was already abbot of Peterborough, the same office at four other houses, Burton, Coventry, Thorney and Crowland. Although his precise status at each is uncertain, the episode clearly demonstrates the degree of control which the king enjoyed over the religious houses of his realm.[33]

One of the legacies of the tenth-century reform movement in England was the monastic bishop and, to a lesser extent, the monastic cathedral. It has already been mentioned that Dunstan and his monastic colleagues were elevated by Edgar to be archbishop and bishops. This led to the peculiarly English tradition of the monk-bishop, which for decades dominated the English church. Up to 1042 the vast majority of bishops of Anglo-Saxon sees were both native-born and monks. For example, between 1004 and 1049 three monks of Ramsey became bishops of Dorchester. Canterbury was ruled by a monk-bishop until 1052 and Ramsbury until 1045. Between 1042 and 1066 the number of monk-bishops fell, partly as a result of the decline in prestige of some of the abbeys relative to the status they had enjoyed under Edgar, partly because of Edward the Confessor's preference for appointing foreign clerks. Between 1050 and 1066 the proportion of monks within the whole episcopate ranged from about 25 per cent to 50 per cent. One monk-bishop survived the Conquest: Wulfstan of Worcester continued in that see until his death in 1095.[34] The great abbeys within a diocese could, however, inhibit the development of the endowments of the cathedral church and in effect overshadow the bishop's seat. In the late Saxon period at least one bishop cast covetous eyes on a religious house within his diocese: Bishop Herman of Ramsbury, complaining of the poverty of his see, attempted to annex and move into the well-endowed abbey of Malmesbury.[35]

ARTISTIC, CULTURAL AND LITERARY ACTIVITIES

The monastic day was spent in public prayer, the liturgy, which seems to have derived many of its features from the continental monasteries,[36] in private contemplation and in manual work. This last activity could take many forms: it could comprise work in the fields or gardens, or it could be educational or artistic.[37] The Old English monasteries produced, or were patrons of, artistic treasures of the highest quality. The manuscripts of the last century of the Anglo-Saxon monasteries have been recognized for the superiority both of their script and of their illumination. A particular school, the 'Winchester School', has been identified, and associated with work produced not only at Winchester but at monasteries influenced from there. From these centres came manuscripts like the missal of Robert of Jumièges, a fine illuminated manuscript, of a date before 1023. Christ Church, Canterbury, produced a large number of manuscripts of the gospels, while the other Canterbury house, St Augustine's, was responsible for illustrated versions, in the vernacular, of the beginning of the Old Testament.[38] Other types of art flourished. Evesham under Abbot Mannig (1044–58) was famous for its goldsmith work, sculpture, painting and calligraphy. Documentary evidence suggests that English metalwork was highly regarded in the eleventh century, and certainly the Normans were impressed by the wealth, splendour and ornament of English abbey churches.[39]

Monasteries and nunneries had to be equipped with the means to provide education, primarily for their own oblates (children offered by their parents later to become monks and nuns) and novices. Monastic schools are attested at Ramsey, Christ Church, Canterbury and else-where, and contrasting pictures of the life of the boys are portrayed in Ælfric's Colloquies and Eadmer's writing. Schools were clearly on occasion also attended by outsiders. Edith, daughter of Earl Godwine and wife of the Confessor, was evidently educated at Wilton. Wulfstan of Worcester, born c. 1008 and not intended by his parents for the monastic life, was educated at Evesham Abbey and, from the age of seven or eight, at Peterborough Abbey; when as a mature adult he became a monk at Worcester, his first office was that of *custos puerorum*, the monk in charge of the education of the boys, both oblates and lay schoolboys.[40] The state of learning and education under the last years of Anglo-Saxon rule has been the subject of disagreement. Professor Frank Barlow argued that no great literature was produced at this period and that literary output was

'respectable rather than outstanding';[41] others have disagreed, finding
evidence of a vigorous culture on the eve of Conquest.[42] The tenth-
century reform laid the foundations of an intellectual as well as religious
revival, in that it provided the climate and location in which such work
could flourish. In the monasteries of the late tenth and eleventh century
we can find writers and scholars in both Latin and the vernacular, Old
English. One of the leaders of the revival, Æthelwold, was a scholar and
noted Latinist, and at Winchester he trained a number of others to follow
in his footsteps. Among these was Godeman, abbot of Thorney, and
Wulfstan the precentor of Winchester, who wrote a Latin life of
Æthelwold and an account in verse of the miracles of St Swithun, patron
saint of his house. One of two outstanding prose writers was another
product of Winchester: Ælfric, after being sent from Winchester to Cerne
Abbey (987) and later as abbot of Eynsham from 1006, produced works in
both Latin and English. His writings are important because they reveal his
concern to educate both inside and outside the cloister. His two series of
Catholic homilies (sermons) and other homilies on the lives of the saints
were part of a programme of religious education, designed to convey the
truth of the Christian religion, and were aimed both at clergy who were
unable to understand Latin – they were thus almost a source book for
preachers – and at the laity. He also translated and paraphrased portions of
the Bible. Other works, especially his Latin grammar and glossary and the
Colloquies, were directed at the oblates at Eynsham and designed to train
them to speak, read and write good Latin.[43]

A range of other writing was produced within the monasteries of
England. Surviving manuscripts from Christ Church, Canterbury attest an
interest in devotional writings and the cultivation of private prayer.[44]
Scientific work is represented by Byrhtferth, a monk of Ramsey who had
been the pupil of Abbo of Fleury, one of the most outstanding
continental scholars of the day, who was at Ramsey between c. 986 and
988. Byrhtferth produced within the walls of Ramsey a handbook
(*Enchiridion*) to teach his students about the computus, astronomical
science, and historical and hagiographical works. He may also have been
the author of the life of St Oswald written at Ramsey, and compiled at
the request of the monks of Evesham a life of St Ecgwine. These 'lives'
helped to foster the cult of saints and the reputation of the monasteries.
In a recent article Dr Antonia Gransden has discussed the art of biography
in the late Anglo-Saxon period, which she sees as continuing a
Northumbrian tradition from seventh-century Whitby and Jarrow. She
has argued persuasively that some of this work is embedded in the Anglo-
Saxon Chronicle – itself a testimony to vigorous literary activity at
Peterborough, Abingdon and Canterbury – and some survives in later

work from Abingdon, Evesham and Ramsey. All this suggests that there was 'considerable historiographical activity' on the eve of the Conquest.[45]

Little fabric has survived from the abbey churches and claustral buildings of the eleventh century to tell us of their nature, and the influences which shaped their design. A twofold question arises: how far was the period between 1000 and 1066 one of church building, and did that building reflect continental trends or did it derive its inspiration from the native past? The tenth-century revival stimulated rebuilding as liturgical developments demanded new settings,[46] and archaeological investigation has helped to reveal the nature of these at Canterbury and Glastonbury. It is unlikely that church building would have continued at the same rate after the revival had spent its first energies, but there is some evidence of activity in the years between 1000 and 1066. Evesham, for instance, is documented as having been rebuilt, and had its shrines restored, by Abbot Mannig (1044–58). And there is some evidence of foreign contacts. Westminster, so lovingly endowed and rebuilt by the Confessor – it was consecrated just before his death – was entirely rebuilt by Henry III in the thirteenth century, but we have enough evidence from contemporary descriptions and now from archaeological excavation to be sure that it was heavily influenced by foreign models;[47] an idea of its appearance can be gained from the majestic ruins of the contemporary Norman abbey of Jumièges. Edward's wife, Edith, indulged in what has been called 'pious rivalry' by financing the rebuilding of the nunnery of Wilton, evidently for the first time in stone. The church was consecrated a few months before Westminster, in the summer of 1065.[48]

The disappearance of most of the fabric of the monasteries of the late Anglo-Saxon era, and their furnishings, makes it impossible to estimate how greatly they were informed by European models and cultural trends. The same is true of their writings and artistic endeavours. However, although England was, as Ælfric expressed it, 'on the outer edge of the earth's extent', it was not totally isolated from the culture of western Christendom. Travel, by all manner of men and women, brought both ideas and artefacts from Europe and Rome, and further afield. Monks, too, journeyed abroad: Abbot Leofstan of Bury St Edmunds (1044–63) admired the holy cross at Lucca; Ælfwine, monk of Canterbury, doubt-less had much to tell of what he had seen on his journey to Jerusalem in 1055 and his return via Byzantium, Lombardy and Rome.[49] Knowles considered there to be 'no trace of continental influence in English monasticism' between the late tenth century and the reign of the Confessor.[50] Such a statement may apply at certain, perhaps formal, levels, but the sources do not allow us to say unequivocally that the religious of England were not touched at all, through informal contacts, by cultural and artistic developments in the Latin West.

THE NORTH, WALES AND SCOTLAND

In contrast to England south of the Trent, the North, Wales and Scotland knew little or nothing of Benedictine monasticism. There were no institutions in which all the criteria which constituted monastic life in its truest sense, especially stability within the house, could have been found. In the North the celebrated centres of both male and female monasticism had long gone. The only communal institutions to be found were collegiate churches staffed by secular clerks who did not follow a rule, like those begun by Archbishop Ealdred at Beverley and Ripon, or further north at Durham, where a group of clerks served the shrine of St Cuthbert whose body, after ninety years of wandering since the Danes forced the abandonment of Lindisfarne, had come to rest there in or about 995. What other centres of religious or quasi-monastic life survived the Danish inroads and settlement we do not know, for the era is poorly documented. It is only by chance that the charter recording the introduction of Benedictine monks into the church of the Holy Trinity in York (1089) refers to the church as formerly adorned 'with canons and revenues of landed estates and ecclesiastical ornaments, now almost reduced to nothing'; this provides a tantalizing glimpse of what might have gone unrecorded. There were doubtless minster churches, as there were all over Anglo-Saxon England, mother churches served by secular clergy who also went out to the lesser churches within the minster's *parochia*. The minsters go back to the age of conversion, and the missionary activity of those who served in them was directly opposed to the monastic virtue of stability.[51] The North was untouched by the monastic developments of the South in the tenth and eleventh century, and the reintroduction of full regular life there had to await a unique combination of Anglo-Saxon sentiment for the past and Norman political might and patronage. The main reason for the success of the tenth-century monastic revival was that it received the full and enthusiastic backing of the king. Conversely, the failure of the reform movement to reach the North and to revive those monasteries with which the reformers were familiar is explained by the absence of royal authority there. Thus the revival, which laid the basis for monastic development in the decades before the Conquest, was limited to areas where the king was king in more than just name, that is, to Wessex, Mercia and the South-East. The North, in contrast, scarcely offered a political and economic climate conducive to the reintroduction of monasticism.

In Wales the institution which in form most closely corresponded to the monastery was the *clas* church. However, this had more in common with the minster churches of Anglo-Saxon England than its Benedictine monasteries. The Welsh *clas* comprised a church (*eglwys*) in its enclosure (*llan*) which fulfilled the function of a mother, or minster, church, and could have a number of dependent chapels.[52] The head of the *clas* community was the abbot, who ruled the *claswyr*, originally monks, but by the eleventh century secular canons, who were in charge of worship and parochial responsibilities. The *claswyr* each took a share of the revenues of the church rather than their being administered in common. They were often married, and it was accepted practice for them to pass on their share of the *clas* as a hereditary benefice to their sons. Some *clas* churches were associated with commotes, as Bangor on Dee was with the commote of Maelor, others with the larger administrative units, the *cantrefi* – here we may think of the imposing church of Llanbadarn Fawr near Aberystwyth, which once served the *cantref* of Penweddig. The Normans who pushed into the Welsh kingdoms in the 1070s and 1080s neither understood nor appreciated a religious experience so remote from their own, and the days of the *clas* church, at least in those areas conquered by the Normans, were numbered.

Alongside these churches, whose function and purpose were parochial rather than ascetic withdrawal from the world, there existed in Wales in the twelfth and doubtless in the eleventh century a tradition of eremiticism, the solitary life of the hermit. By their very nature hermits are less likely to figure in written records than property-owning corporations, but sometimes we get a glimpse, as we do in the writings of Gerald of Wales, of a lively hermit tradition reinforcing or even replacing communal monasticism. The situation was not so very different in Scotland. Monasticism had arrived with the Columban mission from Ireland, in the wake of which Scotland's first monastery – and perhaps the only one to survive as an organizational structure through to the eleventh century and beyond – was founded at Iona in 565. From here monasticism had spread through Scotland and also to the north of England. By the pre-Norman period, however, many centres had gone into decline, as indeed they had south of the border. What little the sources tell us suggests that religious life was centred on two types of establishment. One was an institution not unlike the Welsh *clas* church, and was composed of a group of secular priests serving a large parish; houses of this kind existed at Brechin, Dunkeld and St Andrews, which were also episcopal centres. The other type of house was eremitical in nature, and comprised a community of hermits. There were accordingly in Scotland establishments which could be described as both secular and monastic; and the inhabitants of either might be referred to as Culdee. When Margaret of Hungary, great-niece of Edward the Confessor, journeyed north around the year 1070 in order to marry King Malcolm III, she encountered religious life in both these forms.[53] The centres of monastic or quasi-monastic life were few and isolated, and only a chance reference in the *Life* of Margaret suggests that, as in Wales, a tradition of individual withdrawal from the world existed alongside communities of secular and monastic clergy. Yet the Culdee tradition remained vibrant and in several cases communities, like those of Whithorn, Inchaffray, Loch Leven, St Andrews and Abernethy, survived into the thirteenth century, when regular life was introduced there.[54]

However, monasticism in Scotland as well as Wales was gradually to be transformed by the Norman Conquest of England. After the Battle of Hastings Duke William of Normandy was able to have himself crowned king of England in a Benedictine abbey, Westminster, in a ceremony performed by the archbishop of York in December 1066. Within the next few years England was conquered politically; slower and more long-term social, economic and administrative change followed. The Scottish rulers were brought into the political orbit of the Norman kings of England while retaining their independence. The Welsh princes of the North were only completely subdued after two centuries, but in the South the instruments of conquest, castle, town and monastery, were soon to appear. What is clear is that changes came – some radical, some piecemeal – for the monasteries and nunneries of Britain. It has proved difficult to generalize about their state on the eve of the coming of the Normans. The greatest cohesion was to be found in the monasteries of midland and southern England, but even here uniformity, which was to be found mainly in daily liturgical observances, is hard to demonstrate. Differences in size, economic assets, patronage and local loyalties meant that the late Anglo-Saxon monasteries presented the Conqueror with a divergent variety rather than a coherent group. The movement away from some kind of corporate identity, which may have existed for a short time in the age of Dunstan, towards more local interests can be demonstrated by the *Liber Vitae*, or 'Book of Life', kept at New Minster, Winchester. This recorded the names of the dead for whom the monks prayed. Until about 1020 these included the king and all his great men, most of the English bishops, and the members of the communities of Abingdon, Ely and Ramsey. After 1020 those for whom the Winchester monks interceded were overwhelmingly men and women of local significance, with whom the monks had reached a private agreement for their commemoration. Even by 1066 it was clear that the welfare of a monastery depended on its local support and its place in the locality.

2

THE COMING OF THE NORMANS

The Norman invasion and conquest of England had a self-consciously ecclesiastical dimension. Norman writers who sought to legitimize William's actions stressed that King Harold, who had had himself crowned the day after the Confessor's funeral, was a perjurer: that during a visit to Normandy he had promised on sacred relics to support the claim of Duke William, and the fact that he had broken that oath meant that he was unfit to be king. The accuracy of Norman propaganda need not concern us here, for what is of more immediate significance is that the Conqueror gained the support of the church for his invasion. Norman churches helped to finance the expedition, and the pope gave it his sanction, thus enabling William to fight under a papal banner promising not only to depose the perjurer, but also to reform the English church. How far the Anglo-Saxon church was in need of serious or thorough reform is open to question. Certainly its reputation then, as since, has been dominated by the bias of the historical sources as well as the existence of the notorious pluralist Stigand, archbishop of Canterbury and concurrently bishop of Winchester. As the previous chapter has argued, there is no evidence of serious moral decay or need for reform among the Old English monasteries.

THE ANGLO-SAXON HOUSES

What did William know about the religious houses of the land he was about to govern? Norman infiltration into the ranks of the upper clergy had begun before the death of the Confessor. In 1065, for instance,

Edward had placed a former monk of the French abbey of St Denis (Paris), his physician Baldwin, as abbot of Bury St Edmunds, an office whose duties he would discharge until his death in 1097/8. Norman monasteries like Fécamp had already before 1066 been recipients of grants of land in England. Certainly the channels of communication between England and Normandy meant that the Normans knew of the wealth of the Anglo-Saxon houses. When William had himself crowned king of the English, he had in his new realm over forty religious houses, between them controlling as much as a sixth of the wealth of southern and midland England. Perhaps twenty of them were extremely rich and powerful. William knew that a number of their monks were bishops, and as he found out more of the way England was ruled he would have learnt that many abbots were involved in governing the country, at least at a local if not also at a higher level. Common sense would dictate that he ensure the loyalty of these institutions and their rulers, and as time passed and the Norman régime encountered resistance this need became more acute.

One result of the Battle of Hastings and the crushing of a series of revolts against the Normans between 1067 and 1076 was that the secular aristocracy of England was destroyed. Ultimately, the Anglo-Saxon ecclesiastical aristocracy too was deprived of power. A number of bishops, notably Stigand, were deposed for ecclesiastical offences and, more gradually, heads of religious houses were replaced by Normans. The earliest casualties, though, appear to have been succeeded by Anglo-Saxons: Ælfwig of New Minster, Winchester, is recorded as having died at the Battle of Hastings; perhaps because of his alliance with the cause of the last Anglo-Saxon king the abbacy was kept vacant for at least two years before a monk of the house, Wulfric, was allowed to succeed, only to be deposed less than three years later. Also present at Hastings, though tradition has not placed him in the thick of battle, was Leofric of Peterborough, who 'fell ill there and came home and died soon after'.[1] To succeed him the monks chose their prior Brand, who, through a bad miscalculation, declared his allegiance not to the victor of Hastings, but to Edgar Ætheling, great-nephew of the Confessor. But William, perhaps acting cautiously in the first days of his triumph, allowed Brand to purchase his goodwill and confirmation of the abbey estates at a cost of forty golden marks (about £25). Others fared less well. Abbot Godric was removed from the rule of Winchcombe in 1066 and placed in the custody of Abbot Æthelwig of Evesham while his abbey passed to a monk of the Norman house of Cérisy. William evidently had reason to doubt the loyalty of Æthelnoth of Glastonbury, for when he returned to Normandy in 1067 the abbot was among those potential troublemakers whom the king took with him, although Æthelnoth survived in office until 1077/8, when he was placed in custody in Christ Church, Canterbury. The new king was definitely trying to stamp his authority on the English church; the chronicle of Florence of Worcester, for one, linked William's deposition of a number of abbots at the council of Winchester in 1070 to his need 'to confirm his power in a kingdom which he had but newly acquired'.[2] The deprivations continued the following year when Ealdred, appointed to Abingdon early in 1066, was removed for his part in the conspiracy of the bishop of Durham and his place taken by Adelelm, monk of Jumièges. So too, in 1085, fell the abbot of Crowland, possibly implicated in the last major rising against William in 1075; the abbey church gave burial to one of the chief conspirators, Earl Waltheof.[3]

The removal of the Anglo-Saxon rulers of religious houses was therefore gradual rather than drastic. Those removed forcibly from office formed a minority and most continued in office until their death, like Brihtric of Malmesbury, whom William moved in 1066/7 to Burton, where he ruled until 1085. At least one abbot, Æthelwig of Evesham (1059–77), demonstrates continuity on either side of the traditional 'great divide' of 1066. He convinced the new king of his loyalty and received from him control over the shires of Worcester, Gloucester, Oxford, Warwick, Hereford, Stafford and Shropshire. Thus Æthelwig filled the gap left by the death of William's trusted earl of Hereford, William fitz Osbern, and with the monk-bishop Wulfstan of Worcester, helped to defend the marches against the Welsh.[4]

However, by the end of the Conqueror's reign nearly all the positions of responsibility in the religious houses of England had been filled by Normans or Frenchmen. Six of these were drawn from the Norman abbey of Jumièges, and three each from Fécamp (which had been the focal point of the reform of the Norman church from the early years of the eleventh century), the Conqueror's own foundation at Caen, and Mont St Michel. There were some good choices and some disasters. To the Normans, whose province had for sixty years been open to the reforming influences of Cluny, via the mission of William of Volpiano to Fécamp (1001), Jumièges, Mont St Michel and others, and where churches had been rebuilt in the latest fashion, the English abbeys must have seemed small and old-fashioned, although they were impressed by their wealth and decoration. They were probably unfamiliar with the way in which the daily services were said or sung. Indeed, some changes in the internal practices of the Anglo-Saxon houses followed in the wake of the appointment of foreigners. For Christ Church, Canterbury, a cathedral church as well as a monastery, Archbishop Lanfranc devised a new series of constitutions, the *Decreta*, which regulated daily life and liturgy and simplified

many of the practices of the *Regularis Concordia*. Further, these customs
were adopted at houses influenced from Christ Church, among them St
Augustine's and Rochester, St Albans, where a kinsman of
Lanfranc was promoted abbot, Battle, where the prior of Christ Church
became head of the community, and Durham, which at its own request
received a copy.[5] Not all changes in liturgical practices were so peaceful,
however, and at least one newly appointed abbot took drastic steps to
enforce his own preference, for the chant used at Fécamp: the Anglo-
Saxon Chronicle records how Thurstan of Glastonbury, a former monk
of Caen, brought his knights into the monastic church and they

> broke into the choir and began pelting the monks in the direction of the altar
> where they were. Some men-of-arms climbed up to the gallery, and shot arrows
> down into the sanctuary, so that many arrows stuck in the cross which stood above
> the altar . . . They showered arrows, and their companions broke down the door
> and forced an entrance, and struck down and killed some of the monks.

The incident left three of the monks dead and eighteen injured.[6] If this
were the only account left to us, we might dismiss it as an exaggerated
attempt by an Anglo-Saxon patriot to discredit the Normans. But others
tell the same tale, and as a result of his behaviour Thurstan was deposed
by the king and sent back to Caen.[7]

   Thurstan – and doubtless other Normans – were clearly set on change,
but fortunately not all took such drastic measures to enforce their ideas.
However, others espoused and even fostered native traditions. Historians
in the past have accused the Normans of undermining the cult of Anglo-
Saxon saints:[8] did not Archbishop Lanfranc demote and remove one of
his predecessors, Ælfheah, from the liturgical calendar at Canterbury?[9]
Did not Abbot Paul treat with disrespect the tombs of his Anglo-Saxon
predecessors at St Albans? And did not the Normans at Abingdon slight
the memory of Æthelwold ('an English rustic') himself? The researches of
Susan Ridyard have modified this view by highlighting the fine but
crucial distinction between disrespect to a former abbot (as at Abingdon
and St Albans) and disrespect to local saints. There now appears little
evidence that the Norman abbots tried to undermine the latter; indeed,
on the contrary, some actively promoted the cult of the abbey saints.[10]
They encouraged the composition of their lives and laid their bodies to
rest in places of honour within their newly built churches. They became
jealous guardians of their relics: the Norman abbot Turold went so far as
to rescue Peterborough's relics from Ramsey, whither they had been
removed for safe-keeping. The transition from Anglo-Saxon to Norman
rule cannot have been easy, especially for those English monks who had
seen themselves as potential abbots of their communities, but apart

from isolated instances, it seems to have been achieved with reasonable smoothness and lack of discord. The monks of Christ Church, Canterbury accepted the customs devised for them by Lanfranc; Thorney accepted those from Marmoutier. Other incidents which have been seen as resistance to Norman rule over English monasteries admit of other interpretations. The first Norman abbot of St Augustine's in Canterbury ruled in apparent peace and equanimity until his demise in 1087. The monks, possibly taking advantage of the death of King William, refused to accept as their new abbot a Norman monk from the neighbouring monastery of Christ Church, named Wido, the nominee of Lanfranc. As the archbishop tried to install the abbot the monks filed out of the church in protest. For a while peace was restored, but after Lanfranc's death there was a further riot which resulted in the monks being dispersed and their servants blinded as a punishment. Knowles interpreted this as a late example of resistance to the Normans, an incident at the heart of which was 'racial feeling'.[11] However, it is just as likely that this was a manifestation of rivalry between the two senior Canterbury religious houses as an anti-Norman gesture.

The Anglo-Saxon monastic chroniclers who charted the progress of the Norman settlement did not, on the whole, complain about the wholesale replacement of their abbots by alien rulers except, as at Glastonbury, where they created havoc by their high-handed methods. They did, however, complain vociferously on other matters, principally that the Normans carried off treasures from their churches to enrich the religious houses of Normandy; that their estates were devastated; that Norman abbots granted away abbey properties; and that estates were lost because of the need to provide land for knights. On the first charge there is sporadic chronicle evidence that the ornaments of English churches were regarded as legitimate spoils of war, rewards for those Norman houses which had financed the Conqueror's expedition. On the second there is the testimony of Domesday Book, some aspects of which have already been considered, and which indeed indicates that some lands which had been in the possession of religious houses in 1066 had been lost by 1086. However, some houses had actually increased their land holdings. Nor should it be assumed that the Normans alone were responsible for those land losses which had occurred. Marjorie Chibnall has shown that when the monks of Christ Church complained that they had lost lands to Odo, bishop of Bayeux and earl of Kent, the property which they claimed had actually been taken from them before the Conquest by Earl Harold and passed from Harold's estates to Odo.[12] However, certain loss of land was sustained by religious houses, not only during the immediate process of conquest as a result of confiscation by the king, but also by nobles newly

settled on English soil, who took advantage of the confused situation to
encroach on monastic lands. Tavistock Abbey had to fight off the
attention paid to its property by Baldwin, sheriff of Devon; Peterborough
lost lands to the rapacious sheriff of Cambridge, Picot.[13] On the whole,
however, there is no widespread deprivation evident in the Survey.

This brings us to a controversial area of scholarship, perhaps the most
difficult question which has to be faced by historians seeking to assess
whether 'continuity' or 'change' is the more appropriate term to describe
what happened to English monasteries during and after the Norman
settlement. Religious houses were major landowners. But did the
Conquest radically change the terms under which those lands were held?
To resurrect the arguments of J. H. Round and F. W. Maitland and
others about the 'feudal revolution' may seem to be beyond the scope of
this study, but the problem, since it so closely involves monastic houses,
must be addressed. Let us first try to define the problem. The monastic
houses of the Anglo-Saxon era, like the secular aristocracy, held lands,
mostly bookland, in return for service to the king; and these public
obligations included providing military service for the fyrd. From a
document known as the *Cartae Baronum* dating from 1166 (so exactly one
hundred years after the Conquest) we know that major landowners,
including many but by no means all religious houses, owed a fixed
number of knights for the army. This was their 'quota', and the *cartae* of
1166 gave the number of knights enfeoffed, that is, granted land in return
for service, by each tenant-in-chief in 1135 and 1166. Fixed quotas, then,
existed in 1135, but how old were they at that date? It was Round's
thesis that both a distinct type of military tenure and the knightly quota
were innovations created by the Conqueror in England in the wake of
conquest.

Much has been written on this famous issue, and historians, although
mainly agreeing that the quotas were introduced by William I, might be
said now to be taking more of a 'middle ground' on the question of
continuity. There is, however, still room for disagreement. Round's
major pieces of documentary evidence for the novelty of knight service
and the quota have recently been examined afresh by scholars, one of
whom has suggested that the quotas represented nothing radically new
in 1066.[14] The evidence supporting this is based on silence: of all the
monastic and other chroniclers writing at the time or shortly afterwards,
none complained of any new exaction by which the Conqueror had
demanded so many knights from such-and-such abbey; this was not
among their general complaints. John Gillingham has indicated that
the sources used by Round to demonstrate that the quotas were a novelty
are late, confused or unreliable. In one case, the Abingdon Chronicle

seems to be reporting not the imposition of quotas, but the grant of land by the abbot to knights, that is, the creation of knights' fees. Gillingham suggests, in fact, that the famous writ, quoted by Round and dated by him to c. 1072, by which King William summoned Abbot Æthelwig of Evesham to Clarendon with 'those five knights which you owe me from your abbey', may be assigned to an earlier date, thus indicating that a knightly quota of five existed for Evesham shortly after, if not before, the Conquest.

Gillingham's reassessment of the problem has not been universally accepted, and Marjorie Chibnall for one still sees the introduction of quotas as the work of the Conqueror; she argues that before the Conquest the obligation of monasteries as landowners to contribute to defence was a general one, which, after 1066, was sharpened and defined to include a quota of knights from the major abbeys. These quotas were reached by personal agreement or imposition on each house.[15] This does not preclude the possibility that such individual contacts had been negotiated before the Conquest, and it is quite possible that Gillingham is correct when he suggests that it was not the *fact* of the quota which distressed abbeys but the increase in their obligation. The conquest of England and the replacement of the secular aristocracy with foreigners gave to William I a chance to define with greater precision the services owed by landowners. That the evidence should come first from ecclesiastical tenants, where there had been less change in tenure, should not surprise us. The greater definition and increased quotas also led to that process of subinfeudation on which the Abingdon chronicler remarked. Even this must not be seen as a product solely of conquest. Before 1066 knights, or thegns, were settled on the estates of Tavistock, Ely, Canterbury and Worcester in return for service, and these 'thegnlands' were taken over by Norman tenants.

What has struck commentators forcefully when considering the size of the abbeys' quotas is their discrepancy. Twenty-six houses – none of them post-Conquest foundations – were assessed in 1166, and their quotas range from 60 (Peterborough, and Glastonbury later reduced to 40), to 40 (Bury, Ely) and 30 (Abingdon), down to 2 (Winchcombe, Sherborne and Milton) and 1 (Muchelney and Abbotsbury). The diversity is evidently not related solely to wealth, since Peterborough and Glastonbury valued respectively in 1086 at £323 and over £827, owed the same number of knights, and Pershore, whose value was half that of Cerne, owed the same number (2). The imposition on a few rich houses, like St Albans (6) and Ramsey (3), was light, whereas for some of the less wealthy, like Bath (20) and Tavistock (15), it was burdensome. Knowles suggested that the explanation for this discrepancy lay in the number of knights brought in by individual Norman abbots.[16] Thus, Peterborough had a high quota because of the need to provide for the knights of Abbot Turold: the monks must have looked on in some horror as he arrived at the abbey in 1070 'and one hundred and sixty Frenchmen with him, and all fully armed'.[17] More recently it has been suggested that the quotas, negotiated early in the Conqueror's reign, were related to the needs of defence.[18] Glastonbury had a high assessment, not so much because it was rich, but because it was strategically placed to guard the Somerset marshes and the invasion route down the river Severn which had been used by the sons of Harold Godwinson in 1068. Ely's quota, like that of Peterborough, was related to the role their knights could play in securing the marshes of the Fenland, the lair of outlaws like Hereward the Wake. Both the number of knights in the retinue of individual Norman abbots and the military needs of defence may have been factors in the assessment of quotas; nevertheless these are unlikely to have been entirely unrelated to the wealth of the abbeys as demonstrated in Domesday Book. Few of the wealthiest houses escaped with a light assessment, and only one or two of the less well endowed ones were burdened excessively. The apparent omission of houses may have been due to particular circumstances, or to favour shown by the Conqueror to individual abbots or abbesses and their communities. Certainly the houses newly founded in the post-Conquest period, such as Battle Abbey, which were still in the process of acquiring endowments and erecting their buildings, escaped the extra burden of knight service.

In general we can see that the Norman Conquest affected the Anglo-Saxon monasteries in a number of ways. Gradually, Norman and French abbots helped to impose foreign customs and practices on some of the monasteries. Monasteries as landowners were drawn more tightly into that system of land tenure and jurisdiction known to historians as feudalism, and although the changes in obligation might not have seemed as radical as once thought, the services owed were redefined and sharpened. The Normans were suspicious of some features of Anglo-Saxon practice, but they accepted, indeed strengthened, others. One of these was the monastic cathedral. The practice of making a conventual church the cathedral of a diocese, its abbot the bishop, and its monks the chapter, was a peculiarly English one, and continental examples are extremely rare. There were in 1066 four monastic cathedrals in England, Canterbury, Winchester, Worcester and Sherborne. The only casualty of the Conquest was Sherborne, which ceased to be monastic when the see was moved to Old Sarum between 1075 and 1078. When he arrived at Canterbury Archbishop Lanfranc (himself a monk) must have considered the monastic chapter a novelty, but despite its unfamiliarity he and other

Norman churchmen supported its adoption elsewhere. Within fifty years
the number of cathedrals served by Benedictine monks had risen to nine.
The ancient see of Rochester had at one time in its long history been
monastic; here Lanfranc revived the monastic chapter by bringing monks
from Bec in 1083; and in the same year the community of secular clerks
at Durham, as we shall see, became monastic. In East Anglia, as part of a
general trend to move sees from rural sites to more populated centres, the
seat of the diocese of North Elmham was transferred to Thetford by
Bishop Herfast, who then made an unsuccessful attempt to relocate it in
the monastery of Bury St Edmunds. When the cathedral was finally established at Norwich (c. 1100) by Herbert Losinga, monk of Fécamp, its
chapter was monastic. In addition three new cathedrals were created in
monasteries: Bath (1088), whither the seat of the bishopric was moved
from Wells; Chester, transferred from Lichfield in 1075 and then to
Coventry in 1121; and Ely (1109). The creation, in 1133, of a new see
with its cathedral church in the Augustinian priory of Carlisle meant that
a majority of English medieval cathedrals – ten out of nineteen – were
served by members of the monastic order. In Scotland the premier
cathedral of St Andrews, too, came to be served by Augustinian canons
(on these see below, chapter 3).

THE CREATION OF DEPENDENT PRIORIES AND CELLS

Many of those who fought with the Conqueror and shared in the
partition of the conquered land were important landowners in Normandy
and other parts of northern France. It was natural, therefore, that when
they came to endow monasteries either in thanksgiving for victory or as
penance for taking part in battle, they should give land to Norman and
French houses, not Anglo-Saxon ones. Between 1066 and 1086 some
thirty continental houses had gained estates in England, the most
prominent being Fécamp and the nunnery of Holy Trinity in Caen. The
scale of their acquisitions has been demonstrated by Brian Golding, who
has pointed out that the assessed income of Fécamp in 1086 was only £70
less than that of St Albans.[19] One consequence of the grant of land to
a Norman or French house was the creation of two types of priory:
daughter houses dependent on, that is, derived from and jurisdictionally
subordinate to, continental abbeys, which constituted the class of what are
generally termed alien priories; and the monastic cells, which were little
more than economic units designed to administer the British estates of
foreign houses. Into the first category fell such houses as Frampton in
Dorset, founded before 1077 as a dependency of the Conqueror's abbey
at Caen, and the Cornish St Michael's Mount, established from its Breton

namesake before 1091. Most of these alien priories were founded in the generations before the reign of Henry I, when ties between the Norman settlers in Britain and the duchy were at their strongest. But the foundations persisted after 1100, and from Bec-Hellouin, the Norman abbey which gave to the English church two successive archbishops of Canterbury, sprang priories at St Neots in Huntingdonshire (1081 or 1082), Stoke by Clare in Suffolk (1090), Goldcliff in Monmouthshire (1113), Wilsford in Lincolnshire (between 1135 and 1154) and Cowick in Devon (before 1144).[20] Another group of priories founded after the Conquest were dependent not on foreign but on English abbeys, and one of the most important mother houses was St Albans, with dependencies in Lincolnshire (at Belvoir, founded between 1076 and 1088), Northumberland (Tynemouth, established before 1089), Norfolk (Binham, founded before 1093, and Wymondham, before 1107), Essex (Hatfield Peverel, after 1100) and at Hertford (before 1093). This marks a significant development in English monastic life.

More numerous than such daughter houses were those administrative units, the monastic cells, over 150 in all, which Knowles called 'unfortunate by-products' of the Conquest. His assessment, that they became 'the most considerable of all the elements of spiritual decay' in the monastic life of England, may be justifiable, especially applied, as he apparently intended his remarks to be, to the later Middle Ages.[21] However, it has to be remembered that cells were establishments whose primary function was economic. The small number of monks placed, for instance, in the small Yorkshire cell of Ecclesfield, were there to administer and manage the local estates of the abbey of St Wandrille. They were not intended to provide an outlet for those who wished to enter the religious life. Although churchmen were constantly aware of the spiritual dangers for monks of living in isolation, there is little concrete evidence, within our period, for the decay and corruption which Knowles's comments imply, even if the contribution of the monastic cell is small compared to houses of major religious groups.

NEW BLACK MONK FOUNDATIONS

Not all monastic benefactors in the post-Conquest period channelled their gifts to houses across the water, and several independent Benedictine houses were founded by Normans in England. Pride of place must go to the Conqueror's foundation at Battle, the abbey whose high altar was said to mark the very spot at Hastings where King Harold fell. The insistence on this location suggests that William was anxious to erect not only a symbol of his penance for the deaths wrought by battle, but a splendid war memorial. The abbey, whose monks were drawn from the monastery at Marmoutier on the Loire, was lavishly endowed and built in glorious style on the model of St Martin of Tours, two miles away from Marmoutier.[22] From Bec came the monks who staffed the monastery at Chester, which they dedicated to the Anglo-Saxon saint Werburgh (1092–3). Colchester was founded in 1096 by William I's seneschal, Eudo, and its first monks derived from the cathedral priory of Rochester. One of William the Conqueror's trusted henchmen, Roger of Montgomery, earl of Shrewsbury, established a Benedictine abbey in honour of St Peter and St Paul on the banks of the river Severn by the east gate of the city. A handful of monks were brought from Séez to begin the abbey in 1083, but it was not until 1087 that an abbot was appointed. Despite the status of Roger of Montgomery (who became a monk at Shrewsbury, died and was interred there) and his successors, it was not until the abbey came into royal hands after the rebellion and forfeiture of Roger's sons that it began to thrive and rise to a position of importance, which it always maintained, in the Welsh marcher regions.

THE NORTHERN REVIVAL

In the North, too, there began the resurgence of regular life, a curious product of nostalgia for the Anglo-Saxon past and of Norman political propaganda. The first stirrings of monastic life are documented in a twelfth-century history of Selby Abbey, which tells how a monk of the French abbey of Auxerre named Benedict settled at Selby, having absconded from Auxerre (in response to a vision of its patron saint, Germanus) with its most prized relic, the middle finger of the saint's left hand. The history is a blend of historical narrative and hagiography which is difficult to untangle, and much remains unclear about the origins of Selby, although its dedication to St Germanus – one of only two in Britain – suggests that there was indeed a link with Auxerre. But that link was not a formal one, and what is certain is that Selby, which rose to be one of only five autonomous Benedictine houses in the North, began as a settlement by that one man, Benedict, who was evidently aiming to live as a hermit.[23] What determined that the community should emerge as a fully constituted Benedictine abbey rather than remaining the refuge of a solitary on the banks of the river Ouse was the notice taken of Benedict, first by William I's sheriff of Yorkshire, then by the king himself. It is evident that both saw the possibilities offered by the creation of a strong, well-endowed and loyal religious house in an area which had recently been the centre of rebellion against the Normans.[24] Estates were granted to the community, a new church was begun, and under its Norman abbots, particularly Hugh de Lacy (c. 1096/7–c. 1122), Selby began to achieve a position of prominence.

The story of the establishment of Selby is overshadowed, understandably enough, by that of the 'northern revival', which owed a conscious debt to the Anglo-Saxon past. [25] The north of England was the centre of two serious uprisings against the Normans in 1068 and 1069, and after the second of these the conqueror ordered a scorched earth policy, the 'harrying of the North', determined to ensure that the countryside could no longer support the rebels. One of the knights in his army was a man named Reinfrid, and during the expedition he visited and was deeply moved by the ruins of Whitby Abbey on their dramatic clifftop site on the North Sea coast. Not long afterwards Reinfrid decided to become a monk, and the place he chose was Evesham, which was thriving under the rule of Abbot Æthelwig, and was, significantly, offering relief to the refugees from William's harrying of the North.[26] At a neighbouring monastery, Winchcombe, Reinfrid encountered Prior Aldwin, a man well-versed in history with a particular interest in Bede's *Ecclesiastical History*. Together with Ælfwig, a monk of Evesham, Reinfrid and Aldwin decided to visit Northumbria, to live a life of poverty there in the places which Aldwin's reading of Bede told them had been the centres of monastic life. Their journey took them first to Newcastle, where they received permission from Bishop Walcher of Durham to settle at the site of Jarrow, Bede's own monastery. Here they attracted considerable attention and were joined by recruits. As the community grew Aldwin moved on in the company of a clerk named Turgot to try and live a solitary life at another ancient site, Melrose, while Reinfrid travelled to Whitby. Aldwin and Turgot were recalled to restore Monkwearmouth, and in 1083 the secular clerks who served the shrine of St Cuthbert at Durham were replaced by twenty-three monks from Monkwearmouth and Jarrow. So began the great Benedictine cathedral priory of the North, where within a few decades there rose on the banks of the river Wear the magnificent Romanesque buildings which still dominate the city. The monastic cathedral faces the castle, the two together forming powerful symbols of Norman political might. At the same time the monastic community was the custodian of the relics of the greatest Northumbrian saint, Cuthbert.

Reinfrid's resettlement at Whitby (1078/9) was to prove no less momentous in its consequences. Although it was made in time to emerge as a Benedictine house of importance in Yorkshire, the indications are that in its first years Whitby, like Selby, was intended to be an eremitical community, where the emphasis was on solitude and individual life. It was endowed by a lay patron, William de Percy, but his relationship with the monks was a troubled one, and hostility between them, combined with pirate attacks, led to temporary disbandments of the Whitby site, resulting in migrations, once to Lastingham, an inland site on the southern fringes of the north Yorkshire moors, and once to Hackness, about four miles inland from Scarborough. From Lastingham a group of monks under their abbot, Stephen, moved to York, where they had been offered the church of St Olave in Marygate. This proved to be decisive. Once established just outside the major settlement of the North, Stephen and his monks were in a position to attract endowments, and in this they were successful. Critical to the development of the community was the patronage of William I – anxious as at Selby to foster a strong and loyal institution in an area of political unrest – and of his son William II. The success of St Mary's, no doubt because of its geographical location, exceeded that of Selby and Whitby, and the charters of the house attest its rapid and unparalleled acquisition of lands from leading Norman nobles, not only in the environs of the city and in the county, but all over England. St Mary's, Durham and Whitby owed their foundation initially to a movement which combined the pull of the solitary life with a devotion to the Anglo-Saxon past, both a reaction to the impact of the Norman Conquest. Ironically, they owed their development and success to the Normans, who saw the political potential to be gained by fostering such religious institutions. Stone abbeys and cathedrals no less than stone castles were a symbol of conquest.

NORMAN INFLUENCE IN WALES

Norman infiltration into Wales began soon after the conquest of England. In 1067 William fitz Osbern, one of William I's most trusted men, had been established on the borders in Herefordshire. By 1086 the Norman invasion had reached as far west as Caerleon, and from the 1090s a number of prominent conquerors and settlers had emerged in mid- and south Wales: Bernard of Neufmarché in Brycheiniog, Robert fitz Hamo in Morgannwg, Arnulf of Montgomery in Pembrokeshire and Gilbert fitz Richard de Clare in Ceredigion, all of whom came to be associated with the development of monasticism. In Wales, as in the north of England, there were no native houses which could attract Norman interest. However, there were three ways in which the conquerors made their impact. As in England, Welsh lands, many of them endowments of the *clas* church, were given to Norman houses. Second, churches and their property were acquired by and for Norman abbots of English houses. Third and as a consequence of the first two, new houses came into existence. One characteristic of the Welsh houses in the eleventh and early twelfth centuries was that they were all dependent priories, that is, they derived from English or continental houses which retained a measure of control over them; only religious houses established on the Welsh borders, like Shrewsbury and Chester, were independent abbeys. Another was that they were nearly all associated with two other Norman institutions, the castle or the borough. Benedictine monasticism was generally urban, but in Wales this association links the emergence of monastic life more closely still with the agencies of conquest.

Seventeen monastic dependencies were founded in south Wales during the course of Norman infiltration; the majority remained cells, and only seven achieved the status of conventual priory.[27] Of these, five were dependent on Norman or French and two on English houses, while of the cells, two administered lands of Norman houses and eight, estates of English abbeys. The names of those with whom the initial grants are linked demonstrate quite clearly the connection with political conquest. Fitz Osbern granted Chepstow to the abbey of Cormeilles which he himself had founded c. 1060. Arnulf of Montgomery founded Pembroke Priory, drawing monks from Séez, that monastery restored by his father, Roger, which had also provided monks for the Montgomery foundation at Shrewsbury. After his victory over the Welsh in 1093 and his construction of a castle at Aberhonddu (Brecon), Bernard of Neufmarché built a priory there, dependent on Battle Abbey; in so doing he completed the classic triple settlement of castle, church and borough. The choice of William I's abbey of Battle as a mother house may well have been designed to emphasize Bernard's own status as a conqueror of Wales.[28] Some of these new houses were based on the *clas* churches, the most famous being Llanbadarn Fawr near Aberystwyth, granted by the Clare lords of Ceredigion to Gloucester Abbey.[29] Most, like fitz Hamo's cell of Cardiff and Bishop Roger of Salisbury's priory at Kidwelly, were built close to their castles.[30] It is small wonder that the Benedictine priories of south Wales were associated firmly with alien settlement. They continued to pay monetary tribute to Norman or English houses, Brecon to Battle, Monmouth to St Florent, Chepstow to Cormeilles and Goldcliff to Bec; as far as we can tell they failed to attract local Welsh recruits or Welsh endowments. We may see the introduction of Benedictine monasticism to south Wales as part of Norman conquest and settlement, as a concrete expression of who was now the ruler.

SCOTLAND

The first steps in the spread of Benedictine monasticism into Scotland are owed not to the Normans but to a descendant of the line of the Anglo-

Saxon kings. Around 1070 the Scottish king Malcolm Canmore married Margaret, sister of Edgar Ætheling, who with her brother and sister Christina, later a nun and abbess of Romsey, had been brought up at the court of Edward the Confessor. The regular life with which Margaret was familiar was, therefore, of the Benedictine type followed in the Anglo-Saxon monasteries. By contrast, in Scotland by 1070 the only forms of religious life were solitary hermits or communities of Culdees.[31] While Margaret does not seem to have despised the Scottish church that she encountered – she made benefactions to the ancient communities of Iona and St Andrews – she did attempt to introduce Benedictine monasticism from south of the border.[32] She consulted with her spiritual adviser, Archbishop Lanfranc, and as a result a small group of monks was sent from Christ Church, Canterbury, to found a Benedictine community at Dunfermline.[33] The house did not, however, prosper until after her son King David I enlarged it in 1128 and raised it to the status of an abbey. Less successful was a monastic settlement which formed part of the 'northern revival'. As already mentioned, Aldwin and Turgot moved on from Jarrow to Melrose, a site associated with St Cuthbert, but their attempt to reintroduce monastic life there ran into political difficulties and foundered when they refused to do homage to King Malcolm. But although Melrose was abandoned, Turgot, as prior of Durham, maintained contacts with Queen Margaret and later, under her son, King Alexander I, became bishop of St Andrews (1107–15). A further connection with Durham came with the grant by Malcolm and Margaret's son, King Edgar, of the shire of Coldingham to the church of Durham (1098), but it was probably not for over forty years that a priory emerged from that endowment. On the whole, the spread of monastic influence into Scotland from the South came in a later period, the reign of David I.

THE CLUNIACS

The patronage of religious houses is a good indicator of cultural identity, and, as a group, the first generation of Norman incomers into England and Wales was more inclined to direct its sympathies and loyalties, concretely expressed in terms of grants of lands, towards Norman houses rather than existing English ones.[34] A general change in attitude would only come when settlers started to think of themselves as Anglo-Norman rather than Norman; for some, perhaps younger sons, landless in the duchy, who achieved status in England, this would happen sooner rather than later. A newly found sense of identity would be expressed by the foundation of a religious house in England, and towards the end of the eleventh century, this is precisely what happened. From 1077 to the end of the century and beyond a significant number of houses were established which had no formal links with Normandy but were influenced by the Burgundian monastery of Cluny. Cluny was a Benedictine abbey, founded in 910, whose impact on the development of the monastic life was already out-standing. First, it had elaborated the performance of the liturgy and set 'the splendour of worship' in a rich architectural setting. Second, and this was a novel step in monastic practice, it developed a federation of houses which surrendered traditional Benedictine independence to create for Cluny a 'vast spiritual empire'. The family of Cluny was a monarchical institution in which each house was constitutionally bound to the centre, Cluny. Monks from all houses were regarded as monks of the Burgundian house, and the authority of its abbot was supreme. The desire of religious houses to band together, first successfully expressed by Cluny, was to become an important feature in the development of medieval monastic life.

There were a number of houses, however, whose association with Cluny was limited to the adoption of its liturgical customs without implying any loss of autonomy. Normandy was already deeply influenced by Cluny in the early eleventh century when William of Volpiano trans-mitted its usages into Fécamp via Dijon.[35] It was thus that many Norman houses, such as Fécamp and also Bernay, Jumièges and St Wandrille, bore the imprint of Cluniac customs while retaining their independence.[36] In England Henry I's foundation at Reading (1121) and later King Stephen's at Faversham (1148), as well as the Scottish house of May founded by King David I, were strongly influenced by Cluny (Reading was colonized by monks from the Burgundian abbey) yet remained autonomous. Seemingly major royal patrons wished to participate in the fashion for Cluniac-inspired houses without founding monasteries which were dependent on, and subordinate to, a Burgundian one.

When new houses were founded as members of the Cluniac family they usually had the title of priory, indicating a status subordinate to the mother of the congregation. England had already experienced some of the influence of Cluny, which can be observed in the *Regularis Concordia*, in the tenth century, but it was not until 1077 that a dependent priory of the congregation was founded there. Some time before 1077 a Norman noble, William de Warenne, decided to establish a religious house on his English estates. The sources for that foundation, Lewes, are not without their problems, and the 'foundation charter' as it stands is a forgery. However, the main outlines of the story appear to be that while on a journey to Rome, William and his wife stayed at Cluny and that it was there that they decided that the house they intended to found should be a Cluniac one. Accordingly they negotiated with Abbot Hugh of Cluny,

who thought long and hard about sending out a colony before he agreed
to do so. The reason for his reluctance may have been connected with the
perceived difficulties of maintaining control over a colony in England. At
roughly the same time Hugh refused William I's request to send him six
monks to aid in the reform of the English church, though in this case the
sources link Hugh's reaction to William's offer to pay £100 per monk;
certainly twelfth-century commentators interpreted this offer as simony.[37]
By 1077 monks from Cluny had made a first foundation at Lewes which
was well endowed by Warenne. In due course it made its own foundations, among them Castle Acre in Norfolk, established in 1089 by
Warenne's son and namesake, and Thetford, also in Norfolk, in 1104. But
the major expansion came, not direct from Cluny or Lewes, but from the
French house of La Charité. Between 1079 and 1100 five significant
offshoots from this house were planted in England: Much Wenlock in
Shropshire (1080/1), where an Anglo-Saxon monastic site was revived,
Bermondsey (1089), Daventry (c. 1090 at Preston Capes, to Daventry in
1107 X 1108), Pontefract (c. 1090) and Northampton (1093 X 1100). The
founders were major Norman nobles, with one important exception, and
this was Alwin Child, founder of the London priory of Bermondsey, and
an English citizen of London. What prompted Child's foundation or the
choice of La Charité and the customs of Cluny is not documented. It
appears, however, that the lands with which Child endowed Bermondsey
and which formed the basis of the priory's wealth throughout the Middle
Ages had been sold to Child by William II, who may in this instance have
been associating himself with a monastic foundation in thanksgiving for
having survived a baronial revolt in 1088.[38]

The British congregation of Cluny was not large, although foundations
continued, in small numbers, to be made until the mid twelfth century
and secured major patrons. One group of monasteries, descended from St
Martin des Champs (Paris), included Barnstaple, Exeter and the Welsh
house of St Clears, about ten miles west of Carmarthen. Two questions
arise: why did the Cluniacs enjoy this vogue in the last twenty years of the
eleventh century and beyond? And how may we characterize the movement? One answer to the first question might be that the foundation of a
Cluniac house gave benefit to a Norman who wished to associate himself
with his English estates and lordship in some tangible way, yet avoided
any connection with existing Anglo-Saxon houses, of which there were
a number which could, presumably, have provided alternative colonies.[39]
Cluny was a French house, and its offshoots had no 'English dimension'.
It was also a form of monasticism with which the Normans were familiar.
This is a persuasive argument, yet we must still ask the second question:
what was distinctive about Cluniac monasticism? Did a founder choose to

endow a Cluniac house because of the observances he or she expected to
be followed there? Or in order to reproduce the splendours of Cluny? To
follow a fashionable trend? Or because in founding a new priory a man or
woman was choosing not just a Cluniac house, but a daughter house of
an existing monastery? When Adam fitz Swane decided to establish a
monastery at Monk Bretton in southern Yorkshire in the middle years of
the twelfth century, he turned for his monks to one of the houses founded
by his feudal lords, the Lacy family. The choice open to him was the
Augustinian priory of Nostell, or the Cluniac house of Pontefract. He
chose the latter. The proximity of Pontefract to his estates, and his own
tenurial and personal connections, rather than the nature of Cluniac
observances, may have dictated Adam fitz Swane's choice. Similar
personal connections might explain the advent of Cluniac monasticism to
Scotland. In the 1140s or early 1150s King David I turned to the abbey of
Reading, founded by his former brother-in-law Henry I, for monks to
found an abbey on the Isle of May. This monastery was not David's first
Scottish foundation, but it was significant as a religious house planted
in the province of Moray, which had only recently come under royal
control. It was an example of an Anglo-Norman institution designed to
strengthen David's authority.[40]

How cohesive were these members of the vast Cluniac empire? The
evidence we have suggests that contacts were usually formal ones, like the
payment of a yearly tax and the recognition of the right of a mother house
to a voice in the election of the prior of a dependency. Even this could be
a vexed question, and Monk Bretton spent much time and effort
trying to extricate itself from the control of Pontefract, a matter which was
only solved when the daughter house left the congregation of Cluny to
become an independent Benedictine priory in the mid thirteenth century.
Certainly evidence for contact with Cluny itself is sparse. The Anglo-
Saxon Chronicle records the visit to England in 1130 of Peter the
Venerable, abbot of Cluny; and a later abbot, Hugh, was in the country
in 1201.[41] On the whole, there seems little reason to question the verdict
delivered on the English Cluniacs by David Knowles, namely that as a
group they were loosely organized and played no outstanding part in
public life. Knowles's statement applied to the period from the late
eleventh to the first part of the thirteenth century, during which time the
Cluniac federation did not attempt to develop any machinery of control
as elaborate as that of the Cistercian Order, which was soon to prove so
successful. It was not until 1231, when Pope Gregory IX introduced the
general chapter and regular visitations, that more direct control over
Cluniac houses was sought.[42] That the British houses should have
developed along independent lines, largely heedless of the mother house,

is consistent with the constraints of distance. Nor is it to be expected that even the greater British houses, like Lewes and Bermondsey, could in any way match the splendours of Cluny itself. As a group, the Cluniacs are of interest as the first wave of foundations on English soil after the Conquest and for the influence of their congregation on the development of church architecture and ornament.

CHURCH BUILDING

Commenting on the coming of the Normans to England, William of Malmesbury did not fail to notice one change in the rural and urban landscape, a major programme of building of greater churches and monasteries 'after a style unknown before'.[43] This was not just the obvious consequence of the founding of new houses; in the latter years of the eleventh and early years of the twelfth centuries, nearly all existing ones were rebuilt. The Normans seem to have considered the English churches (with the exception, presumably, of the recently completed Westminster) small and old-fashioned, and accordingly embarked on a programme of rebuilding which opened the gate for further continental influence already evident at Westminster. Moreover, they consciously introduced into England a new style of church design consistent with the demands of liturgical practices derived from Cluny and Dijon and in use in the churches of the duchy from the early eleventh century.

The architectural style in fashion in Normandy in the mid eleventh century is best illustrated at St Etienne, Caen (from the early 1060s), which influenced the design of Canterbury's two monasteries, Christ Church and St Augustine's, the rebuilding of both of which began around 1070. The best English survivors from the period are, however, St Albans (begun by Abbot Paul in 1077, substantially completed by 1088, and consecrated in 1115) and the transepts of Winchester Cathedral.[44] Here, as in so many other places, later rebuilding has disguised or replaced eleventh-century Romanesque work. Very little remains, for instance, of the well-documented building activity of Wulfstan of Worcester, perhaps rendered necessary because of the rise in the number of monks from twelve in 1062 to over fifty in 1089.[45] Worcester in turn influenced Great Malvern (c. 1085), Gloucester (begun in 1089) and Tewkesbury.[46] It has been suggested that Worcester and Gloucester, like St Augustine's, Canterbury, Winchester and Bury, may reflect, in their complex east end, the design of St Wandrille and Mont St Michel, which allowed for the particular needs of pilgrim churches, that is, protection for the relics and the free flow of pilgrims.[47]

The design and layout of monastic churches was affected, not just by

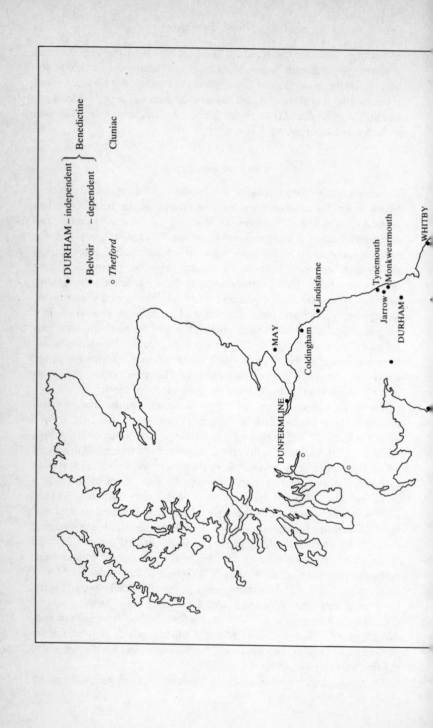

DURHAM – independent ⎫
Belvoir – dependent ⎬ Benedictine
                    ⎭
Thetford ○ Cluniac

MAY

Coldingham
Lindisfarne

DUNFERMLINE

Tynemouth
Jarrow   Monkwearmouth

DURHAM

WHITBY

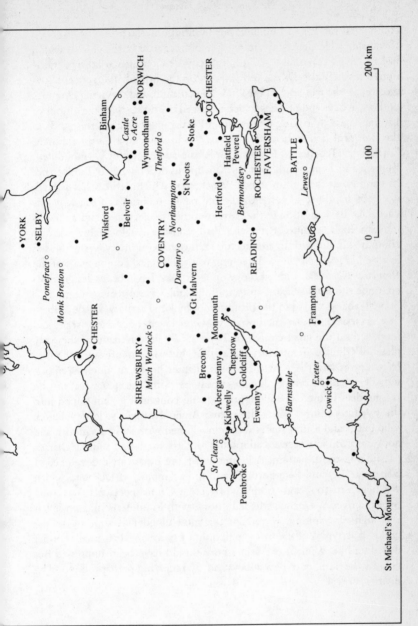

Map 2 Benedictine and Cluniac houses founded between the Norman Conquest and c. 1150

continental models of building, but by liturgical practice. The *Regularis Concordia* had located worship in three distinct areas of the church which had equal architectural and liturgical status.[48] Continental liturgy, transmitted through the *Decreta* of Lanfranc, on the other hand, concentrated worship in the east end, in the choir and crossing; and surviving churches of those abbeys and priories which followed the monastic constitutions of Lanfranc bear a 'striking uniformity' of ritual plan which corresponds to the liturgical demands of the *Decreta*.[49] These include Christ Church, Canterbury, Rochester, Evesham, St Albans and its cells of Wymondham, Binham and Tynemouth, and Durham and its dependency of Lindisfarne. In contrast to this group stands Winchester, which, Klukas has argued, was rebuilt in a style perpetuating the native traditions of the *Regularis Concordia*. Its dedication to the native Swithun was retained and linked to the two highest saints, Peter and Paul, and the Anglo-Saxon calendar continued to be used. In architectural terms this continuity was expressed in a building which allowed free rein to the liturgical complexities of the *Regularis Concordia* and whose west end may have been designed to continue the Anglo-Saxon custom of the king's ritual crown-wearing.

New abbeys added to the profusion of building activity. Battle Abbey, that ecclesiastical war memorial, was conceived on a large scale and modelled on the great church of Tours. Sadly little remains of the early phase of Cluniac architecture in England, but some impressive sculpture from Lewes and the ornate Norman chapter house at Much Wenlock suggest a lavishness of design consistent with the practices of the Burgundian house. Rebuilding of existing communities continued into the twelfth century, and a distinctive Anglo-Norman style developed: solid pillars and round arches were embellished with incised patterns, and doors and window recesses adorned with intricate design and the characteristic dog-tooth pattern. A lighter and more ornate style developed at places like Ely and Peterborough and most famously at Durham, which was begun in 1093 and completed by 1133. On its spectacular site rising over the river Wear the cathedral priory, with its immense incised pillars and high-rib vaulting, is perhaps the most eloquent testimony to the building activities of the first generations of Normans. It is small wonder that men like William of Malmesbury should have been impressed not only by the number of new abbeys and churches, but perhaps above all by their sheer scale.

3

THE REGULAR CANONS

•

A central theme throughout monastic history has been an appeal to the apostolic life, the *vita apostolica*. Men and women have looked to the Bible to discover how the apostles and early Christian community in Jerusalem lived; and they found one key text in the *Acts of the Apostles*, chapter 2, which described how 'all who believed were together and had all things in common. And sold their possessions and goods and parted them to all men as every man had need' (verses 44–5). The true apostolic life was, therefore, one lived in common where there was no private property or possessions. It was, one could argue, monasticism itself, and texts like these inspired early writers on the monastic life such as St Basil and St Jerome. The idea of the *vita apostolica* was, however, given wider significance by St Augustine, bishop of Hippo in north Africa between c. 396 and 430, who was to argue that all priests – not monks – should, after the pattern of the apostles, give up personal possessions and live in common; and he adopted this practice in his own cathedral church. Augustine did not write a rule as St Benedict had done, and only one of his surviving works, Letter 211, written for his sister, who was a nun, was specifically about the practice of the religious life. Some time afterwards this letter was adapted – not necessarily by Augustine – for a male community and became known as the *Regula Tertia*. Together with the *Regula Secunda*, a brief document listing the daily services and regulations on discipline and manual labour, these formed the Rule of St Augustine. The date at which they came together is unknown, but it is likely to have been by the sixth century.[1]

It was, however, much later that the writings by, and attributed to, St

Augustine came to exercise a significant influence on the development of monasticism. From time to time between the sixth and mid eleventh century attempts were made to improve clerical discipline by imposing a regular life on the clergy, but among the documents associated with these attempts none made mention of Augustine or his rule. The idea that groups of clerics serving cathedrals and major churches should live a life in common re-emerged in the eleventh century, especially at first in southern France and in Italy, where it was associated with two important movements: the revival of the eremitical tradition[2] and the Gregorian reform movement. During the middle years of the century the papacy emerged from a long period during which it had deteriorated into little more than a local power. Now it began to assert its status and to turn its attention to the reform of the church.[3] There were many problems to be faced; but most reformers felt that the majority of these could in some way be traced to private possessions and money. One abuse was simony: the buying of an ecclesiastical office which would then yield profit. A second was nepotism: the granting of an office to a relative, frequently a son. A third was clerical marriage, which might also lead to the further problem of hereditary clerical benefices, the passing of a parish church, or a position within the church, from father to son. Perhaps the best answer to all these dangers might be the adoption of a quasi-monastic life by clerics. They would then not marry; they would hold no personal possessions; they would derive no revenue from their office. Here we can begin to see the attraction of the kind of celibate clerical community envisaged by Augustine and others. The Lateran Council of 1059 gave authority to the adoption of a common life by the clergy, and by 1100 a number of communities of clerics had in fact begun to live in common, in accordance with papal decrees.

Many formulae were used to describe these clerks, but the most common came to be regular canons, that is, canons who followed a rule; and that came to be the Rule of St Augustine, adopted gradually as the canons searched for an authority for their way of life. Thus the development of the regular canons did not follow a rediscovery of the Rule; rather, it came into gradual use as the canons, the 'clerical monks', sought to give a weight of authority and historical respectability to their way of life. The Rule of Augustine came to be the standard one for houses of canons, and so successful was it that it was adopted and adapted by other orders like the Premonstratensians, to whom we shall turn in due course. Part of the reason for its pre-eminence was that it acquired the backing of popes as a means of enforcing a sensible way of life for the clergy, and it suited the twelfth-century desire to find precedent and historical authority for a way of life. Another reason for the popularity which it came to enjoy was its adaptability. It was not just that it could be supplemented, as it was to be by the Premonstratensians, Gilbertines and Dominican Friars. It could also provide the basis for the way of life of a variety of communities. The documents which came together to form the Rule of St Augustine laid down only the basic requirements and could therefore encompass local customs. The regular canons lived a common life according to a monastic timetable, but the wish to emulate the life of the apostles meant that it was desirable to adapt that timetable to accommodate concerns of a pastoral or social nature. The Rule of St Augustine was suitable for use by communities serving collegiate churches, cathedrals and hospitals, and this wide variety can be seen in Britain. Here the houses which followed Augustine's Rule were to be the most numerous religious houses in the country, and their popularity among founders was to continue well into the thirteenth century.

ARRIVAL OF CANONS REGULAR IN ENGLAND AND WALES TO 1135

There was a brief 'pre-Augustinian' period in England when, as on the continent, communities of clerics adopted a common life without using the Rule.[4] At Canterbury, for example, Archbishop Lanfranc instituted a hospital in St Gregory's between 1085 and 1087. Dickinson suggested that to begin with, the priests within the establishment 'were a minor element' and that it was not until the time of Archbishop William of Corbeil (1123–36) that we may speak of them as regular canons.[5] However, it remains the case that the foundation charter refers to six priests placed in the church 'to serve in it [and] to live a common life according to a rule'. The priests did not yet follow the Rule of St Augustine, but they were committed to a full common life and may appropriately be described as regulars. The care of the sick entrusted to them anticipated one of the subsidiary functions of the Augustinian canons. Another early foundation – traditionally identified as the earliest – represents a second type of establishment. The house of St Botulph in Colchester was a secular college which was converted into a community of regular canons. The date of 1095 which various authorities assign to its foundation probably refers to the establishment of the secular college; all that can be said of the adoption of the regular life is that it had occurred before 1107, when canons from St Botulph's helped to staff a new foundation in Aldgate. We know little of a third early house, St Mary in Huntingdon, except that it was apparently established before 1092, when it sent a colony to found a tiny and short-lived house in the church of St Giles in Cambridge.[6]

The heyday of Augustinian foundations – and after about 1100 we may

more confidently call them this – came during the reign of Henry I
(1100–35) and was indeed associated with the patronage afforded to the
canons by the king and his first wife Matilda (d. 1118), daughter of Queen
Margaret of Scotland. Investigation of the chronology of foundation is
rendered difficult by the usual types of problems, either the lack of a
foundation charter for a house, or the impossibility of assigning to it a
precise date. It seems, however, that there was a sudden rise in the
number of foundations for canons between 1100 and 1120, and an
explosion between 1120 and 1135, with sixteen houses founded during
the last five years of the reign alone. However, an account of the spread
of the canons in Britain might usefully begin with Queen Matilda's
foundation in London, for this will introduce to us a number of
important factors in the story. In 1107 or 1108 the queen evidently
decided to found a religious house in London. She had already expressed
her concern about the sick of the city by her foundation of the leper
hospital of St Giles, and now sought to extend her charitable activities.
For help with the project she approached Archbishop Anselm of
Canterbury, who had recently returned from a prolonged exile in Europe,
during which he had come into close contact with the reformed papacy.
He had had ample opportunity then, as during his period as abbot of Bec,
to become familiar with the concept of the regular canons, and it is not
perhaps surprising that he suggested to the queen that her new venture
should be a house of canons. We should not try to read too far beyond
the sources; nevertheless, we may suggest that such a house would appeal
to the archbishop as particularly suited to pastoral work in an urban
context, and that it would attract a benefactor like Matilda with a strong
sense of social concern. Aldgate was colonized from Colchester, and its
first prior was the canon Norman, who had studied abroad and who now
became the queen's confessor. The house was well endowed by the queen
(although Aldgate's early years were not without their financial troubles),
and, as would be expected because of the identity of its patron and its
location, it came to prosper. It grew wealthy on the offerings of
Londoners; and its prior even became an alderman of one of the wards of
the city. Further, in the late twelfth century Aldgate enjoyed a reputation
as a centre of intellectual activity under its prior Peter of Cornwall.[7]

   The story of Holy Trinity highlights three crucial issues: the influence
of the royal family in establishing the reputation of the canons; the
importance of the archbishop in promoting their cause;[8] and the expectation, implicit in the urban location of the house, that the canons would
function in a wider context of social and pastoral concern than existing
monasteries. The part played by Henry I and Matilda as founders and
encouragers of others will become clearer as the story unfolds. The role

of the archbishops and bishops must claim our attention for a few moments.

That those entrusted with the running of dioceses should find the concept of the canon, the 'clerical monk', attractive should not surprise us. The office of the medieval bishop was in many ways not an easy one. Some had large dioceses which were difficult to administer; and it was no simple task to try to ensure that clergy were educated and conscientious, and that parishioners received proper spiritual direction. The regular canons were not the answer to all such episcopal problems, but they could make a contribution towards their solution. From their base, a house in which discipline was maintained within a monastic régime and the canons were freed from the ties of family and possession, they could serve the pastoral needs of a district. It may have been for considerations such as these that several of the English bishops quickly began to take an interest in the canons and establish them within their diocese. One way in which they were used was the reform of secular colleges, communities of priests who served a wide *parochia* or parish, which were to be found all over England.[9] William Warelwast, bishop of Exeter (1107–37), was an early enthusiast for putting regular canons in the place of seculars. In 1121 he brought canons from Aldgate to restaff the secular house at Plympton in Devon and in 1127 followed this up with the conversion of the great college of Launceston (Cornwall). Another west-country house revived and placed under the control of the regulars was Taunton, and the guiding light here was William Giffard, bishop of Winchester, whom we shall later encounter as the man who brought the first Cistercian monks to England.[10] He drew his canons from Merton, a priory founded *de novo* in 1114 by Gilbert the sheriff, which was to become one of the most influential of all English Augustinian houses: from there, too, came the brethren who were to revitalize another ancient Cornish minster at Bodmin, whose refoundation was a co-operative effort between the dean of Coutances and the bishop of Exeter. Henry I's chancellor and bishop of Salisbury, Roger, began around 1111 to revive the minster church of St Frideswide in Oxford, a task completed a decade or so later by his royal master, who came to be reckoned as founder.[11] Henry I also founded, from Merton, the great house of Cirencester, one of the few British Augustinian houses to achieve the title of abbey. Most were designated 'priory', which does not (as with Benedictine and Cluniac houses) denote a dependent or subordinate status, but is usually an indication of the size of a community and its endowments, and therefore its status.

It may be assumed that bishops who placed regular canons in the ancient minster churches intended them to fulfil the same pastoral and parochial functions as their predecessors; and we may suggest a similar motive for the early conversion of at least one *clas* church in Wales. Around the year 1110 Henry I had given the church of St Peter, Carmarthen, together with the *clas* church of nearby Llandeulyddog, to Battle Abbey, which had established a cell or dependent priory. Bishop Bernard of St David's evidently saw greater potential in the Carmarthen site and succeeded in wresting the church from Battle, which was compensated for its loss. From this point his part in the development of the community at Carmarthen is undocumented, but given Bernard's connections (he was a former chaplain of Queen Matilda, and had episcopal colleagues who founded Augustinian houses), and the ideal urban location of Carmarthen for such a priory, we may suppose that the acquisition of the church from Battle was the first step in a plan to introduce the concept of the regular canons to Wales and in so doing to oust a traditional *clas* establishment, while retaining its parochial function.[12]

The influence of the higher clergy in the revival of ancient churches and their committal to regular canons may be detected, but to a lesser extent, in the north of England. In 1113, the church of Hexham in Northumbria, once the centre of a bishopric which had now deteriorated into a family possession, had its hereditary priest ousted by Archbishop Thomas II of York and replaced by canons from Huntingdon. Thomas died before he could foster the cause of the canons any further, but they soon acquired an energetic patron in his successor, Archbishop Thurstan (1114–40). The early years of his pontificate saw the plantation of canons regular at Bridlington who evidently replaced 'clerics' – we know no more of the nature of the pre-Augustinian foundation. However, in the North the pattern of expansion was rather different from that in the South, and fewer Augustinian houses came about through the conversion of secular minsters.[13] The influence of the northern archbishop is to be detected more in the foundation charters of priories established on new sites: the Yorkshire houses of Guisborough, Drax, Bolton and Kirkham, and Thurgarton (Nottinghamshire), all founded by barons on the advice, or with the counsel, of Thurstan.[14] That the early endowments of these new priories frequently included a string of parish churches suggests that, like converted secular colleges and minsters, they too were intended to have a pastoral function within the diocese. Although the grant of a church to a religious house was not unique to the Augustinians,[15] they were the major recipients.

Churchmen seem actively to have promoted the establishment of regular canons in their dioceses in order to place the care of parishes in their hands. However, the nature of our sources from the twelfth century makes it impossible to tell how frequently canons themselves did, in fact, serve those churches which they were granted; and it is only with the inception of bishops' registers in the early thirteenth century that we can more easily identify the incumbents of benefices.[16] Perhaps the large number of churches conveyed to them and – in some cases – the small number of canons in priories makes it unlikely that they exercised parochial functions in all or even a majority of them.[17] But there was another advantage to the transfer of parish churches to the canons: even if they did not provide spiritual service for the community, they exercised the right of patronage, the right to choose a parish priest; and the effect of this was to wrest patronage from the laity and give it to regulars who could by wise stewardship and their choice of incumbent improve clerical standards. Either way, the enthusiastic backing given to the Augustinian canons by the higher clergy suggests that those churchmen perceived for them a very real pastoral role within the diocese as agents of reform. If reality fell short of ideal, then neither the early generations of canons nor their ecclesiastical sponsors were entirely to blame.[18]

The expectation that canons would serve in parish churches represents what we might call a practical side to their vocation. Another such aspect is suggested by their work in hospitals, and this may be demonstrated especially well by the foundation of the house of St Bartholomew in London. A fortunate survival from the second half of the twelfth century has been the 'foundation book' of the priory and hospital. This tells us that a royal clerk named Rahere, a man who had risen to considerable wealth, probably through court patronage, conceived the idea of establishing a hospital. Inspired, so the sources tell us, by a vision of St Bartholomew directing him to a place chosen for a church built in his honour, Rahere started work on a site at Smithfield, and with royal support and assistance from other Londoners, he cleared the site and built a church, priory and hospital. He himself became the first prior in 1123. Originally, then, the priory and hospital were founded as one institution following the Rule of St Augustine; but in the course of the second half of the century they diverged and became separate establishments.[19]

The distinction between 'priory' and 'hospital' is not always easy to make. Hospitals for the care of the sick and guests (an increasingly popular target for endowments in the twelfth century) had a religious element, at the very least chaplains who prayed for the sick and for benefactors. Priories had the responsibility for providing hospitality for guests. This close approximation in function led to a lack of definition in the Middle Ages, and some houses are referred to as both priory and hospital. The history of Smithfield shows that some eventually separated and achieved that distinction of function. In other places hospitals were served from a priory and were thus dependent institutions. The abbey at Cirencester, for instance, ran two hospitals in the town. Some Augustinian houses, like Hempton (Norfolk), were founded as hospitals and later converted into priories. At others the development was reversed. Care for others in a different guise is demonstrated by an early foundation made in 1115 by the constable of Chester, who placed canons at Runcorn to serve in his castle chapel and also to look after pilgrims and travellers crossing the river Mersey.[20]

The initial functions envisaged for Runcorn Priory remind us of the diversity of origin of houses of regular canons, and in many ways the beauty of the Rule of St Augustine lay in its adaptability. It also came to be used by groups of hermits, and communities whose members had a leaning towards the contemplative life rather than an active ministry. The transformation of hermit sites into religious houses was not an exclusively Augustinian activity, but the Black Canons do provide us with some notable examples.[21] One such is Llanthony, a house which was to become famed both for its austerity and its learning.[22] In the last years of the eleventh century a knight of Hugh de Lacy called William had cause to take shelter in an ancient ruined chapel in the remote Black Mountains, and here on the borders of Wales and Herefordshire he established a hermitage. He was joined by Ernisius, a former chaplain of Queen Matilda, and together they lived an eremitical life, and constructed a church which was consecrated by the bishops of Glamorgan and Hereford in 1108. Hugh de Lacy became a patron of the hermits, and this connection with the royal court and episcopal colleagues no doubt brought the community to the attention of Archbishop Anselm. Anselm advised that the hermits should become Augustinian canons, and arranged for staff to be brought from Merton, Holy Trinity, Aldgate and Colchester to instruct them. Merton itself was only founded in 1114, so we are looking to the establishment of Llanthony in the years after that date. Their austerity, and the high reputation which the canons soon acquired, gained them benefactors, some of whom, notably Henry I and Matilda, had to be fought off to prevent them almost crushing the community with kindness; but the canons were determined to preserve that solitude and asceticism which made them famous. Their location on the borders of Wales, as well as their association with the king, made them vulnerable to attack by the Welsh; they survived the Welsh rebellion which followed the death of Henry I in 1135, but the following year the bishop of Hereford offered a new and more secure site near Gloucester, which became known as Llanthony Secunda. Some canons went to what was intended to be a daughter house of Llanthony Prima, but others stayed in the Black Mountains, and after 1205 any connections between the two communities were severed. What helped the original community to survive materially was the patronage of the Lacy family, who in the 1180s found themselves among the Anglo-Norman conquerors of Ireland, and who then shared the spoils of war with their Welsh house, as the Norman settlers in England and Wales had done with their Norman houses over one hundred years before.

A group of hermits; a royal chaplain; a Norman baron; bishops; a king; an archbishop: it was this team which therefore brought about the successful foundation of Llanthony Prima. Although the personnel was slightly different, it was a similar combination which ensured the success of a northern venture, Nostell.[23] In the early years of the twelfth century a group of hermits established themselves on the lands of the Lacy lord of Pontefract – a branch of that same family which had founded Llanthony – on an ancient site associated with St Oswald. Some time later, perhaps around 1114, they came to the notice of a royal chaplain named Æthelwulf, or Æthelwold. He decided to join them, and in the next few years with the help of Henry I and Archbishop Thurstan, the hermit community was transformed into an Augustinian one; endowments were provided by the king, and by the supplanter of the Lacy family at Pontefract, Hugh de Laval. Here the similarity with Llanthony Prima ends. While the canons of Llanthony resisted the kind of attention which royal patronage usually brought, those of Nostell welcomed endowments from all the leading barons of the North.

The influence of court and king was paramount in the dispersal of the houses of Black Canons up to 1135; all but about ten of the forty-three foundations were by members of the royal family and their entourage. Henry I himself established five and helped with seven foundations.[24] Other houses we have seen were established by, or at the insistence of, members of the higher clergy who were also frequent attenders at court. Nobles and *curiales*, court officials, were responsible for the remainder of foundations before 1135, including Kenilworth, established by Geoffrey de Clinton, king's treasurer; and Oseney near Oxford, established by Robert d'Oilly, sheriff of Oxford and constable to the king.[25] The canons enjoyed a tight circle of patronage around the royal court. Before we leave the reign of Henry I mention must be made of one further royal foundation: Carlisle.[26] In 1122 the king visited the city, and shortly afterwards a priory of regular canons was established. It was probably as early as this that Henry I conceived the idea of using the Augustinian foundation as a cathedral and creating a new bishopric out of the vast diocese of York. Although the new see did not come into being until 1133, plans – which must have been aided by Archbishop Thurstan – had clearly been in the making for several years. Another person evidently party to the scheme was Henry's former chaplain Æthelwold, now prior of Nostell, to whom Henry had, on the same journey north, issued a charter confirming his house in its considerable possessions. The plantation of a diocese in the North-West was not just an act of ecclesiastical significance; it was a political gesture. Cumbria was an area long in dispute between the English and the Scots. Politically it was difficult for the Norman king to control; ecclesiastically the archbishop of York was stretched to extend his authority this far to the North-West, and had been unable to prevent the bishop of Glasgow from exercising episcopal functions there. The creation of a new cathedral church would in part be a political statement, an assertion that this was an area under Anglo-Norman control. In ecclesiastical terms, it would wrest Cumbria from the bishop of Glasgow, and place it firmly under the control of the archbishop of York. As it turned out it was over ten years before such a statement could be made, but when it was, it was to Prior Æthelwold of Nostell that Henry turned to be his first bishop of Carlisle (1133–56).

Under the government of Æthelwold Carlisle adopted the customs of the French Augustinian house of Arrouaise, where the Rule was used as the basis for an austere and ascetic way of life, and which had become the centre of a small congregation of houses in France and England emulating its ways.[27] In England in the twelfth century there were two northern houses with Arrouaisian affiliations, Carlisle and Warter; and several in the midlands and South.[28] Historians have puzzled as to what prompted the English houses to join the congregation. At one time St Malachy, archbishop of Armagh, who visited both Arrouaise and the north of England in 1140, was a favourite candidate for having promoted the observances of the French abbey. Others have suggested that the link is provided by Æthelwold himself. However, the predominance of houses founded before 1148 in the diocese of Lincoln suggests that Bishop Alexander (1123–48), himself the instigator of the conversion of the secular college at Dorchester on Thames into an Arrouaisian house, may have been active in encouraging the adoption of the customs of the French house.[29] At Carlisle the connection lasted as long as the cathedral did during its first phase, that is, until 1156. At Warter it persisted for some fifty years. Although they may have thought of themselves as distinctive in customs and observance, to outside eyes Arrouaisian canons were probably indistinguishable from others, and whether the English abbots attended the annual meeting at Arrouaise of all abbots is not clear.[30]

THE SCOTTISH KINGS AND THE AUGUSTINIANS

The part played by Henry I and Matilda in furthering the interests of the canons was important, although it should be remembered that Henry's religious interests were not exclusively Augustinian. But influential he and his wife clearly were, and not just in England. The Augustinian expansion was the first major religious movement in Scotland; indeed here the canons had perhaps an even greater role than in England.[31] They succeeded in gaining the patronage of Queen Matilda's brothers, the Scottish kings Edgar (1097–1107), Alexander I (1107–24) and David I (1124–53). The first site in Scotland chosen for an Augustinian house was Scone, the ancient seat of the Scottish kings and a place with political and religious associations; and a foundation here raised the Augustinians to a position of considerable prestige. Some sources date the foundation of the priory as early as 1114 or 1115. However, since there seems little doubt that Scone was colonized from Nostell, the date of the foundation cannot be earlier than c. 1120, when Nostell became firmly established as an Augustinian house and, perhaps more significantly, obtained that royal and archiepiscopal patronage which raised its status and made it a likely place for the Scottish king to look for a colony.[32]

The site chosen for the first plantation of Augustinian canons on Scottish soil was, therefore, highly significant. So too was their introduction into the church of St Andrews, for this was not only an ancient Culdee establishment, but the premier cathedral in the kingdom. Like Scone, St Andrews had close links with Nostell and with its prior, Æthelwold. Before King Alexander's death there had already been moves which indicate that the king intended to convert the Culdee community which served the cathedral into a house of regular canons. In 1124 Alexander appointed the prior of Scone, Robert, as bishop of St Andrews (although he was not consecrated until 1127), and another canon of Nostell was sent to replace him at Scone. The king died in 1124, and the process of introducing Augustinian canons into the cathedral was interrupted; however, it is clear that Alexander's plans coincided with a similar scheme for the creation of an Augustinian cathedral chapter at Carlisle, whose first bishop, as we have seen, was to be Prior Æthelwold of Nostell. The close connections of the Scottish court, the northern archbishop, Thurstan, and the prior of the house which he (along with the English king) had fostered are clear. When Alexander brought canons to Scone and began the process, completed by his brother David I, of establishing regular life in the cathedral chapter of St Andrews, he was bringing to Scotland a new type of monk-priest who represented the ideals of the Gregorian reform movement.[33]

King David I must have known much of the regular canons from his long stay at the court of the English king, and at least one early Augustinian foundation, Llanthony Prima, had felt the benefit of his patronage. As king of Scotland he established three major Augustinian

houses. Holyrood was founded from Merton in 1128 just outside the
royal town of Edinburgh. Some years later (1138) David planted canons
from the French house of Beauvais – the choice of mother house is
tantalizing – at Jedburgh, a site not apparently linked to any previous
ecclesiastical settlement. His adviser here was Bishop John of Glasgow,
possibly eager to use this foundation to mark his reconciliation with
Rome after he had resisted papal attempts to force him to recognize the
authority of the archbishop of York. Finally, Cambuskenneth lay just
outside another royal burgh, Stirling, and was a symbol of royal power
and authority. Connections with northern England are again suggested by
the fact that by 1147 it was, like Carlisle, affiliated to Arrouaise.

David I, as will become clear, was to become a connoisseur of the
religious orders;[34] the Augustinians were not the first group of religious
whom he patronized north of the border, nor were they to be the last.
However, they must have been an obvious choice for inclusion among
the recipients of his generosity. David had long been in England, exposed
to the fashions of the Anglo-Norman world, and eager to import them
into his own kingdom. He encountered current ecclesiastical thinking
through his contacts with men such as Thurstan and Æthelwold. His
contacts with the English court are of paramount importance; but so too
are his dealings with the diocese of York. The Augustinians could tackle
the same kind of pastoral problems north of the border as they could to
the south, and it is for this reason that we find the Black Canons not only
placed on the outskirts of new burghs and in the bishopric of St Andrews,
but also used, as in England, to reform and refound groups of secular
clergy. Culdee communities – both eremitical and collegiate – were ripe
targets for conversion. Before David's death in 1153 he had, at the request
of the bishop of Dunkeld, given the island-hermitage of Inchcolm to
Augustinian canons; and he transferred the island and Culdee community
of Loch Leven to be a dependency of St Andrews, stipulating that the
Culdees were to join the canons, or leave the island.

REASONS FOR SUCCESS

The English and Scottish kings and queens were undoubtedly powerful
advocates of the Augustinian canons, but this in itself cannot explain the
popularity and success they enjoyed. This is a useful point to pause in our
account of the foundations and consider a little more fully the reasons for
that success. In both England and Scotland the Augustinians constituted
the first major religious movement after the Conquest of England and the
extension of Norman influence north of the border. We have seen how
a majority of first-generation Anglo-Norman barons preferred to give

English lands to Norman monasteries rather than found houses on conquered soil. With the reign of Henry I two factors modified this general pattern. The first was that it was now over forty years since the Conquest, and ties, both family and sentimental, had weakened. The second was that there was emerging under royal patronage a group of barons of the first and second rank who had fewer, if any, connections with the duchy. Not all these were, in the memorable phrase of Orderic Vitalis, 'men raised from the dust'. Some were already major barons in their own right. But others were younger sons of aristocratic houses or *curiales*, civil servants, and it was men from both these groups who founded Augustinian houses in the first three decades of the twelfth century; members of the baronage and those who, with no Norman connections, rose to power in England now sought to identify themselves more closely with England, and one mode of expression of this association was the foundation of religious houses.[35]

A sense of group or cultural identity was, therefore, articulated through the plantation of religious houses on what was no longer seen as conquered soil, but this does not explain why barons and *curiales* chose the Augustinian canons as the recipients for their patronage. This is a more difficult question. Indeed it raises the question of how distinctive, to an eleventh- or twelfth-century lay man or woman, the regular canons were.[36] The barons were presumably influenced by fashion – and in this sense the Augustinians made their debut at about the right time to catch the changing tide of benefactions: until about 1130 they lacked serious rivals for patronage. Founders' charters often tell us that they took the advice of archbishops and bishops; and both they and lay patrons may have been attracted by the notion that the canons, as men in orders yet still clerics following the apostolic life, could be thought to have a wider social function than monks who were vowed to a life inside the cloister. A third reason for the popularity of the canons lies on a more practical level. When a layman came to found a religious house, he may have been influenced less by the nature of the establishment (whether it was to be for monks or canons) than by the financial outlay required to endow it. Professor Southern has shown convincingly that the resources needed for a house of regular canons could be considerably less than for a Benedictine or Cluniac abbey.[37] There was a wide variety in the size and resources of Augustinian houses. They could become very wealthy if their founders were of high status and generous nature, or if, as at Aldgate, Merton and Nostell, the initial endowments were augmented by others. In many cases, however, the outlay needed to endow an Augustinian house could be modest. Houses like Cirencester, for instance, took over the revenues of a former college; others were constructed around existing parish churches and chapels, and here again the cost would have been considerably reduced. A house of canons could function with a handful of men and modest resources, and this in itself may have been as (if not more) appealing to a founder as an inclination to parish or pastoral work.

In England and Scotland the reigns of Henry I and David I saw the main period of expansion of the Augustinian canons. After 1135 in England, and 1153 in Scotland, the expansion was by no means over, but by those dates the large and important houses had come into existence. It would be too simplistic to say that houses founded before were large and powerful, and those established after, smaller and less important: indeed the great college of Waltham (Essex) was converted by King Henry II in 1177 as part of his penance for the murder of Archbishop Thomas Becket. However, it is clear that after the first wave of expansion, the Augustinians acquired a widening social circle of benefactors, and many houses were, as a consequence, less well endowed. Their founders were no longer drawn almost exclusively from the ranks of the wealthy and powerful and those with court connections, and the establishment of an Augustinian house – and the spiritual insurance enjoyed by a monastic founder – came within the reach of those of more modest means and political power. The remainder of the twelfth century was for the Augustinians a period of steady but not perhaps spectacular growth. About eighty-three houses were founded, with a concentration in midland and eastern England.[38] In contrast the geographical distribution of houses in the west country, where a number of well-endowed minster and collegiate churches like Bodmin and Launceston had already been converted, was much more sparse.[39]

THE PREMONSTRATENSIAN (WHITE) CANONS

The sustained growth of Augustinian houses between 1135 and 1200 suggests that although the Black Canons faced formidable rivals for attention after the coming of the Cistercian monks and other reformed orders discussed in chapter 4, they were far from overwhelmed by them. From the 1140s a further choice still was offered to monastic patrons in Britain which combined features of both the canons regular and the austerity of Cistercians. The origin of the Premonstratensian canons, like that of several other religious movements, lay in the forests of north-east France, where in the early years of the twelfth century Norbert of Xanten had drawn vast crowds by his preaching and teaching. He had founded for them, both men and women, a house and then an order, and the basis of the observance which he adopted for his followers was the Rule of St Augustine. Later legislators grafted on to it a number of customs borrowed from Cîteaux; and the canons of Prémontré, the White Canons, became, to all intents and purposes, regular canons following a more austere way of life than the Augustinians. They were distinct from the Black Canons in their dress and their liturgy and, in many cases, by the sites which they settled. One contemporary, a canon of Liège, who characterized monks and canons not by their order or family but by their remoteness, included the Premonstratensians with those 'who establish themselves far from men'.[40] How they appeared to founders is more enigmatic.

There is, for instance, no record of the impulses which led a minor Lincolnshire noble named Peter of Goxhill to apply to the French monastery of Licques for a convent of canons, but by 1143 the first Premonstratensian foundation on British soil was established at Newhouse, about six miles from the centre of his estates. By 1267 there were thirty-seven abbeys, three nunneries and six cells. The British Premonstratensian houses have many features in common with the Augustinians and show a similar diversity in origin. H. M. Colvin, historian of the order in England, has demonstrated the importance of family relationships in the spread of the houses: in particular he has elucidated the intimate connection of half a dozen houses founded by kinsmen and associates of Ranulf Glanville, royal justiciar.[41] Only two founders were barons of the first rank, Eustace fitz John (Alnwick) and William de Warenne (Croxton); the rest, like so many Augustinian patrons, were honorial barons (those who did not hold in chief from the king) and lay administrators. Some of their houses lay, as Alnwick did, in the shadow of the castle of the founder. Some transformed ancient minsters like Easby, whose canons took the endowments of the minster of St Agatha, which continued to function as a parish church. Cockersand (Lancashire), as remote as any British house of any order, was successor to a hermitage and a hospital, which was initially served by the Premonstratensian canons. The establishment of Dale (Stanley Park, Derbyshire) serves as a useful reminder that the foundation of a religious house could be a hazardous business. The abbey, which achieved foundation at the turn of the twelfth and thirteenth centuries, was the last in a chain of attempts to introduce canons into what had begun life as a hermitage. First an Augustinian colony from Calke, then Premonstratensian offshoots from Tupholme and from Welbeck all failed, through lack of resources, to maintain conventual life there.

The White Canons pushed north of the border, first either at Soulseat (founded by Fergus, lord of Galloway, traditionally in 1148)[42] but more probably at Dryburgh, established in 1150 by Hugh de Morville, constable of Scotland, from Alnwick. The canons took possession of the

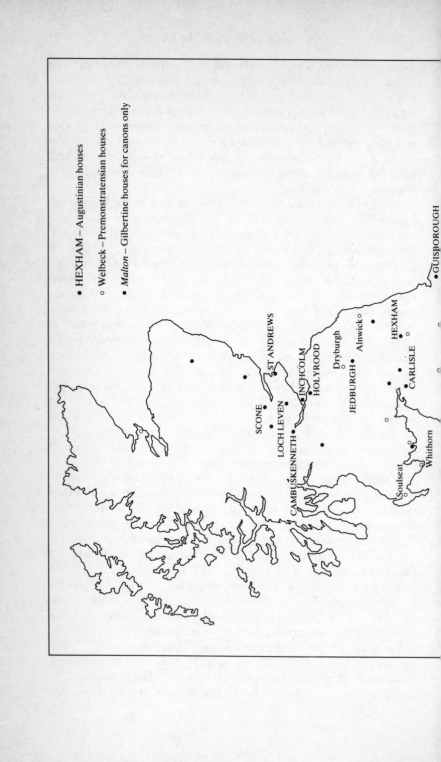

● HEXHAM – Augustinian houses

○ Welbeck – Premonstratensian houses

■ *Malton* – Gilbertine houses for canons only

ST ANDREWS

SCONE

LOCH LEVEN

CAMBUSKENNETH

INCHCOLM

HOLYROOD

Dryburgh

JEDBURGH

Alnwick

HEXHAM

CARLISLE

Soulseat

Whithorn

GUISBOROUGH

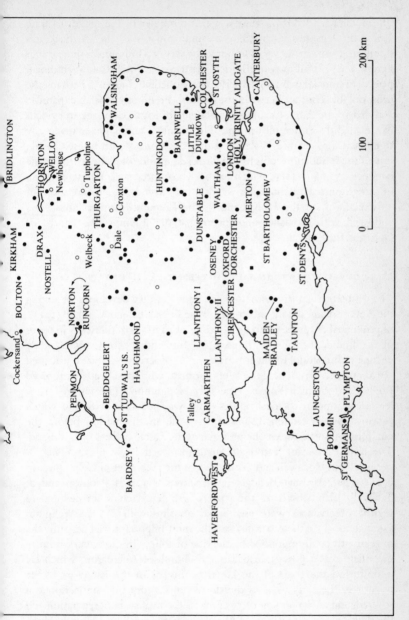

Map 3 Distribution of houses of regular canons by c. 1300

site in 1154, and this provides a useful reminder of the length of time which the legalities surrounding a foundation could take. A third, and significant, plantation was Whithorn, the seat of a bishopric, where either Fergus, lord of Galloway or Bishop Christian of Candida Casa (Whithorn) placed Premonstratensians to serve the cathedral church.[43] Perhaps the most notable contrast between the Scottish Premonstratensian expansion and that of the Augustinians is the absence of royal patronage so evident in the slightly earlier movement. The White Canons never made any significant inroads into Wales, and there was one Welsh house, Talley, one of the foundations of Rhys ap Gruffydd, prince of Deheubarth, made between 1184 and 1189, which has been associated with Rhys's decision not to go on crusade; in other words it may have been a substitution for an expedition to the Holy Land.[44] The Premonstratensian house was endowed with the lands and income of the foremost *clas* church of Deheubarth, Llandeilo.[45]

DEVELOPMENTS IN THE THIRTEENTH CENTURY: WALES

The thirteenth century witnessed one constitutional development among the Augustinians, the introduction, by the Fourth Lateran Council (1215), of provincial chapters, periodic meetings of all heads of houses.[46] In terms of the foundation of new houses the thirteenth century saw a steady decline in England. However, a new centre of activity – as yet untouched – was north Wales, where the Welsh princes, who had already patronized English Augustinian houses, especially Haughmond (Shropshire), now lent their support to local houses. This was not an area within which Norman power stretched, and it was still, in this period before the conquest of north Wales, the preserve of the native princes of Gwynedd. The most significant feature of Augustinian activity in north Wales, as previously in Cornwall and Scotland, was the take-over of Celtic sites. In four places, Bardsey, Beddgelert in Snowdonia, and Penmon and St Tudwal's Island, both off the coast of Anglesey, churches devoted to regular observances were established on sites with a Celtic religious significance.[47] Of these Bardsey was the most important, and certainly the only one to be distinguished by the title of abbey. In the twelfth century the island was a possession of the *clas* church of Aberdaron, which lay opposite on the coast of the Lleyn peninsula. In the last years of the twelfth or the early years of the thirteenth century the connection was severed, and an agreement of 1252 marks the final stage of separation and the division of the revenues of Aberdaron between the *clas* church which continued to exist there and the Augustinian house. The island of Bardsey, Ynys Enlli, enjoyed fame as the burial place of thousands of saints, and became one of the foremost pilgrimage centres of medieval Wales. By the time that the Augustinians had made their debut in north Wales the Cistercians were already well established, at Basingwerk, Valle Crucis and Aberconwy, and were recipients of the patronage of the Welsh princes. But the churches now converted to regular observance exercised a parochial function, and Bardsey was, moreover, a centre of pilgrimage. To encompass them within the orbit of the Cistercians of north Wales would have been incompatible with the desire of the White Monks for solitude, and it was therefore appropriate that their charge should be committed to the clerical monks. The princes of north Wales, like the Scottish aristocracy and clergy, saw the Augustinian canons as worthy successors to the Celtic traditions of the *clas* church and the Culdees.[48]

Augustinian expansion continued, modestly, in south Wales. Like the houses of the North, Haverfordwest Priory, which was founded some time before 1213, was associated with a Celtic site, not a *clas* church but the traditional site of the hermitage of St Caradoc at St Ishmael. A feature which it shared with the other southern house, Carmarthen, however, was that it too lay close to an urban settlement. Initially these two southern houses, Carmarthen and Haverfordwest, probably recruited locally, but their fortunes were linked to the ups and downs of royal power, on which Carmarthen in particular was dependent. In the early thirteenth century the priory came briefly under Welsh control, but the re-establishment of royal power in the reign of Henry III ended this native influence, and from then onwards it was associated both in its interests and in its personnel with Anglo-Norman dominance. For this reason the Augustinians of Carmarthen (and probably Haverfordwest and the small house of St Kynemarks near Chepstow) may have failed to attract Welsh recruits in any great numbers, and accordingly present a contrast with Augustinian settlements in the North, who, like the Cistercian, show evidence of native Welsh recruitment, indicating their identification with local interests and local aspirations.[49]

In a challenging and compelling essay exploring the nature of the vocation and spirituality of the regular canons Caroline Bynum has argued that the canon's life was marked by a sense of outward vocation that extended beyond the cloister, and by a desire to teach by example. Some have challenged her argument on the grounds that the comparative sparsity of sources tell us little about what the canons thought of themselves, let alone how they were perceived by others.[50] However, the exploration of this chapter into the origins of the houses of regular canons in Britain has suggested that many of those who founded them perceived and appreciated just that sense of outward purpose in the life of the canon.

They were patronized as agents of clerical reform, to serve the cure of souls, or to minister to the sick in body within their hospitals. Yet that is not the whole story; for although many Augustinian houses took over, or took in, collegiate, *clas* or Culdee churches, or served hospitals, most were founded *de novo*; they were new establishments. It is perhaps this very diversity that has made the canons the least accessible of all the religious orders, the least easy to discuss as a group. There was no Augustinian style of architecture, no imposed uniformity such as the Cistercians sought to achieve. Moreover with very few exceptions – notably Waldef, the Augustinian prior of Kirkham who afterwards sought the rigours of the Cistercian way of life – the British Augustinians of our period lacked prominent public figures; they produced no Ailred of Rievaulx, no St Hugh, the Carthusian bishop of Lincoln, no Samson of Bury St Edmunds, the latter captured for us in the pages of Jocelin's chronicle of life at the Benedictine abbey. Yet in a modest, perhaps unspectacular way, the canons regular came to enjoy a significant influence in the religious life of medieval Britain, in cathedral chapter, collegiate church, hospital and hermitage, and achieved enduring popularity among both recruits and patrons.

4

THE NEW MONASTIC ORDERS OF
THE TWELFTH CENTURY

Perhaps the most striking feature of medieval monastic history is the proliferation of new religious groups and orders in the late eleventh and early twelfth centuries. These were the product of a search for the purest, indeed the perfect, form of monasticism, and are characterized by two main features: the desire to return to primitive monastic observances, either to the eremiticism of the Desert Fathers or to a stricter interpretation of the text of the Rule of St Benedict; and the appeal of apostolic poverty. Both these carried implicit, sometimes indeed explicit, criticisms of the religious life as practised in contemporary monastic houses, and led to what has been termed the 'crisis of monasticism'.[1] These new trends and new religious emotions can be investigated through an examination of four religious orders which, in a greater or lesser degree, transformed monastic life in Britain. These are the orders of Tiron, Savigny, Cîteaux (the Cistercian Order), and La Grande Chartreuse (the Carthusian Order). This is also an appropriate place to consider the military orders, which, although their aims differed widely from those of the conventional orders, were nevertheless heavily influenced by the Cistercians, and made a unique contribution to the development of the monastic life of the period. Of all these groups, the Chartreuse was the first to be founded and the last to reach Britain. And it was the Cistercian Order which was to exert more influence in Europe than any other medieval religious order, although it perhaps had the least auspicious beginning of all.

The desire to return to a life of poverty, the eremitical element, and devotion to the Rule of St Benedict cannot easily be separated, for those men who were inspired to establish communities with a strict interpretation of and adherence to the Rule were often also hermits.[2] Up to a point, Bernard of Tiron, one of the most influential of these, had a conventional career as a Benedictine abbot, but he was also a preacher, and at times a hermit. The desire for the solitary life led him to settle in the forest of Craon on the borders of Brittany and Maine; but in 1109, having gathered around him a number of recruits, he founded the abbey of Tiron. A similar person was Vitalis of Mortain, formerly a secular clerk in the household of Count Robert of Mortain, who, like Bernard, lived for a while in the forest of Craon. When he found it difficult to achieve the solitude he desired, he left to establish for himself a hermitage in the forest of Savigny in Normandy (c. 1089). Again, he was joined by disciples, and so he composed for them a simple rule, based on that of St Benedict. The community rose to the status of an abbey between 1112 and 1115. Both Tiron and Savigny became the heads of orders, spreading across the channel into England, Wales and Scotland. Tiron achieved modest success, and Savigny, within thirty years, numbered a congregation of thirty-three houses, fourteen of them in Britain. Tiron kept its independence, while Savigny, under internal pressure, merged with Cîteaux in 1147.

Both Tiron and Savigny produced ways of life which were based on the Rule of St Benedict, but which also incorporated an eremitical element. They have something else in common: they were communities which gathered around an individual. An initial contrast is presented here by Cîteaux, for although the ideals of one man, Robert of Molesme, were influential there, Cîteaux affords an example of a group of men deciding to convert to a harsher régime.[3] Robert, like many of his contemporaries, seems to have found it difficult to mould his career into the existing pattern of monastic observance, and in 1075 founded a monastery at Molesme, in Burgundy, where he attempted to live a more austere life, though still within the framework of a community. His failure to do so was the result of success, the appeal of his vision, and in 1098 some of his disciples had little difficulty in persuading him to move on in order to found another community where a stricter interpretation of the Rule might be applied. This was the *Novum Monasterium*, the new monastery, Cîteaux. However, it was not Robert who was to be the formative influence, but the two men who followed him as abbot, Alberic (1098–1109), and the Englishman Stephen Harding (1109–34), who was probably the author of the primitive *Carta Caritatis*, the Charter of Love, which lays out the basic Cistercian principles. A third powerful force in the formation of the Cistercian identity was a man who entered Cîteaux in 1113 and went on to be abbot of Clairvaux and one of the most influential voices in western Europe, St Bernard.

If we ask *how* Cîteaux differed from Tiron and Savigny in its conception of the monastic life, we may give two broad answers. First, the founders of Cîteaux and successive generations of their abbots laid down the basis of their observances in legislation, which was to be followed by all houses. Second, they created a machinery for enforcing the observance of their statutes, through the system of visitation and the annual general chapter. It is the organization of Cîteaux, the creation of an international order which followed common statutes and bound house to house by a system which overrode political boundaries, which was the unique contribution of Cîteaux to the monastic life of the twelfth century. The customs and statutes, which were added to over the years, are witness to the developing aims of the White Monks, to their search for solitude and divorce from the world, poverty and simplicity. The documents lay down the following requirements: that Cistercian houses were not to be built in towns and cities, but were to be remote from the 'habitation of men';[4] that churches were to be plain and unadorned; that the liturgy was to be unaffected and simple. Cistercian economy was characterized by the prohibition of the traditional forms of revenue enjoyed by Benedictine houses, which yielded income derived from the work of others. The White Monks therefore rejected manors, rents, labour services, mills, churches and tithes. Although their statutes reinstated manual work as a central feature of the timetable, they revolutionized the management of the economy by the creation of a whole new class within the monastery, the *conversi* or lay brethren. In traditional monastic parlance a *conversus* was a man who entered a religious house as an adult, in contrast to one who had been offered as an oblate. It is at the Italian abbey of Vallombrosa that we first encounter the existence of the new *conversi*, the lay brethren, but it was among the Cistercian houses that the idea was most successfully developed. The unique conception of the lay brethren was that they were not servants: they were members of the community. The Cistercians therefore opened up to a whole new set of people – the illiterate laity – a chance to enter a religious community and enjoy its benefits. They provided an outlet for both peasants and men of higher social status who managed and supervised the innovative system of grange-farming which the Cistercians pioneered. The chronology of the early documents is still not clear, and it must be stressed that we are not talking of a house, or an order, that conceived its ideals overnight. These developed gradually, and what has come down to us does not always represent the thinking of the founders of the New Monastery. However, they were very probably part of much Cistercian thinking by the 1120s and 1130s, that is, by the time the order reached Britain.[5]

The *Carta Caritatis*, which was first composed by Abbot Stephen

Harding before 1119, certainly envisaged that the order would grow. However, it could not have foreseen that before 1152 there would be over three hundred abbeys in Europe; this figure alone is eloquent testimony to the success of the Cistercian appeal. Even more striking is the fact that the Cistercians developed a system of government to oversee this great number of houses. In contrast to the Cluniac, the Cistercian congregation throughout Europe was not seen as a monarchical institution, but rather as a family, with each house bound as a daughter to the mother house from which it was founded. The ties of love and discipline were to be maintained by the annual visitation of each daughter house by the abbot of the mother house. Cîteaux itself was not exempt, and lacking a mother house itself, was visited by the abbots of its four eldest daughters. Furthermore, each year the abbots of every Cistercian house were to gather for the general chapter at Cîteaux. In time, and as Cistercian plantations became more remote, this dual system placed an intolerable burden on individual abbots, and their responsibilities were commuted. Abbots of Scottish houses, for instance, only had to attend the general chapter once every four years.

THE BRITISH HOUSES OF TIRON

Of the three congregations, Tiron was the first to make a foundation in Britain, but its contribution to the general monastic expansion was small. Indeed, it hardly touched England at all, numbering only a handful of modest houses.[6] However, Earl David, later king of Scotland, brought a group of monks from Tiron (probably in 1113) to settle at Selkirk and form his first monastic foundation in Scotland; their number was increased after a personal visit by David to Tiron in 1116. Indeed there are two significant features of the early history of the Scottish Tironensians. First, continental reform came to Scotland, as indeed it did to Wales, independently from and even ahead of similar developments in Norman England.[7] Second, Selkirk enjoyed strong connections with the mother house, at least on a personal level, for two of its abbots, Ralph and William, went back to rule Tiron. The Selkirk community was transferred in 1128 to Kelso, where it was one of the most successful and wealthy of all Scottish monasteries and became by 1300 the mother house of a congregation north of the border which numbered four abbeys and three priories. Among these were William the Lion's foundation at Arbroath, made in memory of the murdered archbishop, Thomas Becket, and Lindores, established by William's brother David, earl of Huntingdon, and colonized from Arbroath.[8] The coming of the Tironensians was a significant chapter in Scottish monastic history.

Roughly contemporary, but far more modest, was their settlement in Wales. Between 1113 and 1115 Robert fitz Martin, lord of Cemais, brought thirteen monks from Tiron to found a priory on the coast of Cardigan Bay at St Dogmaels; and the colony was increased by a further thirteen monks a few years later. The monks were able, with the patronage of Robert's mother, to establish a dependent cell on Caldy Island off the Pembrokeshire coast, although they seem not to have been able to sustain a permanent colony there, and founded another at Pill (Glamorgan) c. 1200. The Welsh Tironensians lacked the royal support they enjoyed in Scotland, but St Dogmaels at least was adequately endowed by its founder. Despite Tiron's place among the reformed orders of the twelfth century, however, the economy of its Welsh houses at least was more akin to that of the Benedictines.[9]

THE CONGREGATION OF SAVIGNY IN BRITAIN

The growth of the Savigniac congregation in Britain began in 1124, with the foundation of the important house of Tulketh in Lancashire, which transferred to Furness in 1127.[10] By 1147 it had fourteen houses in England and Wales,[11] all but Rushen on the Isle of Man, the Yorkshire abbeys of Byland and its daughter house of Jervaulx, Swineshead (Lincolnshire) and Calder (Cumberland) founded directly from Savigny. These four were offshoots of Furness, although in 1147 Byland argued, successfully, at the annual general chapter that it was dependent on Savigny rather than the Lancashire abbey. The founders of the Savigniac houses were powerful men, and one of the order's most influential advocates was the man who, as count of Boulogne and Mortain, founded Furness in 1124. Later as King Stephen he planted monks at Buckfast in Devon in 1136 and with his wife established Coggeshall (Essex) a few years later. As a prestigious patron, the count of Mortain, favourite in his later years of Henry I and one of his 'supermagnates', was almost unparalleled, and the favour he showed them could well have contributed to the great vogue for the Savigniacs in the first half of the 1130s.

Little is documented of the growth of the Savigniac houses in Britain, but the early history of the abbeys of Byland and Calder, and their relationship with Furness, hints at many of the problems which plagued the congregation in Britain. It also reminds us that monastic foundations were not always trouble-free.[12] In 1134 Furness Abbey sent a colony of thirteen monks to Calder in Cumbria to settle on land donated by Ranulf Meschin. No reason is given in the sources for what motivated Meschin, but subsequent events suggest that the monks of Furness themselves would have welcomed the foundation of a new colony because of pressure of increasing numbers at the abbey. In 1137, however, Calder was burnt by the Scots who raided and devastated the Cumbrian countryside, and had to be abandoned. The monks returned to Furness but were refused entry, and the abbot of Byland who, sixty years later, set this event down in writing from an eyewitness account suggested two reasons for the attitude of the Furness monks: the refusal of the abbot of Calder to resign his abbatial status; and an unwillingness on the part of the Furness monks to share their resources. Refused entry at Furness, the monks decided to look for another patron, and to approach Thurstan, archbishop of York, for help. On their journey over the Pennines they encountered Gundreda, mother of the young baron, Roger de Mowbray, who persuaded her son to become their patron. After moving four times in an attempt to find a suitable site, the colony settled in 1177 at New Byland on the southern edge of the North Yorkshire Moors, where it prospered.

The early history of Byland accordingly reminds us that life was uncertain, and that experiment was often necessary before a final, appropriate site for an abbey was acquired. The vicissitudes of the community are paralleled by those of its daughter house, Jervaulx in Wensleydale. Jervaulx began with a group of monks from Savigny who (for reasons which are not documented) were in Richmondshire, and who were offered the site for a new religious house at Fors by Acaris, son of Bardolf. At a ceremony to mark the erection of the first building, Acaris's lord, Count Alan of Brittany and Richmond, offered the monks his own support. The sequel to these events is instructive. Count Alan soon after returned to his Breton estates, and visited Savigny to inform its abbot of the new foundation. The reaction can scarcely have been what he expected, for Abbot Serlo refused to ratify the existence of the latest daughter house. His opposition was apparently based on the dangers and hardships encountered by other Savigniac houses in England – could he have been thinking of Byland here? He did all he could to bring the monks back to Savigny and was only reluctantly persuaded to let the colony continue when Byland offered to assume responsibility as its mother house. At the same time, Byland was having its own problems, and like Jervaulx these seem due, in part at least, to the ineffectiveness of the Savigniac system of filiation. In an important way, Byland could be said to have had no mother house, since Furness, arguably, had shed that role in 1138. By 1141, when Byland had acquired patrons and benefactors, and was beginning to flourish, the monks decided to place their house directly under the subjection of Savigny, and the plan was accepted. Years later this was contested by Furness, and we may see the episode in the context of the resistance of the Lancashire monks to the merger of Savigny with the Cistercians. The history of the northern Savigniac houses, which is better documented than that of other houses of the congregation, is suggestive of weakness within the Savigniac system, of a lack of central control. Both the failure of Abbot Serlo to maintain his authority and his personal admiration for the White Monks led him to petition for the entire congregation to be accepted into the order of Cîteaux in 1147. Savigny was a monastic experiment which had failed. The surrender to the authority of the White Monks was opposed by Furness, which saw its freedom of action curtailed. There were also reservations on the part of some Cistercians, who took steps to ensure that the advent of the Savigniacs did not result in falling standards (something of which they stand accused); in 1148 Ailred as abbot of Rievaulx sent monks to the Savigniacs of Swineshead 'to illuminate it with the Cistercian way of life'.[13]

THE COMING OF THE CISTERCIANS

The fortunes of the Savigniacs in Britain, who were part of a loose organization which failed as an independent congregation, and the houses of Tiron, which never gained a foothold in England, contrast sharply with the success of the Cistercian Order. Here the British expansion began later, in 1128, and despite the general chapter's attempted ban on new foundations in 1152, continued into the late twelfth century and beyond until there were over eighty houses in Britain. The expansion began modestly enough. In 1128 the elderly bishop of Winchester, William Giffard, settled monks from the French house of L'Aumône on his estates at Waverley. From L'Aumône, too, came the monks to staff the second British Cistercian house, that of Tintern, established by a relative of Giffard, Walter fitz Richard de Clare, one of the early Norman conquerors of south Wales, who placed the monastery not many miles from that other symbol of his power and 'Normanness', his castle at Chepstow. Although Waverley was a foundation that did not achieve the celebrity of the northern Cistercian houses, like Rievaulx, it was an important one and became the mother house of a notable monastic family.[14]

Waverley was one of three main springboards of Cistercian expansion. The others, both northern, began more publicly. In 1131–2 a group of monks from Clairvaux arrived at the court of King Henry I of England bringing with them a letter from their abbot, Bernard. In characteristically forthright language Bernard told the king: 'In your land there is a possession of my lord and your lord . . . I have arranged for it to be taken back, and have sent men from our army who will (if it is not displeasing to you) seek it out, recover it and restore it'.[15] We know nothing of the negotiations which must have preceded the advent of these monks, who were to go on to found Rievaulx Abbey in Yorkshire, but the Englishmen who had entered the monastic life in the Cistercian houses of Burgundy must have supplied Bernard with valuable local knowledge of conditions in the North. Among them was William, Bernard's secretary, sent as first abbot of the new plantation. As a result of discussions between the king, the archbishop of York and one of the royal justices named Walter Espec, the monks were settled on a site in the Rye valley only a few miles from Espec's castle at Helmsley.

Their arrival caused quite a stir. As they passed through the city of York they were seen by a group of monks from the Benedictine house of St Mary's, a rich foundation which enjoyed much prestige as the foremost abbey of the North. These Black Monks were so impressed by the poverty and simplicity of the Clairvaux group that they immediately petitioned for the reform of their monastery. We may perhaps think of the arrival of the White Monks in the diocese of York as the event which set alight smouldering discontent within the community of St Mary's, but whether it was a catalyst or a final straw, the event was catastrophic.[16] The reforming party led by the prior argued that the monastery's wealth should be given away and a more rigorous and ascetic lifestyle adopted; the abbot and his supporters refused to listen. On an October day in 1132 the two parties confronted each other, the abbot backed by religious leaders from other houses within the diocese. Archbishop Thurstan of York was there too, supposedly to mediate, but his role, as things turned out, was to take into his own household thirteen monks of the reforming party who were forcibly ejected from St Mary's. At the turn of the year he provided them with land in the valley of the river Skell near his manor at Ripon. Here a new house was built, not at first Cistercian, but some time after 1133 taken into the order as a daughter house of Clairvaux. Thurstan could afford to supply only the bare minimum of resources, and until the arrival, a few years later, of two members of the cathedral clergy of York Minster as recruits, the continuation of the community, Fountains Abbey, was by no means assured.

These four early Cistercian houses illustrate for us the diverse nature of Cistercian foundations and show how the initiative for expansion came from the White Monks themselves, from archbishops and bishops, from kings and barons. It was from these centres that the Cistercian movement in Britain blossomed. Waverley's contribution was to spread through three generations within the South and midlands. Rievaulx dominated Lincolnshire and pushed north into Scotland, and Fountains became the mother of seven daughters and three granddaughters in Yorkshire and the eastern counties of England. There is no single explanation for the phenomenal success of the Cistercian Order and its domination of monastic foundations in the years after 1131. The British experience is part of a European one. In the twelfth century the White Monks were themselves convinced, and convinced others, that if monasticism had 'exclusive possession of authentic Christianity', then theirs was the highest form of monasticism. But can we go beyond this kind of general observation, and discover what motivated lay men and women to found Cistercian houses? Why did the White Monks enjoy such outstanding popularity? Often our only source for a monastic foundation is the charter, a legal document couched in formal language which records the transfer of land to a community. In a few fortunate instances we can learn more from foundation narratives and chronicles. We know, for instance, that a baron named Henry de Lacy fell ill, and vowed that if he recovered he would found a monastery. Accordingly when he was well again he went to Fountains Abbey to ask for a group of monks to establish a daughter house. Fountains also provided the colony for Meaux Abbey, whose founder had made a vow to go on crusade, but who, as he grew older and fatter, became less enthusiastic for the enterprise; he was easily persuaded, by a Cistercian monk, to endow a monastery instead. But instances like these can only explain so much. They may tell us why Henry de Lacy and William of Aumale founded monasteries, but they do not tell us why they founded Cistercian ones.[17]

The main Cistercian expansion was confined to the two decades between the sending of the Cistercian mission from Clairvaux in 1131 and the ban placed on further expansion in 1152. Spiritual movements are not immune from the pressures of fashion; a new order with a reputation for austerity and sanctity might enjoy a great appeal. This attraction would have been magnified by the patronage of royalty – Henry I of England and David I of Scotland – in the same way as the count of Mortain enhanced the prestige of the Savigniacs in the 1120s and early 1130s. The Cistercian founders of the twelfth century were among the greatest in the land; in the early years it was from those intimately connected with the royal court that the White Monks found their most powerful patrons. The spread of one particular order could be facilitated by family and tenurial connections, and a glance at the names of those who founded Cistercian houses confirms this as an important factor. Within the Waverley group, the first daughter house was founded by Robert de Beaumont, a close adviser of King Henry I. In 1133, two years after the arrival of the Clairvaux monks at court, he founded a Cistercian house at Garendon in Leicestershire. Robert's twin brother, Waleran, had inherited the family estates in Normandy, and was a benefactor of various religious houses there. But in 1138, when he acquired estates and high office in England, he decided to found a Cistercian community at Bordesley in Worcester-shire – and he brought monks from his brother's house to do so.[18] A second daughter house of Garendon, Biddlesden (1147), was established by Robert de Beaumont's steward. Here we see family and feudal relationships perhaps not influencing the decision to found a monastery, but more certainly directing the choice of the Cistercian Order, and the mother house within it. The importance of personal connections is also indicated in the fortunes of the order in Scotland, where it was closely associated with one man, King David I (1135–53). We have already encountered David as the man who introduced the order of Tiron north of the border, and as a monastic patron he had interests which were far from exclusive. His first contact with the Cistercian Order may well have come in 1134 when a man to whom he was very close, his steward, Ailred, became a monk at Rievaulx. Two years later David made his first Cistercian foundation in Scotland at Melrose, colonized from Rievaulx; and Rievaulx it was which provided monks for Dundrennan Abbey, also founded by the king. From Rievaulx, through the mother houses of Melrose and Dundrennan sprang eight of the nine other Scottish abbeys of the order, most of them intimately connected with the royal house.[19]

A Cistercian founder, then, might have been influenced by those to whom he was related, with whom he had political associations or from whom he held lands. He might be impressed by the sanctity and repu-tation of the White Monks. He might also be attracted by their desire – enshrined in their legislation – for remote sites, and for lands which they could cultivate themselves. They wanted no manors, and no estates which brought income from the work of tenants and peasants. In short, they wanted the type of site and lands with which it might best suit a founder to part. A baron like Walter Espec could found Rievaulx at very little expense to himself; and Rievaulx only prospered because its reputation, which it built up especially under Abbot Ailred, attracted other benefactors. It was in the uplands of Yorkshire and Wales, where uncultivated lands were still to be had, that the Cistercians grew richest and most powerful, their wealth coming from their ability to farm their own lands, to develop sheep farming and from it a trade in wool. The small expense involved in setting up a Cistercian house may accordingly have influenced a founder trying to decide what kind of house to establish. However, not all their sites were remote, and the researches of historical geographers have indicated many cases where lands given as Cistercian endowments were far from marginal. The foundation of Meaux Abbey in East Yorkshire, for instance, entailed the reduction of a village to the home grange (farm) and the removal of its inhabitants; and when Revesby Abbey was founded in 1147 three villages were destroyed, whereupon a handful of peasants were relocated and the rest became lay brothers. It was doubtless cases such as these which led to accusations of greed and ambition levelled against the Cistercians. One critic, Walter Map, commented that:

> because their rule does not allow them to govern parishioners, they proceed to raze villages, they overthrow churches and turn out parishioners, not scrupling to cast down the altars and level everything before the ploughshare.[20]

Founders and patrons are only one side of the story, however, and we have seen how the impetus for a foundation might come from the monks themselves: how, although Rievaulx was founded by Walter Espec, the initial idea for the Cistercian colonization of Yorkshire came from St Bernard – a man whose powerful personality and high European profile is often quoted as an important factor in itself in the spread of the order; how Fountains was a result of monastic pressure, albeit unplanned; and how Meaux was established at the suggestion of a Cistercian monk. Many Cistercian convents grew quickly in numbers.[21] In the 1160s, when Walter Daniel wrote the life of Ailred, abbot of Rievaulx, he claimed that there were at the abbey under Ailred's rule 140 monks and 500 lay brothers.[22] We need to allow here both for exaggeration by Walter Daniel and for the particular appeal of Rievaulx in Ailred's time. However, we should also consider the possibility that Cistercian monks themselves actively sought new patrons and new houses as the growth in numbers placed a strain on resources. Such economic problems may have been a reason for the rejection of the Savigniac monks of Calder who returned to Furness in 1138.

One fact which did not escape the notice of twelfth-century chroniclers was that the rate of monastic foundations increased dramatically during the reign of King Stephen (1135–54). Expansion in these nineteen years was dominated by two groups: the Cistercians, and religious women. The reign, during which Stephen's cousin, the Empress Matilda, contested the throne, is sometimes characterized as a period of anarchy, or breakdown in royal government, and although conditions were not uniform throughout the country, it is clear that in many areas there was a great deal of confusion about who were royal officials and about who held land. And it was amid this tenurial uncertainty that the Cistercians flourished. Some foundations can be directly linked to the climate of disorder, and it is instructive to look again in this context at Garendon and its daughter houses. The foundation of Garendon by the earl of Leicester in 1133 was part and parcel of his conflict with the earl of Chester over lands in the Charnwood area: it was founded on Chester property.[23] The establishment of Bordesley by the Norman twin Waleran of Meulan coincides quite precisely with his elevation by King Stephen to the earldom of Worcester (1138). Was the abbey intended to furnish a symbol of Waleran's newly found power and authority in the Midlands? A more explicit example is provided by Biddlesden (1147). The land on which the abbey was built had reverted from its tenant to the lord of the honour, the earl of Leicester, and he had granted it to his steward Ernald de Bosco. Ernald was worried that the previous holder might try and claim the land from him, and so on the earl's advice he founded an abbey there. He now enjoyed the status and privileges of a monastic founder but had at the same time effectively prevented the reclamation of the estate.[24]

The same kind of underlying motive in a period of tenurial insecurity can be seen in the foundation of Sawtry (Huntingdonshire), a 'grand-daughter' through Warden of Rievaulx, and it provides another demonstration of the importance of David I as a link in the chain of monastic patronage.[25] The earldom of Huntingdon was held by King David and from 1136 by his son, Henry; but in 1138, when David supported his niece Matilda against King Stephen, the English king confiscated the earldom and granted it to one of his own men, Simon de Senlis II. During the period of Scottish tenure of the earldom strong links had been forged, and tenants of King David there, like David Olifard, resented the new earl and rebelled against him. Olifard's fee at Sawtry was confiscated, and it was here that Simon built a Cistercian abbey (1147). In one stroke he had provided himself with a community of monks who would pray for him; erected a symbol of his power and status as earl; and denied to his enemy Olifard the opportunity to regain his estate at a later date. Whether or not the White Monks were innocent victims is unclear. Certainly in some instances the insecurity of their title to land caused long legal wrangles. The rather jaundiced pen of Walter Map, on the other hand, blamed Cistercian greed: 'how gratefully do they enter upon lands that are given by someone who is not the true owner . . . caring not so much how they get them as how they may keep them', he wrote.[26] Certainly the connection between the Cistercian foundations and the anarchy introduces a more overtly political dimension to monastic foundation and patronage.

By 1152, when the Cistercian general chapter tried to place a ban on further foundations, the main expansion in England was over, and between then and the end of the twelfth century only a handful of houses were established. However, the order enjoyed a resurgence of foundations under royal patronage after 1204, when a colony founded the year before by King John moved to Beaulieu. The foundation was in part a peace offering made after John's reconciliation with the order following his attempt to impose heavy taxes upon its English houses.[27] The number of monks grew, and the house sent out colonies to establish Netley (1239), Hailes (1246), Newenham (1247) and later still St Mary Graces in London (1350), all founded by kings and members of the royal household. The second half of the twelfth century saw further foundations in Scotland, but the major area of expansion after 1152 was Wales. Already by this date there were six houses of White Monks there. On the eastern borders in Herefordshire but straddling the ecclesiastical boundaries was Abbey Dore, the only English daughter house of Morimond; in the South were Tintern, Margam and Whitland; the remaining two houses, Basingwerk in the North and Neath in the South, joined with the congregation of Savigny in 1147. Most of these houses played no further part in the Cistercian expansion. Tintern, Margam and Neath were in an area which had been conquered by the Normans and never really succeeded in gaining the respect or the benefactions of the native Welsh. Indeed they were identified with the Anglo-Norman conquerors and from early in their history were likely to be attacked.[28]

It was the Carmarthenshire house of Whitland which was to become the key to further expansion, to a movement which became identified with the native Welsh princes. It did not start that way, for the first foundation in Welsh Wales, Strata Florida (1164), was made by the Norman constable of Cardigan castle, Robert fitz Stephen. The following year, though, Ceredigion passed from Norman control into the hands of Rhys ap Gruffydd, lord of Deheubarth and leading baron of south Wales. Rhys took over the patronage of Strata Florida and came to be regarded as its founder. He also took over the patronage of Whitland, and now that the Cistercians were no longer completely identified with the Norman invaders (Strata Florida was a daughter house of Whitland, and Whitland of Clairvaux, so neither had constitutional links with an English house) there was no barrier, no Welsh opposition, to expansion. The Welsh princes, contacts of the Lord Rhys, founded houses in their turn. From Whitland were established Strata Marcella, founded in 1170 by Owain Cyfeilog, prince of Powys, and Cwmhir, founded in 1176 by the prince of Ceri and Maelienydd. From Strata Florida sprang the communities of Llantarnam (Caerleon) and Conwy (Aberconwy), whose effective founder, Llywelyn ap Iorwerth, was the leading Welsh prince of the late twelfth and thirteenth centuries. His benefactions established Conwy as the most substantial of Welsh Cistercian landowners. The Cistercians' own initiative also contributed to their Welsh success. Valle Crucis near Llangollen was founded as the last Welsh abbey of White Monks in 1201 at the request of the abbots of Whitland, Strata Florida, Strata Marcella and Abbey-Cwmhir.

Welsh success was partly due to the chord struck by the Cistercians among the native princes, and their ability to become identified with Welsh self-awareness and aspirations. Although the Welsh abbots were forced to co-operate with the English at the time of the Conquest (1282), this close native connection continued: Welsh princes were buried at Cistercian abbeys; Strata Florida for a while compiled the *Annales Cambriae*, the Welsh annals, and it was here between 1175 and 1332 that the *Brut y Tywysogion*, the chronicle of the Welsh princes, was composed. Another reason for Cistercian success in Wales – as in the north of England – was the suitability of the Welsh terrain for the needs of Cistercian communities. Remote sites there were to be had in plenty, and uncultivated lands ready to be opened up. However, as in England some opposition was aroused by Cistercian methods of land acquisition. Gerald of Wales quoted a contemporary proverb: 'they are bad neighbours just like the White Monks'. But he could also admire their technical expertise: 'settle the Cistercians in some barren retreat which is hidden away in an overgrown forest: a year or two later you will find splendid churches there and fine monastic buildings, with a great amount of property and all the wealth you can imagine'.[29] As in northern England, the coming of the Cistercians was accompanied by an expansion of arable farming, but particularly in the uplands by large-scale sheep farming and wool production.

The Cistercian story is therefore one of rapid and resounding success, which transformed the primitivist aspirations of Robert of Molesme and his companions for a more austere lifestyle, and the intention, articulated by their successors in the 1130s and subsequent years, to restore a life based strictly on the Rule of St Benedict. Indeed, Cistercian legislation went far beyond the Rule in its deliberate attempts to impose uniformity in the design of its buildings, its provision of books, its liturgy and its administration.[30] The White Monks succeeded in translating into a reality that desire, characteristic of monastic communities from the tenth century onwards, to band together, to coalesce into an order, by creating a network of houses over which authority could be maintained. As with all success stories, the Cistercians were to find it difficult to maintain their ideals, and their popularity with founders and benefactors put them under pressure. The sites available were not always remote; and financial necessity might force the acceptance of prohibited resources. One early victim was the ban on the grant of churches, and from as early as the 1140s the White Monks, in direct contravention of the statutes, began to accept these gifts. However, in many ways the Cistercians remained true to the intentions of their fathers. Their innovative grange economy enabled them to remain outside the traditional manorial system; and the *conversi* continued to act, as they had been intended, as a buffer between the monks and the outside world, able to act for them in commercial and business affairs, and leave the brethren free from worldly distractions. The creation of a class of 'pseudo-religious' suited the economic and social conditions of the time, a period of rising population and labour glut, and the number of lay brethren remained buoyant until economic changes of the fourteenth century reversed labour trends. However, by the end of the twelfth century there are indications that *conversi*, in the Cistercian Order as in the Gilbertine, were beginning to find their inferior status, as neither monks nor lay men, irksome and unable to satisfy their own aspirations.

As the Cistercian Order in Britain grew in maturity it began to assert itself in the wider church. When in 1141 William fitz Herbert was elected archbishop of York at the request of King Stephen, the Yorkshire Cistercians objected and insisted on the right, newly proclaimed at the Lateran Council of 1139, of the religious orders, the *viri religiosi* of a diocese, to participate in the election of its bishop. Their actions led ultimately to William's deposition and the election in 1147 of a Cistercian archbishop of York: Henry Murdac was the first diocesan since the Conquest to be elected and consecrated without royal assent.[31] From its remote origins in the marshes of Burgundy, the Cistercian Order had come to occupy a powerful place in church politics.

THE CARTHUSIANS

Discussion of one other initiative of the twelfth century will bring us back to where this chapter opened, to the aspirations of those men who came to found new orders; but it will also present us with a complete contrast to the rapid success of the White Monks. This initiative was the order of the Grande Chartreuse, which has survived to this day, but whose growth in the twelfth century was slow. High in the French Alps near Grenoble, Bruno of Cologne, former master of the cathedral school of Reims, founded a small community in the 1080s. We know little of the observances or way of life in the Chartreuse in these early years, but its inspiration seems to have been that same rejection of wealth within the contemporary church and the desire to return to a more primitive observance and worship that we have encountered elsewhere. More direct influence might have come from Robert of Molesme, with whom Bruno had spent some time after leaving Reims. By 1128 the Chartreuse, and its colonies which were beginning to be founded, had acquired a set of customs which drew on a number of familiar traditions: the institution of the lay brothers was borrowed from Vallombrosa and Cîteaux, and in

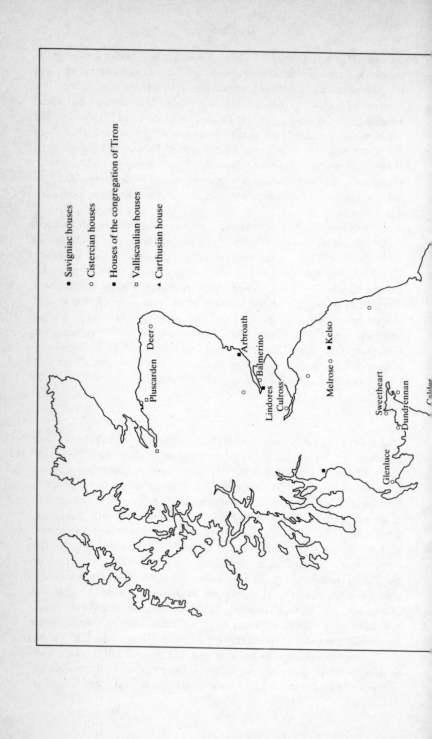

- • Savigniac houses
- ○ Cistercian houses
- ■ Houses of the congregation of Tiron
- □ Valliscaulian houses
- ▲ Carthusian house

Pluscarden □ Deer ○

Arbroath ■
Balmerino ■
Lindores ○ Culross ○

Melrose ○ ■ Kelso

Sweetheart ○
Dundrennan ■
Glenluce ○ Calder

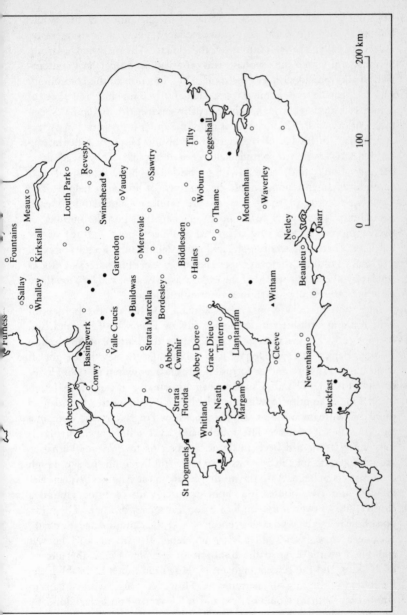

Map 4 The new orders in Britain

1142 the general chapter was introduced on the model of the White Monks. What the Carthusians succeeded in doing was to recreate, psychologically, the conditions of the desert. They created a group hermitage in which the emphasis was on isolation, on personal contemplation and individual spiritual striving. The function of the community was to provide the stability of a shared dwelling and a degree of communal support through only two daily services (Matins and Vespers) in the priory church. The conception of the order is explained by Adam of Eynsham in his life of the Carthusian bishop Hugh of Lincoln: the Carthusians 'combined solitude with community life. They lived alone lest any should find his fellows an obstacle to him; they lived as a community so that none should be deprived of brotherly help.'[32] The Carthusian customs strictly limited the numbers admitted into each community: there were to be no more than the apostolic number of twelve monks, a prior and a limited number (about sixteen) of lay brothers. There was accordingly, and quite deliberately, no possibility of a repetition of the Cistercian experience of abbeys of hundreds of monks and lay brothers. The spread of the order was slow, too, and by 1200 there were only thirty-nine Carthusian priories in Europe.

In Britain there was only one, Witham, located on the borders of Somerset and Wiltshire. Its founder was King Henry II of England, and his motive was repentance and restitution for the murder of Archbishop Thomas Becket in 1170. Despite its royal founder the new house got off to an uncertain start, and its fortunes only changed when in 1180 Henry brought from La Grande Chartreuse the procurator of the house, Hugh of Avalon, to be prior of Witham. The life of Hugh, written by Adam, a monk of Eynsham around 1212, describes how Hugh found at Witham a tangled state of affairs.[33] The monks and lay brethren were living in huts; no attempt had been made at building or to provide alternative accommodation for the peasants who were still living on the site. Hugh took matters in hand. As in the mother house in the Alps, so Witham was divided into two houses, the upper house, built of stone around a cloister, and a lower house, built of wood, for the lay brothers. The prior, one of the few men who could venture to face the famous Angevin wrath, became a close friend and adviser of Henry II, and in 1186 he was appointed by the king to the bishopric of Lincoln.[34] Both the interest of the king and the respect enjoyed by Hugh did much to establish the reputation of the English charterhouse. However, Hugh worked hard to ensure that Witham would not expand as Cistercian houses had done, by adhering rigidly to the custom which made certain that the number of aspirants always exceeded that of recruits; and such selectivity helped to ensure the high standards of observance for which the Carthusians –

although they had their critics among other orders – were famous throughout the Middle Ages.[35] There were no Carthusian houses in Wales, and Scotland had only one, Perth, founded in 1429. Scotland was, however, influenced by one movement, which had affinities with both the Cistercians and the Carthusians, and which never reached England or Wales. The rule of the order of Val des Choux, founded by a Carthusian *conversus*, was confirmed by the pope in 1205. William de Malvoisin, bishop of St Andrews, is credited with the introduction of the Valliscaulian monks to Scotland (1230), and King Alexander II founded a house at Pluscarden, one of three Scottish monasteries of the order.

The flowering of the Carthusian Order in England proved in fact to be a late phenomenon linked to the aftermath of the Black Death.[36] In the fifteenth century the last charterhouse had as its founder yet another king with a bad conscience: Sheen on the Surrey bank of the Thames was established by Henry V in recompense for his father's execution of Archbishop Scrope. The spirit and aspirations of the Carthusian Order can best be appreciated by visiting a Carthusian site. Remains like those at Mount Grace in Yorkshire, whose foundation falls outside the chronological scope of this study, nevertheless speak volumes about the way the Carthusians institutionalized the desert: the church is small, reflecting the lesser demands of community worship, and around the large cloister are not the traditional communal buildings but individual cells each with its own garden, in which the monk said the remainder of the offices, ate, slept, worked and read. This reminds us of the desire for solitude and simplicity which inspired and characterized the new religious movements of the twelfth century.

THE MONASTIC KNIGHTS

The military orders of the Knights Templar and Hospitaller were, in one sense, a culmination of the development of the concept of Christian warfare and Christian knighthood, which received its most significant ratification at the preaching of the First Crusade in 1095. The process by which the fighting instincts of the aristocracy were approved, even sanctified, is a complex one and owes much to tenth-century movements, like the Peace of God, as well as to the crusades. Yet the military orders were also a product – albeit a paradoxical one – of the new monasticism of the twelfth century, and as such deserve mention in this chapter. They are, too, a part of the development of the religious orders in Britain, for although the main arena of their activities lay in the Holy Land, where the Hospitallers cared for pilgrims visiting Jerusalem and the Templars guarded the routes which approached the Holy City, and where both played a major role in the military victories and disasters of crusader battles, the knights acquired estates in the West, where they founded small houses. These acted as centres from which to administer property and to recruit from the local population.[37]

Both the Hospitallers and the Templars had been in existence for some considerable time before they were incorporated into the body of monastic orders, but from their earliest days they had developed a style of life which was, in essence, monastic. They took vows of chastity and obedience, and lived a common life. Very little, in fact, was needed to transform these quasi-monastic groups, and this was achieved when both acquired a rule. That of the Templars, which was devised by St Bernard, and which received papal approval in 1139, was based on the Rule of St Benedict and not unnaturally bore the imprint of Cistercian observances and influence.[38] The Rule of the Knights Hospitaller, in its surviving form a later composite document, owed much to the Rule of St Augustine, and thus cast its members in the role of canons regular. By these rules the 'New Knighthood'[39] was firmly established as monastic and cenobitical. Whether stationed in the East or in one of the outposts in the West, the knights followed a monastic régime; they were committed to poverty, lived in common, and, except when they were engaged in military duties, followed the religious offices.

Both orders divided their western houses into provinces (called priories by the Hospitallers), comprising individual preceptories (Templar) or commanderies (Hospitaller). The Knights Templar were the first of the two to establish themselves in Britain.[40] Around the year 1128 the founder of the order himself, Hugh de Payens, created their headquarters at the Old Temple in London. It was in London, too, that the Hospitallers chose first to settle.[41] Here c. 1144 Jordan of Bricett, a Suffolk landowner, granted land in Clerkenwell for the creation of the Hospital of St John of Jerusalem. From their London bases the knights were successful in attracting endowments, and all over the country preceptories and commanderies were established, sometimes on the initiative of lay folk, sometimes by the knights themselves, as their possessions in a region made it expedient to have a local centre for administration and collection of revenue. Most preceptories and commanderies probably comprised a preceptor, one or two brethren (often those who had retired from active duty), serjeants (serving men of humbler social origin than the knights) and a chaplain or two. By the end of the twelfth century there were roughly thirty-four houses of each order in England and Wales and one of each in Scotland. In the following century nearly fifty more establishments were created, indicating that the knights retained their popularity and continued to increase their centres of operation well after the number of new foundations of other orders had contracted. Their well-wishers included members of all sections of society, from the tenants of the major honours to the king himself. Those who gave estates on which houses were founded included King Stephen and Queen Matilda, King David of Scotland, and earls, archbishops and bishops. The chronology of foundation and expansion indicates that the success of the knights had, as we might expect, some correlation with the crusading movement, for it was when crusades were being preached – in the 1140s and again in the 1190s – that endowments appear to have increased. Land and property were given both by those, like Roger de Mowbray, who took the cross, and by those who stayed at home.[42] Papal mandates and bishops' letters show that many who in a fit of enthusiasm made a vow to go on crusade lived to regret it; and the commutation of such a vow by the endowment of the military orders fighting in the East must have seemed an appropriate gesture.

The knights did not always rely on the pious instincts of the laity to expand their territorial holdings. On occasion they exchanged property in one area for land in another in order to consolidate their estates and facilitate their exploitation. They used cash to purchase land; and, like the Cistercians, were active in the clearance of scrub and waste land for cultivation. Around the preceptories of Temple Newsham (Yorkshire) and Temple Bruer (Lincolnshire) the knights were active in the clearance of marsh and fen and their reclamation for agricultural use.[43] The great inquest into the extent of the lands of the Templars, which dates from c. 1185, demonstrates not only the size of their land holdings by that date, but how enmeshed they were, as landowners and landlords, in the rural life of England.

The Knights Templar and Hospitaller were a radical concept, and provide perhaps a fitting climax for this discussion of the impact of the new orders of the twelfth century. Quite how contemporaries regarded them – as monastic knights or fighting monks – is not clear; nor is it certain which half of their *personae* would have been more easily identifiable. In the Holy Land their military role was obvious. In Britain the number of knights must always have been relatively small, and their duties mainly administrative. For this reason it could be argued that the activities of the knights in Britain belong more properly to a discussion of the economic and agricultural development of the country. However, the knights certainly have a place in the history of the religious orders in Britain as elsewhere. It was the achievement of St Bernard and others successfully to fuse the fighting talents of the knightly class with their religious aspirations. They sanctioned the ideal of a Christian knighthood dedicated to holy war, and made it possible for men who had no inclination to enter the traditional spiritual retreat of the cloister still to become members of a monastic order. In time the knights outgrew their original purpose. In the East, military defeats, culminating in the fall of Acre in 1291, undermined their credibility, while in the West their role as bankers and international financiers laid them open to charges of corruption and arrogance, and prey to royal greed. At the very end of our period the Templars were on the brink of disgrace and dissolution, as one of the monastic adventures of the twelfth century came to an end.

5

5

WOMEN AND THE RELIGIOUS LIFE

·

THE PROBLEMS

It has been common in accounts of medieval monasticism to omit or marginalize the role of women. David Knowles's masterly study, for instance, is primarily one of male monasticism; he makes only a few comments on two aspects of female monasticism, the Old English nunneries between 1066 and 1100, and the origin of the Gilbertine Order. The notable exception was the pioneering work of Eileen Power, *Medieval English nunneries c. 1275–1535*, published in 1922. Recent years have seen, as part of the surge in women's studies, the advent of works devoted specifically to medieval nuns. Particularly pertinent for this survey are two monographs treating English women religious after the Conquest.[1] There has yet to be a modern study of British monasticism which places the contribution of women within the context of both male and female religious life. The study of religious women and their communities in the Middle Ages poses a number of problems. One – and possibly a major reason for their neglect in the past – is the scarcity of source material, specifically a lack of records produced within the communities themselves. Nunneries may figure as prominently as some male houses in the visitation returns preserved in bishops' registers, but fewer than twenty English female houses have left cartularies, those collections of copies of charters and other legal documents which enable us to build up a picture of the growth of the landed estates of a house, and to analyse the identity of benefactors and the motives for their grants. Elsewhere the survival rate is also dismal: there are no such records for the small number

85

of Welsh nunneries and only a partial cartulary for one Scottish house, Coldstream. Although foundation charters often have to be treated with caution in an attempt to date the inception of regular life in a religious house, the lack of many of these most basic of documents means that the chronology of the establishment of women's communities and in some cases the identity of the founder remain uncertain.[2] In contrast to the number of nunneries in medieval England – over 150 by the third quarter of the thirteenth century – Wales and Scotland were less well served. In Wales there were only four small houses, one of them short-lived,[3] and in Scotland ten can be identified within our period. So poorly documented are they that when referring to Eileen Power's study of English nunneries between the late thirteenth and sixteenth centuries a leading authority could write that 'no comparable account of the contemporary Scottish nunneries has been attempted nor indeed is it possible, since the material for such study is very scanty'.[4]

Not only the chronology of foundations, but the affiliations of female houses are often difficult to identify. Women in the nunneries of medieval Britain followed either the Rule of St Benedict or the Rule of St Augustine, perhaps in modified form. Some of their houses belonged to organized congregations, like the Gilbertine Order or the order of Fontevrault. Others were affiliated to groups with particular observances, like Arrouaise and Prémontré. A substantial number were, became, or claimed to be, Cistercian. As we shall see, these houses pose a particular problem for the historian. Because we lack so many foundation charters and because the documentation in many cases is so thin, it is often difficult to know to which order religious women belonged. Sometimes the first record occurs at the Dissolution, indicating the order to which houses belonged in the sixteenth century, but we cannot assume that they were consistent in affiliation throughout their history. It is therefore more appropriate to treat the foundation and expansion of houses of religious women in a separate chapter, rather than discussing them like men according to order or congregation. To do this would be to squeeze women into categories which may better describe male rather than female congregations.

A further factor which complicates general discussion of the way medieval society viewed communities of nuns is the changing attitude which is apparent in the course of the period under review. We have already seen how the tenth-century monastic revival, which was led by men, nevertheless took account of women's aspirations in that several nunneries were founded, most of them sponsored and fostered by the royal family.[5] Medieval male and female houses were separate entities; there was no attempt to reproduce the famous double houses of the early

Saxon period, like Whitby, where the Abbess Hilda ruled women and men. However, in one sense monasteries and nunneries of this period were of equal status. On the whole, male houses were larger and wealthier than their female counterparts, but both were charged with the responsibility of praying for the king and queen and their realm. We can be in no doubt that the reformers favoured the development of female monasticism by their encouragement of both patrons and professed women. The late eleventh and early twelfth centuries in England saw the continuation of participation by churchmen in the promotion of female religious vocation, both those within the ranks of the ecclesiastical hierarchy and those outside it. Bishops, monks, preachers and hermits in their own ways contributed to the opening up of opportunities for women in the monastic life. By the 1130s on the continent as well as in England a gradual change becomes perceptible. The easy association of men and women within communities fell under suspicion. The Cistercians did not, until the thirteenth century, waver in their determination to keep women out of the order, but their rigid attitude began to be shared by others who had previously looked with favour and sympathy on the female religious vocation. The reasons for this change are complex, but its consequences were far-reaching. Whereas the history of male monasticism within the period 1000–1300 may be seen as exhibiting a continued growth of variety of opportunity, that of female monasticism is full of checks and of setbacks; it has less of a unity. The early to mid twelfth century witnessed the foundation of two orders designed specifically to cater for women: those of Fontevrault and Sempringham (the Gilbertine Order). By the thirteenth century, although women were allowed to join in the great experiment of the mendicant orders of friars, their involvement was limited. Such an association was resisted by the male mendicants; and the women's way of life, a strictly enclosed one, varied little from that of their precursors in the two previous centuries.

FEMALE VOCATION

Very few of the women who entered the nunneries of medieval Britain are known to us by name, but those we can identify provide us with a glimpse of the variety of vocation and motivation which led to their becoming brides of Christ.[6] We know enough about the nunneries of late Saxon England to know that they were aristocratic institutions. After the Conquest the ranks of these nuns were swollen by the arrival of Anglo-Saxon women, those who had lost their husbands, fathers and sons at one of the three battles of 1066 or whose families had been dispossessed to make land available for the conquerors.[7] We do not know their numbers, and only a few of their names, but we may be reasonably certain that they were still confined to the well-to-do of society. Queen Edith, widow of Edward the Confessor, entered Wilton abbey, where she was later joined by the daughter of King Harold Godwinson. Wilton may also have been the temporary home of the sister and nieces of Edgar Ætheling, the last claimant of the Anglo-Saxon line. There is more certain evidence of his sister Christina as a nun of Romsey, where she may also have been abbess; with her was her niece Edith. As a short-term relief from the pressure of enforced marriage, the nunnery served a useful function. But problems might emerge at a later date, and from the letters of two successive archbishops of Canterbury it is clear that they did. The question the latter were faced with was this: if a woman entered a nunnery through fear or under duress, should she be forced to remain there for her whole life or could she be released? Archbishop Lanfranc was clearly sympathetic and ruled that, so long as no vows had been taken, a woman was free to leave the nunnery. For his successor, Anselm, the problem assumed a political dimension. Edith, niece of Edgar Ætheling and daughter of the Scottish king and queen, Malcolm Canmore and St Margaret, had been sent to England at an early age with her aunt Christina. It is unlikely that she was intended to make her profession as a nun, since from 1093 at least she became a pawn in the matrimonial/political plans of her father. When in 1100 Henry I of England saw the sense in arranging his own marriage to the daughter of the Scottish royal house who was at the same time a descendant of the house of Wessex, the question was asked, quite seriously, whether Edith could marry or whether she was, in fact, a nun. Anselm investigated and found that, although Edith had worn the veil of a nun, she had done so unwillingly, had never made profession, and was therefore free to marry. His decision was criticized by some, but a fruitful friendship grew up between Edith, who became known as Matilda, and the archbishop as her spiritual adviser.[8]

The case of Edith/Matilda and her aunt Christina reminds us of one aspect of the history of nunneries. Both were high-born and well-connected women. One found her vocation within the cloister; the other did not. The motivations of those who entered the religious life are difficult to assess. They are rarely explicitly stated and not necessarily straightforward. We have from the early twelfth century, however, two contrasting examples of women who entered the religious life which illuminate the various pressures through which medieval nunneries originated. The first, Eve, was an oblate.[9] In 1065, at the age of seven, she had been placed by her mother and father in the abbey of Wilton, where she had progressed to take her vows. Far from resenting the choice made for her, Eve found that the wealthy and aristocratic ambience at Wilton was not strict enough: an account written shortly after her death indicates that she chose to live a reclusive life within the confines of the abbey. Around 1080 the eremitical pull drew Eve away from Wilton and took her to France to live as an anchoress, an *inclusa*. In all this she enjoyed the spiritual and material support both of women and particularly of men: her confidant at Wilton, the monk Goscelin, who wrote for Eve the *Liber Confortatorius*, and the hermit Hervey, with whom she lived in France.[10]

The second woman was Christina, the daughter of well-to-do merchant parents from Huntingdon. They chose for Christina the way of marriage, not that of the cloister, but their daughter had already laid out the course she would follow when at an early age in the abbey church of St Albans she made a personal vow of chastity. The following years illustrate the heroic determination of a young girl who had dedicated herself to a life of celibacy to resist the pressure of her parents, of the young man they had chosen for her, and of the bishop of Durham, who tried first to seduce and then to rape her. Unable to persuade those with the power to shape her life of the seriousness of her vocation, Christina was forced to flee on horseback dressed as a man and to escape to the relative safety of a hermitage. She spent the next six years in hiding, two at Flamstead with the anchoress Ælfwen, and four at Markyate, where she lived with the recluse Roger, a former monk of St Albans. It was only on the death of Robert Bloet, bishop of Lincoln, who had refused to honour her vow of virginity, that Christina was able to live openly as a religious woman and make her profession before the new bishop. Around her and Roger, at Markyate, there grew up a group of women devoted to a life of chastity and seclusion, and some years after Roger's death, at which he bequeathed his hermitage to Christina, the community of Markyate was transformed into a priory with his protégée as its first prioress. The development was aided by Christina's close friendship with Abbot Geoffrey of St Albans, and possibly due to his initiative.

Christina of Markyate is unique in that she was the only twelfth-century female hermit of whom a biography was written, a work whose vitality makes it likely to have been framed by one who knew her well.[11] Both her story and that of Eve of Wilton tell us several important things. First, however difficult to isolate are the motives of those who entered the religious life, there was a strong spiritual element, that same desire for solitude and retreat that we encountered in male monasticism.[12] True divorce from the world is more manifest in the life of Eve than that of Christina, for the one chose the solitary life while the other had it forced upon her. For Christina the dominant motivation seems to have been the desire to live as a holy maiden (*virgo*), to preserve her virginity, either because she saw it as a spiritual concern, one way to live a holy life, or because on a different level it gave her a means to control her own destiny and escape the social and economic expectations of marriage. Christina's *Life* is a warning to us not to interpret the word 'hermit' too strictly or as synonymous with 'anchoress'.[13] The hermit life was not one of unremitting solitude.[14] Christina associated with like-minded women and men, and the picture that comes through her biography is of a network of lively hermit communities, both male and female, with strong links with the abbey of St Albans. The eremitical life enabled men and women to live in seclusion, poverty, chastity and prayer without being subject to the formal constraints of a religious house. Yet their spiritual aspirations were a powerful factor in the emergence of such monasteries.

  Although Christina found her ambition to live the religious life frustrated by men, both she and Eve at times received help and support from them, and at times lived in their company. At Markyate Christina had frequent communication with Geoffrey, abbot of St Albans, with whom she maintained a close friendship. It may have been on Geoffrey's advice that gradually monastic discipline and observance was imposed on Markyate. From the early twelfth century we can detect a trend towards what we may call the institutionalization of hermitages, the tendency to make them subordinate to religious houses, and this is apparent in male as well as female houses.[15] A number of medieval nunneries – possibly many more than the sources reveal – began life as hermitages and were moulded into dependent priories.[16] Markyate gives us one example; another is provided by Kilburn (Middlesex). At a date between 1127 and 1134 the abbot and prior of Westminster issued a notification to the effect that they had given to three maidens (*puellae*) named Emma, Gunhild and Christine 'the hermitage of Kilburn which Godwin built, with all its land and all those things which they will have [need of] for the sake of living a holy life'. The hermit Godwin was designated master of Kilburn for the term of his life, and after his death authority over Kilburn was to pass to a senior maiden chosen by the convent. Here we have the rudiments of a monastic community. In another charter, roughly contemporary, the abbot referred to the *ancillae Dei*, the handmaids of God (a term often translated as 'nuns') in the church of St John the Baptist, Kilburn.[17] Thus fostered by the great abbey of Westminster, Kilburn began its development as a centre of regular life. Similar links between female or mixed hermitages and male monasteries emerge. At Sopwell a group of female recluses were helped by Abbot Geoffrey of St Albans. Sopwell lies less than half a mile from the monastery, and it is possible that the women may have had some previous association with the abbey, and almost formed a double house.[18] The relationship was regularized by Geoffrey in the same way as with Markyate, by the creation of a female monastery; and Sopwell became a house of strictly enclosed nuns dependent on the monks of St Albans for help with administration and having one of their number as its master.[19] Sopwell is another manifestation of that tendency, apparent as the twelfth century wore on, to segregate more rigidly male and female members of mixed communities.

Like Herbert of Westminster and Geoffrey of St Albans, Abbot Hugh of Bury St Edmunds was responsible for the conversion of an eremitical community into a priory. His abbey had a cell at Thetford (Norfolk) occupied by a number of religious men, but their numbers dwindled to two whose resources could no longer support them. At their suggestion, the abbot transferred the cell at Thetford to a group of female recluses from Ling, in the hope that the combined resources might be sufficient for the upkeep of a community of nuns who would continue the tradition of religious worship at Thetford and that women might succeed where men had failed.[20] Other priories, too, may have had their roots in the kind of informal community described so vividly in Christina's *Life*. The very name of Ankerwyke (Buckinghamshire) hints that the priory was preceded by a hermitage.[21] The *Ancrene Wisse* ('Guide' or 'Rule for anchoresses') written in English in the early thirteenth century for a group of anchoresses, and surviving in thirteen manuscripts, demonstrates the enduring popularity of this form of life.[22] It also shows that the dividing line between nunnery and anchorage could be a fine one. More than we can know from documentary evidence, the spiritual aspirations and vocation of medieval women were prime influences behind the formation of nunneries.[23]

WOMEN AS FOUNDERS AND PATRONS

If the role of female religious women is often obscured by the nature of our sources, then so too is the part of women as founders and patrons of nunneries. For one thing, female involvement may be masked by the formality of the language of the charter. Although we have examples of women who issued charters in their own right, this was the mark of a woman of high rank, usually a widow. Sometimes men and women are associated together in the foundation and endowment of a house, and here as well as in cases where the man alone is recorded as the donor, female influence may have been much greater than the written record suggests. Husband and wife acted jointly in the foundations of Blackborough, Norfolk (c. 1150), Bungay, Suffolk (1175 × 1176) and Gokewell, Lincolnshire (1147 × 1175) and several others. That the women played a leading role is indicated by the occasions on which the

nunnery was sited on lands forming part of a woman's dowry.[24] The
Yorkshire house of Baysdale is stated in a charter of Adam de Brus to have
been founded initially by Ralph de Neville at Hutton, which land was
'the free dowry of his wife'.[25]

Only one female foundation by a lay person can be assigned to the
immediate post-Conquest period, the Bedfordshire convent at Elstow,
established between 1076 and 1086; the Norman settlement did not,
apparently, result in the foundation of alien priories for women in the
same way as it did for men. There is no evidence that Elstow was created
in order to satisfy the religious vocation of one who wished to become a
nun; rather, it has been suggested that it was to salve the conscience of
its founder, Countess Judith, widow of Earl Waltheof, who had been
executed for treachery in 1076. The countess may have been implicated
in his betrayal, and her religious foundation has been interpreted as an act
of atonement.[26] Another notable female founder provided for herself. At
some time before 1133 Edith, widow of William de Lancelene, took to
the solitary life. Later she decided to form a community at Godstow, a few
miles north of Oxford, made over property to the house, received the
agreement of her lord, and herself became a nun and first abbess. A
charter of Bishop Alexander of Lincoln confirming the foundation leaves
us in no doubt as to the dominant role of Edith, 'who with her own
wealth and by her own work, and with the alms collected from the
faithful, wisely built from the first stone the church of this place'. The
charter goes on to describe the dedication ceremony of the church in
1138, attended by King Stephen and Queen Matilda, earls and barons, and
a host of ecclesiastical dignitaries, and the grants which were made by the
faithful.[27] Quite what drew these eminent men and women to the
ceremony we do not know, but there can be no doubt as to the outcome
of their patronage and later that of Henry II, whose mistress, the fair
Rosamund, was buried at Godstow: Godstow not only enjoyed the title
of abbey – a rare distinction outside the circle of pre-Conquest
foundations – but became one of the wealthiest post-Conquest nunneries
in England.

Another widow who founded an abbey and then became its head was
Ela, countess of Salisbury. Her plan had been to associate the community
at Lacock (Wiltshire) with the order of Cîteaux, but she was unsuccessful,
and the nuns followed instead the observances of the Augustinians.
Stixwould Priory in Lincolnshire, too, boasted an aristocratic founder,
Lucy, dowager countess of Chester. It is not certain if Lucy became a nun
at Stixwould, but she certainly exhibited a fierce determination not to
remarry – after the death of her third husband she paid the king 500 marks
to be allowed to remain unwed.[28] This reluctance to re-enter the state of

matrimony was shared by the founder of Marham Abbey (Norfolk), Isabel, countess of Arundel, who received burial at the house she established, one of only two female abbeys incorporated into the Cistercian Order early in their history. Wealthy widows of the nobility did not found the majority of medieval English nunneries, but the ones for which they were responsible were of high rank: Elstow, Godstow, Lacock, Marham and Canonsleigh, for instance, were all accorded the title of abbey. The differentiation between abbey and priory does not, as it does with male Benedictine houses, denote whether an institution was independent or subordinate to another. Rather it conveys a distinction acquired through wealth or association with a powerful lay patron. The two fully incorporated Cistercian communities, Tarrant and Marham, were abbeys, while others calling themselves Cistercian, in keeping with their lack of status within the order, were priories. The small group of pre-Conquest abbeys for women were thus joined by an equally small and select band of post-Conquest ones whose powerful patronesses brought them prestige and, equally importantly, wealth. Very few twelfth-century houses achieved resources and income comparable with those of the earlier foundations. Elstow and Godstow, building on significant twelfth-century endowments, managed to rival the ancient foundations, and at the Dissolution were among the wealthiest female houses in the land. Even then, the value of each was under £300 per annum, significantly less than prestigious male monasteries.

In the North, where an outburst of women's foundations was initiated by Archbishop Thurstan's establishment of St Clement's between c. 1125 and 1133, we encounter a number of female founders. Within a short period three family nunneries were founded in Yorkshire: Nunkeeling by Agnes de Arches, Nun Monkton by her brother William and his wife Ivetta, and Nun Appleton by Alice de St Quintin, daughter of Agnes de Arches.[29] In roughly the same period Yedingham was founded by Helewise de Clere, and William de Clerfai and his wife Avice de Tany were jointly associated in the foundation of Hampole. Partly as a consequence of the lower status of these founders, who were of knightly rather than baronial families, the priories founded by women for women in the North did not attain the wealth of those southern houses established by aristocratic widows. At the Dissolution all but one of the Yorkshire nunneries had an income of less than £100 per annum. In Scotland two nunneries have been associated with female founders: Haddington, about twenty miles east of Edinburgh, was established by Ada, countess of Northumberland and mother of King Malcolm IV; and a countess of March may have been responsible for Eccles, about fifteen miles from Berwick, although this has also been ascribed to King David I.[30]

MEN AS FOUNDERS AND PATRONS

A wide spectrum of men, both lay and ecclesiastical, were involved in the fostering of the religious life for women. Some of them we have encountered already, but the abbots who lent their support to female hermits were not the only ones to encourage women. The monks of Peterborough established a nunnery at Stamford (St Michael's), over which they retained authority through overseeing the administration there and the reception of nuns. In contrast to the dependencies of Westminster and St Albans, the degree of control exercised by Peterborough over its subordinate women was considerable. The link goes back a long way. Domesday Book recorded a number of women present at Peterborough, and the community at Stamford very possibly represents their successors, moved away from the abbey as part of a general trend towards segregation. Another group of men who were instrumental in the furthering of the female religious vocation were members of the episcopate. Commentators have differed in their opinion as to how significant, as sole founders, bishops were. Elkins suggests their role was an important one, while Thompson more moderately differentiates between those ecclesiastics who founded houses *de novo* and those who acted in their pastoral role to confirm the foundations of others or to protect communities of women who lacked a strong lay patron.[31] The first post-Conquest bishop to act was apparently Gundulf of Rochester, who around 1095 built and endowed an abbey for women at Malling in Kent and placed the nuns under his authority. Another episcopal founder, the man who in effect reintroduced female monasticism north of the Trent, was Thurstan, archbishop of York, who established a community of nuns in the church of St Clement.[32] The archbishop had hoped to persuade Christina of Markyate, then a recluse, to be prioress, but she declined. Elsewhere bishops acted – Anselm at St Sepulchre in Canterbury, William Giffard of Winchester at Ivinghoe, and Roger de Clinton of Lichfield at Brewood Black Ladies and Farewell – to offer protection to the nuns or simply to confirm their endowments.[33]

Lay men, alone or acting with their wives, were also involved in the foundation of nunneries. If one general observation can be made about England, it is that the lay men who founded female houses tended to be of a lower social and political status than those who established male houses: this has been found to be the case at a regional level in the North and more generally.[34] Over seventy post-Conquest English nunneries were founded by non-baronial founders, men who enjoyed neither title nor office. It is less true of Wales, where the Lord Rhys ap Gruffydd added to his male houses of Strata Florida and Talley a nunnery at Llanllŷr, or

Scotland, where the lords of Galloway and of the Isles were founders of Lincluden and Iona, and the earls of March and Fife, of Coldstream and North Berwick. In contrast to male houses, only three English nunneries were royal foundations. King Stephen and Queen Matilda founded Higham (Lillechurch) in Kent as a daughter house of the abbey of St Sulpice at Rennes around 1150 for their daughter Mary. She had first become a nun at Rennes, so the choice of mother house is not surprising. When her father became king of England in 1135, Mary and a group of nuns moved to take up residence at the Middlesex nunnery of Stratford, but tensions ensued. These have been attributed to the different customs that Mary had become used to at Rennes,[35] but we may suppose as well that the arrival at Stratford of a king's daughter, perhaps too aware of her royal birth and worldly status, may have increased discontent. As a way out of the impasse Higham Priory was founded to provide this member of the ruling family with an institution to rule.[36] In Scotland David I established at least one nunnery, at South Berwick, and possibly another at Eccles; while his daughter-in-law established Haddington, and her son, Malcolm IV, the largest Scottish nunnery, Manuel, some twenty miles west of Edinburgh. As with the expansion of male monasticism the Scottish royal house was instrumental in the widening of opportunities for religious women, and female foundations were largely aristocratic.

Stephen and Matilda's foundation at Higham was partly motivated by family considerations, the desire to provide for a female relative. At Wroxall a priory was built by a crusader, Hugh fitz Richard, and it was here that his wife and two daughters made their profession. Another crusader, Roger de Glanville, with his wife Gundreda founded a house at Bungay, the most important role being played by Gundreda. Roger died in the Holy Land and she may then have entered Bungay as a nun. In both these instances the association of the foundation with the crusading movement suggests that the establishment of the nunnery was intended as an insurance policy: it provided a community of religious to pray for the soul of the crusader, and a place of retirement for his wife and family. Often the evidence for this kind of motivation is obscured. Another joint husband/wife foundation was the Yorkshire house of Nun Monkton, and the charters of William and Ivetta de Arches make no mention of why the foundation was made. But the casual reference that their grant was made to 'God and St Mary and their daughter Matilda' suggests that this was another foundation made for the provision of a female relative.[37] A chance mention in a charter of the steward of the honour of Richmond makes it clear that the daughters of the constable of the honour, Roger de Aske, had become nuns at their father's foundation at Marrick.[38] The charters of founders, patrons and benefactors might make a grant of property to a nunnery with a daughter, a sister or a niece, and this practice continued into the thirteenth century and beyond. It may well have been more common than we know. For one thing charters, as we have noted already, are much scarcer than for men's houses; for another, canon law had come to associate this kind of grant with simony, the buying of ecclesiastical office, and we can suppose that donors might obscure rather than proclaim openly the reason for their gifts.[39] It is for these reasons that the opinion of historians as to the frequency of the dowry grant, a term which compares a gift offered to a nunnery when a woman entered the religious life there with her marriage portion, have differed. Elkins concluded that the evidence was insufficient to confirm the 'typical assumption that lay founders were acting in order to aid their own kin', while Thompson found that a 'significant number' of female relatives entered foundations made by their family.[40] Certainly, if the net is cast wider to include benefactors as well as founders, then there would appear to be evidence to support Thompson's argument. An early example is provided by the pre-Conquest nunnery of Shaftesbury, whose cartulary preserves, from the late eleventh or early twelfth century, a list of thirteen donations which 'men gave with their daughters to the church of St Edward of Shaftesbury'; those daughters were both Anglo-Saxon and Norman.[41] In the North, where nunneries were smaller and places in them restricted, the number of dowry grants as a proportion of the surviving charters is striking.[42] But motivation is a question on which it is difficult to generalize. Founders of female as well as male houses show a combination of spiritual motives and the desire through their religious establishments to build a network of patronage.

MONASTIC ORDERS FOR WOMEN: FONTEVRAULT AND SEMPRINGHAM

In the early to mid twelfth century the work of two men, Robert of Arbrissel and Gilbert of Sempringham, opened up more opportunities for women in the religious life, yet neither had set out to be a monastic legislator. Robert was one of those hermits and preachers who in the last years of the eleventh century lived in the forests of northern France, and as with Bernard of Tiron and Vitalis of Savigny the response to his call to the apostolic life and to repentance was overwhelming. Both men and women congregated around Robert, and what might have been a cause for satisfaction, his success in converting sinners, became a cause of potential scandal, the free and easy association of his male and female followers, and led to the foundation of the house and then the order of Fontevrault. Robert was concerned above all to minister to the poor

and the outcasts of society, and his critics accused him of being more
concerned with prostitutes than with those aristocratic women who were
attracted by his teaching. Robert's foundation of an order for female
religious has been interpreted in a number of ways, and current scholarship suggests that his motivation was mixed: a desire to avoid scandal;
his own search for a way to serve the weak and the poor and especially
the outcasts; his need to test his own virtue through association with
women.[43] It was above all a response to a situation as it arose, not a
carefully planned enterprise. At Fontevrault (c. 1101) separate buildings
were constructed for Robert's male and female followers, but the
community was evidently regarded, jurisdictionally, as a single one for
both sexes. However, the early documents give prominence to the
women of the community, and its head was the widow Petronilla, who
after Robert's death became the first abbess of Fontevrault. The male
component was there, but the status of men was lower than that of
women.[44] The power of the abbess Petronilla and her successor
Helisende, both ironically women of high birth, was supreme, but as the
years passed the lowly status of men within the house and order became
a matter for discontent.

In one important respect Fontevrault developed on lines not envisaged
by its founder. From being a haven for the poor and disadvantaged, it
became a refuge for aristocratic ladies. One reason for this was
undoubtedly the prestige which accrued to Fontevrault through the
patronage of the English royal house. Eleanor of Aquitaine, wife of
Henry II, was a benefactor of Fontevrault, and it became her burial place
and that of her husband and her son Richard I. The order was brought to
England by Earl Robert of Leicester, who with his wife Amicia established a house at Kintbury which by 1157 had moved to Nuneaton
(Warwickshire). If, as has been suggested, Kintbury was founded around
1154 – the year of the accession of Henry II and the joining of the
territories of Anjou and Aquitaine to those of Normandy and England –
then Robert's choice of the order of Fontevrault might have had political
overtones and been a recognition of the ascendancy of the Angevin power
in England.[45] A further, and perhaps more significant, house of the order
was Amesbury (Wiltshire). Here in 1177 a Benedictine house which had
been the subject of scandal was disbanded and reconstituted by Henry II
as part of his penance for the murder of Archbishop Thomas Becket.
Female houses needed the service of male chaplains, and an associated
house for men was founded at Grovebury as a source of assistance for
the English houses of the order. Fontevrault was a federated order: it was
held together by governmental devices adopted from the Cistercians, the
general chapter and internal visitation, and early charters show how

closely the English houses were associated with the continental mother house.[46] However, the subsequent history of the English houses indicates that such closeness was difficult to maintain, and as early as 1155 the abbess of Fontevrault allowed Nuneaton to forgo some of the formalities normally expected and to receive its own nuns and brethren without recourse to the mother house. The redrawing of political boundaries following King John's loss of Normandy and Anjou by 1205 made contact with the centre even more difficult, and this, along with the prestige of acquiring a royal patron, led to an increased status for Amesbury at the expense of Fontevrault.[47]

The association of the priest Gilbert of Sempringham with holy women began after he had left service in the household of the bishop of Lincoln to take charge of two Lincolnshire parishes in the patronage of his father. He found a number of women in the parish of Sempringham who wished to live the enclosed life, and so, around the year 1131 and on the advice of Bishop Alexander of Lincoln, he built for them a cell adjoining the church. This act marked the very humble beginnings of the order of the Gilbertines. How the movement developed is told to us in the *Life of Gilbert*, composed by an unknown canon in 1201 as part of the campaign for Gilbert's canonization, and expanded and revised in 1205. Gilbert himself related how he soon realized that if the women were to be strictly enclosed they would need to be served, and so he placed some village girls under a simple vow, and converted them into lay sisters. Soon, after a visit from the abbot of Rievaulx, he added lay brothers on the model of the Cistercians. Events soon accelerated. The anchorage at Sempringham grew and developed into a priory possibly c. 1139 but definitely by 1154 on the basis of grants of land by the laity,[48] and in 1139 an associated house, Haverholme, near Sleaford, was established by Bishop Alexander of Lincoln. His charter refers to the handmaidens of God 'under the guardianship and teaching of Gilbert the priest', who follow 'the life of the monks of the order of Cîteaux as far as the strength of their sex allows'.[49] Although at this stage the Gilbertine houses had no formal organization or affiliation, it is clear that Bishop Alexander associated the austerity of their observance with the Cistercians. And it was to the White Monks that Gilbert turned when in 1147 he felt that some more concrete regulation was needed; the movement which he had begun was growing in popularity, and he himself was unwilling to take on the responsibility of its administration. At the momentous Cistercian general chapter of that year the White Monks were asked to take charge of the two Lincolnshire convents. Their refusal is usually attributed to the fact that at this date they acknowledged no Cistercian nuns, and although it is true that two contemporary Lincolnshire nunneries claimed to be Cistercian, these were outside the official fold and were to remain so for some time to come.[50] The Cistercian rejection of the Gilbertine nuns was apparently due to their desire to remain an exclusively male organization.

Gilbert's journey to Cîteaux had, however, a fruitful outcome, for the pope encouraged him to compile regulations for the communities under his charge. How far others aided his efforts is not clear; the life of Gilbert states that he received advice from St Bernard and Archbishop Malachy of Armagh, who was visiting Cîteaux.[51] The innovation in the second phase of Gilbertine development, that is, after 1147, was the introduction of a fourth element, regular canons, into their houses. Gilbertine organization was now an amalgam of customs. The nuns followed the Rule of St Benedict and were rigorously enclosed. The lay brothers owed their way of life to the Cistercian customs, while the canons observed the Rule of St Augustine. Other elements of Cistercian organization were prominent, in particular the annual general chapter. Gilbert's mature thinking seems to have been governed by a conviction that the presence of literate priests was necessary for the well-being of the nuns, to allow them to follow a religious vocation within the strict confines of the nuns' cloister. The necessary domestic work was done by the lay sisters and the labouring tasks by the lay brothers, while the canons served to the spiritual needs of the women.[52] In the years after 1147 the Gilbertine Order grew in popularity, especially in Gilbert's native Lincolnshire; it was primarily a local order. Before 1154 new double houses had been created at Alvingham, Bullington, Catley, North Ormesby and Sixhills in Lincoln-shire, Chicksands in Bedfordshire and Watton in Yorkshire, but attempts to found Gilbertine houses outside England, at Dalmilling in Scotland, and in Rome, failed.[53] At the same time began the establishment of male-only houses of the order, such as Malton in Yorkshire, founded at roughly the same date and by the same person at Watton and possibly intended, like other male houses, to be a training ground and retreat for Gilbertine canons, or to fulfil an eleemosynary function.[54] After the middle of the twelfth century most new Gilbertine foundations were for men only, with the important exception of Shouldham (Norfolk).

The existence of a male element in the Gilbertine nunneries was not unique; indeed we have already encountered it at Fontevrault. Nunneries of all orders housed men within or near their walls, particularly as priests or chaplains, but also as servants and agricultural workers, or as administrators. Recent scholarship has been more inclined to recognize the co-existence of men and women within 'female' communities, and therefore to question the traditional use of the term 'double house' exclusively to describe priories of the orders of Sempringham and Fontevrault. Yet such a label is useful, for although the priories of these

two orders were not the only nunneries to include men, their constitutions alone incorporated a male element within the formal organization
of the order. And this may have been the reason why they apparently
served the needs of women better than did the other new monastic and
canonical orders of the eleventh and twelfth centuries.[55]

MALE CONGREGATIONS WITH ASSOCIATED FEMALE HOUSES: PRÉMONTRÉ AND ARROUAISE

The attempts by Robert of Arbrissel and Gilbert of Sempringham to
accommodate female religious vocations were experiments which
lasted. Others were ultimately less successful. Women formed a sizeable
proportion of those who responded to the preaching of Norbert of
Xanten, and in its early years the monastery of Prémontré included both
men and women. Like Robert of Arbrissel, Norbert was aware of the
dangers of close proximity, and the men and women were separated into
single-sex but adjacent houses so that the women could attend the services
in the canons' church. By 1137, however, Premonstratensian attitudes
began to change, and gradually women were ordered to remove their
houses to a more respectable and safe distance. Quite when, and why, this
happened is not clear. One contemporary suggested that as the original
fervour of the movement passed, the moral dangers of proximity of the
sexes increased. There was no clear-cut decision by the chapter to distance
its women; rather it seems to have been left to individual abbots to decide
their fate. However, the final consequence of the more rigid attitude was
the refusal in 1197 or 1198 to admit any more women into the order.
This loosening of links is paralleled in the history of the English
Premonstratensian nunneries, Orford (Irford), Broadholme and
Guyzance. All three were initially closely linked with the first two
male foundations of the order, Orford (Lincolnshire) and Broadholme
(Nottinghamshire) with Newhouse, and Guyzance (Northumberland)
with Alnwick; and analysis of charter material has shown that they may
originally have been regarded as double houses, that is, the nunneries
were a dependent but integral part of the male houses, and thus of
Premonstratensian expansion in England.[56] The history of the English
houses accordingly parallels the continental experience. The late twelfth
century also saw attempts to lessen the part played by women in the
houses of the congregation of Arrouaise, a movement which, as we have
seen, influenced a number of the English and Scottish houses of canons
regular.[57] The one English nunnery of the order, Harrold (Bedfordshire),
was contemporary with the expansion of male houses in England, and
Gervase, abbot of Arrouaise, was closely involved with the foundation. By

the end of the century, however, Harrold had broken its ties with the French house; on whose initiative it is not clear.[58]

In one sense the Cistercians represent the reverse of the trend which we have so far encountered. Instead of beginning with an open attitude towards women and moving towards exclusion, they began by excluding them and then, in the early thirteenth century, admitted them into the order. In the twelfth century, although individual Cistercians encouraged female religious vocation, the order as a whole refused to countenance the existence of Cistercian nuns. Unlike Prémontré and Fontevrault, Cîteaux had begun as a monastic, not an evangelical movement. From the first secession of Robert and his companions from Molesme to the *Novum Monasterium* the movement was a male one, and it is not to be wondered that to the White Monks 'Cistercian nun' was a contradiction in terms. By the 1190s, however, the general chapter was forced to take notice of the claims of certain nunneries to be Cistercian, and in 1213 these semi-autonomous convents were placed under the tutelage of neighbouring male houses. Male support was grudging: the number of houses was to be severely limited; their women were to be strictly enclosed; their opportunity to make confession to male confessors was curtailed. Three years later the general chapter decreed that Cistercian nunneries were to be six leagues from a male monastery, and in 1228 it forbade the future affiliation of female houses and refused to allow visitation and pastoral care to those convents which they had previously acknowledged. The admission of the existence of Cistercian nuns was a triumph for female persistence, for in the latter half of the twelfth century nunneries had called themselves Cistercian, followed Cistercian customs and adopted their practices to the extent, in France and Spain, of holding provincial chapters on the precedent of the general chapter at Cîteaux. But this admission could scarcely have been more reluctant, and although the male Cistercians were unable to maintain their rigid attitude to their sisters, the official line towards women was always discouraging.[59]

One of the problems of writing the history of the British Cistercian nunneries is therefore that of identification, since until 1213 female houses calling themselves Cistercian were not a recognized part of the order. How their daily life differed from that of convents of other affiliations is accordingly problematic. In England twenty-seven nunneries have been identified as described as Cistercian at one time or another in their history, sixteen of them also having other attributions. Only two, Marham (Norfolk) and Tarrant (Dorset) are mentioned in the thirteenth-century statutes of the order, and only the first of these was actually founded as a Cistercian abbey. In Wales two nunneries may well have been founded as Cistercian, since they enjoyed close contacts with male houses, Llanllŷr with Strata Florida, with whom it shared a common founder in the Lord Rhys ap Gruffydd, and Llanllugan with Strata Marcella, whose abbot, Enoch, evidently founded that nunnery at Llansantffraed which was probably the precursor of Llanllugan.[60] In Scotland there were eight nunneries in existence by 1300 which were later designated Cistercian; whether they would have been described as such in the twelfth century is not documented, but North Berwick for one may have begun as a Benedictine house.

Documentary evidence suggests that some English nunneries were attempting, within the restrictions placed upon them, to follow a way of life which approximated to that of the White Monks without the governmental procedures of chapter and visitation. Their attempts evidently received some recognition. Thus Pope Alexander III in 1172 referred in a bull to the nuns of Sinningthwaite (Yorkshire) following 'the Rule of St Benedict and the institution of the Cistercian brothers';[61] it may be significant that the founder of Sinningthwaite at a date before 1155 was Bertram Haget, the father of Ralph Haget, a Cistercian monk of Fountains and later abbot of Kirkstall and of Fountains. A further bull of Alexander III in favour of Swine and Nun Cotham priories, situated in Yorkshire and Lincolnshire respectively, indicates that the nuns were claiming to be exempt from the payment of tithes in the same way as Cistercian monks.[62] Other houses which later claimed to be Cistercian definitely began as Benedictine, among them St Michael's, Stamford, which had been founded from Peterborough. Between 1268 and 1272 Stamford and five other Lincolnshire houses were claiming exemption as Cistercian houses from the payment of tithes, much to the annoyance of the abbot of Cîteaux, who strenuously denied that they were of his order.[63]

Among those twenty-seven nunneries in England which were or became Cistercian, eighteen lay in the North, and at least half are documented as having a male presence, with evidence at seven of lay brethren.[64] By the mid 1170s five priories had 'masters', and the number rose in the thirteenth century. Masters were drawn from local monastic communities – like William de Bardney, monk of Whitby, appointed guardian of Hampole and Baysdale in 1267/8 – or from the ranks of the secular clergy, incumbents of parish churches: in the late thirteenth century Hampole was committed to the custody of the vicar of Wath, and Arthington to the rector of Kippax. When we extend this line of enquiry to Scotland we find that there are references to 'masters of the brethren' at five Cistercian nunneries, Berwick, Coldstream, Eccles, Haddington and Manuel. In many senses these were double houses, akin to the Gilbertines. In some instances the distinction is difficult to discern, for Swine Priory in the twelfth century contained three of the four elements of the Gilbertine organization, nuns, canons and lay-brethren, and Archbishop Giffard's visitation of 1267 found all four: nuns, lay sisters, who were criticized for wearing the black veil of the nuns, and canons and lay brothers, who were accused of enjoying conversations with the nuns and who mismanaged funds, keeping the women short of food while they had plenty.[65] For another Cistercian house, Nun Cotham, Bishop Hugh de Welles of Lincoln (1209–35) approved regulations which indicate the presence of nuns, lay brethren, chaplains and lay sisters.[66] These two examples suggest a lack of formal and rigid organization in the nunneries of the North and a degree of adaptability to suit local needs and conditions. Elkins has argued that the presence of men in the nunneries of the North – and they were certainly not confined to the 'Cistercian' houses[67] – was dictated by economic necessity: that the type of endowment which the northern houses received, lands which needed clearing and which were most useful for a pastoral economy, in contrast to the income-yielding property common in the South, needed a male – particularly a lay male – presence, and that accordingly the Cistercian and Gilbertine component of the lay brethren was more suitable for northern conditions.[68] This argument has merit, but there were other reasons for the success of the Gilbertines and the popularity of Cistercian nunneries in the North. The local associations of Gilbert help to explain the achievements of the order in Lincolnshire, and the presence of prestigious Cistercian male houses in Yorkshire may have nurtured a desire among female religious to emulate their male counterparts.

But it was not just that there was more choice available to women religious in the North, the midlands and the East, where the Gilbertines and Cistercians were dominant. The distribution of nunneries in medieval Britain was uneven, and it is striking that there were far fewer in Wales, in the marcher counties, in the west country (indeed there were none at all in Cornwall) and in the South. The density of houses in the North and East cannot have been solely due to the intensely local appeal of the Gilbertines and the dominance and influence of the northern Cistercian houses; it also reflects the lower status and poor endowments of the post-Conquest female foundations. Houses multiplied because existing ones were unable to provide enough places for women wishing to live the religious life. Moreover, a small nunnery might be founded to meet the needs of the female members of a family. It did not need to be large. Where a male house, even a modest Augustinian one, might be expected

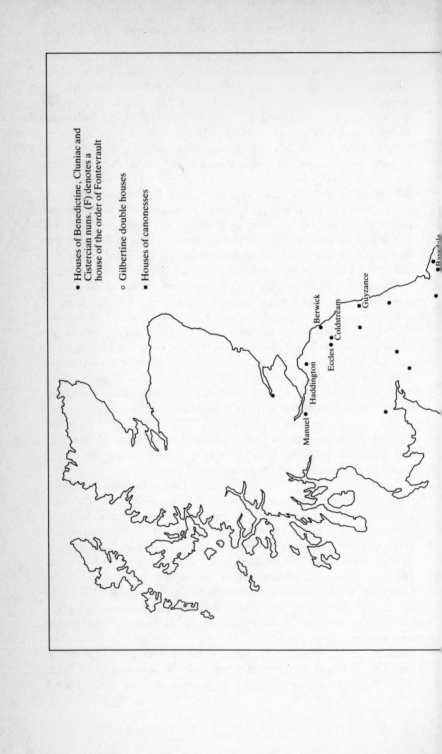

- Houses of Benedictine, Cluniac and Cistercian nuns. (F) denotes a house of the order of Fontevrault

○ Gilbertine double houses

■ Houses of canonesses

Manuel

Haddington

Berwick

Eccles

Coldstream

Guyzance

Bewsdale

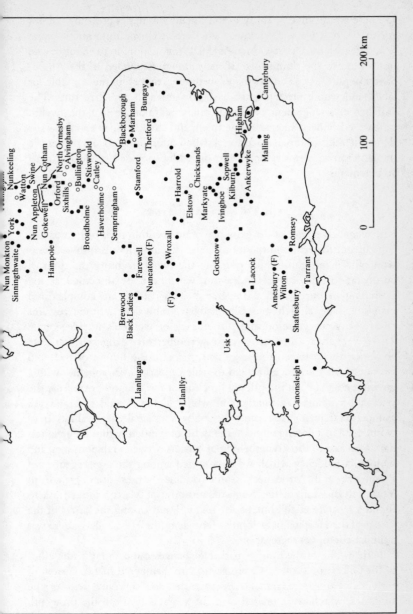

Map 5 Religious houses for women by c. 1300

to house twenty-five or thirty canons, many nunneries probably did not rise to a dozen; and well-endowed and sizeable female communities were few. The paucity of post-Conquest female foundations in the South owed not a little to the dominance of the nunneries founded in the Anglo-Saxon period, whose endowments were set early before the scramble for lands, and whose prestige must have continued to attract recruits. The varieties of arrangement of British nunneries indicate that the twelfth century was indeed an era of experiment and change. They also show the difficulties the historian encounters when attempting to discuss female monasticism in terms which were originally intended to denote male arrangements.

THE LOOSENING OF LINKS

Cistercian acceptance of the existence of nuns within their order was to a large extent forced upon the monks, and despite it few British convents won official recognition. Throughout the twelfth century the spirit of co-operation and mutual endeavour which can be discerned at the beginning of our period disintegrated. The reasons are complex and manifold. The church generally had an ambivalent attitude towards female religious vocation and the efficacy of women's intercessions.[69] There were always men who were eager to perceive dangers in too close an association between the sexes and to see in the houses of men and women a threat to discipline and to male celibacy. This, together with a growing emphasis on the priestly function of the religious, especially the celebration of mass (a function in which women could not, and still cannot, participate), and more generally a gradual marginalization of women led to a downgrading of the status of women within the religious life. It led also to the strengthening of barriers between religious men and women, a tendency which we have noted among the congregations of Prémontré and Arrouaise.[70] Some double houses disintegrated: in Yorkshire the nuns at the Augustinian house of Marton moved out to found a separate establishment at Moxby;[71] and among the sisters of the Order of the Hospital of St John of Jerusalem (the Hospitallers) there was a similar attempt at segregation.[72]

Perhaps one of the most remarkable changes came about in the ethos of the Gilbertine Order. We are particularly hampered in a discussion of early Gilbertine arrangements because the one surviving text of the Institutes, which were revised over the years, dates from the thirteenth century. Other sources, however, enable us to be certain that change took place, as a result of both the general climate of opinion, and more importantly of two internal events within the Gilbertine Order. One was the affair of the nun of Watton, and the other, the revolt of the lay brethren at Sempringham. Our source for the first of these episodes is a letter written before 1166 by Abbot Ailred of Rievaulx, who was called in by Gilbert to investigate events at Watton Priory. Here a young novice who had been placed in the convent at an early age by the archbishop of York took the veil despite showing little inclination towards the religious life. Subsequently she had an affair with a man of the house – whether canon or lay brother is uncertain – by whom she became pregnant. When her pregnancy was discovered, the nuns took their revenge on her lover by forcing the girl to castrate him, and on the nun by placing her in irons in a cell. Ailred was summoned to investigate the supposed miracle when the girl claimed to have been restored to her virginal condition through the intercession of the archbishop of York, now deceased.[73] Ailred's report shows him to have been dismayed – perhaps in this case with reason – at the ease with which male and female religious were able to meet. By extension this could have led to a general distrust of Gilbertine arrangements for the accommodation of both sexes within the same establishment. As it was, the affair seems not to have become public knowledge. In the 1180s or 1190s Walter Map could write of the Gilbertines that 'nothing sinister is as yet reported of them'.[74] It was not the events at Watton but the revolt of certain lay brethren of Sempringham which led to a more public debate on the issue.[75]

Around 1165 rumours were heard that complaints had been received by the pope about certain aspects of the Gilbertine Order. These prompted the writing of a number of letters, one by the king and the rest by churchmen, in support of Gilbert, stressing his integrity and that of his order; the underlying assumption was that the accusations were somehow related to sexual scandal. The letters ranged from persuasion to threats to urge the pope not to interfere with the Institutes which his predecessor had confirmed.[76] Henry II strongly supported the order and threatened to confiscate its possessions if Gilbert's arrangements were tampered with; he further urged the punishment of the rebellious lay brethren, hinting that part of their discontent hinged on the presence of canons within the Gilbertine communities. When the official episcopal enquiries were held in England in the late 1160s the suggestions of sexual misconduct, real or potential, had faded and attention was concentrated on the lay brethren. Part of the latter's complaint may have been the strictness of the régime laid upon them, and certainly Gilbert afterwards modified his regulations on food and drink. However, the overwhelming impression left by their demands, that Gilbert return to the primitive arrangement of the order, is that their main objection was the addition, some twenty years earlier, of the fourth element in the composition of Gilbertine houses. The inclusion of an educated male élite must have had a detrimental effect on the status of the male laity, and that this was the cause of their discontent is reinforced by Gilbert's own identification of the ringleaders as lay men he had brought into the order in its early years. These two events, occurring within a decade, had a serious effect on the internal arrangement of the Gilbertine priories. They led to far more rigorous segregation in daily life and worship, and the houses of Gilbert's order probably never again enjoyed the easy co-operation of their early years.

However, the medieval church was never free from a sense of unease when dealing with women and their vocation. The twelfth and thirteenth centuries saw women attracted to the religious life in unprecedented numbers,[77] yet in many ways the new orders of the era may have failed their female aspirants. This rejection of their participation continued, for although St Francis had women followers and St Dominic himself founded a female house, it needed continued bullying by popes to force the mendicant orders to acknowledge their women associates. Although Pope Innocent III encouraged St Clare in her desire to involve herself with the movement inspired by Francis, and confirmed what was in a sense a new form of convent life which relied not on endowments but on the receiving of alms and the profits of manual labour, the convents of Poor Clares became indistinguishable from their forerunners.[78] On the continent, women turned increasingly to new forms of religious life, some of them deemed orthodox and some heretical, and it could be argued that it was left to informal groups like the Beguines of Flanders to respond to their needs by developing a less structured, less aristocratic and more evangelical way of life appropriate to the rising urban centres of the late twelfth and thirteenth centuries.[79] Whether the religious women of medieval Britain felt that the church responded successfully to their vocation we cannot know. The lack of documented activities of groups like the Beguines suggests that their spiritual needs may, on the whole, have been fulfilled. But the key word here could be 'documented'. Although there is no evidence of beguinages in Britain, it is quite possible that women turned to some form of organized spiritual and religious life outside the nunnery, perhaps within small eremitical communities of the kind which were sometimes transformed into nunneries following the Rule of St Benedict. It is quite clear that the anchorite tradition continued to be a vibrant one in Britain, and it may have been this that satisfied the spiritual vocation of medieval women religious, especially in areas for which there is little evidence of traditional cloistered female monasticism.[80]

6

THE MENDICANT ORDERS

·

In the third decade of the thirteenth century Britain was engulfed by a new and radical religious movement which challenged all accepted notions of the monastic life. The friars were not, like Benedict's monks, to live their lives within the cloister; nor were they to support themselves by ownership of property. They were itinerant and they were mendicant, that is, they wandered from place to place and were allowed to beg for their livelihood. They were to live in poverty, in imitation of the apostles. Four main mendicant orders, with diverse geographical and ideological origins, became influential in Britain: the Franciscans (Friars Minor), the Dominicans (Friars Preacher, or Black Friars), the Augustinian (Austin) Friars, and the Carmelites (the White Friars).[1] A little needs to be said about how these orders emerged and developed, for it is only in the context of their purpose and aspirations that their migration into Britain can be appreciated.

The intention and message of St Francis was at one and the same time simple and powerful. The son of a wealthy merchant of Assisi, Francis underwent a religious conversion, and in a dramatic gesture renounced both family and possessions. His purpose was to embrace absolute poverty, own nothing, and to live as Christ himself had done, teaching and preaching by word and example. Francis was not the only individual to give voice to such an intention, or the only one to gather disciples around him. Some twelfth-century groups which renounced ownership of property and followed the apostolic life ended up on the wrong side of that sometimes very thin line which separated orthodox belief from heresy.[2] What was distinctive about Francis was that he received papal

support for his way of life, and in 1210 approval for the simple rule which
he composed for his followers. The rule was for a way of life, not for an
order, but the congregation grew beyond Francis's wildest imaginings. By
1217 the barefoot friars began sending their first members across the Alps,
to live in poverty, to beg for their food, and to preach the gospel to all.
From now on we can begin to detect tensions among the brethren,
between Francis and his close adherents who resisted any formal
organization and those who urged greater formality. It was pressure that
was difficult for Francis to resist; and by 1221 he had composed the first
written rule (*Regula Prima*), which was followed two years later by the
second rule (*Regula Secunda*, or *Bullata*).[3] Before his death in 1226 Francis
felt it necessary to compose his *Testament* in order to emphasize the
simplicity of the way he had intended his message to be conveyed to the
world.[4] Even then there had been developing the threat – which later
became bitter controversy – of a split between those who, like Francis,
emphasized that the Franciscan movement was essentially a movement
of the spirit, and those who wanted to mould it into a more stable
organization.[5]

From the outset St Dominic (c. 1171–1221) had a different conception
of the nature and method of his friars. He was not a layman like Francis
but an Augustinian canon, who in 1204 began to undertake missions
among the Cathar heretics in southern France in the region of
Montpellier.[6] Slowly he conceived the idea of gathering together a group
of poor men dedicated to preaching and combating heresy, and in 1206
founded a religious house at Toulouse as a base from which to send out
travelling preachers. Like Francis, Dominic sought papal approval for his
ideas; but the Fourth Lateran Council, which met in 1215, had forbidden
the creation of new religious rules, and there was no question, therefore,
of a 'Rule of St Dominic'. However, approval was given for Dominic and
his group to form a congregation following the Rule of St Augustine, and
in 1217 the order of Friars Preacher was confirmed. Dominic's ideas began
to develop. In 1217 he dispersed his companions from their headquarters
in Toulouse and ordered peripatetic missions. He renounced legal rights
in property, and in 1220 followed this by rejecting the possession of
revenues from land and houses; like the Minors, the Preachers were now
wedded to an ideal of corporate as well as personal poverty. From
Toulouse some of the friars went to Paris and others to Bologna. Here is
the key to Dominic's intentions. Paris and Bologna were university
towns. If the friars were to preach effectively against heresy, they would
need to be well-versed in theology; they would need to be university-
trained.

The Minors and the Preachers at the outset of their mission had both common and distinct features. Both embraced poverty, though the Franciscans more absolutely than the Dominicans. Both abandoned the traditional monastic virtue of stability; they were of necessity travellers. Both had achieved the success they so far enjoyed because of papal backing. The distinctive feature of the Dominicans was their attitude towards preaching. Although this was an activity which both orders pursued, the Friars Preacher – as their name suggests – initially placed greater emphasis on the learned preparation which they considered to be necessary for their role in the church. The brethren were to be clergy devoted to the pursuit of learning, study and intellectual activity, and all else was to be subordinate to this aim. As we shall see, moreover, the Franciscans were soon to develop along the same lines. Although their initial conception differed quite considerably, the Minors and Preachers shared a common aim, evangelism. In this they present a considerable contrast to the Austin and Carmelite Friars. During the early thirteenth century in the Italian regions of Tuscany and Lombardy there were a number of amorphous eremitical groups of a kind which the church had always held in suspicion. In 1243 Pope Innocent IV united the hermits of Tuscany, ordering them to follow the Rule of St Augustine, and in 1256 the hermits of Lombardy joined them to form the Order of the Hermits of Augustine, or Austin Friars, though it was not until over thirty years later that the order received its constitution. These constitutions, of Rattisbon (1290), owed much to the Dominican observance. From the 1250s the friars had ceased to be hermits and became urban-based and a preaching order. There was a parallel development among the Carmelites. A rule had been drawn up for the Order of Our Lady of Mount Carmel (Palestine) around 1210 by the patriarch of Jerusalem, and this rule continued to be followed by the colonies which migrated to Cyprus and Europe from the late 1230s, during the decline of the Latin kingdom of Jerusalem. In 1229 the White Friars had been recognized by the pope as mendicants, but even more significant was the reframing of the rule which came to be associated with the name of St Simon Stock, and which allowed more time for study and active work. The earliest statutes of the order to survive, from 1282, show borrowing from the constitutions of the Dominicans. This redirection in the order, which was strongly resisted by some, coincided with a growing preference for urban rather than rural sites. It was therefore in the towns of Europe with their increasing population that the mendicant orders of friars flourished and found their largest, and perhaps their most receptive, audience. Their appeal to the apostolic life was not new; we have encountered it already in the formation of the notion of the regular canons. However, what the friars succeeded in doing was to combine a sense of apostolic mission and evangelism with the concept of complete poverty; this was a new, and powerful, message.

THE COMING OF THE FRIARS TO BRITAIN

The mendicant orders in Britain have left us with scant remains, both physical and documentary. Their houses were not intended to be landowning corporations, as monasteries and nunneries were, and it may be for this reason that only a handful of cartularies have survived; the few that have, notably from the Carmelite priory of Kings Lynn and the Austin friary of Clare, indicate, however, that such records of land acquisition were kept. Scarcely more fortunate in their survival have been the archaeological remains of mendicant houses, and only fifteen or so have left any substantial trace. This chronic lack of sources hampers any attempt to reconstruct the history of the mendicants in Britain.

The Dominican mission

The Friars Preacher held their first general chapter of the order in Bologna in 1220, and the following year began to organize themselves into geographical provinces. At the chapter of 1221 the decision was taken to dispatch a mission to England, and twelve friars, led by Gilbert de Fresney, a man trained at the University of Bologna, travelled to Dover under the protection of Peter des Roches, bishop of Winchester.[7] With the bishop they went on to Canterbury – a route which was to be followed three years later by the Franciscans – and in the cathedral city they were presented to Archbishop Stephen Langton, who ordered Gilbert to preach a sermon. If this was a test, Gilbert passed with flying colours, and his party received enthusiastic support from Langton. It is quite clear what plan the friars had in mind, for leaving no rearguard in Canterbury or in London (their next brief stop) they went straight to Oxford, England's main seat of learning. As they were thirteen in number the friars were able immediately to establish a fully constituted priory, which they did on a site acquired for them by merchants and townspeople.[8]

The Dominicans, unlike the Franciscans, had no English chronicler to chart the progress of their early foundations. However, a scheme for early expansion can be discerned in the few years that followed the creation of the Oxford friary. From Oxford a group moved back to London, where a priory is first mentioned in 1224, founded on property in Holborn given by Hubert de Burgh, earl of Kent. This was a part of the suburbs of London already densely populated by the religious orders, and the Black

Friars found themselves within easy reach of the Knights Templar at the Temple, the priory and hospital of St Bartholomew's, and the nuns and the Hospitallers of Clerkenwell. Later they would be only a few hundred yards from the Carmelite Friars.[9] It may have been this proximity which prompted them in 1275 to accept from Edward I an extensive new site at Baynard's Castle just inside the city walls. After London the Friars Preacher turned their attention north and east, to Norwich (1226) and York (1227). In the 1230s they moved west, to Bristol (1230) and Shrewsbury (1232), reaching the North-West at Carlisle (1233). The 1230s saw a consolidation of foundations in towns such as Northampton, Canterbury, Cambridge, Chester, Derby, Exeter, Lincoln, Newcastle and Winchester. In this decade expansion moved north of the border, and by 1240 the friars had established themselves at Berwick, Edinburgh, Elgin, Inverness and Perth, and possibly at Ayr and Aberdeen. Some members of the order had reached Wales as well, for in 1237 two Dominicans witnessed a grant by Llywelyn ap Iorwerth in favour of Penmon Priory. Whether the order had yet founded a friary, however – the date of the north Wales houses of Bangor and Rhuddlan is uncertain – is not known. By 1260 the Friars Preacher had about thirty-six houses in England, five in Wales and nine in Scotland. By the end of the century their total was in the region of sixty, not far short of the number of foundations made by the Cistercians in their first century.

The Friars Minor

It was at their general chapter of 1217 that the Friars Minor decided to establish outposts beyond Italy, but not for another seven years that a group of Franciscans were sent to England. They were nine in all, four clerks and five laymen, led by the former guardian of the Paris house, Agnellus of Pisa; of the nine, three were Englishmen. Their arrival and subsequent events within the English province are well documented by Thomas of Eccleston, himself an English Franciscan, who in 1258/9 produced a tract *De Adventu Fratrum Minorum in Angliam, On the coming of the Friars Minor into England*.[10] It is Thomas who tells us that the friars had their passage across the Channel arranged by the Benedictine monks of the Norman monastery of Fécamp; and that they landed in Dover on 10 September 1224 and went straight to Canterbury. Here they stayed two days at Christ Church, after which five, including Agnellus, were accommodated in a 'hostel of priests' until they were given the use of a room in a school established by the monks. The other four members of the group were sent on to London, where they stayed for fifteen days with the Black Friars, and then rented a house in Cornhill. Richard of

Ingeworth and Richard of Devon left shortly afterwards for Oxford. Again, they stayed with the Dominicans until they were able to rent a house in the parish of St Ebbe. Within six weeks, then, the Friars Minor had made three settlements, in contrast to the Preachers, who took over five years to achieve the same number. Only months after their arrival at Oxford, the Minors settled in Northampton. The reason for the difference in the speed of foundations seems to be that while the Dominicans were insistent on establishing a full priory of thirteen in Oxford before making new settlements, the Franciscans were happy to initiate a convent with only a handful of brethren and rely on rapid recruitment to make up numbers. Their faith was justified, for by 1230 – within six years of their arrival – they had set their sights on, and captured, twelve other towns: Norwich, Stamford, Kings Lynn, Cambridge and Lincoln in the East, Worcester, Hereford, Bristol and Gloucester in the West, and Leicester, Nottingham and Salisbury. By 1240 settlements had been made further north, in York (c. 1230) and Carlisle, where the Franciscans arrived in the same year as the Dominicans (1233), and in Scotland at Roxburgh (1235) and Berwick (by 1244). They were in north Wales at Llanfaes (1237), and in south Wales at Carmarthen and Cardiff. Between them, the two major mendicant orders had by 1300 made over 120 foundations in Britain. Only four cathedral cities lacked friaries (Bath, Ely, Rochester and Wells), and few towns of any size were without a mendicant presence. By the end of the Middle Ages over thirty towns had both the Friars Preacher and Minor, and fourteen sustained convents of all four major orders, a sure sign of the economic pre-eminence of these boroughs.[11]

The Carmelite and Austin friars

The coming of the Preachers and Minors was the result of a decision by their respective general chapters. The advent of the two other major mendicant orders seems – although the story is far from clear – to have been the consequence of invitations by lay patrons. Thomas of Eccleston noted that among the achievements of William of Nottingham as prior provincial (1240–54) of the Minors he 'welcomed a close fellowship between our brethren and those of the Order of Mount Carmel, which had been introduced into England by Lord Richard de Grey when he returned from Syria with Duke Richard of Cornwall'.[12] Certainly before 1242 Richard de Grey had founded a Carmelite house at Aylesford in Kent, although the order's own lists of foundations suggest that priority should be given to Hulne, near Alnwick, founded by William de Vescy, which preserves some of the most important archaeological and architectural remains of the order in Britain.[13] From the mid thirteenth century the Carmelites' reliance on mendicancy and their moves towards scholarly pursuits brought a migration into towns where new houses were established: in 1247 at London, located on a site in Fleet Street donated by Richard de Grey; in the 1250s at York; in 1256 at Oxford. Some houses established in earlier years were transferred from isolated rural sites. The colony at Chesterton (c. 1247), for instance, moved in 1249 to Newnham; in 1290 it petitioned to settle in Cambridge because the conditions in winter made it difficult for the brethren to get into the town for food and to attend the schools. By 1300 the White Friars were the third largest mendicant congregation, with about twenty-six houses in England, one in Wales and five in Scotland.[14]

The Austin friars reached England before the union of the hermits of Italy in 1256, probably from Gascony.[15] According to John Capgrave, Austin prior provincial from 1453 to 1457, his order had received papal licence to settle in England in 1230, but there is no other evidence to suggest that a foundation had taken place before 1248, when the friary of Stoke by Clare (Suffolk) came into existence. Knowles drew attention to the rural isolation of both Stoke and the second Austin friary at Woodhouse near Cleobury Mortimer in Shropshire,[16] but this should not be exaggerated. Stoke by Clare was a significant market town, and the friars were settled by Richard, earl of Gloucester and Hereford, at the foot of his castle there.[17] Earl Richard had had frequent occasion to be in Italy on diplomatic business and may well have come across, and been influenced by, the order's protector, Cardinal Richard Annibaldi. From the rural areas the Austin friars, like the Carmelites, moved into the towns. In 1253 another noble patron, Humphrey de Bohun, earl of Hereford and Essex and constable of England, settled a convent at London. Oxford was colonized in the years after 1266, when King Henry III gave money to purchase a site and persuaded others to donate land to the friars.[18] By 1300 a dozen or so other urban centres, including Cambridge, and five sites in Scotland had been settled.

THE ESTABLISHMENT OF MENDICANT PRIORIES

In order to flourish and expand the mendicants needed two things: recruits and benefactors. The rapid expansion of the Franciscans from their very first arrival in Britain, and the more cautious explorations of the Dominicans in the 1220s followed by their own mounting success after 1230 tell us that sufficient recruits were made to staff new establishments. Thomas of Eccleston again gives us a vivid impression of the variety of Englishmen who joined the Minors in those early years. Among those who entered the London house at Cornhill were local recruits, members

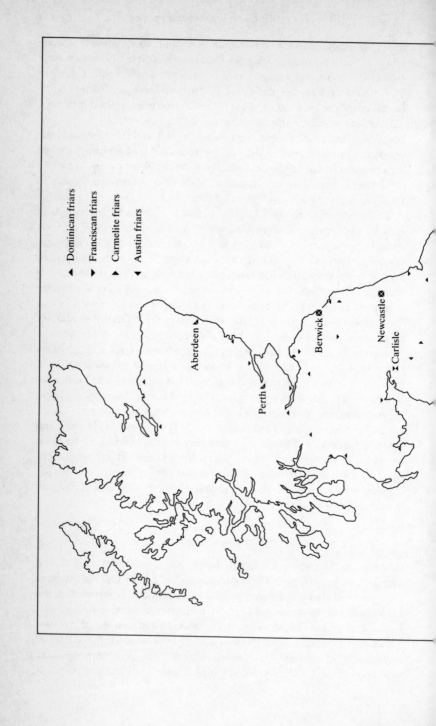

Dominican friars
Franciscan friars
Carmelite friars
Austin friars

Aberdeen

Perth

Berwick

Newcastle

Carlisle

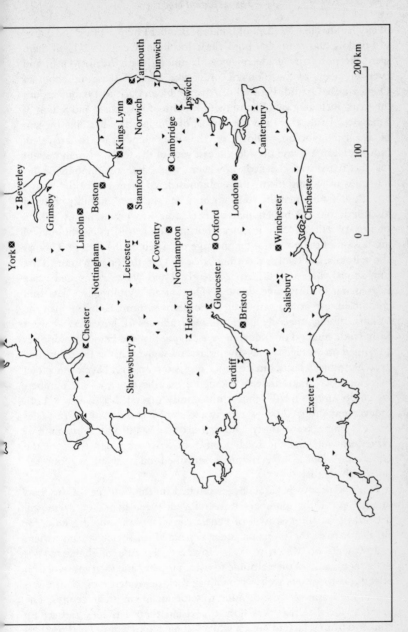

Map 6 The friars in Britain: location of priories of the four main orders by c. 1300

York
Beverley
Grimsby
Lincoln
Nottingham
Boston
Chester
Leicester
Shrewsbury
Coventry
Stamford
Kings Lynn
Norwich
Yarmouth
Dunwich
Ipswich
Cambridge
Hereford
Northampton
Gloucester
Oxford
London
Cardiff
Bristol
Salisbury
Winchester
Canterbury
Chichester
Exeter

0   100   200 km

of city families like William of London, Brother Philip, a priest and native of London, and the nobly born cleric Jocelin of Cornhill.[19] Then there were the university graduates, notable among them Adam Marsh, and even members of the monastic order like John of Reading, abbot of Oseney near Oxford. Paris scholars were drawn back to Oxford to join the friars, including two Englishmen, Haymo of Faversham and Simon of Sandwich. Lastly there were members of knightly families, like the son of Richard Gobion, who gave the first mendicants to arrive in Northampton a house outside the east gate of the town. His enthusiasm for the friars was checked, however, when his son announced his intention of joining them, and Gobion ordered them out of the house; but at the last moment his son's sincerity and the friars' humility changed his mind. No doubt Thomas of Eccleston was providing us with a cautionary tale in this instance, but it still leaves us with a vivid impression of the power of the message preached by the friars.[20] Thomas also tells as a fact 'worth recording' that in 1256 the Friars Minor in the English province, which included Scotland and Wales, comprised 1,242 friars living in forty-nine houses.[21] Dominican recruitment is less well chronicled, but at this early date the order was more exclusive than the Minors, aiming especially for clerics and graduates. If, however, we use a fairly crude method of estimating, we can say that the Franciscan priories contained on average twenty-five friars, and suggest that in the thirty-five or so Dominican houses in existence by 1260 there may have been a total of around 900 friars. Indeed this figure may be too low, for numbers which do survive for the thirteenth century suggest that friaries of both orders rarely dropped below twenty and some had many more. In Wales in 1285 there were thirty Dominicans at Cardiff and thirty-nine at Haverfordwest, and the total number of friars exceeded those of the Cistercian monks.[22] Recruitment remained buoyant throughout the thirteenth century.[23]

Many friaries were doubtless established on the initiative of the friars themselves as the number of recruits allowed, but they were still dependent on the goodwill of benefactors. This was nothing new, for all members of the monastic order depended on society to give them endowments on which to live. However, the case of the friars was different because of their attitude towards property and their insistence on poverty, corporate as well as individual; their dependence on charity was one of the reasons for the decision to settle mainly in urban centres. The problem for the friars was how to expand their activities and set up convents from which to preach while still remaining poor. The Preachers (and we may include here the Carmelites and Austins, who modelled their practices closely on them) initially differed from the Franciscans in their attitude towards the ownership of their priories. The Dominicans rejected the ownership of property from which to draw revenue, but they were prepared to own their houses. So they were happy, for example, to accept seventeen acres of land on which to build in Bamburgh.[24] Or they might purchase a site, as they did in Gloucester with forty marks given by the king. In contrast the Franciscans would not own a house or site, nor would they handle money in order to purchase one. Thomas of Eccleston explained how they managed. In Canterbury Alexander, warden of the priests' hospice, transferred land to the city council, which then held it in trust for the use of the brethren, and Alexander 'built them a chapel large enough for their present needs'. In London, Master John Iwyn bought land and 'presented it to the city, piously designating it for the use of the brethren at the discretion of the city fathers'; his donation was augmented by John fitz Piers, sheriff and alderman, and William Joyner, lord mayor in 1238, built a chapel. In a similar way land was held in trust for the use of the friars in Oxford, Cambridge, Shrewsbury and Northampton 'since the brethren refused to accept any property as their own'. An alternative method of finding accommodation for the friars was for a benefactor to retain legal ownership of property and allow the friars to use it.[25]

The evidence shows that a mendicant foundation, the acquisition of land and the erection of buildings, was often a corporate effort. In Southampton the king gave the site of the Franciscan friary; Richard Pride, a burgess, built the church; while Laurence Cox financed the construction of other buildings. Royal records, in particular the close rolls, show how important the kings were in providing building materials for mendicant houses. In York all four friaries received royal grants of timber for building. In 1237 Henry III ordered that a lime kiln be constructed in Windsor for the building of the church of the London Black Friars. The Carmelites of Newnham received a royal grant of rafters for the fabric of the church in 1267, and the close rolls record gifts of timber for the new Carmelite church of Oxford in 1258, 1260, 1266, 1267, 1268, 1276 and 1286.[26] In the 1280s the Dominican house of Bangor was destroyed by fire, evidently in the war or the rebellions which followed, and the king gave £100 compensation and timber for rebuilding.[27] The king was a prominent benefactor, but others made similar kinds of grant, the earl of Pembroke to the London Black Friars in 1235, and the abbess of Barking to the same in 1250.

PATRONS, BENEFACTORS AND OPPONENTS

The nature of mendicant foundation, the degree of initiative taken by the friars, and the way in which urban property had to be acquired piecemeal make it difficult in many cases to assign one single 'founder'. However, historians have rightly stressed the importance of royal patronage in the success of the friars. Henry III and Edward I in England and Alexander II in Scotland were all enthusiastic patrons of the mendicant orders. The royal house was associated with the foundation of eight houses of Black Friars in England: the site was donated by the king at York, Canterbury, Ipswich, Bamburgh and Salisbury and by Queen Eleanor of Provence, wife of Henry III, at Guildford. Henry III was also remembered as the founder of the York priory of Grey Friars, to whom he gave an important site opposite the castle, and he was a principal benefactor of Norwich and Shrewsbury. He also made over three hundred grants to the Minors and a similar number to the Preachers.[28] Some priories were particular favourites, and the Black Friars of London and Canterbury received monetary grants from the king every year between 1237 and 1250. Edward I was especially generous to the London friary, which during his reign moved to its Ludgate site.[29] In Scotland too the Black Friars stood high in royal regard, and all but three houses of the order were credited as foundations of King Alexander II. The earliest Welsh Franciscan priory, Llanfaes in north Wales, was established in 1237/8 by Llywelyn ap Iorwerth, prince of Gwynedd, in memory of his wife Joan, daughter of King John and half-sister of Henry III.

The patronage of the kings of England and Scotland was important not only for the material benefits it brought but for the social respectability and distinction which it gave to the friars. The mendicants thus became a novel and fashionable target for pious endowment and found benefactors among the aristocracy. But because the friars were urban-based they relied more heavily still on the citizens and merchants of the towns. We have noted the part Thomas of Eccleston describes the citizens of London and Shrewsbury as playing, but all orders benefited from the patronage of the townspeople. The Norwich Carmelites acknowledged their first founder as Philip de Cowgate and after him the mayor, aldermen, merchants and citizens of Norwich.[30] The social cachet of the friars in the thirteenth century and beyond is illustrated by the way in which they were called on to provide a burial place for many of their benefactors throughout the social scale. Those of great importance were given interment within the friary church. The heart of Eleanor of Provence was buried in the church of the London Grey Friars in 1291. Queen Margaret, second wife of Edward I, was buried there too, and John Pecham, archbishop of Canterbury and himself a Franciscan, was interred behind the high altar in the London church.[31] Hubert de Burgh, founder of the London Dominican house, was buried there in 1243, and when the convent moved to Ludgate the friars took his remains with them.[32] Lesser folk, too, expressed in their wills a desire to be interred within the grounds of local friaries, and this led at times to conflict with the secular clergy.[33] The support of the townspeople might at times dip and waver, as it did when the friars came to the aid of the Jews after they were accused of the murder of the child Hugh of Lincoln, but it was apparently never lost for a long time, and the evidence of wills shows that the mendicants remained the recipients of bequests until the Reformation.[34]

Those who welcomed the friars provided them with land on which to build, the means to build and also the wherewithal to live from day to day. St Francis had envisaged that some of his brethren at least would be engaged in manual work, either the production of food or making and repairing clothes in the priory workshop, but the most important way in which a friar was meant to live is also the least tangible of his activities: begging. Friars generally travelled in twos and were allowed to ask for food and clothes, but not money; they were not, however, to beg while they were preaching. In addition the friars received alms, testamentary bequests and gifts. The king is again recorded as a major benefactor. In 1233 Henry III ordered the sheriff of London to buy 700 ells of cloth for the Friars Preacher and Friars Minor of London, and 100 pairs of shoes for the Preachers,[35] and in 1240 he commanded the sheriff of York to feed the Friars Minor of Scarborough for one day a week at the king's expense.[36] Such alms were particularly welcome as they enabled the friars to be supplied with their needs without handling money. Sometimes there were special needs. In 1250, when four hundred Black Friars gathered in London for the thirtieth general chapter, food was supplied in turn by the king, the queen, bishops, abbots and the citizens of London. In 1263 the seven hundred Black Friars who gathered for the same purpose must have been similarly dependent on charity.[37]

The friars also benefited from the testamentary dispositions of their supporters. Wills extant from all dioceses show that the friars of all orders enjoyed a comparatively consistent popularity as beneficiaries, more so than any other groups of religious. An early benefactor was Archbishop Boniface of Canterbury, who in 1270 bequeathed forty marks to the Friars Minor of Canterbury, fifteen marks to those of Oxford, and five marks to every house of Franciscans and Dominicans in the province of Canterbury. Eleanor of Castile, wife of Edward I, who died in 1291, left 100s. to thirty-nine Dominican priories, including the five Welsh ones.[38] This kind of donation raised problems, especially for the Grey Friars, who early in their history had to decide what to do with such gifts in the face of Francis's prohibition of handling of money. Some of their attempts to observe the letter but not the spirit of the law aroused barbed comment. In 1230 the Friars Minor asked the pope for permission to have trustees to administer their funds, and the granting of this request meant that they now had the use of money and were able either to purchase something through a third party as a single transaction, or have their funds held in store by a 'spiritual friend'. In 1232 the Minors are recorded as having a proctor, William le Cuteler, in Oxford, and by the end of the century they were handling their own financial affairs.[39]

The account so far of the coming of the friars suggests that this was the greatest success story of the thirteenth century, and indeed in many ways it was. But success was not achieved without opposition, and in several instances the friars fell foul of vested interests. In some of these cases it was the interests of the established monastic order which were threatened. One example comes from Yorkshire. Since the late twelfth century the church of Scarborough had been appropriated to the abbey of Cîteaux to provide revenue towards the expenses of the general chapter; when the Friars Minor settled in the parish there began a bitter dispute which lasted for about fifty-five years, from 1239 to c. 1294, and which involved many appeals to Rome.[40] A struggle between the friars and the powerful Benedictine abbey of Bury St Edmunds is well documented. In 1257 the Minors obtained papal permission to settle at Bury, and apparently took advantage of a vacancy, when the monks were without an abbot, to move into the town. They settled in a private house, but the monks expelled them and razed the house. First the monks and then the friars obtained official approval for their case, and then in 1263 the friars started to build. The story did not end there, however, for, as the result of another appeal by the monks, they were forced to suspend operations. However, the support of the townspeople for the activities of the friars forced a compromise: the friars moved out of the town, but were allowed to settle nearby at Babwell.[41]

THE ORGANIZATION OF THE FRIARS AND THEIR ACTIVITIES

Government and legislation

A major difference between the Minors and Preachers in the early days was in the degree of organization. Francis was a spiritual leader, not an organizer. Dominic was a legislator of genius, and the creator of the constitutions of the order which were formally passed in 1228.[42] Among the Franciscans the development of the government of the order was slower, and was only gradually articulated in the years after 1239 and the code presented to the general chapter in 1260.[43] Both legislated for an international order divided into geographical provinces. The Franciscans introduced another level of government, the custody, of which there were seven in England.[44] All the major mendicant orders with the exception of the Minors ultimately owed their constitution to the Preachers. In the organization of both orders there was an element of the monastic, such as the general chapter, borrowed from the Cistercians, but what was revolutionary about the Dominicans and their emulators was the degree of representation in their arrangements. The basic unit of the Friars Preacher was the priory, whose head, the prior, was elected by the brethren in chapter, and attended the annual provincial chapter. On this occasion he was accompanied by another member of the priory elected for that purpose who reported on his conduct. The head of the house, then, was not only elected: he was accountable. The province was governed by a provincial prior, elected by the chapter in special session, comprising the conventual priors and two elected delegates from each house. The master-general of the whole order was chosen by a specifically constituted assembly of the provincial priors and two representatives from each province. All the mendicants had their general chapters, but they differed. At first the Franciscan one was an unwieldy meeting of all friars, but it was gradually modified and came to comprise elected represen- tatives drawn from each province who met only every three years. The Dominican chapter comprised the master-general, and one representative from each province; every third year it comprised instead all the provincial priors. When these three different sets of men had discussed any proposed addition or modification to the constitutions, it could be passed. The Dominicans thus evolved a system of government which laid stress on elected officials, although, as commentators have pointed out, this was less for reasons of democracy than efficient government. In contrast the minister-general, not the chapter, was the pivot of Franciscan govern- ment; he it was who appointed heads of custodies. Under the minister- general Elias (1227–39) proof was given of how lack of controls within the Franciscan system could produce monarchical and indeed despotic government, and in the deposition of Elias two English Franciscans, Adam Marsh and Haymo of Faversham, played an important role. The latter became minister-general of the order himself, and among his adminis- trative reforms he introduced elements of Dominican government. Under his rule, too, the growing emphasis on learning and the intellectual preparation for preaching led to a downgrading of the status of the laity within the order in a way which went counter to the spirit of Francis. The number of lay recruits was limited, and lay brothers were barred from holding office. Like the Black Friars the Minors had become a clerical order.

All orders allowed for some system of visitation for the correction of faults. The general chapter of the Dominicans appointed four friars each year to detect and correct abuse; and there are surviving records of England's four visitation circuits from 1250 and 1261. Faults were also corrected in the provincial chapter, and the London chapter of 1250 removed the priors of Newcastle and Ross (Scotland) for putting their friars on a starvation diet and accumulating massive debt in order to build lavishly.[45] Among the Minors John of Malvern was a special visitor who brought to England the bull *Quo Elongati* of Pope Gregory IX in 1230, which modified certain aspects of the Rule. While in England he punished a friar of Gloucester for painting pictures on a pulpit and complained about the glass windows in the friary there.[46] Sometimes, indeed often, comments from the orders' hierarchy were favourable. Thomas of Eccleston quotes the minister-general of the Franciscans, John of Parma (1247–56) as saying, 'how I wish that a Province such as this [England] could be set in the centre of the world, and provide an example to the whole order'.[47]

Preaching

Preaching was the raison d'être of all the major mendicant orders. In their concern for Christian teaching, Francis among Christian and pagan and Dominic among the heretics, the founders of the two largest mendicant orders, were voicing a concern that troubled the hierarchy of the church: the widespread inadequacy of parish priests, few of whom were sufficiently educated to offer doctrinal instruction. It was an issue addressed by the Fourth Lateran Council of 1215, which stressed the need for preaching for the salvation of Christian people, and recognized the great difficulty that providing it could cause bishops. The council therefore sanctioned bishops to 'appoint men suited to fulfil the office of holy preaching . . . who shall diligently visit the flock committed to them on the bishops' behalf'.[48] The friars, therefore, were fulfilling a perceived need. But the church was almost as wary of unlicensed preachers as it was of heretics, and thus it was vital that Francis and Dominic achieve and retain papal support. Francis's early followers were drawn from a wide variety of backgrounds, and the *Regula Bullata* assumed that the brethren would be engaged in two kinds of activity, work 'in such manner that idleness, the soul's enemy, is kept at bay'[49] and, for those approved by the minister-general, preaching.[50] The constitutions of the Friars Preacher were even more explicit. They had three categories of preacher, based on the amount of schooling a brother had received. Those who had been through the priory school were allowed to preach to their companions there. A brother of over twenty-five years of age who had studied theology for one year was permitted to preach within the territory of a priory with the prior's permission. To be able to preach within a province a friar had to have read theology for three years, and received the authority of the provincial chapter.[51]

One of the reasons that the mendicants chose to settle in urban centres was that here they were guaranteed sizeable audiences. The friars' message of salvation was intended for the whole world, but, as the Franciscan St Bonaventure (d. 1274) explained, their numbers were small, and they therefore had to concentrate their efforts where those who would hear that message were most numerous; in the towns, too, the friars (being totally dependent on charity) were likely to receive the most alms. In the early days of the mendicant mission – indeed for longer than that – the friars preached in the open air, in the market place and at the street corner. As they became more established they drew crowds into their own churches; and they preached, too, by invitation in cathedral and parish church. Their main concern was to reach the laity with the message of salvation, and in their attempts to do this they made an important contribution to the art of preaching. They developed new techniques suited to their audience, such as the use of *exempla*, short stories designed to convey a simple truth, rather than learned discourse. They produced handbooks of *exempla* and preaching manuals, and using these exhorted men and women to good behaviour and to repentance.[52] As important, if not more so, as their preaching techniques was the message they brought. The appeal of the friars as preachers lay in the fact that they themselves were not part of the social and political hierarchy; rather, they presented themselves as being as poor as the poorest of those who gathered to listen to them. Their appeal was universal. As well as identifying themselves with the poor they managed to reach the prosperous, for, in this age of the rise of a new urban class whose wealth derived from commerce, the friars preached that a devout life could be lived within a community which made money. No longer was the goal of Christian perfection to be sought only within the walls of the cloister: it was open to merchants, to masters and apprentices, to married people and unmarried. In preaching in this way the friars touched the aspirations of those informal religious groups which had sprung up throughout the late twelfth and early thirteenth centuries in the urban centres of Europe, the Waldensians of Lyons, the *Humiliati* of northern Italy and the Beguines of Flanders. In Britain as in these places men and women responded to a new urban theology suited to an increasingly articulate and educated laity which could question the teaching of the church and be critical of the practices of the established monastic order and parish clergy.

There was always, in the preaching of the friars, an element of the radical, the revolutionary. Had not St Francis himself overturned the social and economic expectations that his parents had had for him? Soon the topics on which some of the friars expounded went beyond an explanation of the gospels and a call to repentance and moral reform. A continental example is provided by the Franciscan Anthony of Padua, who preached in northern Italy and southern France on all manner of topics; in 1231 he preached against civil strife, but he also advocated that members of the lower orders of society be included in communal politics.[53] From Britain, too, derives evidence that the friars implicitly or explicitly criticized the established social and political order. Simon de Montfort, one of the leaders of the baronial movement for reform in the years 1258–65, was a friend of the Franciscan Adam Marsh, who appears to have influenced Simon greatly. The admiration was not one-sided, however, and Adam Marsh praised Simon's plans 'to purify, enlighten and sanctify the Church of God by a government that well befits it'.[54] The correspondence between Marsh and Simon de Montfort does not suggest that the Franciscan was going so far as to advocate rebellion against King Henry III; his concerns were more spiritual than political. However, his support for Simon and for baronial efforts at reform was not unique among the mendicants; other Franciscan friars evidently preached in favour of Simon, who was to be killed in battle in 1265 by the future Edward I. The friars' involvement in his cause shows that their preaching could have a decidedly political element.

Parochial work and the conflict with the secular clergy

The danger of the development of the preaching functions of the mendicants, as perceived by the secular clergy, lay in an escalation of their parochial and pastoral activities; and these had financial implications. When friars settled in a town, they began to preach and call to repentance; if they preached successfully they might be called on to hear confessions and pronounce absolution. When they were sufficiently established they built a chapel and constructed a burial ground; members of the laity might then decide to attend services in the friary church and seek burial within its cemetery. This is where the financial dimension arose, for the friars would not only encroach upon the functions of the parish priest; they would draw away revenues in the form of burial dues and other offerings. These fears in time caused concern among the secular clergy. A number of bishops, too, were uncertain as to the status of the friars within the established diocesan structure. There was an early crisis in 1230–1 when the bishop of London, who seems not to have known what to do with the friars, claimed jurisdiction over all of them. The mendicants reacted quickly and obtained a papal bull allowing them power to govern their own activities. Soon, action by the pope was needed to clarify the situation further; and a number of bulls were issued to try and define the activities of the friars.[55] In 1250 the potential cause for conflict was heightened with the issue of the papal bull *Cum a Nobis Petitur*, which allowed burial in friary churches on request. *Etsi Animarum* (1254) tried to draw limits by enjoining all religious orders not to intervene in secular parishes or preach without the approval of local clergy. Right at the end of our period, *Super Cathedram* (1300) reached a compromise by allowing the friars full right to preach in their own churches and in public places at certain times, and also in parish churches by invitation. When they received legacies from the faithful, one-quarter was to go to the parish priest. Friars were to choose suitable brothers to be confessors and present them, through the provincial prior, to the bishop for approval. Accordingly from the mid thirteenth century papal bulls gave sanction to the activities of the friars yet tried to delineate their responsibilities. The increase in their parochial and pastoral functions coincided with the building of second-generation friary churches, larger and constructed for the purposes of public worship, and it was under the pressure of both these developments that tensions between the mendicants and the secular clergy increased. Despite the injunction of *Super Cathedram* that friars who wished to be confessors needed to be licensed by the diocesan bishop, and the attempts to limit their preaching activities, areas of conflict between the friars and the local bishops still existed, because the mendicants were not subject to the kind of episcopal control that the ordinary exercised over the monastic orders of his diocese. In many dioceses there is evidence of cool relations between the friars and the bishops.[56]

It was for these reasons that some parish priests and bishops were hostile to the friars, and with those clergy were ranged the monastic houses which had appropriated parish churches and a financial stake in them. We can see this conflict of interest in Oxford in the aftermath of the settlement of the Dominicans in the parish of St Aldate's. The patron of the parish church was the priory of St Frideswide, and the canons opposed the friars' plan to enlarge their oratory. An appeal to the pope in 1227 produced a verdict for the friars, who were allowed to proceed, but the interests of the canons were safeguarded: the parishioners of St Aldate's were not allowed to attend the oratory; the priory was to have 40s. compensation, and the cemetery of the friars was only to be used for the burial of the brethren and members of their household. The revenues of the parish church were thus safeguarded for St Frideswide's.[57] Similar agreements were reached by the Austin friars of Cambridge and the canons of Barnwell, who held the advowson of the church of St James, in which parish the friars had settled; the friars were obliged to promise not to admit any parishioners to take the sacraments in their chapel and to send their own secular servants to the parish church.[58] It might be thought that these are just isolated instances which have left their mark on the records, but further evidence of hostility to the friars and accusations of encroachment on parochial functions comes from the pen of Matthew Paris, a Benedictine monk writing at St Albans in the 1230s, within a decade, that is, of the coming of the friars.[59]

THE MENDICANTS IN CHURCH AND SOCIETY, AND THE PRICE OF SUCCESS

The friars made a distinguished contribution to church and state in the thirteenth century. Despite the initial hostility of bishops such as London and Hereford and the continued existence of potential points of conflict, the episcopate, among them Edmund of Abingdon, archbishop of Canterbury (1234–40) and Richard of Wyche, bishop of Chichester (1245–53), came to value the friars for their help in reaching the lowliest within their dioceses. After his move from the University of Oxford to the see of Lincoln Robert Grosseteste used the Franciscans within the diocese, and in later years was able to write to Pope Gregory IX that the friars 'illuminate our whole country with the bright light of their preaching and teaching'.[60] Soon friars themselves rose to the ranks of the episcopate. In 1234 the Dominican Hugh became bishop of the see of St Asaph, and in 1268 Prior Anian of Rhuddlan was elected to the same see, over which he presided until 1293. In 1272 Robert Kilwardby, a Black Friar, became the senior English archbishop, and his successor at Canterbury was a Franciscan, John Pecham. On an international level friars acted as papal legates, preached the crusade, and heard appeals, as a Dominican prior and a Franciscan guardian did together in 1252 in a case brought by the dean and chapter of Lichfield against the prior of the Cluniac house of Lenton.[61]

It was not only in the sphere of church activity that the friars made their mark. In return for the patronage of the royal house the friars, in particular the Preachers, proved loyal servants. Thomas of Eccleston claimed that the Franciscan Agnellus of Pisa wore himself out while conducting peace negotiations on behalf of King Henry III.[62] Adam Marsh was a royal confessor, who was twice used by the king on diplomatic missions abroad, and who was, in addition, in correspondence with Queen Eleanor. Friar John of Darlington took on the office of royal confessor after being adviser to Henry III from 1256. Walter Winterbourne was a counsellor of Edward I from 1290, and took part in the negotiations ending hostilities between Edward I and Llywelyn ap

Iorwerth, those concerning the Scottish succession in 1291–2, and the making of peace with France in the 1290s. The Dominicans of Rhuddlan in north Wales took charge of the English wounded during the war of 1277 and carried communications between the king and London; and the Dominican bishop of St Asaph, Anian, also acted as an intermediary.[63]

As we saw in the case of the Augustinian house of Llanthony Prima, the religious could regard patronage almost as a threat, a factor which could change, indeed corrupt, their ideals and aspirations. In the face of the interest taken in them by, and the generosity of, the bishops, the royal house, the aristocracy and the people of the towns, the friars had to work hard to preserve their ideals. Thomas of Eccleston, thirty-five years after the advent of the Franciscans, wrote with a certain sense of nostalgia, of a golden age past. When he describes the first chapel at Cambridge as 'so humble that one carpenter erected it in a single day', his approval fairly leaps off the page.[64] It is in the matter of buildings, however, that Eccleston gives the clearest impression of a tendency to depart from the ideals of St Francis. The friars soon became victims of their own success. Ironically, it was the rich and powerful benefactor who desired to see the result of his patronage in a visible and tangible way that was the clearest cause of decline. The Shrewsbury friars evidently allowed Laurence Cox to build in too grand a manner, for 'when Brother William, who was zealous for poverty, saw the stonework of the dormitory, built with devotion and skill and at great cost, he ordered it to be taken down and replaced with cob walls'.[65] Later Agnellus of Pisa destroyed a stone cloister at Southampton, and it was only fear of royal displeasure which prevented him meting out the same treatment to the chapel which the king had built. That by about 1260 the era of simplicity was over is implied in Eccleston's comment that 'in those days the friars were very strict about erecting buildings and possessing pictures'. He is similarly suggestive about a change in their attitude to poverty, noting that 'in those days the friars were so strict in avoiding debts that they would only agree to borrow in cases of dire need'.[66] The friars were forced to face the paradox of the result of their search for absolute poverty: 'it is so easy to be poor by chance, so difficult by policy'.[67] Yet their commitment to 'Lady Poverty' was probably the main reason for the support they enjoyed.

Despite this, and despite the criticism of the practices of the friars by fourteenth- and fifteenth-century writers and poets, the documentary evidence suggests that their popularity remained steady among their urban flock. In York the late medieval probate registers show that the mendicants far exceeded the monastic houses of the diocese as recipients of testamentary benefactions. The mendicants owed much to the tradition of the wandering preachers of the twelfth century, to men like Robert of Arbrissel, Vitalis of Savigny and Norbert of Xanten. But they succeeded in taking the sense of the *vita apostolica* a step further, for where twelfth-century experiment invariably ended in the cloister, the friars created a new form of wandering mission rooted in the monastic tradition, yet more suited to an urban environment, and making use of the international academic and intellectual community of the universities of Europe. They were able to grasp the challenge posed to the hierarchy of the church by the increasingly articulate laity of the town, and help to formulate a spirituality which encompassed their ambitions and aspirations. The friars were in many ways responsible for the 'most distinctively and uniquely *urban* contribution made by the church in the long history of Christianity'.[68]

7

THE PHYSICAL SETTING: MONASTIC
BUILDINGS AND THE MONASTIC PLAN

•

The choice of where to locate a monastery or nunnery was very important. It could influence how much attention the community would – or would not – attract, and this in turn might be a powerful factor in its future development, its accumulation of endowments or decline into poverty, its adherence to or departure from its original ideals. The decision of where to build was dictated by a number of different factors. We know little of the process by which most sites were chosen, but their selection must have depended on what land a prospective founder had, or what he or she was prepared to give, as well as on the expectations of the religious orders themselves. In the eleventh century, before the coming of the reformed orders, it would have seemed natural for a Benedictine house to have been built in a town, or an important centre of communication. The majority of English pre-Conquest houses were either located in or near Roman towns or formed (as did Amesbury, Evesham and Shaftesbury) the focus for a new urban settlement.[1] In the post-Conquest period urban locations continued to be a feature of houses of Black Monks and regular canons, and to a lesser extent nuns also occupied sites in towns or on their outskirts. We have already noted the way in which castle, borough and abbey (or cathedral) formed part of the pattern of Norman conquest, and there is evidence that even after the immediate settlement period, founders continued to wish to associate their religious foundation with the centre of their power, that is, their castle. One hundred and seventy medieval British monasteries, the majority founded before 1300, have been identified as lying near a castle.[2] These figures suggest that for houses of Black Monks, independent, alien or Cluniac, as well as of Augustinian canons – only a handful of Cistercian and Premonstratensian houses were so situated – one major factor in determining the general location, if not the actual site, of a house would have been the position of the founder's castle. This emphasizes the role of the founder as protector of a monastery or nunnery, and the closeness of the relationship between patron and religious house.

With the new orders of the eleventh and twelfth century came a totally different expectation of where the religious would settle. The Cistercians, Carthusians, Tironensians and Savigniacs all stressed the need for solitude and divorce from the world which would have made an urban site or one associated with a castle unacceptable. Cistercian regulations limited the sites their monks could occupy and laid down precise rules to be followed before they could be occupied.[3] First, abbeys were not to be built 'in cities, castles or vills . . . but in places remote from the society of men'. Some time before 1152, in response to the expansion of the order, the general chapter added a provision that all its abbeys were to be at least ten Burgundian leagues (fifteen miles) apart from each other. When a new foundation was considered, the general chapter had to receive an invitation to settle and the permission of the diocesan bishop. If the chapter agreed, in principle, to a colony, then two abbots were sent to inspect the lands which had been offered, and choose a site; a colony of monks could then be sent out to take possession. That this rule was generally followed is indicated by the fact that complaints when it was not were infrequent. In 1204 it was noted that Woburn Abbey in Bedfordshire had sent a colony to Medmenham (Buckinghamshire) without the permission of the general chapter: the new convent was recalled without delay, and the abbot deposed. The desire for desert places led to criticisms that when the White Monks were unable to *find* a secluded spot, they created it, and there are certain cases of deliberate depopulation of Cistercian sites. Thus the foundation of Meaux Abbey involved the displacement of the inhabitants of Domesday 'Melsa'; and when Valle Crucis was established, the inhabitants of Llanegwestl were moved to make way for the monks.[4]

Diverse groups of religious accordingly had different general requirements from their sites. But all had basic needs: enough room to build a church and the necessary domestic buildings, and a good supply of water for drinking and washing as well as to carry away waste. Sometimes the first locations chosen proved to be unsuitable, and a transfer became necessary. A significant number of monasteries changed their original site, but the reasons are not always documented. Thus a charter of King

David I stated that his Tironensian foundation had been moved to Kelso on the advice of John, bishop of Glasgow, because the site of Selkirk was 'not convenient'; possibly the king wanted his monks nearer to the royal burgh of Roxburgh.[5] At least thirty English and Welsh Cistercian houses and twenty Augustinian communities moved once or more often before reaching their final site; this accounts for roughly one-third of the houses of either group. And as many as a quarter of Carmelite friaries moved their sites.[6] As has been remarked, given the careful procedure laid down by the Cistercians for approving a site, this high proportion might surprise us. However, there are two factors to be remembered. First, it is perhaps too much to expect that a brief inspection by two abbots who may have been strangers to a district would have told them all they needed to know about conditions throughout the year.[7] Second, there are few transfers which are closely documented, and it is possible that the first site was never intended to be a permanent home, but merely to afford temporary accommodation until the entire monastic complex was completed. This could have been the case with Renfrew (1163 × 1165), the first site occupied by Cluniac monks from Wenlock before their move to Paisley (c. 1169), and with the Cistercian settlements at Pendar (to Margam), and Strata Florida I (Yr Hen Fynachlog, to Strata Florida II). However, where more than one move was made, or transfers deemed necessary after a long lapse of time, it seems that mistakes of location had been made. Some convents were unfortunate time and again. After being driven out of Calder by the Scots, a group of Savigniac monks settled at Hood in north Yorkshire. This site was found to be inadequate for the building of an abbey, and a move made to Old Byland, an existing vill whose inhabitants were resettled. This was unsatisfactory again, for it was only a mile or so away from Rievaulx Abbey and each convent was confused by hearing the other's bells; a third location was tried at Stocking, where the monks stayed for thirty years while the buildings at New Byland were completed.

There are a number of other cases where a site came to be considered unsuitable because of a shortage of space or a lack of adequate drainage. The Cistercian site at Faringdon may have been rejected in favour of Beaulieu because it failed to provide a good water supply.[8] Hood was described as 'too restricted' both by the Savigniacs and by the Augustinians from Bridlington who succeeded them there in 1142 and moved two or three years later to Newburgh. But the clearest instances of locations rejected because they were too crowded come from urban and castle sites occupied by the Black Canons. The canons of Huntingdon moved from the centre of the town because of the noise. Those of Portchester, whose original settlement lay within a castle bailey formed by the walls of a Roman fort, moved within twenty years to Southwick, but not before they had constructed a fine Romanesque church.[9] The migration may have been connected with the proximity of the castle, as was certainly the case with the first foundation of the Cluniacs at Castle Acre; it took less than a year for the monks to realize that the site within the castle precinct was impossible. The need for room for increased numbers might also prompt a reconsideration of the site. The plan to raise the number of canons in the priory of St Giles, Cambridge, made expedient a move to Barnwell in 1112. All these factors contributed to shifts in location by the Black Canons, but a further reason was the influence of the White Monks and their emphasis on desolate, rural seclusion. The Cistercians brought a totally different expectation of where a monastery should be built.[10]

Several migrations were considered necessary or advisable because of adverse climatic conditions. In 1147 a Cistercian colony from Fountains Abbey which settled in the West Riding of Yorkshire at Barnoldswick (a site over 500 feet above sea level) found its life made difficult by the intemperate weather, particularly the heavy rain. An enterprising abbot, Alexander, discovered an ideal alternative spot at Kirkstall (200 feet) and arranged for his patron to take possession of it. We may well believe Alexander's complaints about Barnoldswick, for the canons of the Augustinian priory of Embsay (620 feet), which is situated in the same region of Craven, felt it necessary to obtain a lower site at Bolton (340 feet), and the White Monks of Sallay considered, but did not make, a move.[11] A charter graphically described how the abbey had been founded 'in a land so cloudy and rainy that the crops usually rot on the stalks'. A house, then, might find its site too high and too exposed; alternatively, it might turn out to be too low-lying. Bishop Alexander of Lincoln founded a Cistercian house at Haverholme in Lincolnshire in 1137, but shortly moved it to Louth Park within the same county (although the first site could not have been totally unsuitable since it later provided a home for Alexander's Gilbertine foundation). Another Cistercian plantation of 1137, Otley, also failed, and Bishop Alexander rescued it, providing a site at Thame, near Oxford, which he had been planning to turn into a deer park. In both cases the original site seems to have been rejected as prone to flooding.[12] Certainly this was the reason for the transfer of a Cistercian community to Whalley, near Blackburn, in Lancashire, from Stanlaw on the river Mersey, where the monks had sustained intermittent flooding for over 124 years.

There were also political reasons for site changes. In 1226, after a series of negotiations which illustrates the care with which Cistercian foundations were intended to be made, John of Monmouth settled a group of monks from the Herefordshire house of Abbey Dore at Grace

Dieu on the southern marches of Wales. Seven years later the abbey was burnt to the ground by the Welsh, who alleged that the land on which it was built had been taken from them by John of Monmouth. It was the general chapter of 1234 which considered a move desirable and which deputed the abbots of Bruern and Kingswood to go to Grace Dieu and there 'advise the founder either to make peace with his enemies or to give the monks a more suitable place where they can live without damage'.[13] The second alternative was adopted, and two years later the chapter ordered the abbot of Buildwas to oversee the transfer to a new location. Another Welsh house was moved on royal initiative. Aberconwy, formerly Rhedynog Felen, remained at its second location until 1284, when Edward I, wishing to consolidate his conquest of north Wales the previous year, decided to construct a castle at the mouth of the river Conwy – the precise location of the abbey. The monastic buildings were therefore demolished and a new site provided by the king some seven miles away at Maenan.[14]

THE BUILDINGS OF A RELIGIOUS HOUSE

The location of a monastery affected the way in which the buildings were laid out, since a restricted site might lead to modifications from a standard plan. While the permanent stone buildings were being constructed the brethren lived in temporary wooden buildings. Documentary sources contain a number of references to such structures, most of them too vague to be of much significance. However, a useful description of the early occupation of a site is to be found in the chronicle of the Yorkshire Cistercian abbey of Meaux. The author described how the site was selected by Adam, a monk of Fountains, at the request of the count of Aumale, who:

caused there to be built on the spot where the bakehouse is now sited, a certain large house (although of base mud) in which the convent which was about to arrive might live until he could provide for them more adequately. He also built a certain chapel near this house where the cellarer's chamber is now, where all the monks might sleep in the lower chamber and devoutly say the divine office in the upper one.[15]

Generally the early temporary wooden buildings of a monastery have not survived, but archaeological excavation can reveal their existence and location. At the Augustinian priory of Norton traces have been found of wooden buildings which have been interpreted as the quarters occupied by the canons while the stone buildings were being erected;[16] and at Fountains Abbey two timber structures have been discovered underneath

the south transept of the later church.[17] It has been suggested that the
first of these was a chapel or oratory, and that the second may have been
two-storeyed, like the building described at Meaux. The excavations at
Fountains have provided us with the clearest archaeological evidence yet
for the nature of the earliest buildings of a Cistercian site. They accord
with descriptions in the documentary sources at Meaux and the continental houses of Clairvaux and Foigny, and with Cistercian legislation
which laid down that before a site could be occupied, it had to be
provided with a church, refectory, dormitory, guest house and accommodation for a porter. Neither the archaeological nor the documentary
evidence suggests that the initial temporary buildings of a Cistercian site
were expected to be laid out on the normal claustral pattern which will
be described below. The same may well have applied to houses of other,
less well-documented congregations.[18]

The church

The church was the most important building in the monastic complex,
for it was here that much of the waking day would have been spent in
worship. Accordingly it was common for the church to be the first
masonry building to be constructed. It was usually orientated, with the
choir at the east end, where it would catch the early morning light, but
occasionally this plan had to be modified. The designers of Rievaulx, for
instance, were faced with a need to construct the complex along a narrow
river valley, and this led to a realignment of the usual pattern with the
church lying along a north–south axis. Many Anglo-Saxon churches were
rebuilt by the Normans, and little has remained of their structure.
However, archaeological excavation shows the Anglo-Saxons to have
been fond of the 'additive church'; and sometimes, as at St Augustine's,
Canterbury, more than one church was built end to end.[19] At Deerhurst,
the elaborate design of the church suggests that each part, its *porticus*
(additions to the main body), chambers, galleries and annexes, had a
liturgical function: they provided the space for singers, theatrical
performances and the display of relics. In the late Anglo-Saxon period
churches began to be consolidated to form a single, composite building in
order to fulfil the liturgical requirements of the *Regularis Concordia*, which
demanded three distinct areas of worship within the church: the west end
(*oratorium*), the east end (*chorus*) and the nave (*ecclesia*), each with its own
altar. At the west end it was common for there to be a gallery so that
worship did not interfere with the entrance into the church.

Around the time of the Conquest this arrangement was replaced by the
'coherent' or 'unitary' church, in which liturgical functions were for the

most part concentrated in the eastern arm of the church and the crossing. Most churches were built in a basic cruciform (cross) shape.[20] The main entrance was in the west front, which could have one or two towers, and which might be richly decorated as it is at Norwich and Castle Acre. The west entrance led directly into the nave of the church, which occupied the longer, western arm of the cross. In some abbey and priory churches all or part of the nave was used by the laity, either parishioners if the conventual church also acted as the parish church, or guests, pilgrims and visitors. At Blyth and Leominster the parishioners used the south aisle of the nave, although at the latter a larger parochial nave was built in the 1230s. In a number of nunneries, too, the church was shared with parishioners; at Romsey the laity used the south aisle of the nave, and at the small Yorkshire houses of Marrick (Benedictine) and Nunkeeling (Cistercian), the nuns used the nave of the church and the lay folk of the parish the east end; this is an unusual arrangement which echoes that in some German Cistercian nunneries, where the ritual choir was located at the west end. In Cistercian churches the nave was occupied by the lay brethren. To compensate for this lack of provision for lay visitors the monks occasionally constructed a separate chapel for them. This is probably the purpose of the building of which traces remain off the south nave wall at Buildwas Abbey in Shropshire. In other Cistercian churches the laity worshipped in a chapel in front of the main doors, a *capella ante portas*; several have bequeathed examples of medieval wall painting.[21]

In the eastern part of the nave were two screens whose locations might vary. The more westerly was the rood screen, which was often positioned before the nave reached the transepts (the arms of the cross); it was a stone partition with altars, and a crucifix above. The second was the stone pulpitum, which lay to the east of the rood screen and contained a door leading through to the choir where the monks, nuns or canons sat facing each other in wooden stalls. Good examples of a pulpitum are to be found at the Scottish monasteries of Melrose and Lincluden.[22] In many monastic churches the choir lay beneath the crossing of the transepts, and in some the monks' stalls spread into the nave. East of the choir was the presbytery, containing the principal or high altar with a carved screen (reredos) behind, and here would have been the shrines of the saints like St Alban, and St Cuthbert at Durham. It was in the east end that pronounced architectural developments took place within our period. In the Black Monk and Cluniac houses of the eleventh century and later, the east end tended to be apsidal, that is, it ended in a semi-circular shape and was flanked by semi-circular-ended aisles containing chapels. At some churches the three-apse plan which this arrangement produced was developed to contain five or even seven apses. St Albans and its dependency at Binham, as well as the early churches of Castle Acre and Thetford and the Romanesque church of St Mary's, York, are good examples. An elaboration of this apsidal pattern was the three-apse and ambulatory arrangement, in which a passage ran from one nave aisle around the back of the choir, passing a number of radiating chapels and returning to the nave. This was particularly common in the larger churches, which had many shrines and altars, and could be found at a number in the west midlands (Tewkesbury, Worcester and Pershore) as well as at Christ Church, Canterbury, and most spectacularly at Norwich.

An assumption which developed among founders and patrons was that they would be allowed burial in the church of the religious house which they had endowed, and the tombs of founders are often located in the choir. It was at the east end of Westminster Abbey that Henry III was buried, and at Kirkham that, on a less exalted scale, some members of the Ros family were interred. Burial within a monastic church, especially if it was in the presence of the saints and relics, allowed founders and benefactors to share in the benefits of sacred soil. Until the thirteenth century few lay people, other than founders, were offered burial within the monastic church, but from then onwards it became more common, and late medieval wills can not only contain a request for burial but very occasionally testators specify the part of the church in which they desired to rest.[23]

The Cistercians initially spurned all elaboration, and their churches were to be plain and unadorned. One consequence of this attitude was the rejection of apsidal east ends and transepts in favour of plain, square-ended chapels and presbyteries. It was a fashion which came to be followed by other orders, and can be seen, for example, at the Cluniac house of Monk Bretton. The plans of the earliest Cistercian stone churches, Waverley and Tintern, and now the recently excavated first (c. 1136) stone church of Fountains, reveal these plain, austere structures. The naves lacked aisles, and the transepts were short, and had rectangular chapels in their non-apsidal eastern end. The solidity and plainness of Cistercian architecture can still be seen at Kirkstall, built after 1147, and in some later buildings constructed at convents of modest size and endowments, such as Valle Crucis and Cymmer. The White Monks considered massive stone towers to be superfluous and therefore placed a ban on them. What they considered acceptable – a low structure barely rising above the level of the roof – can be clearly seen at Buildwas, a fine series of twelfth-century buildings little altered in later centuries.[24]

Each group of religious had its own needs. The churches of the Knights Templar reflect influence from another quarter in that they were designed with naves built on a circular plan in order to emulate the Church of the

Holy Sepulchre in Jerusalem; examples may be seen in the layout of the church of the London Temple, and the excavated site of Temple Bruer in Lincolnshire.[25] The requirements of the mendicants were different from those of the monastic orders. In their churches, the emphasis was less on corporate worship than on preaching to the laity, and this rendered impractical the compartmentalized church achieved by the use of screens between the religious and the congregation. In friary churches, therefore, there was no division between the nave, choir and presbytery, but rather a studied openness. Long aisleless structures are a feature of the friars' churches like those of the Franciscans of Lincoln and the Dominicans of Brecon. Second-generation mendicant churches were, as we have noted, considerably larger than their primitive structures, reflecting the pressure of their patrons and their large audiences.[26]

The internal arrangement of a monastic church was modified according to liturgical needs. Thus, in a Cluniac church, many altars were provided for the monk-priests to say mass; conversely in a nunnery the need for multiple altars did not exist. Procession formed an important part of the liturgy in many houses, and accordingly, in some churches processional doorways may be seen leading into the cloister from the south transept, and back into the church from the west range.[27] For part of the Sunday processions, it became common for Cistercian churches to have a porch built on at the west end, which became known as a Galilee. Examples may be seen at Fountains, Byland, Neath, Sweetheart and Tintern, and (in a major Benedictine house) at Durham.[28]

It is at the cathedral priories, like Durham, which survived demolition or decay at the Dissolution because of their dual status, that the clearest impression of a large Benedictine church can perhaps be gained. Durham has already been mentioned in the context of the energetic building campaigns of the Norman conquerors and settlers of the North. It was in 1093 that the foundation stone of the church was laid, and the building was complete by 1133. Since that date only two substantial additions have been made: these are the Galilee chapel at the west end (c. 1175), and the chapel of the nine altars at the east end (dating from the thirteenth century). The fabric of the cathedral priory of Norwich, too, dates almost entirely from the twelfth century, and is a fine example of a Romanesque church. Durham and Norwich are perhaps the best survivals from our period, not just of a Benedictine conventual church, but also of the monastic claustral complex. Both sites give a resounding impression of the extent of a monastic church and the buildings surrounding it.

The importance of the church within the monastic community meant that where funds permitted, it was common for churches to be rebuilt in the latest architectural fashion, either in whole or in part. Early churches, such as the simple aisleless cruciform structures at the Cistercian abbey of Waverley and at the Augustinian house of Norton, aimed to serve the needs of communities of modest size and means. As further resources were acquired, wealth was ploughed back into building activity, and the church was the first part of the monastery to be reconstructed to accommodate increased numbers, and beautified. In the thirteenth century the canons of Kirkham enlarged their mid-twelfth-century church, a simple cruciform building, by lengthening and broadening the east end (the presbytery and the choir); the original nave was kept. At Norton, the first church was retained until a radical programme of rebuilding was undertaken in the first three decades of the thirteenth century, probably as a result of a growth in numbers. Rebuilding usually began at the east end, as at Brecon and Chester (both in the 1190s) and Hexham (c. 1195). Common in these rebuilt churches was an elongated east end: examples are provided by St Mary's, York (nine bays) and Thornton (six bays).

The lengthening of the eastern arm of monastic churches was evidently not a functional development required to meet increased numbers in a community, for it was rare for the monks', canons' or nuns' choir to be moved from the eastern part of the nave and the crossing into the new eastern arm.[29] Rather, the reason seems to have been liturgical. The pronouncements of the Fourth Lateran Council (1215) that defined transubstantiation as a matter of faith led to an elaboration of the liturgy of the mass which may have demanded a richer and more spacious setting. Certainly the introduction of a daily mass to the Virgin resulted in the construction, in many churches, of a Lady chapel at the east end. In addition it was increasingly common for monks to be priests, and priests needed altars at which to say mass. The period also saw the refurbishment of the tombs of saints lying in the east end of churches, such as Wulfstan and Oswald at Worcester (1224) and Æthelreda at Ely. Most spectacular was the sumptuous shrine of Thomas Becket, erected at Canterbury in 1220, which formed 'the visual and liturgical focus of the church'.[30]

Rievaulx Abbey, where the twelfth-century choir, but not the nave, was rebuilt in the following century, provides us with an example of the development from the solid simplicity of early Cistercian architecture. The modern visitor walks down the early nave (dating from the 1140s)[31] with the remains of massive stone piers to either side and faced by the tall, plain and solid walls of the transepts, and then passes through the crossing into the splendour of the east end: the seven bays of choir and presbytery with their shafted piers, moulded arches and narrow lancets of the clerestory have been called a perfect example of 'embryonic Gothic'.[32] Many abbey churches of consequence were rebuilt in the thirteenth century. At Fountains there is harmony between what the written foundation narrative and the stones themselves tell us. Hugh of Kirkstall records that by the beginning of the thirteenth century the church was inadequate for two reasons: the increased number of monks, and the need for more altars so that monk-priests, now as common in Cistercian as Benedictine and Cluniac houses, could say a daily mass. The evidence of the buildings shows how this was achieved, not by using the apsidal plan favoured on the continent, but by the construction of the eastern transept, the 'Chapel of the Nine Altars'. Unique among Cistercian churches, it was emulated at the important Benedictine cathedral priory of Durham.[33]

The cloister and claustral buildings[34]

During the tenth-century revival it became common if not universal for the domestic offices of a religious house to be arranged around a large square or rectangular piece of ground, the cloister, bounded on one side by the church. The classic claustral plan is that of the ninth-century monastery of St Gall (Switzerland), and the first evidence of it in England comes from Glastonbury in the time of Dunstan, and from Canterbury. Here there is clear evidence of the influence of continental monastic practice in England. On all four sides the central area, the garth, was surrounded by a low wall with arcades and a lean-to roof which thus provided covered passage ways around. In northern European countries it was usual for the cloister and surrounding buildings to be constructed to the south of the church, so that its massive structure did not block the daylight and could afford some shelter from the cold. To take advantage of the light from the south, desks and carrels for study and writing were placed along the wall of the church, facing to the south, and it was here that monks, canons and nuns spent the portions of the day allotted for work and reading.[35] Sometimes, however, the constraints of the site meant that a southerly location was impossible. Thus at Tintern Abbey the monastic complex lay to the north of the church to allow for the river Wye to be utilized for drainage, and similarly at Melrose in order for water to be supplied from the Tweed. At the Premonstratensian abbey of Easby in north Yorkshire, in an unusual arrangement, there were major buildings to both north and south of the church. There were, naturally enough, many local variations in the disposition around the cloister of the buildings necessary for the monastery, but as convenience more often than other factors dictated how the rooms were arranged, a general description may be given.

The monks' dormitory generally lay in the east range of the cloister, on the first floor; a flight of stairs at the north end, the night stairs, led directly into the south transept of the church, and thus provided the shortest route from the dormitory when the monks were roused for the night office. Few sets of night stairs have survived, but a good example can be seen at Hexham Priory. Below, on the ground floor of the east range running south from the church was a sacristy, where vestments and vessels for mass were kept, and where books might also be stored. Next came the chapter house, and then a parlour where talking was allowed.[36] As chapter houses became larger and were vaulted, it was impossible to accommodate them in the ground-floor space beneath the dormitory. This came to provide the vestibule or portico only, while the chapter house proper was extended so that it lay on an east–west axis and protruded to the east of the eastern range. The undercroft of the southern end of the east range might be occupied by the novices' room, the monks' day room, or in Benedictine monasteries, a warming house. Somewhere along this range a second flight of stairs, the day stairs, was used by the religious when entering the dormitory from the cloister. In the extreme south of the east range, at first-floor level, was the reredorter, or lavatory, built over a stream or drain. Particularly fine examples of monastic plumbing survive at Castle Acre and Melrose.[37]

The south range generally housed the refectory (frater), at the entrance to which a lavatorium (washing trough) was provided, usually built into the wall, and less commonly free-standing. A richly carved stone lavatorium of twelfth-century date stands in the centre of the garth at the Cluniac priory of Much Wenlock. In Benedictine houses the refectory might occupy the whole of the range, and the warming house and kitchen were free-standing buildings lying to the south. This was a sensible arrangement, for it guarded against the risk of fire spreading quickly in a series of connected buildings. A significant development was made by the Cistercians, for in their houses the kitchen and warming house became integral parts of the south range, flanking the refectory and, in the case of the kitchen, linked to it by serving hatches. In the earliest Cistercian monasteries it was common to build the refectory on an east–west axis, and this persisted later as well in smaller houses like Cymmer in mid Wales, Tilty and Merevale. However, historians have detected from the mid 1160s a distinct tendency among the larger Cistercian houses to rebuild the refectory and create a more spacious room on a north–south axis.[38] Some abbeys founded after the 1170s built their first refectories to this new pattern. Traditionally this realignment has been explained in terms of the increase in numbers in the community; it was easier to build on a larger scale on a north–south line where only the topography of the site would restrict the length of the new structure. This is an adequate explanation as far as it goes, but, as Peter Fergusson has pointed out, if it

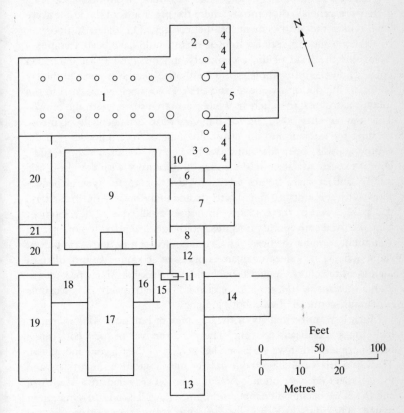

1	Nave	9	Cloister	15	Slype
2	North transept	10	Night stairs	16	Warming house
3	South transept	11	Day stairs	17	Refectory
4	Chapels	12	Day-room, with	18	Kitchen
5	Chancel		dormitory above	19	Lay-brothers' dormitory
6	Library/sacristy	13	Novices' room, with	20	Cellars
7	Chapter house		dormitory above	21	Outer parlour
8	Parlour	14	Reredorter		

Figure 1 A Cistercian plan: Dundrennan Abbey near Kirkcudbright, founded in
1142 from Rievaulx

is the only one, we would expect the rebuilding of the refectory to be accompanied by similar reconstruction of, for example, dormitory or chapter house. This did not apparently happen, and Fergusson has argued convincingly that there was an ideological reason for the development of a north–south refectory: the incorporation of the kitchen and warming house into the claustral buildings meant that all the essential offices were now accessible direct from the cloister for the ritual Sunday procession.[39]

The west range shows considerable variation. At ground-floor level there were generally storerooms where the provisions of the house were kept under the management of the cellarer. On the first floor, in Benedictine and Augustinian houses, there would have been accommodation for the head of the community and his guests.[40] In Cistercian houses, however, the whole of the west range was given over to the lay brethren: the dormitory above, and the refectory below, situated in the south end towards the kitchen, which was often shared with the monks. This was another advantage of the Cistercian arrangement of incorporating the kitchen into the claustral complex. Accommodation in the west range was not needed for a twelfth-century Cistercian abbot, since he was expected to sleep in the common dormitory with the rest of the monks, and separate houses were provided for guests; where the site allowed (as at Fountains) these were situated to the west of the monastery, the 'public' end of the complex. In houses of all types, a development from the thirteenth century onwards was the gradual provision of separate accommodation for the head of the community, comprising a complex of rooms (chapel, hall, sleeping quarters and guest accommodation), often to the east of the church and claustral buildings. Kirkstall Abbey provides us with a substantial, and, for a Cistercian house, remarkably early example (thirteenth-century) of an abbot's lodging.

Much less can be said about the complex of buildings which went to make up a mendicant convent. The poor survival of their conventual buildings means that we are much less certain of their layout and design. The loss of friary buildings is due in large measure to their urban sites; and the fact that they were often located in the most crowded areas of a town, and therefore occupied cramped sites, must have led to great variation in design. The friars had basically the same requirements as monks and canons, and like those of the monastic orders, the domestic buildings of the mendicants were arranged around a cloister; moreover, where evidence exists, it indicates that the chapter house was located in the usual position in the east range. However, the sources, both archaeological and documentary, suggest that the variation in the disposition of offices around the cloister could be great. Moreover it seems certain that in some convents communal life gave way early to the needs of study; and at the

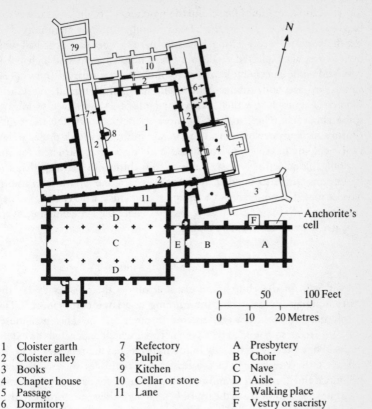

1	Cloister garth	7	Refectory	A	Presbytery
2	Cloister alley	8	Pulpit	B	Choir
3	Books	9	Kitchen	C	Nave
4	Chapter house	10	Cellar or store	D	Aisle
5	Passage	11	Lane	E	Walking place
6	Dormitory			F	Vestry or sacristy

Figure 2 The house of Dominican friars at Norwich. The large open nave and the walking place which communicated with the domestic buildings are characteristic of mendicant churches (see p. 139)

Dominican priories of Gloucester and Bristol there is evidence that the common dormitory was subdivided into cells.[41] Both the deficiencies of their sites and the special needs of their orders meant that the domestic offices of the mendicants may have been distinctive from those of their monastic brethren.

The infirmary

The infirmary lay a little way from the main monastic buildings, often to the east. It provided accommodation for the resident sick and the elderly monks, canons and nuns for whom the rigid régime of the cloister was too harsh, and was also used by the healthy members of the community during the periodic blood-letting. The infirmary comprised a large hall with beds along each wall, rather like a modern hospital ward, and a chapel at one end. The surviving remains of monastic infirmaries show great variety in size and arrangement, from the grand structure at Christ Church, Canterbury, which, with its length of 237 feet, was as long as some abbey churches, to halls of more modest size. In the thirteenth century further developments in monastic infirmaries took place; and at Norwich, for instance, an additional building was constructed for the periodic blood-letting. It was also in the thirteenth century that the Cistercians began to build their infirmaries in stone, and fine examples have survived at Fountains of a complex containing hall, chapel, kitchen and infirmarer's lodging, and at Waverley, where the same buildings were arranged around an infirmary cloister.

The inner and outer courts

To the west of the church and claustral offices there generally lay the other buildings necessary for the running of a large corporation.[42] The whole monastic precinct was entered through one or more gatehouses and came to be surrounded by a precinct wall which delineated the extent of the abbey site, and especially in towns protected the religious from the bustle of the streets. Precinct walls survive in places such as Bury St Edmunds and Cirencester, and at non-urban sites, for example, Fountains and Furness, and at Sweetheart Abbey, where they are constructed of massive hewn boulders. The gatehouse needed to be wide enough for carts to pass through and was generally a two-storey edifice, the upper floor providing a school, or court house (as at York), or frequently in Cistercian houses, a chapel for the lay people, who were not allowed into the church. There are many English examples: Kirkham Priory has a fine thirteenth-century gatehouse carved with the arms of its patrons. Fewer gatehouses have survived in Scotland; noteworthy ones are St Andrews and Arbroath.

Within the precinct there were an inner and an outer court. The inner court, lying nearer to the claustral complex, generally contained the guest houses (those of Fountains have already been mentioned) and accommodation for corrodians (on whom see below, chapter 8). Also in the inner court were the domestic workshops, including bakehouse, brewhouse and laundry, and granaries and storerooms, the servants' quarters, and stables. In the outer court lay the larger industrial and agricultural buildings. Some of the most extensive outer courts, like that at Rievaulx,

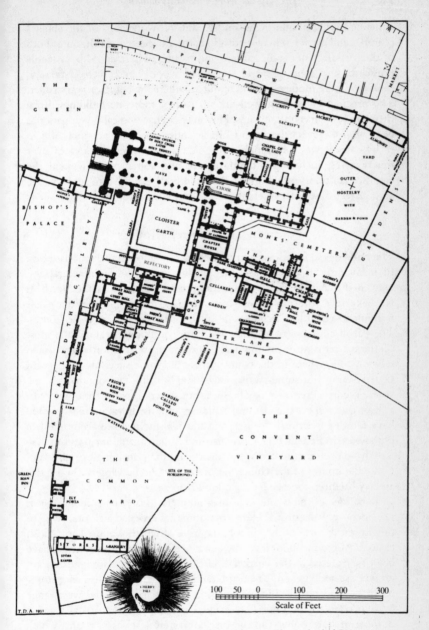

Figure 3 The precinct of a Benedictine house: Ely Cathedral Priory

contained mills, a tannery, a smithy, and the workshops of the abbey's plumber and glazier. There were also barns, dovecots and fishponds (both of them sources of food), gardens and pasture. There could be a wool-house for the collection and sorting of wool. There were, naturally, houses of more modest size and resources where the complex was smaller. The precinct is the least well-known part of monastic buildings, since there are few surviving remains. However, archaeological investigation is beginning to reveal the extent of the entire monastic precinct, and in many cases it was surprisingly large: Rievaulx covered an area of over ninety acres, including fifty of pasture and water meadow; and the Augustinian priory of Thornton (Lincolnshire) extended to seventy-one acres. Areas of seventy to eighty acres are not uncommon.

NUNNERIES AND DOUBLE HOUSES

The buildings so far discussed have been those found in male monasteries. In many respects this reflects the relative paucity of architectural and excavated archaeological evidence for nunnery buildings. In the North, as we have seen, the nunneries were small and poor, and they have left nothing to equal the architectural splendours of the large male houses. The parish churches of Marrick and Nun Monkton are about the most substantial remains of the physical environment of the northern women religious. Elsewhere in the country there are some survivals; Butler and Given-Wilson list some twenty-seven English sites and one Welsh one where medieval remains may be seen, but select none for comment.[43] In at least one respect the claustral buildings of a medieval nunnery would have differed from male houses, and this was the need to accommodate both sexes. In Benedictine, Cistercian and Augustinian nunneries this may only have been the master or guardian[44] and the nuns' priest or chaplain; in double houses of the Gilbertine or Fontevraudine Orders, the canons and lay brethren too needed accommodation.

Some idea of the layout of a small nunnery in the late Middle Ages is provided by Wilberfoss.[45] Here excavation has revealed a cloister lying to the liturgical north of the church, the nave of which was used as a parish church. At ground-floor level the east range contained rooms which have been interpreted as the chapter house, the day stairs, dairy, storeroom, brewhouse and kitchen. The north range revealed two larders with store-room beyond, a hall, buttery, kitchen and a chamber; the west range leading back to the church contained a buttery, a set of stairs and a number of storerooms. On the first floor were a series of rooms which extended above the cloister walk. These were a chamber and dormitory and granary beyond (east range), chamber and buttery (north range), and a series of chambers (west range). To the north of the claustral buildings, across a court, lay the nuns' priest's chamber, a poultry house, pantry and bakehouse, and at first-floor level, chambers and a granary. There are analogies for this arrangement at other small nunneries, the distinctive feature of which is the intrusion of the domestic buildings – dairy, brewery, etc. – into the cloister complex. Unfortunately all are late medieval and cannot be said with certainty to represent the circumstances in the era of foundation and beyond. However, given the general poverty of the nunneries and the unlikelihood of there being substantial sums for rebuilding, the later medieval layout might represent the primitive one also.

The best example of the layout of a double house is provided by the excavated site of the Gilbertine priory of Watton (Yorkshire).[46] The solution adopted at Watton to the need to accommodate both sexes in rigid segregation was to provide two of everything. The church was divided down the centre by a wall; the nuns, on their side of the church, could hear the canons saying the offices on the other without seeing them or having contact of any kind. From the nuns' side of the church the transept led to a parlour and chapter house, and the usual offices arranged around the cloister on a Cistercian-type plan, with accommodation for the lay sisters in the west range. From the nuns' cloister leading to the canons' cloister was a passage containing a window house, through which all communications had to be made. This archaeological evidence is consistent with contemporary descriptions of the 1160s.[47] It is possible that the disposition of the buildings at Watton was followed at nunneries inspired by the fourfold Gilbertine arrangement. A visitation report for the nunnery of Swine refers to the careless guarding of doors and windows through which food was passed, which had allowed conversations between the canons and the nuns.[48] The excavated plan of Watton is resonant with the ideology of the order in the aftermath of the scandal of the 1160s, and the urgent need for segregation which the planners of the house felt to be necessary. But although what we have at Watton is a mature Gilbertine plan, it is likely that the buildings always reflected the needs of a strictly secluded nunnery.

RESOURCES FOR BUILDING

Three kinds of resources were needed for the planning and construction of a medieval religious house: human skill and labour, materials, and patronage. The availability of these three determined how quickly the work could be completed, and we know that there was great variation in the time it took to finish a project. When Ailred of Rievaulx visited his

Scottish daughter house of Dundrennan (founded in 1142) in 1165 he found that 'the abbey had only begun to build its regular offices a short time before'.[49] Beaulieu Abbey took forty-three years to complete. Arbroath Abbey was founded in 1178; the founder was buried next to the high altar in the completed east end in 1214, and the abbey was all but complete by c. 1230. In contrast, the abbey of Hailes, to the north-east of Gloucester, demonstrates what good resources and royal patronage could achieve: started in 1246, the church was dedicated in 1251.

Monastic buildings were designed and built by professionals, but this is not to say that abbots, priors and patrons did not take part in discussions about the form buildings would take. Indeed, Professor Fergusson has drawn attention to the close involvement of a number of abbots, monks and lay brethren of Cistercian houses in the work of construction.[50] However, there is little doubt that in most cases the details of planning were the task of the master mason, or as he was called in some houses, the master of the works. Few are known to us by name. We know that three men, Leofsi Duddensunu, Godwin Gretsith and Teinfrith, the first two described as masons and the last as a churchwright, were in charge of the work commissioned by Edward the Confessor at Westminster Abbey.[51] From Norton Priory we have an incidental reference which tells us the name of the builder: Eustace fitz John, who came to hold the patronage of the priory and who died in 1157, made a grant to Hugh of Catwick of pasture for a hundred sheep on condition that he finished the construction of the church 'in every part according to the first foundation of William fitz Nigel'.[52] Generally, however, those who planned and supervised the construction of religious houses great and small remain anonymous, as do the armies of masons, carpenters, metalworkers, tilers, glaziers and labourers who worked under their command. Sometimes the documentary sources allow us a glimpse of how work proceeded. At Selby, Abbot Hugh de Lacy (1097–c. 1122) began the building of the first stone church, a process in which he took more than a passing interest. 'Everyday, dressed in a workman's cowl along with the other labourers he used to carry to the wall on his shoulders stones, chalk and other materials which were needed for the work, and every Saturday he received his pay like any of the other workmen, and gave it away to the poor.'[53] In a massive rebuilding programme hundreds of workers were employed during the building seasons. In the first week in July 1253 there were 426 men at work on the rebuilding of Westminster Abbey: of these over half (220) were labourers; the remaining included white cutters (free masons) (56), marblers (49), layers (masons) (28), carpenters (23), polishers (15), smiths (17), glaziers (14) and plumbers (4).[54]

Wherever possible monastic builders used local material resources, and

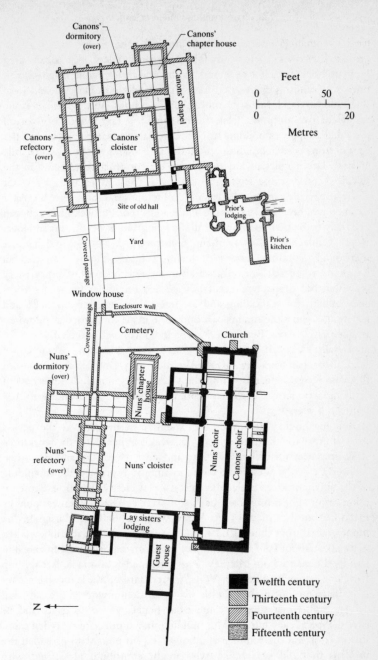

Canons' dormitory (over)

Canons' chapter house

Canons' chapel

Feet

0   50

0   20

Metres

Canons' refectory (over)

Canons' cloister

Site of old hall

Prior's lodging

Covered passage

Yard

Prior's kitchen

Window house

Enclosure wall

Covered passage

Cemetery

Church

Nuns' dormitory (over)

Nuns' chapter house

Nuns' refectory (over)

Nuns' cloister

Nuns' choir

Canons' choir

Lay sisters' lodging

Guest house

N

■ Twelfth century

▨ Thirteenth century

▧ Fourteenth century

▦ Fifteenth century

Figure 4 Plan of the excavated site of a double house of the Gilbertine Order: Watton Priory, Yorkshire, founded c. 1150. Some portions of the monastery were rebuilt in the fourteenth century, and the prior's lodging, which has survived, dates from the fifteenth

tried to obtain access to quarries, mineral sources and woodland to provide them with their needs. The Norman builders of St Albans used Roman brick in the tower and in the transepts reused Anglo-Saxon turned columns. Tintern used locally quarried sandstone, Maenan local shale and Strata Florida slate rubble; all three houses brought finer stone for decorative purposes from further afield.[55] The manor of Norton provided a supply of building stone for the Augustinian priory, and 99 per cent of stone used in building was sandstone brought from only half a mile away.[56] The magnesian limestone used for construction at Selby in the twelfth century came from Monk Fryston eight miles away by water along a specially constructed canal.[57] Sometimes transport over a greater distance was necessary. From the 1150s and 1160s Purbeck marble began gradually to be used in churches all over England; it occurs, for instance, in the Galilee chapel of Durham, constructed c. 1170–5, and became increasingly common in the thirteenth century. Timber was also an important resource. Not only were the earliest buildings of a monastery of wood, but timber was constantly needed for use in frames for roofs and ceilings, for scaffolding and for internal fittings, screens, stalls and partitions. Sometimes grants of wood were made for particular purposes. Biddlesden, Cleeve, Beaulieu, Stanley and Thame all received wood for choir stalls; Henry III granted twenty-six trees, including six oaks to Grace Dieu after it had been burnt by the Welsh in 1233. Detailed expenses from the Vale Royal ledger covering the years 1278–81 included the cost of bringing wood from Delamere forest for building, amounting to 108 journeys a year.[58]

Building could certainly be an expensive business. Over the period from 28 April to 6 December 1253 the weekly expenses for the workforce at Westminster varied between £16 and £109 (week 20) and amounted to over £1,500.[59] Westminster was an ambitious project, the rebuilding of the abbey of kings under the patronage of Henry III, but expenses at other major abbeys must have been comparable. These expenses could be met in a number of ways. At Shrewsbury Abbot Henry assigned the money raised from tithes at Ellerdine to building work at the abbey (1234 × 1244).[60] Abbot Paul's rebuilding of St Albans was evidently financed in part by the man whom Matthew Paris identified as his uncle, Archbishop Lanfranc; while Wulfstan of Worcester reorganized the episcopal estates in order to provide money for massive construction work at the cathedral priory. Sometimes support came from benefactors who gave land or revenue specifically intended for building. In a number of recorded cases, however, it was the founder of a house and his heirs who provided the impetus to build or rebuild, who might contribute ideas, and who furnished resources to finance the project. The rebuilding of the second church at Tintern, completed in 1301, evidently owed much to Roger Bigod, who provided the funding – a debt which was acknowledged by the chronicler of that house.[61] We have already encountered Abbot Alexander of Kirkstall (1152–82), who determined on a move from the site at Barnoldswick and persuaded the founder, Henry de Lacy, to acquire for him an alternative at Kirkstall. From the description in the chronicle of the house – 'a place covered with woods and unproductive of crops' – it is difficult to see what attracted Alexander to Kirkstall, although there is here an element of conventional description of the wilderness sites occupied by the Cistercians. But it is clear from what follows that Alexander had an eye for what was needed for a good site: 'a place well nigh destitute of good things save timber and stone and a pleasant valley with the water of a river which flowed down its centre' – building materials and a supply of water. The same source records that Alexander constructed of stone and wood 'the church and both the dormitory of the monks and that of the lay brethren, and both refectories, the cloister and the chapter [house] and other offices necessary within the abbey, and all these covered excellently with tiles'. The evidence of the stones harmonizes with the written word; and little was added to the core of the monastery after the second half of the twelfth century. Such a sustained building programme must have demanded a constant supply of money, and the chronicle tells us who found it: Henry de Lacy, 'now supplying money as the needs of the establishment required. He had part in providing the buildings, laid with his own hand the foundations of the church, and himself completed the whole fabric at his own cost.'[62] Lacy was not the only patron to take an interest – personal and financial – in the building of his monastery. Henry II gave £880 towards building work at Amesbury, which he refounded.[63] King John not only financed Beaulieu, but made frequent visits to inspect the progress of the work;[64] and his son and successor, Henry III, was generous in his contribution towards the completion of the church. Henry's special interest in building also resulted in the reconstruction of Westminster, begun by 1245, and his completion of Netley (founded in 1239). The progress of work therefore depended as much on the finances of a patron as it did on the economic fortunes of the monks.

THE MONASTIC CONTRIBUTION TO ARCHITECTURAL DEVELOPMENTS, AND THE DISTINCTIVENESS OF THE ORDERS

One final question should be addressed before we leave the subject of monastic buildings: just how distinctive, if at all, were the design and buildings of particular groups, congregations and orders in the twelfth and thirteenth centuries? It is usually the Cistercians who are the focus of such discussion. The Benedictine houses were autonomous and could act independently in the matter of their buildings as in other aspects of their daily life and government. The Augustinians, smaller than many houses of Black Monks, also lacked the kind of constitutional control of the Cistercians. There has been no detailed general study of the buildings of the British Augustinians, and few individual houses have been examined.[65] Much has been written about the Cistercian attitude to art and architecture, and little can be done here but summarize a few of the most salient points. The main documentary source for austerity in architecture comes from that most famous of all Cistercians, St Bernard, abbot of Clairvaux. His biographers paint a picture of a man impervious to his physical surroundings, to whom beauty, whether natural or man-made, was irrelevant. Whether this accurately portrays Bernard or tells us more of his biographers need not concern us here. Bernard's own words, in his *Apologia*, his debate with Peter the Venerable, abbot of Cluny, which was written by 1125, are witness to his concern about the use of elaborate architecture, sculpture and painting in monastic churches.[66] We should note that Bernard does not condemn them in all contexts, but he does regard them as unnecessary for monks, and superfluous in their churches. But what of the official Cistercian attitude as expressed in legislation of the general chapter?[67] We have already noted that the chapter attempted to achieve some degree of uniformity in the buildings of a new foundation – the restriction on sites, and the types of buildings to be erected before occupation and so on. But as has recently been pointed out, there is curiously little in the early legislation about the design and decoration of churches. Some time before 1135 – and therefore possibly though not certainly influenced by Bernard – the general chapter forbade sculptures and pictures in Cistercian churches and monastic buildings; only painted crosses of wood were allowed. As to architectural detail, it was not until 1157 that stone bell towers were prohibited; and in 1159 coloured windows were banned and it was stipulated that those which had already been installed were to be removed. In 1188 the general chapter denounced 'grand and sumptuous buildings'. Four years later the chapter reported that the abbey church of Vaucelles (France) was 'too sumptuous and superfluous and a cause of great scandal', while the new dormitory of Longpont was 'against the form and custom of the order'.[68] In the first instance the fault committed by the abbot and monks of Vaucelles was vague; who was to define what was 'sumptuous' or 'superfluous'? The second case was even more ambiguous, for the abbot of Longpont was apparently breaking an unwritten rule; nowhere is the 'form and custom of the order' written down. In fact there is no mention in twelfth-century Cistercian legislation of the size, form, number or arrangement of the monastic buildings. This leads us to conclude that the 'form and custom of the order' was referring not to written regulations, but to a state of mind, an acceptance that Cistercian ideology naturally preferred buildings which were austere and unadorned, in the same way that their adherence to the Rule of St Benedict was unencumbered by accretions. It was also in keeping with their insistence on monastic poverty.

Although, then, there was a distinctive Cistercian attitude which would favour an austerity in design and lack of decoration in monastic buildings, was there any other factor which might lead to uniformity among the houses of the White Monks? One obvious meeting point was the annual general chapter, where news and views on matters of all sorts could be exchanged. A second was the annual visitation of daughter houses. A third is suggested in a number of documentary sources, and that is supervision of the erection of buildings by a senior monk. Again, the English evidence is most plentiful from the northern houses. When the first monks settled at Fountains they built a hut covered with turf and a chapel of wattle, and cleared land for a garden. Next they asked to be received into the Cistercian Order, and in response to their request the abbot of Clairvaux sent brother Geoffrey d'Ainai to instruct them in the Cistercian way of life. Among Geoffrey's duties was to give advice about the erection of buildings. Geoffrey may have only just returned to Clairvaux from Rievaulx, where he had doubtless performed a similar function, when he was sent back to Fountains. It was while Adam, a monk of Fountains, was supervising the construction of buildings at its daughter house of Vaudey that he met the founder, William of Aumale, and arranged for a further foundation at Meaux.[69]

The architectural evidence for this period also speaks of close contacts with the cradle of Cistercian monasticism, Burgundy. Rievaulx is the earliest example (probably mid 1140s) of a Cistercian church built by English masons under the instruction of a man who was fully conversant with Burgundian customs.[70] It shows affinities with Cistercian houses in that region, notably Fontenay, which is probably the best survival of an early Cistercian church and claustral complex. Rievaulx in turn influenced in its nave and transepts the second stone church at Fountains, followed at Louth Park (late 1140s) and Kirkstall (c. 1152). These show 'family' or 'local' ties, the passing of influence from mother to daughter or from one abbey to another in the same region. The same may be observed in Wales, and affinities here were due to the adherence to a similar plan at Whitland and its descendants at Strata Marcella, Strata Florida and Valle Crucis, and to the coincidence of similar building periods at Margam, Neath and Tintern. Further similarities emerge from archaeological investigation: dimensions at Neath and Tintern; length of crossing and transepts at Strata Florida, Strata Marcella and Valle Crucis; refectory size at Valle Crucis and Cymmer; and masons' marks at Strata Florida and Strata Marcella.[71]

A departure from the primitive austerity of the first and second-generation Cistercians came with changing architectural fashion, and may be observed both in those abbeys founded at a later date, and thus enjoying their first building campaigns in the 1160s and 1170s and later, and in the rebuilding of sections of houses such as Waverley and Rievaulx which have been mentioned already. The otherwise undistinguished abbey of Roche in south Yorkshire is often signalled as the first truly Gothic Cistercian church because of its persistent use of the pointed arch and clustered piers (although Christopher Wilson points out important stylistic features at the slightly earlier Kirkstead).[72] The Cistercians were the first group in the North to use the Gothic style of architecture.[73] They created a distinctive regional school and in so doing lost some of their peculiarly Cistercian features. It was from the northern Cistercian houses that elements of Gothic were transmitted to the cathedrals at York and St Andrews, and to the minster church at Ripon, and from Kirkstead to the Benedictine abbey of Bardney. Since in the early thirteenth century a number of Cistercian churches adopted the elongated eastern arm favoured by the Benedictines, it could be said that the differences between the Black Monks and the White were contracting.

Yet the developments in the architecture of the White Monks were not uniform or generalized. The crucial factor now was not so much, or not solely, the order to which a house belonged, as diversity in size and wealth.[74] Some distinctive features of twelfth-century Cistercian architecture remained, for example, the narthex or Galilee, and the aisleless presbytery with square chapels in the transepts. The latter feature, which contrasts with the Gothic presbytery at Rievaulx, and the aisled structures at Hailes, Netley, Margam, Kinloss and others, nevertheless persisted in Wales at Basingwerk, Valle Crucis and Aberconwy, in England at Cleeve, Sallay and Furness, and in Scotland at Melrose, Sweetheart, Glenluce, Balmerino, Culross and Deer.[75] It is houses which apparently lacked the wealth or the incentive or the need to rebuild which preserve the character and spirit of early Cistercian monasticism. Yet Nicola Coldstream has argued that even late or rebuilt Cistercian houses like Tintern, Netley and Hailes show a restraint and lack of ornament that is distinctively Cistercian, and that the White Monks retained a 'sense of their own identity at least until the end of the thirteenth century'.[76] This may well be so, but could it not be suggested that a thirteenth-century patron or pilgrim, although able to observe a distinct difference between the external appearance of Buildwas and Bury St Edmunds, may (if he or she thought about it at all) have attributed it to wealth and status as much as order? And would there have been a discernible difference, to them, among the richer Cistercian, Benedictine and Augustinian houses or among their more modestly endowed counterparts?

The answer to this last question may well lie in that feature of monastic buildings now lost to us almost completely, that of the furnishings and internal decoration of monastic churches. It is not only at those monasteries and nunneries which are now in ruins that this aspect of their appearance has been lost, for even at those churches which survived the Dissolution, either because they were cathedral churches, or because they were taken over and used as parish churches, the events of 1536–40 were far-reaching. From 1536, for instance, their shrines began to be dismantled and destroyed.[77] Since then, changes in fashion and liturgy have altered much of the medieval appearance of the churches. It is difficult, for example, for the modern visitor to appreciate how richly painted the walls of many monastic churches would have been. A few survivals serve to remind us of this fact, like the early twelfth-century chapel of the Holy Sepulchre at Winchester, which contains wall paintings depicting the crucifixion, deposition and burial of Christ, and the pillars of the nave of St Albans with their crucifixion scenes dating from the thirteenth century. More ubiquitous would have been the coloured geometric designs painted on pillars and arcades and over windows. Much medieval wall painting has not survived, and accordingly comparisons between the decoration of houses of different orders is difficult. However, investigation of surviving Cistercian wall painting suggests that in the twelfth century it may have been common for Cistercian churches to be painted with white limewash and decorated with a simple masonry design, thus conforming to the spirit of the order. By the late twelfth and early thirteenth century other colours began to be used, but there is no surviving figure painting earlier than the fourteenth century.[78] A similar conclusion has emerged from recent research into other aspects of Cistercian church decoration such as tiled pavements[79] and window glass.[80]

It is highly likely that the plainness of Cistercian churches, and those houses of canons regular influenced by them, and the lack of images therein, would have contrasted sharply with the decorated interiors of Benedictine churches. Many of the latter would have been attended by lay people, for whose benefit the painted depictions of the fundamentals of the Christian faith would have been intended. Although there is evidence to suggest that the type of decoration used in Cistercian and other churches became less distinct as the years wore on, it is unlikely that a Cistercian church would have had anything comparable to the shrine of St Edmund at Bury, for which Abbot Samson commissioned a new canopy of gold and silver; or with the work initiated by Abbot William of Trumpington of St Albans (1214–35), who 'put some elegant structures up round the high altar, together with a beam on which the history of St Alban was figured'.[81]

8

INSIDE A RELIGIOUS HOUSE: DAILY LIFE AND THE CHAIN OF COMMAND

—— • ——

What kind of people were to be found in religious houses, and how did they spend their day? Any attempt to answer that question must bear in mind some fundamental points. For most monks and nuns the basis of their working life was the Rule of St Benedict, but Britain in the period covered by this study is far removed, chronologically and geographically, from Benedict's own monastery of Monte Cassino, for which the Rule was written. Even in the houses we call Benedictine (though this was not a term used at the time) modifications and alterations had taken place in monastic life and observances by the eleventh century. We must remember, too, that much of the documentation we have gives us details of theory: it is evidence of legislation, not necessarily of practice.

DAILY LIFE AND WORSHIP

In his rule Benedict devised for his monks a careful, rigid and, to modern perceptions, monotonous routine of work, prayer, study and sleep, designed to subdue the flesh and the will and to make the mind and the soul receptive to God. The overwhelming monastic concern was with the self, however much the world might benefit from the monks' intercessions. The pattern of the day, in which every minute was accounted for, varied only according to the seasons of the year and the liturgical calendar. However, a major development had taken place by the beginning of our period which had upset the delicate balance sought by Benedict. In the monastic world which gave birth to the *Regularis*

Concordia, the liturgy had become the overwhelming element, relegating manual work to almost a token gesture. Although there is no direct evidence at the English monasteries as at Cluny that on some days the liturgy assumed such a part of the *horarium* (timetable) that there was no time for anything else,[1] nevertheless the greater part of the day would have been spent in the church, in corporate worship of God. Below is a reconstruction of the monastic day according to the *Regularis Concordia*, which would with some variations have been in force from the early to mid eleventh century.[2]

WINTER		SUMMER	
		1.30 a.m.	Preparation for night office; trina oratio and gradual psalms
		2.00 a.m.	<u>Nocturns</u> (night office) (later known as matins) including prayers for the royal family and for the dead
2.30 a.m.	Preparation for night office; trina oratio and gradual psalms		
3.00 a.m.	<u>Nocturns</u> (night office) (later known as matins) including prayers for the royal family and for the dead		
		3.30/ 4.00 a.m.	<u>Matins</u> (<u>lauds</u>) at daybreak; change and wash
5.00 a.m.	Reading	5.00 a.m.	Trina oratio Reading
6.00 a.m.	<u>Matins</u> (<u>lauds</u>) at daybreak <u>Prime</u>	6.00 a.m.	<u>Prime</u> Morrow mass; Chapter
7.30 a.m.	Reading	7.30 a.m.	Work
8.00 a.m.	Wash and change <u>Terce</u> Morrow mass; Chapter	8.00 a.m.	<u>Terce</u> Sung mass
9.45 a.m.	Work	9.30 a.m.	Reading
		11.30 a.m.	<u>Sext</u>
12.00 p.m.	<u>Sext</u> Sung mass	12.00 p.m.	Dinner
1.30 p.m.	<u>None</u>	c. 1.00 p.m.	Siesta

2.00 p.m.	Dinner			
		2.30 p.m.	None	
2.45 p.m.	Work		Drink	
		3.00 p.m.	Work	
4.15 p.m.	Vespers			
5.30 p.m.	Change into night shoes	5.30 p.m.	Supper	
	Drink			
6.00 p.m.	Collatio	6.00 p.m.	Vespers	
6.15 p.m.	Compline			
6.30 p.m.	Bed			
		7.30 p.m.	Night shoes	
			Collatio	
		8.00 p.m.	Compline	
		c. 8.15 p.m.	Bed	

It will be seen from this that the summer timetable has been modified to fill the increased hours of daylight. In winter roughly nine and a half hours were spent in church, one and a half reading, three and three-quarters in works, one and a quarter eating, and eight sleeping. In summer roughly the same proportion of the day was spent in communal prayer, rather more reading and less working, another hour eating and only just over five hours sleeping.

The liturgy

The basic framework of Benedict's day was provided by the eight services of communal worship, and this pattern was followed both by the canonical orders and by the friars. It was never forgotten that the primary function of those who were professed to the monastic life was prayer, the performance of the *Opus Dei*, God's work. Their intercession would help to save the human race, and this made them the spiritual equivalent of earthly soldiers. The way in which the liturgy was performed had developed since the sixth century, and one major change was that, whereas Benedict had assumed that mass (eucharist) would be celebrated only once a week, on Sunday, and on feast days, Cluny and other reform movements of the tenth century added two daily masses: the morrow or chapter mass and, later in the day, a sung high mass. We find both these in the *Concordia*, together with instructions on the performance of the liturgy during important seasons and on feast days. Processions, though not as common as they would become, were used as part of the Easter celebration, along with rich vestments, and song and gesture to emphasize the emotion of the occasion. During the Easter service four brethren, dressed in copes, took their places by the empty sepulchre in imitation of the angel and the three women. There was no attempt here to act, and the Easter trope (ritual) was more liturgical than dramatic, but it was a significant development in the performance of the monastic office.[3]

The constitutions drawn up by Archbishop Lanfranc between 1079 and 1089 are a second major source for the nature of the *horarium* and liturgical practice.[4] We know that these were followed not just at Christ Church, Canterbury, but also at Durham, St Albans and Westminster, and probably many other houses.[5] The constitutions follow the pattern of the *Regularis Concordia* but were compiled from a number of customals and were particularly influenced by Cluny. They therefore make no mention of specifically English features, such as the prayers for the royal family and the Easter liturgical trope, but they elaborate the recitation of psalms. Processions became a more common feature of liturgical practice, and as in Cluniac ritual those celebrating mass on principal feasts were clothed in rich vestments. These solemn festivals increased in number over the years. During the reign of King John the prior and convent of Westminster granted to the abbot of the house an increase in the number of feasts to be celebrated with copes and processions, and with wine and pittances.[6] From the twelfth century a daily office of the Virgin was introduced, probably first at Bury St Edmunds, although it was not until the following century that William of Trumpington, abbot of St Albans, realized that his house was out of step by performing this office, with albs (white vestments), only on Saturdays. He therefore ordered 'that a solemn mass of the blessed Virgin should be celebrated daily with music'.[7] It is worth noting the common practice, expunged from the calendar of Christ Church by Lanfranc, which nevertheless re-emerged in the twelfth century at Bury, St Albans, Gloucester, Winchcombe, Worcester and others, of celebrating the feast of the Immaculate Conception of the Virgin Mary. This was a doctrine much debated in the period, and English monks and scholars were among those who rose up to defend its orthodoxy.[8] Finally it may be noted that a number of further adjustments to the *horarium* took place in Benedictine houses in the thirteenth century: a period of sleep was allowed between matins and lauds; the night office began at midnight; and one of the masses was brought forward to allow greater time for study. Private prayer now occupied three short periods: before the night office when the monks had left their dormitory and processed into church; before terce, and after compline before retiring.[9]

A considerable elaboration which took place in post-Conquest days was the performance of masses for the dead. According to the *Regularis*

Concordia masses were said for thirty days for a dead monk, and prayers were recited for monks of nearby houses and for lay benefactors under agreements of confraternity.[10] Apart from the common observance laid down by the *Regularis Concordia*, confraternity, a liturgical and social bond, was the only link between monasteries. Mention has already been made of the *Liber Vitae* of New Minster, Winchester, in the late Anglo-Saxon period.[11] After the Conquest it became more common for houses to bind themselves together by a promise that monks should receive the prayers of both or all the communities. Thus shortly before 1077 Worcester, Evesham, Gloucester, Pershore, Bath, Winchcombe and Chertsey reached an agreement to act as if the seven houses were one.[12] A confraternity list from St Mary's, York, dates from c. 1180, but the text indicates that many of the houses entered into this special relationship much earlier (for instance, the agreement with Ramsey can be assigned to 1091 × 1112), and shows links with houses all over England and in Normandy.[13] From a simple act of prayer for each other's monks, a spiritual union, confraternity sometimes came to be extended to allow a monk full rights in other houses: entry into the choir, chapter and cloister.

The same basic framework of liturgy as laid down by Benedict was followed in Cistercian monasteries and in the churches of the other reformed congregations. Here the difference was less in the organization of the liturgical day and more in the emphasis. With their desire to follow the Rule in a simple manner the Cistercians considered that the elaborate liturgy, the addition of psalmody and chanting, had upset the delicate balance sought by Benedict. The restoration of manual work to its place in the timetable meant that the Cluniac-inspired liturgy was pruned and simplified. Processions, gorgeous vestments and costly altar vessels, as well as bells, were prohibited, and services became plain and unadorned, like the early buildings of the order.[14] The Carthusians, too, followed the main services, but only three of these (matins, mass and vespers) were sung in church; the remainder were said by the monks in their cells or at private altars in the church. The practices of the regular canons are less easy to detect, and only two of their customaries survive, from Barnwell (1295–6) and from mid-thirteenth-century Llanthony Prima; however, it is perhaps worthy of note that more than one contemporary commentator considered it a great merit of the Augustinian canons that their church services were marked by their moderate length.[15] The friars also followed the pattern of monastic offices, but an innovation was the great emphasis laid on one of the minor services, compline. The reason for the elevation to a central position of this, the last office of the day, was the need of the congregation. Attendance by the laity of the night office, or prime, or any other office, would not have been possible, but the friars encouraged their presence at compline, at the close of the working day.

Work and reading

Much attention has been devoted to the vexed question of what Benedict intended when he said that the brethren were to be engaged in manual work and reading, *lectio divina*. The purpose is clear: to fill the day with suitable activities in order to avoid *accidie*, idleness, the 'enemy of the soul'. Work had formed an essential part of the monastic tradition since the days of the Desert Fathers. But what kind of work? And what kind of reading? The pursuit of study and learning will be considered later.[16] Here we may just note that at appropriate times of the day monks, canons and nuns engaged in reading and meditation, probably in the cloister. And what of manual work? There had been many changes since the days of Benedict. Cluniac monasticism had all but expunged work from the timetable, partly because of the proliferation of services which simply left no time for it, and partly because of developing attitudes which regarded manual work as fit for peasants and not for monks. Gradually the daily work of the monastery fell to hired servants. The early Cistercians insisted that work be restored to its rightful place: 'food for monks of our order ought to come from manual labour (*de labore manuum*), agriculture and the raising of animals'.[17] St Francis saw a place for manual work in the daily régime of his friars, but from the beginning the Friars Preacher sacrificed it to the needs of study and preaching.

Of what did this work consist? There were a number of alternatives. The Cistercian statute quoted above suggests a certain amount of hard, physical labour in the fields and garden, but the White Monks, too, used the services of hired servants: the tasks of even the lay brethren were mostly managerial. Monks might be engaged in domestic tasks. In addition, those brethren with artistic or writing skills could be employed in the scriptorium in copying manuscripts and service books necessary for the performance of the liturgy, and charters and legal records, as well as decorating more sumptuous productions. An interesting case is immortalized in the muniments of Westminster Abbey: between 1124 and 1134 the abbot and prior wrote to the prior of Worcester to tell him that they were sending back a monk who had absconded from the priory of Great Malvern, one of their dependencies. They had been about to let him stay at the mother house, 'but he told us that he had begun a certain work for you, namely, a missal', and everyone now agreed he should complete it.[18] Monks with special talents as craftsmen – goldsmiths and carvers, for instance – could be usefully employed, and for many in a sizeable monastery 'manual work' meant the performance of managerial tasks necessary for the smooth running of a large corporation.[19] We perhaps come closest to understanding the type of activity which made up the work periods for most religious in the pages of the twelfth-century *Dialogue between the master and his disciple concerning the Rule of St Augustine on the life of clerics*. Here a canon of Bridlington Priory in Yorkshire, possibly its prior, Robert, gives us a list of the suitable occupations allocated to a canon by his superior for those periods when he was not in church. These are reading, explaining and preaching the Word of God (although he does not say whether this is in the cloister or in the parish); practising for divine worship; preparing parchment; writing, illuminating and correcting books; making and repairing clothes; making implements, such as wooden spoons and candlesticks, and weaving mats. Then come the outdoor pursuits: digging the garden, laying out beds and sowing seeds, pruning and grafting, weeding, ploughing, reaping and mowing.[20] There is a range of activities here; it shows us the monastic world at its most ordinary.

Silence

The monotony of the monastic routine must have been compounded by the long hours spent in silence. The *Regularis Concordia* appears to have allowed talking in work periods in the cloister, but it also suggests that the monks while at labour should recite the canon and the psalter. Lanfranc allowed silence to be broken, again in the cloister, between the daily chapter and sext.[21] The Institutes of the Gilbertine Order laid down that during the work periods while the nuns were occupied in tasks such as sewing, reading and copying manuscripts, they should sit in silence face-to-back to avoid communication. Gradually there came to be two recognized places in the monastic complex where talking was permitted: in the parlour which adjoined the chapter house (where the monks and officials talked) and near the superior's lodging, where the guests and the poor could converse with the monks, canons or nuns. The emphasis on solitude and contemplation in Carthusian houses meant that outside the services held in church, silence must have been all but total. The Rule of St Augustine laid down no precise injunctions on the question, and the customs which have survived suggest moderation. There was generally silence in the church, refectory and dormitory, but on other matters, such as the periods in which talking was allowed, local custom prevailed. The Bridlington author stated 'some prefer to use signs instead of words, some object to signs more than words, some employ a few fundamental signs'. There was evidently diversity within the one priory.

The daily chapter

Once a day the whole community of monks, canons or nuns met in the chapter house, so called because the proceedings usually began with the reading of a chapter of the Rule. The purpose of this assembly was to give opportunity for the confession of individual faults and their correction, and the discussion of business that concerned the house. Often it was a lively affair when the monks, released from their customary silence, could give vent to their opinions on matters great and small. It could be the scene of momentous events. It was in the chapter of St Mary's Abbey, York, one October day in 1132 that Archbishop Thurstan of York and abbots of neighbouring Black Monk houses heard the intense debate between two factions within the convent about their observances – and witnessed the ejection of the prior's party which had demanded reform. Less far-reaching in their effects, but no doubt of great concern at the time, were the disputes in the St Albans chapter between Abbot William of Trumpington and his monks on a variety of matters, including the abbot's alleged association with lay men and his practice of exiling monks to the abbey cells.[22] But for many monks the chapter and its investigations into personal behaviour and vocation must have been an ordeal. In one of his spiritual writings Adam of Dryburgh puts this answer into the mouth of one asked what troubled him most about the monastic life:

It is the chapter. There is too little love and tenderness in those sitting around, no pity or compassion whatever in the superior presiding, but there is very great discomfort and unrest in my heart as I sit there.[23]

Food

The Rule of St Benedict again anticipated the different demands which the summer and winter timetables placed on the monks. In winter, when sleep occupied eight hours of the day, only one meal was allowed, at about 2.00 p.m. In the summer two meals were taken, *prandium*, the main meal, at midday, and *cena* at 5.00 or 5.30 p.m. In the northern climate this was considered to be on the frugal side, so the *Regularis Concordia* added a drink (probably beer), to be taken in the evening in winter and in mid afternoon in summer. The thirteenth century witnessed attempts to allow two meals throughout winter. Meals generally consisted of bread, cheese, vegetables, beans and cereal, with pittances (extra dishes) of fish and eggs on special occasions.[24] The Benedictines and Cluniacs were frequently the target of criticism for their eating habits, and the Cistercians aimed to restore a more rigorous diet. There was a ban on the consumption of eggs and cheese during Lent and Advent, and monks were only allowed a coarse type of brown bread. Despite their austerity the early statutes allowed small pittances on occasion, but there is evidence that at least one convert, Waldef, former prior of Kirkham, found the diet one of many aspects of Cistercian life which was hard to take.[25]

Waldef had been an Augustinian canon, and at Kirkham may have enjoyed a more generous diet than even the Black Monks. Whereas it was assumed that for most monks meat would be prohibited – and the Premonstratensian canons followed the Cistercians in banning the use of meat and lard except in cases of severe illness – the evidence for the houses of Black Canons is more mixed. Gerald of Wales noted as a characteristic of the canons that they ate meat three times a week.[26] Partial abstinence seems to have been a popular compromise. Among the monks there came to be occasions when monks who were thought to need more fortifying food could partake of meat. One such circumstance would be illness, and Lanfranc allowed monks who were, or had been, sick to eat flesh. This leniency could be abused, and bishops during visitation sometimes had to lay down that those who pretended to be ill in order to be allowed meat should be punished.[27] Sick monks would have eaten meat in the infirmary, but a later development on many monastic sites was a separate room in the complex where the eating of meat was allowed. In addition, meat might be consumed at the abbot's table, where guests were entertained, and where from time to time monks were invited to join their superior. Before long, a third circumstance allowed monks to eat meat. This was after blood-letting, which was considered to be beneficial for the health, when a monk was thought to need meat in order to restore his strength. Lanfranc's constitutions clearly assumed that blood-letting would be an irregular occurrence, sought only by those who were sick. However, by the late twelfth century it had come to be a regular if infrequent event, like shaving and bathing, none of which were intended to be enjoyed. Despite injunctions to the contrary, blood-letting became a recreation to be anticipated with some pleasure, for meat-eating was not the only advantage. Those who had been let could miss the night office, have early meals and talk. It was a time when an astute brother could learn a lot. Jocelin of Brakelond, recording some opinions among the Bury monks as to who should be abbot, added:

I once saw Samson the subsacrist sitting in the kind of little groups that used to form at blood-letting time, when cloister monks would tell one another their private thoughts and discuss things together. I saw him sitting silently, smiling and noting what everyone else said, able to recall twenty years later some of the comments I have recorded above.[28]

THE GOVERNMENT OF A RELIGIOUS HOUSE AND ITS PERSONNEL

Abbots and priors

The abbot was the head of an independent house of Black Monks, and of a Cistercian and Premonstratensian house, and his second-in-command was the prior. One Cluniac house (Bermondsey) and a handful of Augustinian communities enjoyed the title of abbey, but all their other houses, as well as Benedictine dependencies, were designated priories; their head was a prior, who had as his deputy a sub-prior. The powers of an abbot and a prior of an independent priory were, within their own houses, the same. In the Rule of St Benedict, the abbot was simply *primus inter pares*, first among equals; he was chosen from among the community as a pastor to profess novices and administer the house. Though he was urged to take the advice of his monks, his authority was absolute. By our period the office of abbot had developed considerably. As we have seen, he could be involved in government; he could be sent abroad on royal business; he could be a major landowner. At the abbey he had responsibility for entertaining guests and so might mix on a social and political level with the influential and powerful. For these reasons medieval writers, though they praised piety and holiness in an abbot, frequently assumed that he had to be a man of business, and these qualities were seen as essential – ironically as much so as his pastoral duties.[29] The increasing demands on the head of a community had two implications for the office. First, more responsibility for the everyday oversight of administration was delegated to the prior or sub-prior. Second, the development was a factor in the gradual separation of the revenues of the abbot and convent, which took place at major abbeys at different times.

The Rule of St Benedict laid down that the abbot should be elected from among the community by the *maior et sanior pars*, the wise majority, which doubtless meant the more senior monks. However, the political and economic importance of the abbot meant that the king took more than a passing interest in who was elected to this high office, and the *Regularis Concordia* laid down that abbatial election was to be according to the Rule of St Benedict and with the consent of the king.[30] The practice of royal intervention by Edward the Confessor continued under the Conqueror and his sons, William II and Henry I, both of whom discovered that failing to appoint an abbot and thus enjoying the abbey revenues during the vacancy was a useful supplement to their own income. After the ending of the Investiture Conflict, when Henry I was forced to concede that he had no right to invest bishops and abbots with the symbols of their ecclesiastical office, it became the practice for monks to 'elect', in his presence, a candidate proposed by the king. With the weakening of royal authority under King Stephen, the church had a chance to assert its own rights, and this period coincided with the coming of the Cistercians. The new orders of the twelfth century were determined to avoid this kind of interference in their affairs. The statutes of the Cistercian Order, for instance, left no room for royal interference, and specified a free election, in the presence of the abbot of the mother house, by the monks, assisted by the abbots of any daughter houses. Documented cases seem to show that the White Monks managed to uphold their own independence and obtain the candidates of their choice. However, among Benedictine houses there was growing tension between the expectation of the king that he should influence the choice of an abbot, and the claim of a monastic community to free election.[31]

From the monastic writers of the twelfth and thirteenth centuries we have a number of descriptions of the process by which an abbot was elected. In 1180 following the death of Abbot Hugh of Bury St Edmunds the convent wrote to the king to inform him of the vacancy. One year and three months later the king wrote back to the convent, and under his instruction, the prior chose twelve monks to accompany him to the royal court; the thirteen were expected, in the royal presence, to agree on a candidate. The Bury monks did not consider this to be a free election, and decided on a middle course. Six of them were nominated by the convent, and they in secret chose three monks, whom they considered to be best qualified for the post of abbot. Their names were written down in secret and sealed, so that if the king were to allow the convent its free choice, the seal could be broken and the names revealed. When the thirteen appeared before the king, he agreed to a free election, but not before six other candidates were proposed. By gradual elimination one of the three original nominees, Samson the sacrist, was chosen.[32] Similar evidence from St Albans, Battle and Peterborough shows the emergence of the practice of election *per compromissum*, by a committee of electors chosen by the convent.[33]

The thirteenth century witnessed attempts by certain religious houses to secure elections which were free from interference, whether royal, papal, or from a lay patron. The best documented case comes again from Bury St Edmunds, where an account was written of the dispute surrounding the election of a successor for Abbot Samson, which occupied the years 1212–15. The matter split the convent into two factions, those who upheld the election of Abbot Hugh of Northwold, and those who advocated submitting to the pressure of King John, who refused to confirm the election.[34] How far the stand made by certain of the monks against the king was typical, or symptomatic of a movement towards free elections, is uncertain. For one thing, the episode is unusually well documented; for another, it occurred at a time when the king was under pressure, both from the church and as a result of baronial discontent. What is certain, however, is that after 1215 the kings of England gradually conceded the right of free election to the religious houses of their realm. This presents a contrast to Scotland, where the royal house seems to have retained control over abbatial appointments. Indeed, the fourteenth century witnessed rivalry between the kings of Scotland and the popes to secure positions of importance for their own nominees, and in practice free election in Scotland meant, not freedom from royal intervention, but rather 'royal nomination without papal interference'.[35]

The practice of royal intervention in elections, more particularly the regalian right of collecting the revenue of vacant abbeys, led to a significant development in the office of abbot, the gradual separation of the income of the abbot and monks. Religious houses as holders of land were part of the political, economic and social order. They were tenants-in-chief of the Crown, and this gave the Crown a right to administer abbey lands during a vacancy in the same way as it would a lay fief. Occasionally an abbot might be persuaded to pay a sum of money after his election – the equivalent of the lay entry fee or relief. This could come dangerously close to simony, the ecclesiastical sin of buying office. To a monarch such as William II the practice of keeping an abbey without a head in order to enjoy its revenues was not a strange concept. When Archbishop Anselm remonstrated with him, the king is alleged to have replied 'What business is it of yours? Aren't they my abbeys? You do what you want with your manors. Why can't I do what I want with my abbeys?'[36] There is an element of genuine surprise here. Therefore, in order to protect themselves and to minimize financial damage when an abbot had died or been removed from office, the monks began to divide the revenue of the house, a proportion for the abbot and the remainder for the convent. Only the abbot's portion now became subject to seizure by the king. This was a gradual process which can be traced from the reign of Henry I (1100–35), and it hastened the process by which the abbot came to have a distinct household.[37] The extent of this divergence worried the papal legates who from the thirteenth century visited English houses, and they attempted to set limits to the abbot's establishment. The growing apart of abbot and convent is also illustrated by the way in which the two issued charters or acquired property separately: at Westminster the formal division of estates did not come until 1225, but throughout the twelfth century the abbot and the prior and monks (sometimes just the monks) are shown by their charters to be acting independently.[38]

Abbesses, prioresses and the rule of female houses

Nunneries could have the status of abbey or priory, generally depending on their wealth and antiquity, and heads were therefore designated abbess or prioress. The process for election was much the same as in a male house, although the lesser status and importance of most female houses meant that they were more likely to enjoy an election free from royal intervention. A description of what was probably a fairly typical process survives from the nunnery of Nun Cotham in a memorandum of the election of Prioress Lucy in 1271.

First a mass of the Holy Spirit was celebrated. Then as the convent entered the choir the grace of the Holy Spirit was invoked and *Veni Creator Spiritus* was sung. Third, the convent entered the chapter house with great devotion and solemnity. The inquisitors were then chosen, [namely] the master of the house with two canons and four nuns, and they made everyone leave the chapter so that they alone remained. Then they individually examined the vote of each one, and questioned each other closely . . . that they should testify on the salvation of their souls, as to who would be most suitable and fit for the office of prioress; and they gave their votes to the said lady Lucy . . . [then] N. on behalf of the whole chapter [asked] if there was common consent among them all, or the greater and wiser part of them, [and declared]: I elect N. [Lucy] as prioress.[39]

At least one thirteenth-century bishop, Oliver Sutton of Lincoln (1280–99), took care to ensure that the procedures for election were followed correctly.[40]

The authority of the abbess or prioress was frequently circumscribed by the presence of a master or *custos*, a guardian to whom the bishop could grant charge of the temporalities of the nunnery, partly no doubt in order to preserve the seclusion of the prioress from the secular world. We have already seen these male masters in both Benedictine houses and those which became Cistercian, though they are less frequently documented from the middle of the thirteenth century onwards.[41] The extract from Nun Cotham quoted above indicates a position of some priority for the master, at least during a vacancy. The designation given to male guardians in Scottish Cistercian nunneries suggests that they enjoyed a certain amount of authority. At North Berwick we find mention of James, described on one occasion as master of the nuns and on another as prior. There was a master of the nuns at South Berwick, St Bothans, Haddington (where there was also a reference to a prior), Coldstream and Eccles. A charter of 1296 for Coldstream mentions, in this sequence, the master, prioress and nuns, and this may well reflect their descending importance in the hierarchy of the house.[42] The chaplains within nunneries may have had some authority, and it has been suggested that it was their own religious affiliations which influenced internal observances at female houses.[43] The group of influential English nunneries whose foundations date from before the Conquest rewarded their chaplains not with salaries but with prebends; they were canons of the nunneries holding property in the form of revenue from their appropriated churches.[44] Among the Gilbertines the power of the prioress was limited still further by the structure of the order. At its head, and a symbol of its unity, was the master. Next, scrutators oversaw the internal discipline of the houses, and in individual houses there were three prioresses who acted in rota. When one died a replacement had to be elected within fifteen days, or the master would impose his own choice. Women accordingly had some authority within individual houses and the order, but the organization was still one which recognized male superiority.[45]

The obedientiaries

Autocratic though Benedict's abbot was, even the saint recognized that authority would have to be delegated. The Rule mentions the presence, in the monastery, of a prior, deans to assist the abbot in the management of the affairs of the house, a cellarer, who had charge of provisioning it, and monks charged with the care of guests, novices, the infirmary and the kitchen. By the late Anglo-Saxon period in accordance with the Rule of St Benedict, there were below the abbot in the structure of command within the community a provost or prior, who was concerned with economic and external affairs, and deans, who took charge of internal discipline.[46] The growth in the size of religious houses and their endowments led to a more complex structure of organization, with the appointment, by the abbot, of obedientiaries, monks with special responsibilities. In a large abbey there may have been fifteen, and perhaps as many as twenty. The chief obedientiary was the prior or sub-prior, to whom general oversight of the monastery would be given. In Lanfranc's constitutions there was also a claustral prior, in charge of internal discipline. Among his other tasks, he had to watch the brethren leave the church after compline and then 'take a dark lantern if it be night and go through the crypt and other such parts of the church as may harbour irregularity, through the cloister, also, chapter-house and other offices, looking carefully to see that no brother remain there who should not'.[47] In his vigilance the claustral prior was aided by roundsmen who patrolled the monastery, noting any fault which would be denounced in chapter.

The sacrist was responsible for the security and cleanliness of the church, and the provision of the vessels for the altar. The precentor or precentrix had to make sure that there were available the correct number of liturgical books for the services, and with the succentor (succentrix) led the chant in church; and he or she generally also looked after the library. The novice-master or mistress prepared postulants for the taking of their vows, and the almoner distributed charity to the poor, sick and needy. This was an important function of the medieval religious house, and most almoners had a separate income which was used to care for both casual and long-term indigent, sometimes within the monastery or nunnery and sometimes outside. An almonry house was constructed at the abbeys of Abingdon and Evesham about 1125; and at Christ Church, Canterbury, it was the custom for the almoner to visit the poor and sick in their homes. Gerald of Wales stated that of all the Welsh Cistercians, the monks of Margam were most noted for their charitable works, and illustrated this point with the story of a miracle which occurred during a famine when a vast crowd of poor and needy had gathered outside the gates of the abbey and a boat had been sent by the monks to Bristol to buy corn to 'meet this demand on their charity'.[48] A number of obedientiaries were responsible for the material welfare of the monastic community, and chief among these was the cellarer (cellaress), who had charge of all the property, rents and revenues of the house, supervised the servants and, where they existed, the lay brothers and sisters, and bought supplies. The kitchener overlooked the preparation of meals, and the infirmarian cared for the sick. At Christ Church, Canterbury, the chamberlain provided garments, shoes and bedding and cleaned the dormitory once a year. The disadvantage of the obedientiary system was that it led to the fragmentation both of authority and financial management, particularly when a monastery lacked a strong abbot. Jocelin of Brakelond's chronicle of life at Bury St Edmunds gives us a vivid picture of the growth of power of the obedientiaries, especially the cellarer and the sacrist, their rivalries, and the problems caused by their control of the revenues of their office. The financial implications of the system, which will be considered in a later chapter, were very great.

The religious community: monks, canons, nuns and novices

We have few fixed points in the period 1000–1300 which enable us to say how large any monastic community was. Abingdon had a population of twenty-eight in 1100, which had grown to seventy-eight only seventeen years later. St Albans numbered fifty in 1190 and double that twenty years later. Bury St Edmunds had between seventy and eighty monks in 1213, and a northern house, Whitby, thirty-six in 1148. Around 1235 it was proposed that Coldingham Priory should increase to thirty monks and a prior, but by the early fourteenth century it had dropped to seven. The cathedral priory of Christ Church, Canterbury, housed one hundred monks in 1087, between 140 and 150 in c. 1125, and 140 in c. 1190. In the thirteenth century political and economic factors caused numbers to fluctuate: by 1207, in the aftermath of the long quarrels between the convent and two archbishops, Baldwin and Hubert Walter, numbers had fallen dramatically to seventy-seven; and in 1298, possibly in consequence of the support given by the monks to Archbishop Winchelsey against the king, there were fewer than thirty monks. At the very end of our period the convent was apparently beginning to increase once more, and by 1315 there were seventy-three monks.[49] Among the Cistercians, Rievaulx was at its height under Ailred, with 140 monks, but the more usual size for the larger Cistercian communities, like Rievaulx and Fountains, would have been between sixty and seventy. The more substantial Augustinian houses probably contained thirty or so canons, while smaller priories and nunneries probably struggled to maintain the apostolic number of twelve and a head which the Cistercians considered to be the minimum complement of a convent. It has been estimated that by the thirteenth century the total number of monks, canons, nuns, and members of the military orders was in the region of 18,000–20,000, or, at a rough calculation, one in every 150 of the population.[50]

Benedict assumed that there would be two kinds of novice: those of mature years who came seeking admission to the religious life; and those who, as children, were offered to a monastery by their parents. Here the oblates received their education along with other aristocratic children until at the age of seventeen they made their vows of poverty, conversion to the religious life and obedience. Some oblates, like Eve of Wilton and Orderic Vitalis, took to the religious life; others, like the nun of Watton, did not. One of the first groups to set their minds against this practice were the Cistercians, who insisted that fifteen should be the minimum age for a novice, and that no boys were to be taught at the monastery except novices.[51] The White Monks were closely followed in this attitude by the Carthusians. Their objection was not solely – as might at first appear – concern for the child and his or her freedom of choice, but also that the presence of children was a disruptive influence within the cloister. In Benedictine abbeys, too, oblates were already being restricted. Under their combined pressure, the class of oblate disappeared during the twelfth century, until by its close seventeen to nineteen years became the usual minimum age for a postulant, who then undertook the year-long noviciate prescribed by the Rule.[52] The class of oblate was officially abolished at the Fourth Lateran Council of 1215. Literate adults, clerical and lay, came to be the usual recruit. However, a religious vocation of itself did not guarantee acceptance within a monastery or nunnery. A poorly endowed house would not be able to maintain a large convent, and a lack of resources could mean that an abbey had only two or three vacancies for novices each year. It was a delicate task to balance the intake of recruits with the material means for their upkeep.

A Cistercian novice: St Ailred

Ailred of Rievaulx was no ordinary monk, but the account of his entry into a Cistercian monastery as a novice is not so exceptional, and contains details worthy of note as describing common practice. Ailred was the son of a hereditary priest of Hexham, Eilaf, who had been supplanted by the Augustinian canons installed in the ancient church by Archbishop Thomas II of York. His upbringing shows us how close were the contacts between the north of England and Scotland, for young Ailred became steward to that noted monastic founder, King David I. By the time he was sent on the king's business to York (c. 1134) Ailred had already thought of becoming a monk. He had, moreover, heard of the coming of the Cistercians to the North, and decided to visit Rievaulx Abbey, founded about three years before. When his mission was over he stayed at Helmsley Castle, seat of Rievaulx's founder, Walter Espec, before next day setting out for Scotland. He could not resist a second visit to the abbey, and here he was met once more by the prior, the guest-master, the gate-keeper and a number of monks. Having decided to become a monk he gave up all his goods and for four days was kept in the guest house to test his purpose. After that he was examined by the whole convent as to his vocation and was then allowed to proceed to the novice-house or *probatorium*, where he spent a year before making his written profession:

before the altar in the church in the presence of all, as the blessed Benedict commands. There he is vested with the sacred robe, that is the habit sanctified by the abbot's blessing, and henceforth is regarded as a member of the monastic body.[53]

The personal qualities of Ailred ensured that he would not remain a simple monk, and he went on to be novice-master at Rievaulx (1142–3), first abbot of Revesby (1143–7), and then abbot of Rievaulx until his death in 1167. The story of his entry into Rievaulx, however, is instructive. It was conducted according to the letter of the Rule. Although a recent commentator on Ailred's conversion has argued that he received special attention – the 'extravagant' welcoming party, and the fact that he was not kept waiting at the gate for four days to test his purpose, as the Rule required, but allowed to retire to the guest house – and that his entry was smoothed by King David I and Archbishop Thurstan,[54] nevertheless it remains clear that there were no shortcuts, even for one so exalted.

Ailred is one of only a small group of men who entered the religious life whose social origins can be discovered: generally, the evidence we have allows us to identify only a handful of those who became monks, canons and nuns in the religious houses of Britain. But what we have suggests that a number – perhaps a considerable number – were drawn from the baronial and knightly class, or from among the burgesses of the towns. They were either literate or well-born or both.[55] We cannot claim that all monks and canons were educated, well-connected men, or that all nuns were high-born, but there is sufficient evidence to suggest that the monastic life in the twelfth century appealed to this type of novice, and was a respectable alternative to life within the world. There are numerous examples of important clergy as well as laity attracted to the monastic life, such as the dean and canon of York Minster, who entered Fountains in the 1130s and saved it from near extinction. Our examination of recruitment by the friars revealed entry by a wide spectrum of persons, including noted scholars. Ailred had been to school in Hexham and Durham. His great friend from his days in Scotland, Waldef, was educated at the court of his stepfather, King David I. Waldef chose the path of the Augustinians, becoming a canon of Nostell, and, at about the time Ailred entered Rievaulx, he was prior of the Espec foundation of Kirkham. Not without some backward glances Waldef converted to the Cistercian way of life and became abbot of King David I's foundation of Melrose, a daughter house of Rievaulx. Here indeed is a tight web of patronage and kinship.[56]

Welsh novices

The pattern of the noviciate among the Welsh houses is complicated by the tendency to fragment along political lines; monastic houses were either Welsh (notably the Cistercian houses of the North and West) or Anglo-Norman/English (the Cistercian houses of the South, and the Augustinian and Benedictine priories). The analysis by F. G. Cowley has suggested that the former never attracted English entrants and the latter failed to find Welsh ones. The alien cells of the South were staffed, from what we can tell, by monks from the mother house, either French or English, although there was the odd exception: Iestin ap Gwrgant, prince of Glamorgan from 1081, was deposed and entered the priory of Llangenydd, a dependency of St Taurin, Evreux.[57] The seven conventual priories may have had some local recruits drawn from those connected with Anglo-Norman patrons and the sons of burgesses of Brecon, Monmouth and so on. They tended to be small houses, rarely (apart from Ewenni) reaching the figure of thirteen inmates. Only Goldcliff, the richest of the Welsh Benedictine priories, exceeded this number, reaching twenty-five in 1295. Even this was thought to be beyond its resources, and in the following two years ten monks were removed.[58] The Augustinians, having no constitutional ties with English houses, recruited locally, but their composition was related to the realities of political power. Thus Carmarthen Priory was for a time in the early thirteenth century a Welsh house with a Welsh prior, but after the resurgence of English royal power under Henry III it became once more a house dominated by the English.

A complete contrast is presented by the Cistercians of north and west Wales, Welsh Wales. From what we can tell they drew their recruits from the sons of married priests (for example, Cadwgan, monk of Strata Florida and later abbot of Whitland) or from the leading Welsh families. David Williams has drawn our attention to a list of monks from Valle Crucis Abbey in 1275 which shows them all to have been Welsh; two-thirds of known monks of Aberconwy and the majority of those of Strata Florida and Llantarnam also have Welsh names. However, the question of the racial origin of the monks of Welsh religious houses cannot be over-simplified. The names of the 750 or so monks which are known to us range over a long period and are not evenly spread among monasteries. Moreover, the concentration of monks of undoubted Welsh origin in certain houses may have been simply the result of intensely local recruitment, rather than an indication of political or cultural loyalties. At least one northern house, Basingwerk, which lay near the Dee estuary, shows little evidence of Welshness, and indeed drew many of its novices from the Chester area. Like Margam Abbey in south Wales, Basingwerk apparently attracted entrants from a wider geographical area than some of the other houses.[59] Despite these reservations, however, the evidence indicates that until the Edwardian Conquest the majority of religious houses of north Wales were overwhelmingly Welsh in their recruitment, and that even after the 1280s the Celtic element remained dominant.

This raises a question of wider application: how much is it possible to know about the localities from which religious houses recruited? This is a notoriously difficult question to answer, since so few lists of monks, canons and nuns have survived. However, we may suggest that, allowing for the particular appeal of celebrated houses at certain times in their history, many religious houses may have recruited locally. The chronicle of the election of Abbot Hugh of Bury St Edmunds, mentioned earlier in this chapter, allows us to identify the geographical origins of a number of its monks. It has been suggested that, out of a total of seventy-one monks, forty-four or forty-five either have surnames which identify their place of origin, or can be located using other evidence. These locations are widely scattered geographically – one monk evidently came from Wales and another, possibly, from Scotland. However, the vast majority hailed from Norfolk and Suffolk, the 'heartland of the cult of St Edmund'.[60] Bury was a prestigious house, and its celebrity may well have drawn recruits from further afield. What we know of more modest houses, and certainly of the small, post-Conquest nunneries, suggests that their intake was intensely local, thus cementing their place within the fabric of society.[61]

Lay brothers and sisters

The new orders of the eleventh and twelfth centuries owed some of their success to their incorporation into the community of a group who fell midway between the professed religious and the laity. The word *conversus* (*conversa*), once applied to an adult convert to the religious life, now described one who was not a monk or nun, yet was still under vows and a full member of the community. As we have seen, it was the Cistercian Order which first realized the potential of the lay brothers as an essential part of the administration of their abbeys and granges, but they were to be found, too, among the Carthusians and, with their female equivalents, among the Gilbertines and in nunneries which were described as Cistercian. In the twelfth century, lay brothers/sisters may well have outnumbered professed monks and nuns; certainly they did at Rievaulx, where the relative numbers during the time of Ailred (1147–67) were 140 (monks) and 500 (*conversi*). Their own accommodation was a distinctive feature of the architectural arrangements of the Cistercian, Carthusian and Gilbertine houses.

Lay folk within the house

Every monastery or nunnery would have contained a number of lay people: servants, guests and more permanent residents. A sizeable community would have required an army of servants to help with the agricultural and domestic tasks. Indeed, there were probably twice as many servants as monks, canons or nuns, except in Cistercian houses, where some manual work would have been undertaken by lay brethren, and Gilbertine houses, where there were lay sisters to undertake the preparation of food, cleaning, and other domestic duties as well as to serve female guests. Monastic servants performed all kinds of work necessary for the smooth running of a large establishment. Sometimes they make their appearance as witnesses to charters or in accounts. At Westminster the allowances from abbey income included portions set aside for the servants of the bakery, brewery, infirmary, kitchen, yard and vineyard, and other documents mention the servants, or serjeants of the almonry, buttery, sacristy and vestibule. Some of the more prestigious lay offices could become hereditary: in 1209, for instance, Nicholas son of Geoffrey granted to Robert of Croxley and his heirs his office of summoner in Westminster Abbey, for twelve years. For this Robert paid 50s., and £5 when the grant was made permanent.[62] At Shrewsbury each abbey servant had an allowance for the support of his horse as well as himself.[63]

St Benedict had laid on his monks an obligation and a duty to provide hospitality; thus guests were also a permanent feature of life in a monastery, especially those which lay in urban centres or, like St Albans, on major routes, or where relics and shrines attracted large numbers of pilgrims. Guests, who were usually entertained at the abbot's table, might bring with them a retinue of servants and followers who also had to be accommodated and horses to be stabled. Jocelin describes for us the custom at Bury: the abbot received all guests, whatever their status, except monks and clerics. If the abbot was not at home, the guests were to be received by the cellarer, and the maximum number of horses they were to bring was thirteen; if they brought more than this number, the remainder were to be charged to the expense of the abbot. The cellarer entertained all clerical guests, including bishops, and the expense fell on the convent unless the abbot chose to invite selected guests to his own table. However, there could evidently be some divergence from this practice, for when the archbishop of Norway visited Bury during the period after the death of Abbot Hugh (1181) he stayed in the abbot's lodging, and the king, out of the revenue he was enjoying as a result of the vacancy, made him an allowance of 10s. a day.[64]

In addition to guests and pilgrims, there was in many abbeys and priories a special class of lay folk known as corrodians, composed of a variety of persons. They could be monastic servants, provided with a corrody, that is, board and lodging, as a supplement to their wages, or with similar maintenance after their retirement. Corrodians could also be former officials and servants of the Crown, imposed on the house by a king eager to reward past service; royal grants of monastic corrodies became increasingly common – and often burdensome – during the thirteenth century. Corrodies could also be purchased by lay persons. Perhaps for a sum of money, more frequently for the transfer of a parcel of land, a monastery or nunnery would undertake to provide board and lodging for the rest of the grantor's life. One example, from Shrewsbury, will suffice to illustrate this practice. In 1272 the abbot reached an agreement with Adam of Bispham and his wife, by which each day for the rest of their lives they were to receive two loaves from the convent, three gallons of ale 'of the better sort', one dish of food from the abbot's table, and when he was at home, two; their servant and maid were to have two of the loaves allotted to abbey servants, two gallons of less good ale, and one of the servants' dishes; each year Adam was to receive a robe, like those worn by the more important of the abbey servants, and his wife 10s. to purchase a gown; Adam was to receive the same allowance towards a horse as an abbey servant; in addition they were to have, for the rest of their lives, the house which was formerly given to Stephen de Stanleg and his wife, and when one of them died, the corrody was to be reduced by a half. For all this, the two promised their movable goods to the abbey after their death.[65] It can be seen that corrodies posed an even greater potential burden than hospitality on the resources of a house, particularly one meagrely endowed. Bishops' registers of the thirteenth century warn the religious orders to be circumspect. Often those who could least afford it fell into the trap of accepting ready money to eke out poor finances, only to find themselves supporting a corrodian, and maybe his family and servants, for years to come.

MONASTIC DISCIPLINE

The White Monks and their emulators

Within all religious houses there existed some way of detecting and correcting faults, both in the regular confession by individuals, privately and in chapter, and in the activities of the claustral prior of Christ Church, Canterbury and his roundsmen and their counterparts elsewhere. The White Monks took things a step further, and one of their great achievements, adopted and adapted by their emulators, was the creation of a machinery for the maintenance of monastic discipline. Not content to lay down the rules and regulations for observance, they made sure that these could be enforced by the dual method of annual visitation of each house by the abbot of its mother house, and the attendance of all abbots of the order at the general chapter of Cîteaux. The latter became the forum for the disciplining of abbots, discussion of decisions affecting the order as a whole, and passing legislation. How far were these obligations met? The evidence does not allow us to say for certain with what degree of diligence the British abbots attended the general chapter; there are, for instance, no records of attendance. Clearly to be present at the general chapter would have taken them away from their houses for a considerable period. The abbot of Basingwerk in north Wales would have needed to allow five weeks for the return journey – about a week longer than his counterpart at Tintern.[66] Added to the time the journey took there was the expense, which would have made quite an impact on the finances of some of the smaller and poorer houses of the order. From 1157 the

Scottish abbots, few in number, received permission to attend only every four years.[67] Although a petition was sent by the Welsh abbots in 1209 asking that one representative alone might be allowed to attend, this request was denied, and throughout our period it was assumed that the abbots of all English and Welsh houses would be there. Not until 1305 were they required to attend only every second year.

Abbots can be assumed to have been at the chapter when they were the recipients of commissions to investigate matters or when they themselves were involved in a dispute. Roger of Byland was there in 1149 when the issue of the filiation of Jervaulx was decided, and it was doubtless also in the chapter that Ailred of Rievaulx, to whom the case of Byland against Furness was delegated, delivered his judgement in the presence of a good many British abbots.[68] On the other hand, some evidence for non-attendance derives from the records of the general chapter. In 1190 the abbots of Quarr and Stanley did not appear and were placed by the chapter on punishment for three days. In 1195 the abbots of Combermere and Rievaulx failed to attend, and in 1198 those of Ford and Furness. The evidence has been variously interpreted. Knowles considered that in the twelfth century attendance was at an acceptable level, while more recently Hill claims to detect a serious falling-off of attendance, in which the Savigniac abbots were the worst offenders.[69] While the nature of the records means that our knowledge is incomplete, it has to be said that, bearing in mind the number of English and Welsh houses by 1200 (over eighty), there is no evidence of serious neglect. Circumstances in the thirteenth century were perhaps a little more difficult. Petitions to be excused were made by Neath in 1267, Margam in 1271, Whitland in 1278, and Tintern, Strata Florida, Caerleon and Strata Marcella in 1281. The difficulty of attendance in the latter year may well have been connected with the Edwardian conquest of Wales.[70] The British abbots as a whole had trouble in attending during the last years of the thirteenth century. In 1298 King Edward I forbade any Cistercian abbot to go to the chapter, or to send money. For some time the considerable expense for Cîteaux in accommodating several hundred abbots and attendants had been offset by a contribution levied on each abbey. It was the sending abroad of funds which might fall into the hands of his enemies, as much as the attendance at chapter, which concerned the king. Edward repeated his prohibition on a number of occasions, but this did not end all contact; individual abbots were able to obtain royal permission to attend, but a limit was placed on their expenses.[71]

The faults of individual abbots and communities could be reported to chapter, and action taken. Thus visitors sent in 1188 by the general chapter deposed the abbots of Tintern, Bordesley and Dore; in 1195 they removed the abbot of Garendon and in 1199 another head of Bordesley.[72] Another problem which emerges from the records of the general chapter is that from the late twelfth century onwards the order as a whole was having trouble with its lay brethren. In 1196 the abbot of Whitland was ordered to investigate problems in his daughter house of Strata Florida caused by the *conversi*, and in 1206 there were serious problems at Margam. Two conflicting accounts exist; the official one blamed the lay brethren for 'conspiracy', pursuing the abbot, barricading themselves in their dormitory and refusing food to the monks. However, Gerald of Wales, though his testimony is not unbiased, lays the blame firmly at the door of the abbot.[73] The problem of lack of discipline among the lay brethren was not confined to Wales, for at Garendon the lay brethren attacked and wounded the new abbot, Reginald, while he was in the infirmary. The motive for their assault may have been the abbot's attempts to get to grips with a problem which had plagued his predecessor, namely excessive beer-drinking among the lay brethren. As a result of the incident the chapter ordered the *conversi* to be sent to other monasteries throughout the country.[74] What we see here are localized instances of more general dissatisfaction among the Cistercian lay brothers about their standing within the order.

Equally hard to determine is the evidence for visitation, for which there are no systematic records. What is certain is that in the years of great expansion the burden which this obligation imposed must have been intolerable, if not impossible, for the major mother houses of Waverley, Fountains and Rievaulx, to say nothing of the continental mothers, Clairvaux and Savigny. The problem was addressed by the *Carta Caritatis Posterior* (a form of the *Carta Caritatis* which came into existence between 1165 and 1190), which allowed an abbot to appoint another as proxy to visit in his stead. Surviving references suggest that visitations may have come to be associated with particular problems encountered by a daughter house. In the mid 1160s Ailred visited Dundrennan 'to visit and comfort' the house, and in the same sentence Walter Daniel speaks of a war raging in the area.[75] In emulation of the system created by the White Monks, the Premonstratensians, the Gilbertines and the mendicants all incorporated elements of the chapter and visitation. In the Gilbertine hierarchy, directly below the master were three male scrutators (two canons and one lay brother) who visited each house once a year, and three female scrutators (two nuns and one lay sister) who visited all female houses; there were also scrutators of the cloister responsible for the detection of day-to-day faults. The only check on the power of the master was the annual general chapter which comprised all six scrutators, the general confessor, the prior and cellarer of each monastery and two prioresses from each house. These, together with a third nun, canon and lay sister from each house, were entrusted with the election of four canons, who in turn chose nine more to help select a new master.[76]

The Benedictines and Augustinians and the introduction of provincial chapters

The Lateran Council of 1215 ushered in an era of monastic reform. It put an end to the proliferation of new orders and recognized the existence of the friars. Moreover it tackled the problems posed by the autonomy of the houses of Black Monks and Black Canons: in particular, the bull *In Singulis Regnis* established the principle of three-yearly meetings of heads of houses, modelled on the Cistercian general chapter. In England there were to be meetings in the northern and southern provinces. In the South the opening meeting was at Oxford in 1218 under the presidency of the abbots of Bury St Edmunds and St Albans, assisted by the Cistercian abbots of Thame and Warden. The northern provincial chapter met first at Northallerton in 1221. Both tackled matters such as the limitation of abbatial expenses, the prohibition of private possessions by monks, and dietary regulations. On the whole, however, we have little record of any further activities for many years.[77] There were similar developments among the Augustinian canons. A provincial chapter was held at Leicester in 1216 under the auspices of two Premonstratensians from Welbeck and Croxton. A further chapter was held at Bedford, probably in 1220; thereafter the northern and southern provinces met separately.[78] For the northern province we have a fairly complete set of decisions of the chapters from 1223 to 1302.[79] The difficulties faced by the abbots and priors acting in chapter are amply demonstrated by the attempt to distil the customaries of all the houses into a single code. In 1265 when the chapter met at Worksop, a resolution was passed that representatives from seven leading houses should meet at Drax with a written record of the customs of all houses; from these the best were to be selected. The *Statuta de Parco*, taking their name from the Yorkshire house of Healaugh Park, were probably drawn up soon afterwards. However, they were not accepted by all, and still in 1288 protests were being heard against this effort to enforce universal observance over local custom. One argument raised was that the chapter had exceeded its powers and ought to confine itself to matters to do with the observance of the Rule of St Augustine.[80]

Episcopal visitation

Throughout the period before 1215 a bishop had enjoyed, in canon law, the right to visit the religious houses of his dioceses; and we have isolated instances in the eleventh and twelfth centuries of a bishop intervening in their affairs. There were several exceptions, however, to the bishops' right to visit. They were excluded from visitation of the houses of the 'exempt' orders, that is, the Cistercians, Premonstratensians and Gilbertines, of the Cluniacs, who were directly under the authority of the pope, and individual Benedictine houses which had secured the rights of exemption. By 1215 these were St Albans, St Augustine's, Canterbury, Battle, Westminster, Bury St Edmunds, Malmesbury and Evesham.[81] However, it was not until the thirteenth century that episcopal intervention became formalized: in particular the twelfth decree of the Lateran Council of 1215 ordered bishops to make strenuous attempts to improve the monastic houses of their dioceses. From 1215 the right of visitation was accordingly sharpened, and became, moreover, a visible symbol of episcopal power to reform.[82] From the mid thirteenth century onwards episcopal visitations became common, their records being particularly fruitful among the registers of the northern metropolitan, York. When studying the evidence of visitation, however, we must remember its limitations. The geographical extent of many English dioceses – notably Lincoln and York – meant that visitation could be a difficult and time-consuming exercise, and few houses were visited regularly.[83] Moreover, by the very nature of the occasion a bishop made note of the bad rather than the good or the ordinary (although in isolated cases a house might receive a 'gold star' for achievement, as the Augustinian priory of Newstead did in 1252). The visitation process was designed to root out faults, great and small. One example must suffice to demonstrate its nature and process.

The visitations of Archbishop Wickwane, 1280–1[84]

In 1280 and 1281 over a period of just a few months, Archbishop Wickwane of York (1279–85) visited twenty-three religious houses in his large diocese, and appointed delegates to investigate three others on his behalf. The injunctions which he issued after each visitation reveal his meticulous concern for every aspect of monastic observance. At four houses all was well: there was no need for action at Whitby, St Mary's, York, Warter and Nostell 'because they conduct themselves well in all things'. Elsewhere there are repeated instructions which betray some common problems, not all of them serious and most to be expected in small, closely knit communities. One frequent suspicion was that monks, canons and nuns were in possession of private property, in contravention of the Rule. Sometimes, as at Nun Appleton, a general prohibition against private possessions was made; on other occasions specific instructions were laid down. The priors of Newburgh and Worksop were charged with the inspection of chests and carrels (individual workrooms around the cloister) and with breaking open locks four times a year to see that no private possessions were being kept; the prior of Healaugh Park was to see that his canons received only gifts of clothes and shoes and not money. There is evidence at Newburgh, Bolton and Kirkham that the canons were not attentive at the services, and were inclined to rush through the chant in an undignified manner. The rule of silence was not being maintained at Worksop and Healaugh Park and, in the latter, rules about the eating of meat were not being observed. Wickwane was clearly worried about the way canons and monks were associating with guests, or leaving the house without permission. The canons of Newburgh were ordered not to wander around the cloister after compline in search of food and drink, either to consume alone or with guests; no woman was to be admitted into the house, with a single exception – the wife of the patron was allowed to stay for one night only; there was to be no hunting or other expeditions from the house. The canons of Healaugh Park were warned against allowing women to stay, and against going out after compline; canons of Bolton who went out without special permission were to be put on bread and water for a day. The nuns of Nun Appleton were not to leave the house or receive strangers in the refectory and cloister. Wickwane realized that some absences from the house were legitimate, but he was still concerned about their possible dangers, and at Thurgarton he stated that no canon was to be away for more than two weeks. The injunctions showed a number of houses in a state of poverty and warned against the granting of corrodies (Healaugh Park, Drax, Worksop), the entertaining of expensive guests (Worksop) and the reception of more novices (Bridlington). They also laid down stricter rules for financial management (Newburgh, Healaugh Park, Bolton, Nun Appleton).

Several visitations made complaints about individuals. A canon of Bolton was sent to undergo penance at Hexham. The sub-prior of Drax was deposed because he was ill-tempered, made no attempt to get on with his fellow canons, and was too fond of staying in bed. At the same house it was ordered that Hugh of Ricall, a quarrelsome canon, was not to hold office. Elias, the sub-cellarer, was too much inclined to wander off, and was ordered to stay in the church and the cloister. But by far the most serious problems were found at Selby, where the visitation revealed a veritable catalogue of faults in the abbot. He did not observe the Rule of St Benedict, did not sing mass, preach, instruct, attend chapter or correct faults. He rarely ate in the refectory, never slept in the dormitory, was hardly ever out of bed in time for matins, and ate meat in the company of lay men both on the abbey manors and in the monastery itself. He treated the monks badly, was contentious, alienated abbey property without consent and in so doing had caused considerable financial losses. He appointed favourites as obedientaries and to oversee manors, men who were unsuitable to the task. He stood accused of immoral behaviour with a local woman and with the daughter of a man called Bodeman who resided by the abbey gate; the second woman was alleged to have had the abbot's child. He was not just immoral: he was violent, and had attacked William of York, William of Stormworth, whom he threw out of chapter, and a clerk named Thomas of Snaith. Finally, and the most bizarre accusation, he had spent a great deal of money on employing a sorcerer to locate the body of his brother, who had drowned in the river Ouse. Abbot Thomas was deposed and sent to Durham to undergo penance.

The time period spanned by this study is a wide one, and in 1300 we are far removed from the forty or so houses of Anglo-Saxon England, autonomous, bound by a common rule, but following local custom too. Few generalizations can be made, but we may ask how distinctive the houses of different orders and congregations were perceived to be, in their daily life and observances. It has already been suggested that to an outsider the divergences might not have seemed great. What were the everyday differences between a small Cistercian abbey and a Premonstratensian house? Or between a modest house of Black Monks and one of Black Canons? Or a Cistercian and a Benedictine nunnery? We can suggest that at the close of our period the divergences were less. The White Monks and Canons were perhaps, through political pressure, loosening their ties with France. By their constitutional developments the Black Monks and Canons were moving closer to the White. In the twelfth century, to be sure, differences were perceived, even if some were becoming stereotyped. Gerald of Wales for one was quite certain that 'Augustinian canons are more content than any of the others with a humble and modest mode of life'.[85] He could distinguish the Cluniacs and the Cistercians and be clear, in his own mind, of their faults and their good points.[86] Although he wrote in a satirical mode not uncommon in the twelfth century, Gerald was an exceptional observer. He was a natural story teller, had an eye for description, and was well travelled among the religious houses of Wales. He also had old scores to settle which naturally coloured his tales. Nevertheless, there are occasions when his observations harmonize with those of others. His description of the moderation of the life of the regular canons surely recalls, in a quite different tone, the life of Waldef, the saintly Augustinian who, having converted to be a Cistercian, found the harshness of the way of life, the dullness of the food, the monotony of the services and the exacting manual work almost more than he could bear.

9

LEARNING AND LITERARY ACTIVITIES

ATTITUDES TO LEARNING

The Rule of St Benedict envisaged that a certain amount of each day not spent in the performance of the divine office or in manual labour would be devoted to reading and meditation, *lectio divina*; and at the beginning of Lent monks were to be given a book from the library for their personal study.[1] Scholars have long debated what Benedict meant by *lectio divina*, and how far his monks were meant to engage in intellectual and literary activities beyond the contemplation of monastic and Christian classics such as those named at the conclusion of the Rule.[2] Whatever his intention, by the beginning of our period the monasteries of western Europe were the channels through which both classical and Christian learning were diffused. Reading was important, therefore, because it was prescribed by the Rule; but it had an added significance in that it was a part of the transmission of eternal values in a society which felt a constant longing for and need to preserve the past. As well as reading, it was under-stood that those with talent would be allowed to engage in writing, and this had become an accepted and acceptable form of manual labour. Learning was not, however, encouraged for its own sake, but as a means to an end: to aid understanding of the Scriptures and pursuit of knowl-edge of God.[3] The Cistercians were anxious to redress the imbalance, as they interpreted it, caused by the excessive emphasis on the liturgy at Cluny and by the rejection of manual labour. They did not forbid literary activities completely but tried to control them by ruling that no one should write a book without first seeking the permission of the general chapter. Individual Cistercians, however, were sometimes encouraged to write: Ailred of Rievaulx was asked to compose the *Speculum Caritatis* by St Bernard, himself a prolific author. It is not possible to say with any degree of certainty how far the statute was obeyed, but in the 1170s we find Baldwin of Ford complying by asking permission to compose the treatise *De Commendatione Fidei*.[4] Moreover, the commissioning of certain works by Cistercian abbots, such as the biblical commentaries of Robert of Bridlington, undertaken at the request of Abbot Gervase of Louth Park, and the *Historia Rerum Anglicarum* of William, canon of Newburgh, urged by Abbot Ernald of Rievaulx because his own monks were not allowed to write, suggests a strict adherence to the ruling of the order. There was no official Augustinian policy towards learning, but the adaptability of the Rule of St Augustine meant that literary activities were possible within its framework; and the British houses produced some distinguished writers. The Premonstratensians did not have any great intellectual ambitions, and although they were not restricted by statute as the Cistercians were, the British Premonstratensians boasted no intellectuals of note and no writers except for Adam of Dryburgh. Similarly within our period the Gilbertines failed to produce any literary works, and few names have been associated with nunneries.[5] With the coming of the friars emerged a totally new concept of the place of learning within the monastic framework. The Dominicans were a self-consciously learned order, and the original Franciscan distrust of intellectual activity was soon lost as they too cultivated a scholarly basis for their preaching activities. Education became central to their training.

EDUCATION INSIDE AND OUTSIDE THE CLOISTER

It would have been assumed that those who took monastic vows had enjoyed a certain amount of basic education, and would have been able to read the Latin texts they needed to know in order to recite the divine office. In the monasteries and nunneries of Anglo-Saxon England, and in the Benedictine houses of the Norman era, education was provided within the monastery for both oblates and for outsiders.[6] However, as the practice of receiving oblates disappeared, there was less need for the education of young children, certainly those who were intended for the cloister. Monasteries, like cathedral, collegiate and the Welsh *clas* schools, continued to provide some basic education for non-oblates – the Beaumont twins, for example, learnt their letters, philosophy and knowledge of the Scriptures at Abingdon[7] – but such cases were not common, and education for the laity was more likely to be provided at schools run under the auspices of the religious houses and staffed by secular masters, rather than at the monasteries themselves. Within the cloister there was still a need to provide education for novices, but the subjects taught were restricted. Only two of the three components of the Trivium, grammar and rhetoric, were pursued, and of the Quadrivium, only music was really appropriate to the cloister. The type of studies which generally flourished, therefore, tended to be literary and historical rather than scientific or legal.[8]

The entry of learned men into religious houses as adults was bound to affect the intellectual character of each house, perhaps give it academic distinction, albeit temporarily. Individuals whom we know to have pursued their studies or to have achieved a reputation for learning before they made their monastic profession include Alexander Neckham, educated at the school at St Albans and then in Paris, later a master at a school in Dunstable and then teacher of theology at Oxford, who in 1197 became abbot of the Augustinian house of Cirencester. Samson of Bury St Edmunds, so Jocelin tells us, was 'well-versed in the liberal arts and the scriptures, a cultured man who had been at university, and had been a well-known and highly regarded schoolmaster in his own region', but he was untutored in canon law, and therefore surprised to receive a commission as a papal judge-delegate. Master Warin, abbot of St Albans (1183–95), had been a student at Salerno, and his successor, John de Cella (1195–1214), had studied at Paris. Thomas of Marlborough, abbot of Evesham (1229–36), was a pupil of Stephen Langton in Paris, and before entering the religious life had taught law at Exeter and Oxford.[9] Men such as these provided a vital link between the learning of the schools and the monasteries. However, not all scholars carried on with their studies, and some evidently deliberately eschewed their former pursuits, possibly as a sign of their conversion.[10]

The need for a high standard of learning among their preachers meant that the mendicant orders placed great emphasis on education. The Dominicans expected each priory to have its own school for the basic study of theology, and the Oxford school opened soon after the foundation of the priory in 1221. They allowed a certain proportion of the more academically able friars to go on to a *studium artium*, a regional school attended by the brethren of a group of priories, where logic was studied for two years; from there they might proceed to a *studium particulare* (provincial school) or a *studium generale* for the advanced study of theology. Oxford had, somewhat reluctantly, accepted its status as a *studium generale* by 1261. The Franciscan educational system developed along similar, though less well-documented, lines. The connection between the mendicants and the University of Oxford began within years of the arrival of the friars. Robert Bacon, a regent master of the university, joined the Dominicans (probably in 1229 or 1230), and in 1229 Agnellus of Pisa built a school at the Oxford Franciscan friary and invited the distinguished theologian Robert Grosseteste to lecture there, which he continued to do until his election to the see of Lincoln in 1235. The Franciscans were taught by three other eminent secular masters, and acquired their first regent master in 1247 in the person of Adam Marsh.

The Franciscans, like the Dominicans, accordingly developed an impressive international system of education, but not without moments of tension between them and the universities. The mendicants' *studium generale* was a place for the study of theology, and they restricted the study of arts to their own schools. This led to a conflict within the university, whose authorities required a student to graduate in arts before proceeding to a degree in theology. The tension, increased perhaps by the growing eminence of the friars in the field of theology, reached its height in 1253, when the Franciscans put forward Thomas of York to be regent. The university objected that he had not graduated in arts, and refused to allow the promotion. The issue was resolved by the granting of a dispensation for Thomas to incept in theology; and the episode did not result, as did a similar contemporary attempt to restrict the freedom of the friars at the University of Paris, in a breakdown of relations between the mendicants and the university authorities. At Oxford, however, the friars were forced to comply with university regulations, and it became normal practice for a friar who wished to incept in theology to apply for a personal dispensation.[11]

During the course of the thirteenth century the friars became dominant in the study of theology at the universities, and their importance in this field of study was acknowledged: in 1275, for example, the cathedral school at Canterbury appointed a Franciscan to lecture in theology. Before the end of the thirteenth century there was no corporate move by the monastic orders to participate in university education; to do so would threaten to undermine the monastic linchpin of stability. Monks were either educated to university level before their entry into the religious life; or, like the brethren of Christ Church, Canterbury, they attended lectures within the monastery. Evidence for the attendance of individual monks and canons at university in the twelfth and first three quarters of the thirteenth century is sketchy, but it seems likely that canons of the two Augustinian houses in the city and suburbs of Oxford (St Frideswide's and Oseney) had connections with the schools.[12] The White Canons established a college for their order, in Paris, in the years after 1252, but it is not clear whether or not British Premonstratensians attended.[13] In 1245 the English Cistercians began to send their monks to the universities, and in 1281 they and their royal patron, Edmund, earl of Cornwall, requested the general chapter to grant permission to establish Rewley Abbey, near Oxford, as the first Cistercian house of study within the university. In 1292 the abbot of Cîteaux ordered all Cistercian houses within the province of Canterbury which had over twenty monks to send one of them, with an allowance of 60s., to study at Rewley. Not all English abbots concurred wholeheartedly with this proposal, but the general chapter managed to deal effectively with the would-be defaulters, and by 1300 there were sufficient White Monks at Oxford for them to take part in university processions.[14] The English Benedictines made a move towards participation in university education just a few years earlier than the Cistercians. In 1277 the Benedictine southern provincial chapter decided to establish a house of study at Oxford, and imposed a tax on its houses – resisted by a handful of alien priories – to raise money for this purpose. It was to be a lengthy process, and although a site was acquired in 1283, it was only after several years of difficulties that the house of study became firmly established as Gloucester College. A project to found a college for Benedictines of the northern province was begun by Prior Richard of Hoton of Durham (1290–1309) but not fully completed for nearly a century.[15]

THE TOOLS OF LEARNING: LIBRARIES AND THE TRANSMISSION OF TEXTS

In order to fulfil the Rule's requirement concerning reading, let alone make possible progress to the production of literary or theological works, a religious house needed to amass a library. Recruits, especially those who came from a career in the secular church or the schools, might bring their collections of books when they entered the house. It was in this way that Fountains Abbey acquired the books of Dean Hugh of York, that Llanthony Prima received the theological books of its prior, Walter de Haya, and that Evesham received volumes on canon and civil law, and medicine, from Abbot Thomas of Marlborough.[16] Some abbots were great collectors of books, and the activities of men like Abbots Paul of St Albans and Godfrey of Malmesbury laid sound foundations for intellectual activities at their respective houses.[17] Patrons might procure volumes for their monasteries: a benefactor of Whitby Abbey made a grant of land to provide money 'for making and writing books for the church', while a knight granted St Albans two-thirds of his demesne tithes for the support of the scriptorium.[18] Benefactors sometimes bequeathed books in their wills; Robert Grosseteste, bishop of Lincoln, left his library to the Oxford Friars Minor because of his close friendship with Adam

Marsh;[19] Thomas Becket left a fine collection of classical works to Christ Church, Canterbury.[20] Less scrupulous methods of acquisition might also be used. The enmity of Gerald of Wales towards the Cistercians of Strata Florida evidently stemmed from the time when he reached an agreement with the monks to take his library of theological works as a pledge for a loan which he required when he was going to the Holy Land. At the last moment the monks claimed that their statutes forbade them to acquire items in such a way, and in order to raise the necessary money Gerald was forced to sell his books to the abbey.[21]

Other volumes were copied in the monastic scriptorium either as duplicates from books already in the library, or from ones borrowed from other religious houses for this purpose.[22] The process of copying fulfilled two functions: it was a way to discharge the Rule's requirement for manual work; and, in the same way as reading, it transmitted knowledge. It was thus consistent with the need and the desire to preserve the past. A wide variety of material was copied: from the basic liturgical service books needed for the *Opus Dei* to more sumptuous productions of illuminated psalters and bibles.[23] Liturgical developments of the eleventh century and later stimulated the copying of treatises explaining liturgy and ceremonial, as well as the lives of saints for reading in private and, on saints' days, in public. It was not just sacred texts which were reproduced, however, and in many cases vernacular texts are preserved for us only in monastic copies. Most Welsh vernacular poetry from the Middle Ages survives in four manuscripts: the Black Book of Carmarthen (Augustinian, copied between 1170 and 1230, probably during the period of Welsh ascendancy after 1208), the Book of Aneurin (Basingwerk, from the second half of the thirteenth century), the Book of Taliesin (Margam, c. 1275) and the Red Book of Hergest (Strata Florida, c. 1400).[24] This is not to argue that poetry was necessarily composed within the walls of monasteries: most was written outside. What we can see here, however, is the role of the Welsh houses, bound as they were by ties of patronage to those with whom they shared a language, as 'transcribers, editors and custodians [responsible for] the transmission of a part of what remains of the Welsh literary heritage of the middle ages'.[25]

The friars had a particular need for books for study, and the constitutions of all the mendicant orders made detailed provision for their acquisition, use and circulation. The books of a priory library could be borrowed by a friar for life, and after his death they reverted, not to the library itself, but to the province, to be assigned by the provincial chapter to houses and individual friars as their needs were assessed. The orders also developed a 'primitive system of inter-library loan' so that books could be transferred from one convent to another. Catalogues and yearly inventories of the contents of priory libraries are also indicative of the care for the provision of books evinced by the mendicants, and their over-whelming concern for the materials of study.[26] Three library catalogues of the mendicants have survived, the fullest being those from the Austin friars of York and the Carmelites of Hulne. From these, it has been possible to suggest that the library of a mendicant house might have comprised four sections, a collection in the choir, another in the refectory, a chained reference section, and a library of books which could be borrowed by individual friars.[27]

Library catalogues such as these, as well as surviving manuscripts which can be assigned to particular houses, provide us with evidence for the contents of monastic libraries. There are very few intact library collec-tions; most of those that we have survive from cathedral monasteries like Durham and Worcester. Dr Neil Ker's study (1964) identified over six thousand extant books from religious houses, colleges and cathedrals. These represent only a small percentage of the total number of books of the five hundred or so libraries to which Ker was able to assign the volumes. Fourteen libraries are prominent, among them the monasteries of Durham (550), Worcester (350), Christ Church, Canterbury (300), St Augustine's, Canterbury and Bury St Edmunds (250), and Norwich, Reading, Rochester and St Albans (all over 100). All of these are Benedictine houses; the other house to which a sizeable number of surviving books have been assigned is the Augustinian priory of Llanthony Secunda.[28] Surviving books from Cistercian libraries in England have been analysed by Professor Cheney. The largest number of the 240 or so books whose provenance he has been able to identify as Cistercian are from Buildwas Abbey, and more recent research by Jennifer Sheppard suggests that forty-three, possibly forty-six volumes survive from its library and scriptorium.[29] Although, as Cheney pointed out, the surviving evidence has to be treated cautiously as representing only a fragment of the whole, he was able to suggest that the interests of the White Monks were conservative. Some of the works found in their collections are those which would have been necessary for the assigned reading of the monks; otherwise they represent a narrower focus of subjects than monastic libraries of other orders. There is no evidence of the renewed interest in the classics which was characteristic of twelfth-century intellectual activity as evidenced in libraries of some Black Monk houses, but there was an emphasis on works of a historical nature.

The evidence of library catalogues from monastic houses must also be used with caution. They do not survive in any great number, and where they do, may not be a complete inventory of the holdings of a house. Moreover they tend to be extant from larger Benedictine male houses;

thus, to estimate the size of libraries of more modest houses and those of the canons, still less of nunneries, is impossible. The few surviving catalogues we have suggest that the libraries of many Black Monk houses could have been of considerable size. The late twelfth-century catalogue from Christ Church, Canterbury lists several hundred volumes; so too do catalogues from Durham (mid twelfth century), Bury and Peterborough.[30] Two identifiable Cistercian catalogues survive, from Rievaulx in the twelfth century (212 books) and thirteenth-century Flaxley (79).[31] Such catalogues are of interest in that they indicate the extent of single monastic libraries, although no general conclusions can be drawn. They may also – again used circumspectly – reveal something of the interests developed in individual houses. All libraries and catalogues tend to show a concentration of patristic works, and biblical and scriptural commentaries. Twelfth-century Whitby Abbey (Benedictine) had several grammar books, whereas Rievaulx in the same period had a collection of history books, both classical and contemporary, which may reflect the interests of Abbot Ailred. The presence of a number of historical works in Cistercian catalogues led Cheney to the same conclusion as his study of the surviving books, namely that the British White Monks generally demonstrated an interest in historical narrative and biography.[32]

WRITING

The writing of history, saints' lives and biography

The past can be kept alive and transmitted to future generations by the copying and collection of texts; it can also be preserved by writing and composition. Monks saw it as their role to commit the past to the written word, not necessarily for others then and there, but for themselves and for posterity. Most histories or biographies written within monastic houses were compiled to be read by members of the author's community and to serve its needs.[33] This is clearly demonstrated by the spate of historical writing, both narrative and hagiographical, stimulated by the Norman Conquest. The impetus was provided partly by what has been called 'conscious revivalism', a kind of emotional response to foreign domination, and partly – perhaps mostly – by the practical reasons of corporate survival. Here, then, is a major reason for writing history: the protection of the rights of a monastery in time of threat.[34] The Norman settlement put at risk the landed wealth, and hence the existence, of the Anglo-Saxon monasteries and nunneries; and the histories and saints' lives which were written within a generation of the Conquest were therefore designed to stress the antiquity and continuity of monastic houses, and to safeguard their lands and possessions. History, biography, hagiography and the copying of archival material from the monastic scriptorium combined and merged into one another. We can see this at Worcester and Evesham, where, within a decade of the coming of the Normans, the lives of two Anglo-Saxons, Wulfstan and Æthelwig, were written. Hemming, significantly, wrote his life of Wulfstan in Old English, although only the Latin translation survives. This is more than a biography; it is a reference work, almost a gazeteer of the lands of Worcester, and its purpose was this:

Wulfstan, bishop of this see, caused this book to be written to teach his successors about the things which have been committed to their care, and to show them which lands justly belong (or ought to belong) to the church and which have been unjustly seized by evil men.[35]

Similarly, works composed at Durham stress continuity with the past, and indeed two of them bear witness to this link through the influence on them of the works of Bede. They are the *Historia Regum* (*History of the Kings*) and *Historia Dunelmensis Ecclesie* (*History of the Church of Durham*), both attributed to Simeon of Durham.[36] The climax of the *History of the Church of Durham* is the introduction of monks into St Cuthbert's church, and a dominant theme throughout is the saint's protection of his monks, their church and their possessions. Historical writing at Durham did not, however, emerge solely after the Conquest and in response to foreign domination, for here already there was a tradition of chronicle writing. The *History* was, in part, modelled on the works of Bede, but it also drew on the *Historia de Sancto Cuthberto* (*History of St Cuthbert*) composed by a Durham monk in the mid tenth century, an account of the wanderings of the Lindisfarne monks which brought them, and the body of St Cuthbert, to Durham. It also contains a meticulous attempt to identify the estates of the church of Durham, and to delineate their boundaries, which was employed by later Durham writers.[37] The recording of the past was harnessed to present needs.

The Norman Conquest also stimulated the writing and updating of the lives of saints. However, this was not just an Anglo-Saxon response to the imposition of foreign rule, for Norman churchmen, like their Anglo-Saxon predecessors, could see the advantages which a powerful patron saint would bring to the protection of their temporal interests.[38] It was on Norman initiative, therefore, not just as a result of Anglo-Saxon sentiment for the past, that hagiographical works and biographies of abbots were produced at monasteries such as Bury St Edmunds, Norwich and Canterbury. The updating of the life of St Edmund at Bury coincided with the abbey's quarrel with Bishop Herfast of Elmham, who was attempting to transfer his see there: St Edmund presumably helped his monks to resist this and so to avoid the financial implications which would have followed.[39] Renewed interest in local saints and the protection they could afford was a feature of post-Conquest historical writing all over Britain. In Wales, too, the Anglo-Norman monks of the southern Benedictine priories took an active interest in the Welsh saints. They collected their relics and compiled collections of their lives, in such a way as to link their present foundations to the age of the Celtic saints.[40] Continuity brought legitimacy, and that continuity was made possible by corporate monastic memory committed to writing.[41]

A monastic historian might write simply to inform his audience of the glorious past and tradition which his church enjoyed. At Canterbury the compilation of saints' lives provided the early training for Eadmer's two major works, the life of Anselm and the *Historia Novorum in Anglia* (*History of Recent Events in England*), the one an account of Anselm's private life, the other of his public role. However, dominant in Eadmer's work is a love of his cathedral church of Canterbury and glory in its past achievements. This distorts his judgement on occasion, but it reminds us that he, and other monks like him, were writing primarily for their own communities. Devotion to Canterbury and dedication to its interests also informed the work of a later writer from the cathedral priory, Gervase. His own research was provoked by the events of the 1170s and 1180s, first the murder of Archbishop Thomas Becket in 1170 and his canonization in 1173, then the disastrous fire of 1174 and finally the quarrel between Christ Church and Archbishop Baldwin. The last decades of the twelfth century saw a continuing interest in the writing of saints' lives, the main purpose of which was to promote the interests of a religious house and to foster local cults. The production of two lives of Becket by Canterbury monks would doubtless have stimulated the cult of the archbishop and pilgrim traffic to the cathedral church.[42] Saints' lives also fulfilled an edificatory purpose, holding up shining examples of holiness to the present generation of monks. The biography *par excellence* – not of a saint but of a living man – must surely be Jocelin of Brakelond's chronicle, which describes the abbacy of Samson of Bury, and which is part of a long tradition of historical writing at the monastery. Devotion to the abbey and its patron saint is dominant in the work, but what it is most remarkable for is the contemporary portrait of the man himself. It is revealing, too, of the conflicting loyalties of its author. Until 1187 Jocelin was the abbot's chaplain, and his great champion; from 1200 he held the post of guest-master, and more often than not sided with the convent against the abbot.[43]

Instruction about the past as a means to edification in the present is discernible in the foundation histories or narratives produced in certain northern monasteries. An early example is that attributed to Abbot Stephen of St Mary's, York (d. c. 1112); and another, from the latter part of the twelfth century, derives from Selby. But of more interest because they form a group, and because they were compiled at Cistercian houses despite the official attitude of the order towards writing, are foundation histories from Byland (of the abbey and its daughter house of Jervaulx), Kirkstall and Fountains. Part of the concern of the narrative written by Abbot Philip of Byland at the dictation of the retired Abbot Roger was legal, in that it aimed to lay to rest any uncertainty about the constitutional status and filiation of the two houses. It drew heavily on documents in the abbey archives and copied texts of documents into the narrative.[44] Another thread, however, which is shared with the histories of Kirkstall and Fountains and also with the southern house of Ford, was the celebration of the pioneer days of early Cistercian settlement. By recording the dangers and difficulties of the first generation of White Monks, the monastic authors aimed to give to present and future brethren a record of how their houses came into existence, and to extol that sense of austerity and asceticism which a more richly endowed and comfortable life might lead them to forget. The early monks became role-models for a new generation. The Cistercians had their own *exempla* of written history in the accounts of the foundation of Cîteaux and in the life of St Bernard. The Fountains history, in particular, shows how these sources were adapted to fit the circumstances of the English houses.[45]

The histories which we have looked at so far are works written by monks about their own communities, but monks also saw themselves as transmitters of the past in a wider sense. The simplest form of record was the annal, a brief entry inserted into a small space in the Easter tables, noting what the author saw as the main event of the year: the death of a king, a battle, a famine. Some writers started to keep fuller accounts of yearly events, chronicles, whose main purpose was to establish chronology rather than interpret events. Many chronicles are local in their interests, while others show wider concerns. At a time when the Anglo-Saxon Chronicle (kept alive and in Old English at Peterborough Abbey until 1154) became 'increasingly provincial in its outlook',[46] the church of Worcester produced a work, the *Chronicon ex Chronicis*, which, as its name suggests, brought together information from a variety of sources, both native (the Anglo-Saxon Chronicle) and foreign (such as the Universal Chronicle of Marianus Scotus of Fulda). It shows evidence of lively contact between Worcester and other Benedictine houses, especially Canterbury and Malmesbury.[47] Unlike the Anglo-Saxon Chronicle, the Worcester work (which goes under the name of Florence but was probably the work of a monk named John) used archives, and brought together national and local events. Moreover, the way the *Chronicon* was used in other contexts shows links among various Benedictine houses, for copies were made for Abingdon, Bury, Peterborough and Gloucester, where the chronicle was edited and material relevant to its new location added. The Worcester *Chronicon* was the basis for the work attributed to Simeon of Durham; in his turn John of Worcester used Simeon for revisions to his chronicle, and when copies of Simeon reached the Cistercian house of Sallay it was similarly adapted by the addition of material to suit its new home.[48]

Indeed, the emergence of chronicles was the main feature of historical writing in the early thirteenth century.[49] This form was used by John, prior of Hexham from some time after 1167, possibly until 1209, and was adopted in the late twelfth century at Winchester and Winchcombe, and at other houses in the early thirteenth. Many of the chronicles borrowed from each other and were therefore interdependent; their complex relationship is still being worked out.[50] Their purpose was sometimes to continue a historiographical tradition, as at Worcester, Winchester and Bury, at others to record domestic issues and to preserve copies of charters and legal documents; or to record political events (they are important sources for the struggle between King John and the barons), while maintaining anonymity. The tradition of chronicle writing continued into the reigns of Henry III and Edward I. St Albans was an important centre of activity; Bury fostered the keeping of chronicles at a number of East Anglian houses, while they flourished (or continued to flourish) at Winchester, Battle, Burton on Trent, Tewkesbury and Chester (Benedictine), Waverley, Stanley and Furness (Cistercian) and at the Cluniac monastery at Northampton. In Wales, too, the past was recorded by monastic writers. The *Brut y Tywysogion*, which was originally written in Latin but now survives only in Welsh, may have been compiled not long after 1282 at Strata Florida. It used different sources, from St Davids, Llanbadarn Fawr and Strata Florida itself, and shows evidence of contributions from other Welsh Cistercian houses. The *Chronica de Wallia* (Welsh Chronicle) is a series of Latin annals covering the years 1190–1266, probably from Strata Florida or Whitland, while the Cistercian monks of Margam compiled annals for the years 1066–1232.[51]

Indeed, after the mid twelfth century the recording of history was no longer the sole preserve of the Benedictines. As their contribution to historical writing went into temporary decline the torch passed to Ailred of Rievaulx and to the Augustinian prior of Hexham, Richard. Although their embarkation into this field of activity – Ailred with the account of the Battle of the Standard of 1138, the *Relatio de Standardo* (his only historical work) and Richard with the *De Gestis Regis Stephani* (*Concerning the Deeds of King Stephen*) and *De Bello Standardii* (*On the Battle of the Standard*) – marks the beginning of non-Benedictine historical writing, both authors are traditional in a number of respects.[52] Ailred wrote not so much as a Cistercian but as a man of Northumbria, steeped in past traditions. He had sympathy with both major protagonists of the Battle of the Standard, King David of Scotland, his former lord, and his patron, Walter Espec. He put stirring speeches into the mouths of both men, which would presumably have pleased neither. For this reason it has been suggested that Ailred wrote the *Relatio* not for a lay audience or patron, but for his own community at Rievaulx. Certainly he laid stress on the religious apparatus of the battle, especially the relics and standards which were borne before the victorious army. That Richard of Hexham, too, wrote for his canons is suggested by the way the work concentrates on the sufferings of the church of Hexham rather than on political narrative.

The religious houses of twelfth- and thirteenth-century England produced names more celebrated still for the writing of history. One outstanding historian, and a product of the cloister, was William of Malmesbury, who had entered the house as an oblate, taken his vows there, and subsequently become librarian.[53] The grounding which he received at Malmesbury, in canon and civil law, Scripture, hagiography, theology, classics and history, enabled him to produce a number of remarkable works: the *Gesta Regum* (*Deeds of the Kings*), the *Gesta Pontificum* (*Deeds of the Bishops*), the *Historia Novella* (*Recent History*) covering the years 1128 to 1142, and *De Antiquitate Glastoniensis Ecclesiae* (*On the Antiquity of the Church of Glastonbury*). William is an important figure in the development of historical research and writing. Although his aims were conventional, he was a judicious historian, anxious to evaluate evidence, and remarkably free from prejudice. He was not confined to the cloister, and travelled widely in his search for information. He had a keen sense of landscape and topography, and used these, as well as physical remains from the past, as historical sources. William, it has been said, exhibits a 'corporate monastic purpose of recreating the Old English past' which he extended to the whole country.[54] Copies of the works of William of Malmesbury have survived in considerable numbers, and the ownership of some has been traced to houses of several orders.[55] There were in fact a number of religious houses with a strong tradition of historical writing, and prominent among these was St Albans. Here literary activities were matched by patronage of artistic endeavour,[56] and both talents came together in the person of Matthew Paris, a man who spent most of his life at the abbey, and whose universal history, the *Chronica Majora*, spanning the Creation to 1259, has been described as 'the most comprehensive history yet written in England'.[57] Matthew Paris also produced the *Historia Anglorum* (*History of the English*, from the Norman Conquest to 1253), the *Gesta Abbatum* (*Deeds of the Abbots* of the house from 793 to 1255), and a number of saints' lives. The marginal drawings with which he decorated some of his works show him to have been an artist of ability as well as a historian of distinction. All his works were written to edify the monks and to improve their observances by holding up a mirror to the past – a main theme of the *Gesta Abbatum* was the firm adherence to the Rule of St Benedict in the past in contrast to the decline of the present – and to record the privileges and achievements of the abbey. His interest in art and architecture has left us with virtually a guide book of the medieval abbey. The most popular of Matthew's works, to judge by the number of surviving manuscripts, was his abbreviation of the *Chronica Majora*, the *Flores Historiarum*, the *Flowers of History*, which was continued by an anonymous monk of St Albans and became the abbey's 'chief literary export', finding its way to houses such as Westminster, where continuations were written and additions made.

The contribution of the monastic orders to the writing of history, in contrast to that of the friars, was wide-ranging,[58] and the works of William of Malmesbury, William of Newburgh and Matthew Paris show what could be achieved by those who received their education within the cloister and relied on books in the monastic library. There is ample evidence of interdependence of sources, and of the circulation of manuscripts among the scriptoria of various houses. Some works were written at the request of lay patrons: William of Malmesbury, for instance, dedicated the *Historia Novella* and the revised *Gesta Regum* to Robert, earl of Gloucester, and Matthew Paris wrote his lives of St Edward and St Edmund for Queen Eleanor of Provence and Isabel, countess of Arundel, respectively.[59] Despite this contact, and although many works ranged beyond events at the monastery at which they were compiled, most histories produced within the religious houses of Britain were essentially domestic in that they were intended for the glorification of their house, and the instruction, amusement, edification and protection of its monks or canons.

Scriptural and theological studies

Basic to the study and contemplation undertaken by all professed religious men and women was the Bible; and scriptural commentary was a natural progression from *lectio divina*, reading and contemplation on the Word of God.[60] Biblical commentaries, like those of Origen, Cassiodorus and Bede, were the staple of monastic libraries; and their study led to the writing of more works of this kind, as an aid to understanding and worship. At the beginning of our period, however, theology, as opposed to the unsystematic biblical study typical of monastic schools, was not a subject in its own right. The twelfth and thirteenth centuries saw revolutionary changes in this area; the application of logic and rhetoric in the secular schools brought more order into scriptural study and led to the formation of theology as a separate academic discipline. It was in the universities that this change took place. Although, as we have seen, there was opportunity for cultural interchange among monastic houses, there was in their schools less opportunity for debate; the universities, on the other hand, stimulated the production of textbooks and summaries, and provided a forum for discussion and argument, and an atmosphere of 'abrasiveness and challenge'.[61] During the twelfth century in the schools of Paris, men like Peter Lombard attempted to meet the challenge by compiling textbooks for the study of theology as an academic discipline. Glossed copies of key texts, especially the Bible and the works of the Fathers (Basil, Jerome, Augustine), together with commentaries, were circulated in an attempt to define theology and find an effective method of teaching it. By the end of the twelfth century theology had a place of its own in the scheme of university study. It now tried to reconcile two distinct features: the study and exegesis (exposition) of the Bible, and speculative theology, where scriptural passages were used to pose questions (*quaestiones*) or to afford the proof for the solution of problems. Because it was in the universities that the study of theology emerged, it was the friars rather than monks or canons who first took part in it.

The contribution of monks and canons in the twelfth century

Monastic theology was a meditative, not a speculative theology, and most writings produced by monks and canons aimed to provide assistance in the interpretation of the Bible. The traditional method of biblical study was to produce comprehensive commentaries on the Scriptures in which moral teaching and biblical exegesis combined, and the religious houses of twelfth-century Britain produced a number of writers who wrote in this way. A popular subject for study in the twelfth century was the biblical Song of Songs, and among its greatest commentators were the Cistercians. St Bernard's own commentary – soon to become as popular among the Black Monks as the White – was unfinished at the time of his death in 1153, and the general chapter passed the task of completing it to the English Cistercian Gilbert of Hoyland, a former monk of Clairvaux and later abbot of Swineshead, who had acquired a reputation as an author of other biblical commentaries. It was still unfinished at the time of Gilbert's death in 1172, and it is possible that John, abbot of Ford, was his self-appointed successor.[62] Although John was writing in the second half of the twelfth century when the Paris theologians were beginning to leave their traces on contemporary thought, his work was traditional. The influences which shaped his writing are the books which could have been found in most monastic libraries and which formed the basis of the monastic *lectio*. John was not a product of the universities but of the monastic school; however, he was certainly not working in an intellectual vacuum, for Ford at that time produced two other distinguished men, Baldwin and Roger, who wrote commentaries on the Christian faith. Ford could produce 'active, if conservative', writers.[63]

More prominent than English monks of the twelfth century were a number of Augustinian canons. In the North Robert, prior of Bridlington, wrote commentaries on the Pauline epistles, the twelve greater prophets and the Apocalypse, and glosses on the Pentateuch. Llanthony Prima produced a number of writers of scriptural commentary. Robert de Bethune, who went on to become bishop of Hereford in 1131, was a man of learning who had studied under Anselm of Laon, an outstanding teacher of theology who was influential in the development of systematic study of the Bible; Robert de Braci, third prior, brought together for use at Llanthony a collection of theological texts. The most prolific Llanthony writer, however, was Clement, who became prior c. 1150 and was the author of biblical commentaries and a large gospel harmony. Clement's fame spread, and gave to Llanthony a reputation as a centre of learning. William of Nottingham, provincial minister of the Franciscans (1240–54), had Clement's works copied for the friars, and they were still being circulated in the fifteenth century.[64] A similar reputation for learning attached to St Osyths (from which few works remain) and to the London priory of Holy Trinity, Aldgate, whose prior, Peter of Cornwall, was a prolific writer who compiled, among other things, a commentary on the Book of Revelation. Oseney, situated on the outskirts of Oxford, had close connections with the world of learning, and at least two celebrated scholars stayed there.[65] Robert of Cricklade, canon of Cirencester, was previously a master of the schools, and c. 1140 became prior of St Frideswide, Oxford, a house which like Oseney had opportunity for contact with the schools. Robert continued to travel until his death in c. 1180, and took part in the debate about the christological views of Peter Lombard. The English regular canons, or some of them, were accordingly in touch with continental developments in theological debate. Finally, and perhaps most significantly, the Augustinian Alexander of Neckham, abbot of Cirencester (1213–16), lectured in theology at Oxford before his conversion to the religious life in 1197. Neckham was perhaps the first person in the West to know the works of

Aristotle through the Graeco-Latin and Arabic–Latin translations which were just becoming available, and we can accordingly say that in some measure Neckham links the world of the twelfth century with the new scholasticism of the thirteenth.[66]

The friars and the new theology

The Bible remained at the centre of theological study, but increasingly some scholars felt a need to present doctrine in a more systematic way.[67] This is where intellectual activity moves from the preservation of existing knowledge (through the copying of texts) and commentary upon it to the creation of knowledge; and this knowledge emerged with the development of a new scholastic method in the thirteenth century, which applied Aristotelian philosophy to the study of the Bible. The new discipline of theology which emerged in the course of the twelfth century may be described as the rational analysis of the Christian faith, the investigation of the foundations of belief. It still included a study of the Bible, but to this were now joined a speculative theology which derived its methods from secular philosophy and the liberal arts, and a polemical or missionary theology designed to refute the heresies of unbelievers.[68] Because of their links with the universities the friars played a great, indeed a dominant, part in the development of the academic discipline of theological study. The nature of their calling – their evangelism and especially their deliberate movement from one place to another – meant that their contribution was an international one. Three features are characteristic of these developments in the study of theology, in which the friars participated: (i) the widening of the study of the Scriptures to include the liberal arts as well as exegesis, (ii) the scholastic method of exposition, and (iii) the reception of Aristotelian thought through the writings of Thomas Aquinas and others.

The direction which Franciscan scholarship at Oxford would take was determined early when Robert Grosseteste became their lector.[69] Grosseteste was one of the first western teachers to understand the philosophical method of Aristotle and apply it to Christian theology, and his contribution was to introduce the liberal arts, natural science and philosophy to the study of theology. But his approach, which must have been influential, was conservative and centred on the Bible rather than the *Sentences* of Peter Lombard, which were coming to be used by Paris theologians as the core of their teaching of speculative theology.[70] Grosseteste was not himself a friar, but since he was the first lector to the Franciscans at Oxford and, moreover, maintained close contact with the mendicants after his appointment to the see of Lincoln (1235), his ways of teaching and writing were influential. According to the famous

Franciscan Roger Bacon, commenting in 1266–7, Grosseteste's methods were followed by his successors, including the first friar regent-master, Adam Marsh, Thomas Docking, and the Dominican Simon of Hinton. These masters firmly established at Oxford the study of science, mathematics and languages which was developed further by Roger Bacon to include optics.

Their approach differed from that of the late twelfth-century Paris masters, who had begun to separate biblical studies from the exploration of doctrinal, theological issues. This method came to be adopted at Oxford, but it is difficult to pinpoint the change, and it was some time before the traditional method of teaching was abandoned by the conservative element among the English mendicants. However, a glimpse of the new scholastic method is provided by the first Dominican master about whom anything much is known, Robert Bacon, who was already a master of the schools when he became a friar, and taught at Oxford until his death in 1248. To Bacon has been attributed a set of extracts from a commentary on the psalter, known as the *Tractatus*, which appear to have been adapted from lectures as sermons. Parts of the *Tractatus* show a development from the unspecialized scriptural commentary, containing both the doctrinal explanations and moral exhortation which are characteristic of twelfth-century expositions.[71] Robert Bacon's work, in these instances, illustrates the detachment of theological exposition from moral teaching, and his use of the *quaestio* (question), the classical method of speculative theology, shows a perfect example of the scholastic form of thesis, objection, argument for and against, and solution. But despite Robert Bacon's adoption, in the *Tractatus*, of the new scholastic method of disputation, he was still apparently teaching the conservative blend of theology and Scripture which became characteristic of Oxford in the mid thirteenth century. It was his method alone which was new. Robert Bacon and his generation of Oxford Dominicans were traditional in the way they taught and showed no interest in the development of science and philosophy.

The change among the Friars Preacher probably began with Richard Fishacre, who wrote a commentary on the *Sentences* in 1240–3, in which he adapted the new Paris way of teaching. However, for some time Oxford continued to compromise; old and new co-existed, and the new method was not fully accepted until the 1260s. The generation after Grosseteste produced both speculative and exegetical theologians. Among the former were the Dominicans Richard Fishacre and Robert Kilwardby and the Franciscan Richard Rufus; Rufus's clear statement that he wished to 'concentrate on the difficulties and ambiguities of theology rather than propound scripture'[72] and his frequent reference to Fishacre are an indication of the adoption of speculative theology by the English friars. However, exegetical theology was not abandoned, and had its notable Oxford exponents among the friars in the generation after Grosseteste, including Simon of Hinton, lector to the Oxford Dominicans (1248–54) and author of commentaries on Matthew, the lesser prophets and Job; John of Wales, Franciscan lector from c. 1259 to 1262, compiler of *compendia* for the use of preachers, which remained popular for two hundred years after his death, and of sermons and commentaries on the Gospels of St Matthew and St John; and the Welshman's successor, Thomas Docking, lector from 1262 to 1265, whose commentaries on books of both the Old and New Testament incorporate theological and moral questions and make use of natural sciences and, unusually, show an interest in contemporary political affairs. In the generation after the coming of the friars, the mendicants at Oxford trained and nurtured some outstanding names in the writing and exposition of theology, scriptural, speculative and moral.[73]

From the late thirteenth century there is more evidence of the existence of a speculative theology at Oxford; this is revealed, not only by extant student notebooks and theological literature, but also by the active contribution of members of both the major mendicant orders to the theological debate sparked by the writings of the continental Dominican Thomas Aquinas.[74] Aquinas was influenced by the metaphysical writings of Aristotle, and one of his great contributions to philosophical and theological studies was sharply to define the difference between reason and faith. Many Christian truths lie beyond the capacity of human reason, Aquinas taught, but they are not contrary to reason even if they depend on faith. The aspect of Aquinas' work which caused controversy, however, was his adoption of the Aristotelian antithesis of form and matter, which stated that form is common to a species, but matter is peculiar to the individual. Although these were metaphysical, rather than theological questions, conflict arose among theologians because of the implications for the view of the human soul and its relationship to the body.[75] Aquinas further employed Aristotle's philosophy of substance and accident to describe the doctrine of transubstantiation, the process by which the bread and wine of the eucharist are held to become the body and blood of Christ. The individuation, or distinction, of form and matter was fiercely opposed by many in the church, including the Franciscans, who held to the plurality of forms, and for the first time the Oxford friars took part in a major theological debate. In England in 1277 Aquinas' views were condemned by the Dominican Robert Kilwardby, formerly (1261–72) prior provincial of England, by then archbishop of Canterbury, who forbade the public teaching of Aquinas' thirty propositions in grammar, philosophy and logic, many of which related to the Thomist view of form. Kilwardby, however, represented the conservative wing of the Dominicans, and his actions were disapproved of and condemned by the order. From 1278 the Aristotelians took the intellectual lead among the English Black Friars, and when in 1284 the Franciscan archbishop of Canterbury, John Pecham, who had succeeded Kilwardby, condemned the teaching of Aquinas, the Oxford Dominicans united to defend the Thomist doctrine. During the controversy a wave of tracts appeared, at first the anti-Thomist *Correctorium Fratris Thomae*, which was followed by at least five Dominican defences of Aquinas. England in the last years of the thirteenth and in the fourteenth century produced distinguished exponents of Thomism, such as Thomas Sutton and Nicholas Trivet, as well as articulate supporters of the contrary, Augustinian view, notably Roger Marston. Their contribution to the debate was played out on an international stage.[76] At the very end of our period the dominance of the Oxford mendicants in theological writing, thought and debate was at its height, and the contribution to scholasticism of the works of Duns Scotus (d. 1308) and William of Ockham (d. 1347) was in many ways its zenith.

Treatises on the religious life, devotional and instructional works

The friars were not totally preoccupied with scholastic theology. Theirs was a practical theology, which was geared to the needs of preaching and the refutation of error. As part of their programme of education of the laity in line with the canons of the Fourth Lateran Council, the friars produced handbooks for penance and sermons. Two examples will illustrate this. The Franciscan *Liber Exemplorum* (*Book of examples*), of English provenance and dated c. 1275, is a collection for the use of preachers. It deals with biblical events, such as the nativity and the passion and resurrection of Jesus, and with human virtues and vices, all arranged alphabetically, with illustrative stories suitable for a lay audience. Similar is the *Speculum Laicorum* (*A mirror for the laity*) written in the late thirteenth century and surviving in eighteen manuscripts, which was dedicated by an English Franciscan to a fellow-friar recently appointed to the cure of souls, who had asked for material suitable for the instruction of the laity.[77] Two other manuscripts, one of Franciscan and the other of Dominican provenance, suggest something of the taste of the friars. These have been described as 'friars' miscellanies' and contain, in Latin, English or Anglo-Norman, poems of a religious and didactic nature, songs, stories, verse-sermons and *exempla*. Oxford, Jesus College MS 29 contains, among other things, one of two copies of the poem *The owl and the nightingale*, a

number of homilies, and the famous *Luue-ron* of the Franciscan Thomas
of Hailes. Oxford, Bodleian Library MS Digby 86 contains items of a
comparable nature, including an early fabliau, *The fox and the wolf*, and
English verse-sermons. Both indicate some of the methods by which
friars reached their lay congregation.[78] They also show their importance
in other ways. Derek Pearsall writes that the friars were 'responsible for
the production of most English poetry of a learned cast in the thirteenth
century', and a similar importance has been detected in Wales.[79]

From among the monastic orders a considerable body of Latin sermon
literature has also survived, which would probably have been intended for
personal meditation, and use within the monastery. The sermons come
from many houses of different orders, mainly though the Benedictines,
Cistercians and Augustinians. Ailred of Rievaulx was a prolific sermon
writer. He was also foremost among the spiritual writers of twelfth-
century England, although he himself tells us that he had no formal
training in the schools or in scholastic method.[80] Ailred's writings deal
with a wide range of monastic and human experience. His earliest
devotional work, written in 1142–3 at the repeated requests of St Bernard,
was the *Speculum Caritatis* (*Mirror of love*), which takes as its subject true
charity and the difficulties of discovering the perfect love of God. It was
written while Ailred was novice-master at Rievaulx, and one book takes
the form of a dialogue between Ailred and a novice; it uses Ailred's own
experiences to explore the difficulties of the monastic profession. *De
Institutione Inclusarum* (*Concerning the institution of recluses*) was written for
his sister, who had vowed herself to be a recluse or anchoress. In other
writings he explores the nature of spiritual friendship and its importance
in the search for God, and in his final work *De Anima* (*On the soul*) he
shows his affinity with continental Cistercian writers, namely St Bernard,
William of St Thierry and Isaac of Etoile. In Ailred the English Cistercians
found a writer of great spirituality, whose work has overshadowed that of
later authors.

Other works which may broadly be classed as devotional were aimed
at a narrower audience. The small body of Cistercian poetry from Meaux,
Combe, Dore and Rufford may have been entirely personal, or intended
for the community. The anonymous *Dulcis Jesu Memoria* (*Remembrance of
Sweet Jesus*) has been described as 'exquisite verses, so redolent with the
imagery of the Song [of Songs]', which 'would stand out in the literature of
any age'.[81] We know of the existence of verses, now lost, from the Welsh
Cistercian abbey of Margam. The long religious poem written in Anglo-
Norman by Simon, a canon of Carmarthen, was in tune with the trend
towards penitential writing of the thirteenth century.[82] Other writings are
contemplations and explorations of the meaning of the religious life. The

sole Premonstratensian writer of our period was Adam the Scot, abbot of
the Scottish house of White Canons at Dryburgh. Adam was a celebrated
preacher and an advocate of the monastic life (the theme of the *De Ordine,
Habitu et Professione Canonicorum Praemonstratensium, Concerning the order,
habit and profession of the Premonstratensian Canons*), until he withdrew from
the world for the eremitical life of the Carthusian at Witham. He wrote
contemplative works both before and after his entry into the charterhouse, and made a significant contribution to the devotional and ascetic
writing of the period.[83] While at Witham he composed *The quadripartite
exercise of the cell*, which was both an apologia for the Carthusian vocation
and a spiritual exercise, an explanation of the degrees of prayer. Similar in
its conception to Adam's exposition on the calling of the White Canons
was a work by the north-country Augustinian Robert of Bridlington,
who wrote an exploration of the meaning of the Rule of St Augustine,
the *Colloquium Magistri et Discipuli in Regula Beati Augustini*.[84]

Writing and study were not major preoccupations of the religious houses
of Britain, and were activities which engaged only a minority of those
who spent their lives in the cloisters. Those who pursued scholarly and
literary work were of two broad types: those who looked inward into the
cloister, and those who directed their gaze outwards, into the parish,
the market place and the schools. The very concept of their religious
vocations determined that the monastic order should fall largely into the
former and the mendicants into the latter. The fact that monks wrote
mainly for their own communities does not in any way lessen their
contribution. Many of the outstanding historians and chroniclers of the
period were monastic, and it is to them that we owe so much of our
knowledge of local and national events. The learning of monks, canons
and friars (nuns are, for dearth of evidence, excluded from this discussion)
developed considerably over the period covered by this study. The
change is perhaps easier to discern among the friars. They, after all, arrived
on the scene late; the Dominicans were wedded to the idea of scholarly
pursuits from their very beginnings, and the Franciscans, Carmelites and
Austins soon followed them. That they came to be dominant in the
theological faculties of the universities of Europe was a natural – albeit
unforeseen – outcome of two factors: their plantation in towns and in
the seats of learning, and their deliberate and conscious cultivation of a
scholarly basis for preaching. The emphasis placed on study by the
mendicant orders did, however, alter their original conception of
themselves to some extent, for possession of a university degree became
essential for those within the orders who aspired to high office. Development took place in monastic learning, too. The evidence from the

beginning of our period suggests that intellectual activity was, and continued to be, stimulated by the needs of the cloister: Ælfric's *Colloquies* were intended for the boys in the monastic school; saints' lives were compiled to safeguard the rights of the church, or to encourage pilgrim traffic; commentaries expounded upon the meaning of the monastic life and liturgical ritual, and upon the Bible for the purposes of personal contemplation. By 1300 monastic learning was spreading outwards from the cloister; and monks and canons were taking their place alongside the friars in the university halls of Oxford and Cambridge. This does not mean, however, that the two orders were moving closer together. Although the Benedictines of Durham Cathedral Priory produced, in the fourteenth century, a writer and teacher of European stature in the person of Uthred of Boldon, Uthred was an exception. The monks did not, on the whole, produce outstanding theologians or university teachers, and the most common progression for a university-educated monk was not a career at Oxford or Cambridge, but a return to his monastery and high rank within it.[85]

10

RELIGIOUS HOUSES AND THE WIDER COMMUNITY: FOUNDERS, PATRONS AND BENEFACTORS

———— • ————

FOUNDERS

In the course of this book we have encountered hundreds of men and women, by reference if not all by name, who founded religious houses. Why did they? The specific motives which we have been able to isolate, the desire of kings for support, both spiritual and cultural, penance for particular misdeeds, sickness, commutation of a vow, safeguarding of lands, indication of status and so on, are just that, specific. But motives for monastic foundations go deeper than that, and before we look at the relationship between religious houses and their patrons we need to remind ourselves of that most fundamental of questions: why did men and women found monasteries? Medieval society was at basis pessimistic; progress was a downward spiral which could not be reversed, only arrested. The two factors which could retard it were stability and restoration; and these were the two monastic virtues *par excellence*.[1] Men and women therefore viewed the inhabitants of monastic houses as able to contribute to the salvation of the world by arresting its decline and by preserving the eternal values of the past. Such a view also helps to account for fashions in endowment. When the Cistercians claimed to be restoring primitive monasticism, their appeal to the past struck a powerful chord. On a more personal level, founders expected prayers for their soul: they purchased salvation by the endowment of a religious house in the same way that men and women in the later Middle Ages bought indulgences. Fundamental to society in this period was the belief that intercession could be bought, and that vicarious prayers were sufficient to obtain salvation, without interior change (repentance) or alteration of outward behaviour. Penance was undertaken by members of the religious orders on behalf of the world. Finally, by establishing monasteries and nunneries founders created what Milis has called a 'functional reciprocity', an unwritten but well-understood contract under which the founder both offered and received certain benefits. These benefits were primarily, though as we shall see, not wholly, spiritual. This chapter will explore more fully of what that 'functional reciprocity' consisted.

PATRONAGE AND ADVOWSON

A monastic patron was, according to the accepted understanding of the word, the heir, direct or indirect, of the founder. Sometimes the patronage descended in the same family in unbroken line from foundation to dissolution. In the majority of instances, however, it passed, like any other piece of property, from one person to another. This could happen through marriage, and it was in this way that the family of Clare acquired the patronage of Tewkesbury Abbey. It could occur, too, when a direct line died out, and the patronage with the rest of the family estate escheated (reverted) to the king and was granted by him to someone else. Patronage might be voluntarily transferred: after the burial of Rosamund Clifford at Godstow Abbey in 1176 the founder's family ceded that role to King Henry II. Victory in war brought to the Lord Rhys ap Gruffydd the patronage of Whitland, Strata Florida, Cardigan and Llandovery, and to Morgan ap Owain that of Goldcliff.[2] If a religious house held its lands under the terms of feudal tenure, that is, for some kind of service, patronage also meant lordship: the patron was lord of the monastery and exercised wider powers and privileges than a patron who was not lord. Here there was an important distinction between the old and the new orders. When a founder endowed a house, he was in essence enfeoffing a tenant; he was subinfeudating land for service. We have seen how, like lay barons, the major monasteries owed knight service for their lands.[3] The new orders tried, and on the whole succeeded, to get grants of land in frankalmoin, that is, in free alms tenure, quit of any secular demands. This is generally indicated in a charter by a phrase such as 'this gift is made in pure and perpetual alms free from all secular service'. Although it has been demonstrated that some of the abbeys of one of the new orders, the Cistercian, did, by the 1150s and 1160s, hold some land for knight service, the holding of lands in frankalmoin, and the lesser role of the patron, remained an important feature of the new monastic orders.[4] As well as referring to the patron (*patronus*), records refer to the advocate (*advocatus*) of a religious house. On the continent there was a distinct difference between the two. In continental, especially German, terms, the advocate was originally a protector, chosen by a religious house or by the king to act as its agent. In turn, through exploitation, the advocate might become the master rather than the servant. In canon law he or she might be the same person as the patron, but on the continent the practice emerged of separating the two, of having advocates chosen by the religious who were distinct from the hereditary patron. In practice in Britain this distinction, although recognized in canon law, rarely existed, and the patron and advocate tended to be the same person.[5] On occasion and especially where a founder was of knightly rather than baronial status, an overlord might assume the role or title of advocate. Peter of Goxhill was founder (*fundator*) of the Premonstratensian abbey of Newhouse and undoubtedly enjoyed the status of patron, but it was his lord, Rannulf of Bayeux, who was described as advocate.[6]

By the end of our period the monastic expansion had all but come to an end, and few new houses were founded between 1300 and the Dissolution of the 1530s. The king was patron of a high proportion of monasteries and nunneries (over a hundred in England), either because the house was a royal foundation, or because a king or queen had been concerned with its refoundation or reformation, or because the house was too ancient for a founder to be identified. This was the case with the pre-Conquest houses, many of which were in any case associated with the royal family of Wessex and England. Then there were houses (about twenty-seven) which had been founded by bishops; in these, as in the cathedral priories, the role of the bishop as patron and as diocesan is not always easy to distinguish.[7] Finally there were the magnates, and by 1300 there was scarcely a family of this rank of society which was not associated with one or more religious house.[8] The thirteenth century saw a move towards the greater definition of patronage, while in the twelfth it was a more fluid concept; we must accordingly remember that patronage did not necessarily mean the same thing at all times. A distinction must also be made between different groups of religious: the founders of houses of Black Monks and nuns and Augustinian canons enjoyed wider powers of patronage than those of the Cistercians, Carthusians and Premonstratensians, who from the beginning attempted to minimize lay intervention and to separate themselves from the world. The area in which this distinction is most clearly manifest is the procedure when the head of an abbey or priory died or resigned, and the office became vacant.

ELECTIONS AND CUSTODY: THE NON-EXEMPT ORDERS

We have already discussed in some detail how heads of religious houses were chosen, and noted that by the thirteenth century free election, which in the twelfth century had been granted as a favour, was now accepted as a right. Nevertheless, canon and common law accepted that the patron had a role to play, and this role became defined. When a vacancy occurred, the patron, whether the king or a noble, had a right to be informed, and he or she then gave permission for the monks or canons to proceed with the election of a candidate. After election, the favoured candidate was presented to the patron for his or her assent, and then by the patron to the bishop for benediction. There was still potential cause for dispute, one circumstance being the conflicting claims of a patron and the head of a mother house of a dependent priory. The patron might regard the prior as a tenant, whereas the abbot would see him as a subordinate to be appointed by him rather than elected in chapter. One instance of this clash of interest occurred in 1200, when the patron of the Cluniac priory of Lewes, Hamelin de Warenne, complained that the abbot of Cluny had appointed a prior to Lewes although the normal procedure would have been for him to be elected by the chapter and approved by the patron.[9] His claim may well have been true, for an alien priory would have been more dependent for protection on a local patron than on a distant continental abbey. Common sense and self-interest would have suggested to the monks of Lewes that they ensure the good-will of their patron towards their prior by giving him at least the voice of assent to the election.[10] An extreme example of patronal claims was recorded by Matthew Paris: when Abbot John de Cella (1195–1214) removed the prior of the abbey dependency of Binham, this is what happened:

Robert, who was patron of the church of Binham, took offence because the prior, whom he was in the habit of calling 'his' prior, had been removed without his being asked . . . [he] suddenly laid hostile siege to the church of Binham with the monks in it, as if it were a castle, so that the monks, having nothing to eat or drink, and being about to perish through starvation . . . had to take rain-water from the roof-gutters for drinking water, and get bread made from bran down their throats with a struggle.

Fortunately for the monks their patron, Robert fitz Walter, was as unpopular with King John as he was with the abbot of St Albans, and the king sent help to relieve the siege.[11]

Consent and approval were, by the thirteenth century, the theoretical limits of a patron's power in elections, and his or her role was a formal one; however, patrons could still use influence to secure the election of candidates of their choice. There were grounds for conflict here as well. If licence to elect had not been requested, then a patron might refuse to recognize the candidate chosen. In 1296 Philip of Hanworth, the

sub-prior of Nocton, appeared before the bishop of Lincoln to have his
election as prior confirmed, but the patron of the house, Philip d'Arcy,
refused his consent on the grounds that the canons had not asked his
permission to proceed with the election. He agreed to waive his privilege
– on this occasion only – and consented to Philip's election. However,
Bishop Sutton, deeming the election to be invalid and Philip unsuitable,
ordered a new election, and Thomas of Louth was chosen. Philip d'Arcy
objected on the same grounds as before, but, when summoned by the
bishop to explain his attitude, could not convince him to delay the
process further. Clearly, the right to grant permission to elect could be
perceived as a privilege, not a right.[12]

When the vacancy of a religious house was reported, the lands of the
house – or, where the revenues of abbot and convent had been separated,
those of the abbot – passed into the custody of the patron, to be
administered by him or her until a new head be appointed. Custody was
a valuable asset to the patrons of the non-exempt orders. In the reign of
Henry III, where the royal records enable us more clearly and consistently
to see how long the office of head of the house remained vacant, the
average length was from two to six weeks. But the time could vary
considerably, and it was a temptation for an unscrupulous patron to keep
the office vacant and continue to draw the revenue. This practice was
elevated to an art form by William II.[13] The earls of Clare claimed the
right to the custody of the dependencies of Bec during vacancies, and the
records suggest that they may have been guilty of deliberate delay in
assenting to the election of a new prior the longer to enjoy his revenues.
Certainly in 1292 the earl took a considerable time to approve the
appointment of a prior for St Neots.[14] Sometimes the potential abuse of
the right of custody was recognized, as it evidently was in 1256, when
Gilbert Pecche promised the canons of Barnwell that he and his heirs
would not waste the goods of the priory during a vacancy, and would
send only one servant with a horse and groom to take control of the assets
of the house as a recognition of patronage.[15] When she founded Flixton
Priory for nuns in 1258 or 1259 Margery de Crek expressly renounced the
right of custody.[16] To avoid the greed of patrons or royal servants, a house
could apply to purchase its own custody. Thus in 1281 Burton Abbey paid
£40 for the right to administer its own goods in the first two months of a
vacancy, and agreed to pay £20 a month thereafter. The statutes of the
Cistercian Order expressly forbade interference by lay patrons in the
election process and denied them the custody. Houses of other orders,
too, could aspire to this freedom for themselves. By the early thirteenth
century the Augustinian canons of Llanthony Prima claimed that by
custom they elected a prior without obtaining leave from the patron, and

that they, not the patron, presented the elect to the bishop. This right was confirmed by their patron, Walter de Lacy, who also formally renounced for himself and his heirs any rights of custody.[17]

THE EXPECTATIONS OF A PATRON

The patron of a religious house had certain duties towards his or her house, and in return expected certain benefits. The responsibilities of the office and its rewards are not easily separated. Consider the issue of vacancies, which we have just discussed: a patron took a house into custody and was responsible for overseeing its administration. This was a patronal duty. But he or she could also benefit financially from custody: a patronal reward. It was the patron's responsibility to present the elect to the bishop for benediction, but he or she could use that special status of patron to influence election, to promote a relative or to reward service. In general the benefits enjoyed by a patron can be classified as two types, spiritual and material, but just as it is difficult to make a rigid distinction between duty and reward, so too the boundaries between spiritual and material prizes are blurred. Perhaps it is misleading to see the issue in quite these terms, since a medieval patron would probably have regarded patronage as a package of benefits, rather than as component parts, spiritual and temporal. Nevertheless, in discussing quite what kind of returns a patron might realistically expect, it is convenient to divide them into those expectations which were primarily spiritual and those which were of this world and not the next.

Spiritual benefits

A significant proportion of charters granting or confirming land and property to a religious house state that this was done 'for the salvation of the soul of' (*pro salute anime*) or 'for the soul of' (*pro anima*) the donor. This indicates a primary function of the religious: to pray not just for humankind generally but specifically for the grantors. Although monks, canons and nuns could be asked by any benefactors for their prayers, there was an expectation that a founder or patron would occupy a special place in the hierarchy of intercession. On occasion this is made specific. The Cistercian house of Jervaulx in north Yorkshire transferred from a site provided by a tenant of the honour of Richmond to one on the lands of the earl, who then assumed the patronage of the abbey. A charter of confirmation describes the earl as 'wishing to provide for the salvation of my soul' and making gifts to 'God and St Mary and the abbey of Jervaulx of the Cistercian Order, which I founded in honour of our Lord Jesus

Christ, and to my monks there serving God and praying for me'.[18] References to 'my monks' or 'my canons' are not unusual. The origins of Egglestone Abbey, a Premonstratensian house, also in north Yorkshire, are obscure, and all that can be said with certainty is that it was in existence by 1198. After some years its endowment was substantially increased by Gilbert de Leya, who gave a manor for the feeding and clothing of nine canons. Some fifty years later one of Gilbert's descendants, Philip de Leya, brought an action before the royal justices in York against the abbot of Egglestone, claiming the right to present all nine canons when vacancies arose. At first this was unsuccessful, but later the abbot was forced to concede that eight canons, in addition to a clerk to be presented by Philip for admission into the house, should celebrate divine service in the abbey church for ever, for the souls of Philip and those of his ancestors and heirs, and that at the death of each canon Philip should have the right to nominate a replacement.[19] The issue at stake here was really the right to present nominees, and it is instructive to note that the abbot never challenged Philip's claim that there should be, in perpetuity, nine canons praying for his soul and those of his ancestors and heirs. What this patron gained, therefore, was not only the right to nominate a high proportion of the canons at the abbey, but also a chantry within the conventual church.[20] In this and similar cases both the donor and the recipients had to be careful that spiritual favours, that is, prayers, which charters linked to grants of land, were not interpreted as simony. The records demonstrate how a house of modest size and endowments was not independent of its benefactors, but held land of them for spiritual service.

A founder or patron could specifically ask a religious house for rights of confraternity. The precise nature of these rights is not easy to assess; there was no universal definition of the phrase, and charters are rarely specific about its nature. Confraternity might entitle the patron or benefactor to an obit, that is, a mass recited on the anniversary of his or her death, or to distribution of alms or pittances in his or her memory on the same occasion. Confraternity rights usually conveyed the idea that in some way the recipient became a part of the religious community, entitled to certain benefits including the privilege of enjoying, at his or her death, the same prayers as a member of the community would have. The Premonstratensians formalized this right, and the ordinal which records the liturgical practices of the order in the late twelfth century laid down in detail that founders were to receive the same benefits at their death as a canon dying in his own abbey.[21] Their names were to be written into the calendar of those for whom special prayers were to be recited, and were to be read aloud in chapter every year on their anniversary; for thirty days after their death a portion of food (prebend) was to be placed in the refectory of the house and then distributed to the poor; a number of vigils and masses were said for the soul, and every member of the house, priest, canon or layman, was charged with the recitation of a number of masses, psalters or pater nosters, as appropriate. Very special benefactors might be taken into the prayers of the entire order, like Peter des Roches in 1219, and Talley's patron, Rhys ap Maredudd, in 1280, but this was rare and required the consent of the general chapter. This was the practice in other orders, too, and one demonstration of the loyalty felt by the Cistercians to the princes of north Wales was the securing, at the instance of the abbot of Aberconwy, of full confraternity of their order for David, brother of Llywelyn ap Gruffydd.[22]

As their final days approached founders and patrons might go one step further than the rights of confraternity and decide to take the habit, and die as a monk, canon or nun of their house. This was known as entry *ad succurrendum*. It was not common for members of the aristocracy to enter the religious life during their prime, although there are some examples, like Richard fitz Gilbert de Clare, who entered St Neots a few years before his death.[23] However, there are numerous instances of those who took the habit on their deathbed, men like Ralph de Haia, founder of the Premonstratensian house of Barlings (Lincolnshire), who became a canon and was buried there. The founders of Beauchief (Derbyshire), Robert son of Ranulf, and Langley (Norfolk), Robert fitz Roger, both died as canons and thereby became entitled to the full prayers of the community.[24] In Wales Owain Cyfeilog, founder of Strata Marcella, 'having taken upon him the habit of religion', died there in 1197. Prince Llywelyn ap Iorwerth died in the monastic habit at Aberconwy in 1240, and two sons of Rhys ap Gruffydd became monks at Strata Florida and another at Whitland.[25] Hugh de Morville, constable of Scotland, ended his days as a Premonstratensian canon at Dryburgh, which he had founded.[26] Very occasionally, although it was a direct contravention of the statutes, women were allowed to be clothed in the Cistercian habit on their deathbed, notable examples being Alice de Gant, wife of Roger de Mowbray (at Fountains) and Matilda de Braose, widow of Gruffydd ap Rhys and daughter-in-law of the Lord Rhys, who received the habit at Llanbadarn Fawr and was later interred at Strata Florida.[27] To die after converting one's life and becoming a member of a religious order, especially after a life of violence and warfare, gave a better chance of salvation and went one better than, as a lay person, receiving the prayers of the community. The promise of reception into a religious house, should the patron be so minded, was sometimes written into a charter granting land. Gilbert de Gant was patron of the family foundations of Bardney (Benedictine), Bridlington (Augustinian) and Rufford (Cistercian). From Bridlington he received a promise that

> for the redemption of my sins and for the particular love which I have always had for the church of St Mary of Bridlington, I have bound myself to the said church in this way: that wherever I shall end my life, I shall receive a burial place in the monastery of Bridlington. And if by chance God in his grace shall touch my heart and give me the opportunity to leave the vanities of the world behind and serve him in poverty, I shall receive the habit of religion in the aforesaid monastery, and end my days among those with whom I was brought up from my infancy. For it seems to me appropriate that where I entered this world from my mother's womb, there I should leave this world in the mother of all.[28]

This contains a number of interesting details – the reference to the education of a patron's heir at a monastery, for instance. It is also a useful reminder that the relationship between members of a founder's family and his or her religious house was one that could persist literally from the cradle to the grave.

The desire exhibited by Gilbert de Gant for burial in the monastic church was by no means unusual. Patrons, and even benefactors who did not enjoy that special status, could hope to associate themselves in death with the religious. We have already seen in chapter 6 how burial in the churches and cemeteries of the mendicant orders was a cause for jealousy on the part of some parish clergy. It also caused rivalry on the part of monastic houses which had often provided the final resting place for their founders and patrons. Although the Cistercian *Carta Caritatis* restricted lay burial to guests and hired workers dying within its monasteries, this ruling came to be disregarded, and the White Monks like the Black offered burial to lay folk, and principally to their patrons. Many instances of burial within religious houses could be cited. Earl Ranulf of Chester, patron of the Benedictine abbey of Chester, chose that his heart should be interred at Dieulacres, the Cistercian community which he transferred there from Poulton. Sweetheart Abbey took its name from the heart of John Balliol, which the founder of the abbey, Balliol's wife Lady Devorguilla, caused to be buried beside her in the abbey church. The choice of burial place reveals much about the loyalties of a family both to a dynasty and to a religious house.[29] Some prominent families continued to be buried in the same place for generations. Others chopped and changed. During the first generation of settlement in Britain, and beyond, several families took members back to Normandy for burial. Robert de Beaumont, count of Meulan and earl of Leicester, who died in 1118, was buried at the monastery of Préaux, founded by his grandfather, which had been the resting place for several generations of his family. However, the investigations of Dr Golding on the subject of knightly burials have indicated that, although loyalty to Norman houses remained strong, surprisingly few of those people whose intentions can be uncovered chose to be buried in Normandy; perhaps cultural assimilation in Anglo-Norman England was quicker than some historians have been willing to allow.

Where a family was associated with one or more house, preference might be given consistently to one, or favours spread around. The Ros family, heirs of Walter Espec, usually chose Kirkham Priory over Rievaulx Abbey. Members of the Gant family, on the other hand, were buried at both the Benedictine abbey of Bardney and their Augustinian foundation at Bridlington. Although she was patron of Whitby and Sallay, Matilda de Percy chose to be buried at Fountains Abbey, despite the Cistercian ban on lay – especially female – burials. It may well have been allowed because of Matilda's special devotion to the church. A similar devotion was expressed by William de Braose (d. 1211), who asked that wherever he died, whether in England or Wales, his body should be interred in the priory church of St John of Brecon 'because this is the church which I love before all others, and because after God and St Mary I have greater confidence in St John'.[30] In 1200 the earl of Strathearn placed Augustinian canons in the Culdee house of Inchaffray because 'we hold the place in such affection that we have chosen in it a place of burial for ourselves and our successors, and have already buried there our first-born son'.[31] The family of Beauchamp was traditionally laid to rest in Worcester Cathedral Priory, and the wish of one of its members to be buried by the Franciscans of that town was strongly resisted, although his son, the first Beauchamp earl of Worcester, succeeded where his father had failed.[32] By providing the service of burial a religious house fulfilled an obligation to a patron; at the same time it could hope to gain financially, both through the gift often associated with a request for burial and the expectation of further patronage from the family. It was for this reason that there were numerous disputes between churches for the body of a patron. In 1107 when Roger Bigod, earl of Norfolk, died, he was buried at Norwich Cathedral. But his body was also claimed by the monks of Thetford, a Cluniac house which Bigod had founded. The wrangle resulted in a case being brought in the king's court and won by the bishop.[33]

Material benefits

As well as spiritual benefits, a patron might expect material returns by virtue of his or her special status. We have noted elsewhere how places for monks, canons and nuns within religious houses might be limited by the resources of the community, and how as a result of visitations it was not unknown for bishops to place a ban on the reception of further novices. Given these restrictions, it is not perhaps surprising that one of the advantages of patronage was perceived as the right to have entry into a community for a member of family or another nominee. Again, whether the right to nominate an entrant is to be termed a spiritual or material benefit is debatable. Certainly for the nominee it was spiritual, in that it offered entry into the religious life; it also secured his or her prayers for the patron. We have seen in another context one instance of the patron of a Premonstratensian house, Egglestone, claiming the right to nominate a specific number of canons to pray for his soul. But there are also grounds for arguing that the right of nomination could offer a material benefit, since it could relieve the patron of the necessity of maintaining a relative or servant within the secular household; it also secured a place in a religious house for a member of his or her family, one with a religious vocation, or who for some reason was deemed to be unsuited to life within the secular community. On occasion a nunnery appears to have been founded in order to provide for a female relative; and other instances show gifts being made when a kinswoman entered the house.[34] Relatives of founders are known to have been professed at Sinningthwaite, Campsey Ash (where Joan and Agnes, sisters of the founder, both held the office of prioress), the Gilbertine houses of Alvingham and Bullington, and many others.[35] Monasteries and nunneries recognized that in return for material support, they might have to concede to a patron the right of nomination of one or more of their members. And so between 1240 and 1250 the abbot and convent of the Premonstratensian house of Welbeck agreed, for the soul of Hugh son of Simon of Ropsley, to receive two secular clerks as canons.[36] In 1231 the Premonstratensian general chapter authorized Torre Abbey to take account of 'any magnate or noble, who, knowing your poverty, wishes to place and institute one or more canons or lay brethren in your house', and accordingly the abbey granted to Hugh Peverel the right to 'institute in perpetuity one canon in our house, that is an honest and suitable person and one worthy of the religious habit'.[37] Although the fact that the permission of the general chapter had to be sought suggests that this was not a common practice among the Premonstratensians, other instances can be cited. The Benedictines of Great Malvern granted to the family of Beauchamp the right to nominate one monk in succession, to pray for the salvation of its members. As Dr Mason has pointed out, this meant that the family also had a monk who would, in the monastic chapter, be able to look after the interests of the patrons.[38] Sometimes the right of nomination belonged, not to the patron, but to his or her lord, or to another powerful benefactor. Arthington Priory was founded between c. 1150 and 1158 by Peter of Arthington, but it was William de Curcy who, some years later, claimed for his mother Avice de Rumilly, a benefactor of the nunnery, that 'there shall always be in the house of Arthington a nun whom my mother Avice shall place there; when my mother is dead, I, her son and heir, and my heirs, shall have the same privilege . . . in perpetuity'.[39] William de Stuteville specifically renounced a similar privilege at Westwood.[40] The influence which a patron brought to bear to secure the entry of a nominee into a religious house was probably more often informally recognized than expressed in the written word. There may have been financial as well as personal reasons for allowing a patron oversight of the admission of novices. At the nunnery of Flamstead the patron, Roger de Tosny, stipulated that any nuns to be admitted over the agreed maximum of thirteen must be approved by him or his heirs. The motives behind this arrangement may have been control over the resources of the community, to ensure that they were not overstretched by the reception of too many women.

We have seen in an earlier chapter how it was part of the duty laid on his monks by St Benedict to provide hospitality and to receive guests 'as Christ himself'. Although any traveller or visitor could make use of monastic hospitality, it was understood that the patron's status gave an unquestioned right to stay at the house. When a bishop tried, for the financial well-being of a community, to limit the number of guests that might be received, the patron was excepted. Patrons were the only women guests whom their statutes permitted within Cistercian houses, and they were only allowed to stay one night, a restriction which was sometimes repeated by bishops for houses of other orders. As well as providing for their personal well-being when they stayed as their guests, a religious house might furnish financial support for its patrons in time of need. One instance is provided by the d'Oilly family, members of which were benefactors of both the old and the new orders, but more specially patrons of Oseney. Despite this status the family showed as much devotion to other foundations as to Oseney; and it was not until 1232, for instance, that a member received burial there.[41] It has been demonstrated that a newly found interest in the Augustinian house came at a time when the d'Oillys were in financial difficulties. Here the canons were able to assist, for they bought from d'Oilly the manor of Weston on the Green, in order that their patron be able to pay off his debts to the Jews. Roger de Mowbray freed his Cistercian foundation, Byland Abbey, from paying for the use of his seal, so that the monks did not have to pay for any charter giving or confirming their property. But in subsequent years the monks aided Roger by paying him £300, for which they held pasture in Nidderdale in mortgage for ten years. It was, however, not with his monks of Byland or his canons of Newburgh that Mowbray had most financial dealings. It was Fountains Abbey which time and again provided funds 'as testimony and in commemoration of a grant', 'as help for my journey to Jerusalem', and 'in my great need'.[42] In 1243 the abbot and convent of Tewkesbury stood surety for their patron, the earl of Gloucester, for the loan of £100, and nine years later the heads of three houses of which Clare was patron, Tewkesbury, Keynsham and Stoke, went to speak to the king about guaranteeing his loans.[43] Although the Cistercian statutes and later the acts of the English Benedictine provincial chapters forbade monks to stand as sureties, the practice of helping a patron in economic difficulties persisted. Grants by benefactors as well as patrons were frequently sales or loans disguised as gifts in free alms. In other financial matters, religious foundations served their patrons. The abbot of Tewkesbury (1301) and the priors of Canons Ashby (1228), Breamore and Christchurch (1293) all acted as executors for the wills of their lay patrons.[44] Monasteries sometimes held money in security for their patron, as the abbot of Aberconwy did for Prince Llywelyn in 1280,[45] and on occasion they also preserved their documents safe. Although relatively little is known, within our period, of how magnates kept their archives, it is certain that the king used the major abbeys to store royal records. Henry II, for instance, placed a copy of his coronation charter at an abbey in each county, and some religious houses were similarly responsible for custody of copies of Magna Carta.[46]

The duties and responsibilities which were expected of a patron could be rewarded in unexpected and less formal ways. Monastic chronicles might take an interest in the family of the patron, as the Tewkesbury annals, kept until 1263, did in the Clare earls of Gloucester; it has also been suggested that *Tewkesbury II*, an account of the opposition of the barons to King Henry III from 1258 to 1263, may have been composed in order to promote the interests of Richard de Clare, earl of Gloucester, the leader of the moderates among the baronial party.[47] It was at Strata Florida that the *Brut y Tywysogyon*, the deeds of the Welsh princes (1175–1332), was written, and here too were compiled the Welsh annals, which demonstrate the loyalty felt by the monks to their patrons of the house of Dinefwr; and the monks and canons of Abergavenny, Tintern and Llanthony Prima preserved the genealogies of their patronal families. Monastic writers might therefore bolster the prestige of their patrons by celebrating their deeds in battle, and telling of their glorious ancestry.

THE RESPONSIBILITIES OF A PATRON

The first duty of a patron was to provide lands for the support of the community. Initial endowments varied considerably in both the amount and quality of land and in the value of other resources; if they proved inadequate, later patrons might be expected to increase this endowment. Patrons were certainly expected, on succeeding to their lands, to confirm a monastery in possession of its property. On very rare occasions charters reveal how deeply this duty was felt. Matilda de Percy granted the church of Tadcaster to the monks of Sallay because 'the greatness of their poverty redounds to the shame and disgrace of my father and all his heirs'.[48] New sites might be provided or secured.[49] A patron was also expected to guarantee lands and secure agreements, as Richard de Morville, constable of Scotland and patron of Dryburgh, confirmed agreements between its canons and those of St James, Northampton, concerning transfers of lands.[50] He or she might also encourage the provision of grants by family and tenants. We have already remarked how Jervaulx Abbey was founded by a tenant of the honour of Richmond. Even before the community transferred to a location on the lands of Earl Conan, the earl's father had taken an interest in the foundation of his tenant. A tradition recorded in Jervaulx's foundation narrative tells how Count Alan had asked to be informed of the progress of the work.

When all the preparations for the construction of the first building had been made, brother Peter sought out the count as he had been ordered. When he [the count] came to the place where the house was to be built, he called four or five of his knights who had come with him, and said to them, with a smile on his face, as if he were joking: 'we have all got great lands and possessions. Therefore, let us now help with our own hands and build this house in the name of our Lord, and each one of us shall give land or rent in perpetual alms for the upkeep of the part he has raised.'[51]

This graphically illustrates the influence of a powerful patron, in this case the lord of the founder. Not all Count Alan's knights apparently shared his sense of humour and were only willing to agree to his proposal on certain conditions.

Lands and property, once given, needed to be retained, and here again a monastery or nunnery might look to its patron for protection against encroachment and for assistance when it encountered opposition. Ranulf of Chester, although a 'pinchpenny patron' as far as the granting of lands is concerned, nevertheless went to the help of his houses on more than one occasion. He intervened in a quarrel between the monks of Chester and Robert of Hastings, the monk of Canterbury whom they had accepted as abbot under royal and archiepiscopal pressure in 1186, and secured his deposition.[52] As well as being patron of Chester, which passed to him as direct heir, and Dieulacres, which he founded, Ranulf was patron of the Lincolnshire house of Spalding, which he inherited in 1198. He intervened in a dispute over land between Spalding and Crowland, although in this case his intervention was unsuccessful.[53] When Roger de Mowbray left England in 1147 his abbey of Byland was harassed by Robert and William de Stuteville, who were trying to regain some of their family lands which had passed to Mowbray and been granted by him to the monks. Other knights started to imitate them. Roger's immediate action was to write to the offenders, ordering them to desist and promising to hold a judicial enquiry on his return to England. He wrote also to his officials commanding them 'to protect and defend Abbot Roger of Byland and his brother monks and their land, as if it were their own land'. This last phrase finds an echo in many a charter.

Protection against physical attack might also be needed, or if this failed, restitution after the fact. Violence suffered by a religious house was some-times the result of its identification with the interests of its founder or patron. The latter's enemies might, in fact, invade and despoil a monastery as they did any other part of his possessions. In 1143, during the troubled reign of King Stephen, the monks of Selby elected as abbot Elias Paynel, cousin of Henry de Lacy, lord of Pontefract, and it has been suggested that the monks were here trying to secure for themselves the protection of a powerful local patron.[54] The plan had its disadvantages, however, for through its association with Lacy the abbey became fair game for attack by his enemy, Earl William. In roughly the same years, rivalry between Gilbert de Gant and Henry de Lacy resulted in so much damage to Henry's monastery of Pontefract that the priory church had to be rebuilt and reconsecrated in 1154x9. Gilbert's Augustinian foundation at Bridlington was attacked by his rival William of Aumale, who 'excluded the regular canons, and invaded and defiled the church' and apparently made his camp in the monastic buildings. Later he made restitution to the canons 'for the wrongs which I have done to them'. Either the culprit, or a patron, or in some cases both, were expected to make good the damage that had been sustained.[55]

THE POLITICAL DIMENSION OF PATRONAGE: WALES

The last paragraph shows instances of how the individual and personal rivalries between magnates could override religious considerations and lead to attacks on abbeys and priories by those who were, in other circumstances, enthusiastic founders and patrons of monastic houses. In

Wales the situation was pushed even further, for religious houses, because of the loyalties of their patrons, could become identified with cultural and political divisions.[56] Wales in the twelfth and thirteenth centuries, that is, before the English conquest in the years following 1277, comprised two distinct types of territory. First there were the lordships carved out by Norman and Anglo-Norman barons and knights, who held extensive powers there; second, there was Welsh Wales, *Pura Wallia*, those areas where the Welsh princes continued to rule, in theory having sworn fealty to the English king, but in practice independent of his control. Some religious houses, such as Tintern and Neath in the South, were founded by and remained in the control of Anglo-Norman lords. Others, especially in the North, were Welsh foundations. Some changed hands. Whitland and its daughter houses of Strata Florida and Cwmhir were located in *Pura Wallia* and in the case of the first two acquired, and in the third, began life with, a Welsh patron. Their recruits were Welsh, their cultural and literary tastes were Welsh, and they were endowed by the local Welsh landowners. In the course of the thirteenth century and by conquest, Whitland and Cwmhir passed to Anglo-Norman patrons. The choice their abbots and monks might be called on to make was between loyalty to a new patron and beyond him to an English king, and loyalty to their brethren and those members of the locality with whom they associated, whose language and culture they shared and whose political aspirations might conflict with those of the patron. From time to time this clash of interests surfaced. In 1217 two Cistercian abbots and five priors were deposed by the general chapter of the order; details of the episode are not entirely clear, but it seems likely that English political pressure had been brought to bear after the abbot of Strata Florida had tried to have lifted the sentence of excommunication imposed on Wales for its support of the French invasion of England in 1216. Some of the actions of the Welsh religious in support of the native dynasties could have been seen as provocative. In 1238, for instance, it was at Strata Florida Abbey that all the princes of Wales gathered to swear fealty to David, son of Llywelyn ap Iorwerth, prince of north Wales; and the abbots of Aberconwy and Strata Florida took a serious personal risk when they journeyed to London in 1248 to ask for the body of Gruffydd ap Llywelyn, who had died accidentally in the Tower. This they were granted, and took back for burial in the abbey of Aberconwy. Finally, when the last native-born prince of Wales, Llywelyn ap Gruffydd, was killed by the English in December 1282 and his head sent to Edward I, it was at a nearby Cistercian house, Cwmhir, that his body was laid to rest.

There was a price to pay for such loyalty, which it would be anachronistic to call national feeling or sentiment, but which went beyond the duty owed to a single patron. In 1212 King John ordered the destruction of Strata Florida, 'which harbours our enemies'. Five years later the Anglo-Norman lords of Cemais, Kidwelly and Carew battered down the doors of Whitland Abbey, stripped the church of its treasures, beat the monks and killed their servants. In 1228 a grange of Cwmhir at Gwern y Gof was burnt in retaliation for help given by the monks to the Welsh. These actions were matched by Welsh attacks on Anglo-Norman foundations. The church of Kidwelly Priory was burnt by Gruffydd ap Llywelyn; Grace Dieu was destroyed when the Welsh disputed the right of the founder to the site; and between 1257 and 1265 Carmarthen Priory, which lay just outside the royal borough itself, was burnt during a Welsh attack. The English Crown recognized that monasteries, whoever their patron might be, could be the victims of war, and there are numerous instances of compensation paid from the treasury to religious houses which had sustained war damage. After the second campaign of Edward I against Llywelyn (1283–4), £1,700 was paid to the Welsh church, of which £897 16s. 8d. went to religious houses. However, there was a disparity in the sums of money paid to individual houses, which may not only reflect the degree of damage, but also represent punishment for those monasteries which actively aided the Welsh cause. When the conquest was over Edward I made a progress through Wales, during which he visited several monastic houses, some of which were recompensed for war damage. Like lay leaders, heads of the religious orders had to conform to the new régime and swear allegiance to the English prince of Wales. They had to serve new masters and new patrons, and were used by the English king as tools in the imposition of the English yoke on Wales.

THE WIDER MONASTIC INTERESTS OF THE NOBILITY

There were some circumstances in which it was difficult for a monastery to identify a founder: we have noted how a number of the friaries of each of the mendicant orders came into being as the result of corporate action, so that there was no single founder. The anchoritic origin of nunneries also makes it difficult at times to associate them with one family. In such circumstances a house might place itself under the protection of a powerful patron. Alternatively benefactors, those who made endowments to a religious house without having the special status of founder, could be more important. One house which found itself in this position was Fountains Abbey, one of the most wealthy and important houses of the North which, as we have seen, resulted from a breakaway movement by a group of monks from the York Benedictine abbey, who were given shelter and then a site for a new house by the archbishop of York. Archbishop Thurstan had had his hand forced, and he probably could not afford to deplete further the lands belonging to the see of York by endowing the house generously. The new foundation was, therefore, forced to rely on magnates, knights and peasants for material support, great and small.[57] Among the baronage of the North, the Mowbrays, Stutevilles and Percys, although closely involved with family foundations of their own, were nevertheless generous in their gifts, and acted at times as patrons or advocates of the house and derived suitable benefits. Roger de Mowbray was called on to settle disputes between the monks and Drogo the forester. William de Stuteville was interred at Fountains. Three members of the Percy family, William II, his daughter Matilda, countess of Warwick, and her nephew Richard, all received burial at Fountains, despite their devotion to their own family monasteries of Whitby and Sallay. Alice de Rumilly, a great benefactor of the house, was described once as 'advocate' of the monks, though this probably meant that she was acting as guarantor of the particular lands which she had given; she was accordingly 'protector' of the monks in a limited sense.[58] Dr Wardrop's close analysis of the Fountains charters has revealed that a remarkable number of spiritual benefits were granted by the monks to members of all strata of society. Over ninety requests for burial were recorded. This illustrates two things: first, the devotion to the Cistercian abbey felt by local people, those of both knightly and lesser rank; and second, the range of monastic interests exhibited by the very well-to-do. Roger de Mowbray was patron of two, and benefactor of over forty, religious houses in England and Normandy. From many he received spiritual succour; from others, notably Fountains, he received also more immediate and tangible rewards in the form of loans and mortgages needed to finance his earthly adventures, rebellion against the king, and crusade and pilgrimage to the Holy Land.

One family whose monastic patronage has been studied in detail is that of Clare, members of which were founders of priories dependent on Bec and among the principal English benefactors of the Norman house.[59] Later branches of the family were founders of the Cistercian abbeys of Tintern and Ford. They acquired the patronage of the Augustinian priory of Little Dunmow, founded the Arrouaisian community at Bourne, established regular canons at Walsingham, and brought the Austin friars to England. Some of the Clare foundations, like Bourne and Clare itself, were honorial, that is, they were connected with the particular honour in which they were located, not with the whole family. When the Clares became earls of Gloucester in 1217 their power base moved from the east of England to the west, and the most important house of which they were patrons was now Tewkesbury Abbey. Here it was that the Clare earls were buried, not in one of their ancestral monasteries. Like many well-to-do monastic founders and patrons, Roger de Mowbray and the Clares and others whom we have noted elsewhere, like David I of Scotland, did not limit their benefactions to one house or one order. Their endowments reveal a wide range of interests and a desire for the prayers of many groups of religious. Their interests were also, in part at least, dictated by the material benefits to be enjoyed by patronage of a religious house.

Like any other piece of property the patronage of a religious house could be a cause of contention. Rival claimants might vie for its ownership. Patron and monastery might fall out. Patron and mother house might dispute each other's rights in a dependent priory. There were arguments over rights in elections and custody, and over conflicting interests of patron and house as landlords and tenants. But however strained a relationship might be, it was one which neither side could afford to neglect. The patron needed the prayers of his or her community; the community, unless very powerful in its own right, needed protection. Small and poor houses, especially nunneries, were vulnerable, and this may explain the voluntary submission to a patron which we meet occasionally. The tiny Yorkshire convent of Foukeholme, for instance, agreed to commit itself to the custody of its patron William de Coleville: this meant that Coleville and his heirs had the right to consent to the election of the prioress, to authorize the appointment of any male master or guardian, and to approve the reception of all nuns, sisters and lay people.[60] Such intervention would not have been welcome at all religious houses, but the economic circumstances of Foukeholme made such dependence a necessity of life.

The relationship of patron and house was one of infinite variety. Some of its aspects were formal, others less so. Just as monastic houses might cement the relationship with their patrons by compiling their genealogies or celebrating family exploits in annals and histories, so too did patrons show their affection and esteem by the giving of gifts. These tokens of esteem were indicative of a special bond. Walter de Gant, founder of Bridlington, presented to the canons a phylactery and relics which his brother Baldwin had sent him from Jerusalem. Edmund of Cornwall gave to Hailes Abbey a relic of the Holy Blood; this was not just a gesture, for it gave the abbey a pre-eminence and a chance to profit from the pilgrim trade. The success of a religious house reflected the success and prestige of its founder and subsequent patrons.

BISHOPS AS PATRONS

We have already considered some aspects of the role of the diocesan bishop in the affairs of the religious houses of his diocese, notably, in the case of the non-exempt orders, his right to hear the profession of monks, to bless the newly elected head of a house, and to visit monasteries and nunneries periodically to ensure the maintenance of discipline. In other instances there was a closer relationship because the bishop stood in the role of patron. Some houses had episcopal patrons because they owed their foundation to bishops, and we might think here, among many, of Bishop Alexander of Lincoln's foundations at Dorchester on Thames, Haverholme, Louth Park and Thame, William Giffard of Winchester's Cistercian house at Waverley, Bishop Roger of Coventry's abbey of Buildwas, and Bishop Bernard of St David's monastery at Whitland. At other houses bishops later acquired the patronage: King John, for instance, granted the patronage of Glastonbury, St Osyth's and Thorney to local bishops,[61] and the acquisition of Glastonbury by the bishop of Bath and Wells marked the end of a long attempt to gain control of the rich abbey, during the course of which many appeals had been made to Rome.[62] Sometimes the functions of patronage might be shared, as they were at the Premonstratensian monastery of Titchfield, founded by Peter des Roches, bishop of Winchester; his successors remained patrons, but the Cantilupe family became the canons' advocates.[63] In addition bishops might act as a kind of unofficial patron, looking after the interests of the houses of their diocese, confirming their possessions and settling their disputes, especially perhaps when they lacked a strong lay patron.[64]

Bishops as patrons enjoyed the same expectations as their lay counterparts. They took advantage of the rights of hospitality. In the latter part of the twelfth century a bishop of Coventry claimed hospitality at Buildwas 'because the abbey was founded by one of my predecessors', and 'I can and ought to go to those brothers whenever I wish, more certainly than to others.'[65] In another diocese and another century John of Pontoise, bishop of Winchester, claimed that Titchfield, of which he was patron, had always given hospitality to previous bishops when they returned from the continent.[66] There are instances when bishops as patrons seem to have rescued a house from mismanagement. In the thirteenth century Archbishop Winchelsey appointed a custodian for St Gregory's, Canterbury, to sort out its debts. Archbishop John le Romeyn of York (1285–96) wrote to the abbot of Clairvaux and to the Cistercian visitors in England to complain about the poor state of affairs at Fountains. Some time later, because of the chaos of its financial management, the king took the abbey into his custody.[67] This is one of the very few instances of an archbishop of York acting as patron of the house founded by one of his predecessors.

There are two abbeys which Knowles singled out for special attention as episcopal abbeys, where, he argued, the bishop enjoyed a special status as patron. These were Eynsham and Selby. The community at Eynsham, an early eleventh-century foundation, had been moved to Stow by Bishop Remigius of Lincoln, but the monks were brought back to Eynsham by his successor Robert Bloet (1093–1123). The bishop of Lincoln thereafter had the right to appoint the abbot and to control the temporalities of Eynsham. Selby in Yorkshire was a Benedictine house in which the kings of England took an interest. Not long after its foundation, William II granted the abbey to the archbishop of York 'to hold as the archbishop of Canterbury holds the church of Rochester'. This terse phrase is difficult to interpret, but it seems to confer on the archbishop some powers of patronage over Selby. Whether these were ever exercised is difficult to know. There are later documentary references to the intervention of an archbishop of York in the affairs of Selby, particularly in the deposition and appointment of its abbots. However, whether these instances represent the actions of a patron or a diocesan is not easy to distinguish; this is a general problem in attempting to assess the role of episcopal patrons.[68]

A similar dichotomy or, perhaps, lack of definition, in the role of the bishop can be observed at the ten English and one Scottish monastic cathedrals. In these institutions the role of the bishop could be interpreted in a number of ways. He stood in the place of abbot, and the resident head of the community was thus the prior. But in a way the bishop of a cathedral priory was also its patron: towards the end of our period the bishop of Winchester claimed to be both abbot and patron of the cathedral priory, abbot because he professed the monks, and patron because he answered for the temporal services due from the community. The monks denied that he was either and claimed the king as their patron.[69] From the Conquest onwards the relationship of bishop and community came under greater pressure than it had hitherto known. Election was a key issue. The *Regularis Concordia* had laid down that the bishop was to be elected by the chapter, but this conflicted with the claims of the king, and in the case of the archbishop of Canterbury, with the bishops of the province. Nearly every election to the southern metropolitan see witnessed attempts by the monks to assert their right to be the sole electors of their abbot. Further, as abbot, the bishop had the right to appoint the prior, but the period under review saw a move towards claims to election by the community. There were also disputes about the administration of priory lands, especially after the separation of the revenues of bishop (abbot) and convent. William Giffard, although a noted patron of the religious orders, nevertheless quarrelled with his monks at Winchester over the temporalities after the division of revenues. Much of the long period of office of Hugh du Puiset of Durham (1153–95) was troubled by his attempts to administer the temporalities of the priory.[70]

Such uneasy relationships led to a number of celebrated disputes, the most notorious of which was probably that between Baldwin, the Cistercian archbishop, and the monks of Canterbury. Baldwin was translated from Worcester by the king in 1184, and was not one of the candidates proposed by the monks. He caused an early clash by depriving the priory of some of its property, but the main problem came with his proposal to found a collegiate church which would have threatened the pre-eminence of the cathedral. The idea outraged the monks, who appealed to Rome. During the course of the quarrel Baldwin kept the monks imprisoned within the cathedral precinct and suspended services. Henry II was in favour of the scheme for a collegiate church, but his son Richard I forced its abandonment.[71] Quite what capacity Baldwin was acting in is unclear. Was it as abbot or patron? The Canterbury dispute is only one, albeit a famous one, of a number of clashes between bishops and monasteries in the twelfth and thirteenth centuries. Not all concerned the relationship of a bishop to his cathedral priory; others were created when bishops challenged title to monastic property or to spiritual jurisdiction over parish churches, or when religious houses sought exemption from episcopal visitation. In these instances the monasteries clashed with the bishop as diocesan. But there can be no doubt that the uniquely British institution of the cathedral monastery brought with it problems, which were not easily solved, for the bishop who was at one time both abbot and patron.

Over the period covered by this study the role of the patron, whether lay or episcopal, was subject to a number of changes. First, and most obviously, by 1300 far more people were involved with religious houses in the capacity of patron than in 1000, when to all intents and purposes the royal house was the special advocate and protector of all monasteries and nunneries. The widening of the social group from which founders were drawn is a common European experience. In the course of the twelfth century the constitutions of the new orders tried to delineate, indeed circumscribe, the powers of the patron, while in the thirteenth, developments in canon and civil law tended to define more sharply a patron's powers, especially with regard to elections and custody. Moreover, it has been remarked that patrons' charters of the thirteenth century are more likely than in previous years to be specific. Not only do they more commonly make endowments for a particular purpose – the buying of books, for instance, or the relief of the poor – but they are also more confident in their demands. No longer did patrons expect spiritual benefits in whatever form the recipients of their generosity thought fit. They were more likely to define the number and type of prayers and masses to be celebrated for their souls, and even impose sanctions for the non-performance of spiritual services.[72] There is much that we do not know, however, of contacts between a religious house and its patron on a less formal level. The vast majority of day-to-day dealings are simply not recorded in the written sources. However, what this chapter has amply revealed is the degree of dependence of a religious house on its local patron in all sorts of ways, and the reciprocal nature of the relationship. It is clear, too, that the withdrawal from the world which monks, canons and nuns sought was far from total, and that their ability to pursue a life of prayer, contemplation and spiritual service within the confines of their house depended in large measure on the material support offered by their lay patrons and benefactors.

II

THE MONASTIC ECONOMY

On numerous occasions the Rule of St Benedict reminds the monks that they are to have no private possessions. But it was assumed that the monastery would have possessions; and this was in no way incompatible with the monastic ideal. Poverty was personal, not corporate. Religious houses became landowners; and their economic practices were affected by a number of factors. First, there was the ethos of the order to which a house belonged. The Cistercians, as we have seen, sought remote sites and rejected all revenue which was derived either from the possession of *spiritualia*[1] or from the work of others. The mendicants were not intended to own property at all, although certain friaries did come into possession of arable land, orchards and gardens in their immediate vicinity.[2] Equally important factors in the economic development of a house were its size and geographical location and the nature and extent of its estates, and their distance from the mother house. These conditions in turn bear upon the records which were generated, and determine what we can know of the management of monastic estates. On the whole, large houses with sizeable holdings produced more records, and are accordingly much better documented than smaller ones. Thus, the following discussion, which looks more closely at two major aspects of the monastic economy, sources of income and the management of resources, centres on the large houses, which cannot but distort the overall picture.

A discussion of the economic assets of religious houses will lead us to the question of their wealth. How wealthy – or otherwise – were they? Any attempt either to estimate the wealth or poverty of the religious houses of Britain or to evaluate their general contribution to the economy or agriculture of Britain is fraught with difficulties. The religious houses are so numerous, and their situation over three centuries so varied, that any generalization is impossible. Yet some remarks can be made. In 1291 and again in 1535 the assets of the monastic houses of England and Wales were valued. Both sets of figures must be used with caution. The one which falls within the period under review, the *Taxatio Ecclesiastica* of 1291, has been shown to be inaccurate in some respects, and almost certainly contains omissions and undervaluations;[3] yet it may be read as an approximate index of monastic wealth and poverty. The same may be said of the *Valor Ecclesiasticus*, compiled on the eve of the Dissolution of the monasteries. What these valuations show us is that the houses which head the list as the most wealthy were those which had their origins in the years before the Norman Conquest, houses like Glastonbury and Westminster. Some post-Conquest Benedictine houses, notably St Mary's, York, Reading and Durham, and a handful of houses of the new orders, like Cirencester, Leicester, Merton and Fountains, made it into the top league, but they were the exception. The pattern of wealth and endowment had in many respects already been set by 1066. In the twelfth century the scramble for land and rivalry for endowments meant that few new houses were able to achieve the wealth and status of the older Benedictine establishments. In Wales the picture is different because of the absence of monastic houses before the late eleventh century. Using the 1291 taxation as our guide, we can see that the Cistercian houses of Margam and Neath appear to have been the most wealthy, with incomes assessed at £256 and £236 respectively.[4] Their nearest challengers were Llanthony Prima (£233) and Goldcliff (£172). In general, in both England and Wales the poorest houses were those of the regular canons and Gilbertines, but more especially the post-Conquest foundations for women. With only a few notable exceptions the nunneries failed to achieve a substantial income, and many must have been existing at subsistence level.[5] The religious houses of Scotland were valued in 1561, when the Crown assumed one-third of the income of all ecclesiastical benefices. In assessing how accurate these figures are likely to be we need to take into account the substantial damage sustained by some houses during the English invasions of the first half of the sixteenth century, and as a result of popular hostility. Nevertheless, these figures may be read as an approximate guide to relative values. They indicate that the most wealthy Scottish communities were the cathedral priory of St Andrews, with an estimated minimum income of £12,500, the Tironensian house of Arbroath (£10,924) and Dunfermline Abbey (£9,630). The foundations for wealth appear to have lain in the endowments of the Scottish royal family in the twelfth century. Houses of friars did not, apparently, rise to incomes of over £100, and, as in England and Wales, the poorest houses were those of the female congregations; only North Berwick, at £1,800, had an assessed annual value of over £500.[6]

INCOME AND EXPENDITURE

Sources of income

Land for arable and pastoral farming

Land was by far the most important economic resource enjoyed by the religious orders. In many cases houses failed to add significantly to their initial endowments;[7] others supplemented their benefactions through further grants or through their own efforts. The main period of landed expansion was from the era of foundation to the end of the twelfth century; benefactions continued to be made in the thirteenth century, but a significant watershed was the Statute of Mortmain of 1279, which prohibited the unauthorized alienation of property to religious houses.[8] Indications of the nature of the land obtained by the religious orders can come from a variety of sources. Sometimes, though not frequently, a charter specified that the land was arable or cultivated land, occasionally indicating its quality: whether it was good, likely to yield profit, mediocre or poor. Other indications of the location of the main arable lands of a house come from account rolls (of which none are extant from before the thirteenth century),[9] which may show how much and what kind of produce lands were yielding. Arable land supplied food for consumption at a religious house, and any surplus could be sold to buy goods; and it has been suggested that it was a need for arable in the vicinity of a house which prompted the site changes of a number of Augustinian houses, among them Bolton and Lilleshall.[10] Although the majority of houses probably operated a mixed economy, it is likely that those in the corn-rich lands of the South and midlands relied more on arable than houses in the more mountainous North and West. However, the Cistercians had a large number of predominantly arable granges in the North, some with over a thousand acres of cultivated land. Among other orders Bolton Priory in the late thirteenth century produced most of its own corn, relying less than it had done previously on sheep, in contrast to Malton Priory, which concentrated on sheep farming and had to purchase its grain.[11] Although in general Wales was a land of pastoral rather than arable husbandry, Welsh religious houses appear to have managed to supply their own needs in normal circumstances. Strata Florida deliberately set out to obtain low-lying land for growing grain on the coastal plain of Cardiganshire as well as further afield in the valleys of

the Wye and Severn.[12] In the late thirteenth century the monks of
Margam possessed over 7,000 acres of arable, those of Neath and
Whitland over 5,000 acres, and even the small nunnery of Llanllŷr over
1,000 acres. The monastic ploughlands could not, however, meet extra-
ordinary needs, and the famine of 1189 sent the monks of Margam to
Bristol to buy corn to feed the starving who gathered at their doors, while
in 1234 the abbot of Neath sought and gained permission to buy corn in
England.[13]

Many houses, in addition to arable, obtained lands which were more
suitable for a pastoral economy, the keeping of cows, sheep and other
animals. Grantors sometimes specified the number and type of animals for
which land was intended, or gave to religious houses a share in the
common pasture of a village, where they were then obliged to
co-operate with their neighbours. A pastoral economy became particularly important for houses situated in East Anglia, in the north of
England, and in Scotland and Wales, where the terrain was suitable for the
keeping of large flocks. In these regions, as we shall see, the White Monks
became particularly important as sheep farmers. The geographical divide
was not clear-cut, however, and southern houses were also major keepers
of animals: cows, sheep and goats for milk and cheese, cows also for their
hides and for ploughing, sheep for their fleeces, and pigs for meat, lard and
hides. Horses were important for travel and haulage, and are recorded on
many monastic estates. The monks of Margam, Neath and Strata Florida
bred horses which fetched high prices, and herds are also recorded on the
estates of Grace Dieu, Basingwerk, Cwmhir and Tintern.[14] Cattle were
very important, indeed may have been as important as sheep on some
Cistercian estates, particularly in the North, the Fenlands and Wales,
where the marshland provided suitable pasture for cows. The earliest
reference to a Cistercian vaccary (dairy farm or breeding station) comes
from Byland Abbey, which within two years of its foundation had one at
Cambe;[15] and Fountains Abbey gave over the whole of its pastures in
Nidderdale to cattle. By the thirteenth century several houses had their
own tanneries.

It was, however, as keepers of sheep that the Cistercians have become
most famed, and wool was the main cash-crop of twelfth-century Britain;
the production and export of this commodity will be treated more fully
later in this chapter. Yet although the Cistercians and their emulators were
foremost in the development of sheep farming and the wool trade, their
importance, or at least their priority, should not be overstressed. Several
large Benedictine houses were also major sheep farmers: already in 1086
Ely had flocks of over 13,000 sheep, and the Norman nunnery of Holy
Trinity, Caen, grazed 1,700 sheep on Minchinhampton common in

Gloucestershire. The numbers of sheep kept by individual religious houses is impossible to determine with any frequency. The grant of pasture for a thousand sheep, for instance, does not mean that a thousand sheep were kept there; often, as pressure on pasture grew, this was intended to denote an upper limit. Moreover, the occurrence of disease such as sheep-rot and murrain meant that the size of monastic flocks must have fluctuated widely. Occasional numerical references do, however, exist. A survey of 1125 shows that the monks of Peterborough grazed just over 1,600 sheep and lambs, nearly half that number on their Northamptonshire estates.[16] In 1270–80 Meaux Abbey pastured 11,000 sheep on their estates, and at roughly the same date the monks of Beaulieu had flocks totalling over 5,000 sheep.[17]

The extension of arable and pasture land

It is generally agreed that the eleventh and twelfth centuries witnessed a growth in the population of Europe. There followed a rise in prices and increase in trade, which in turn led to developments in the way in which religious houses, as landlords, administered their property. An especially urgent need was the extension of land under cultivation, mostly as arable, but also as pasture. In the process of clearance of new lands, of reclamation of fen, marsh, woodland and waste, the religious orders of the twelfth and thirteenth centuries played a major role, in Britain as on the continent. The evidence for monastic activity in land clearance comes from a number of sources. Charters granted to religious houses 'assarts' or 'riddings', that is, areas cleared ready for cultivation; but frequently they received land and permission to assart it as they were able or as they wished. Pipewell Abbey, for instance, received licence to 'assart and reduce to agricultural land'.[18] Although the Cistercians are especially well known in this field of activity, both old and new orders were active. The colonization of Northamptonshire by Peterborough Abbey is well recorded after 1066, and may well have taken place also in the late Anglo-Saxon period.[19] In 1143 the monks received confirmation of all their assarts so far created; and twenty years later they were fined for assarting without licence in four places. Their important manor of Paston in Norfolk was created largely from waste land, and in the area around Oundle nearly a thousand acres were brought into use by the late thirteenth century. Another ancient Benedictine abbey, Glastonbury, was active in extending land under cultivation, not as at Peterborough by clearing forest but by assarting waste around the house, draining meres and building embankments around marshes.[20]

It has been demonstrated that a number of houses of Augustinian canons were also active in the clearance of land, among them Bristol,

Maiden Bradley (Wiltshire), Darley (Derbyshire), Waltham (Essex) and Merton (Surrey).[21] However, it is the White Monks who are most noted as colonizers, and it is significant that many place names make their first recorded appearance in the cartularies of Cistercian and Premonstratensian houses, especially in the North, indicating the creation of new areas of settlement and cultivation.[22] The precise degree to which the Cistercians were involved in land clearance and the size of their contribution have been much debated; but their role was less prominent in Britain than in some other areas of Europe, for the simple reason that England was by the twelfth century already a well-settled land where the opportunities for expansion were limited. Despite the Cistercian ruling that houses should be 'remote from the dwellings of men', few British Cistercian houses could be called truly remote, and most were on the fringes of settlement.[23] Assarting sometimes took place at the site of a house – the environs of Byland had to be drained, and the abbey of Warden was also known as St Mary *de Essartis*, 'of the assarts'[24] – but more commonly the assarting of land was associated with Cistercian granges where lands were cleared to extend the area under cultivation. One of the debated issues is the extent to which the monks resettled land recorded as 'waste' in Domesday Book,[25] or how far recovery had already taken place by the time of the coming of the Cistercians. The evidence suggests that over 40 per cent of twelfth-century granges were settled on lands recorded as waste in 1086, although only one grange, that of Pickering (Rievaulx), seems to have been carved totally from waste. In some areas, notably Wensleydale and Airedale, the White Monks appear to have been agents of recolonization in areas depopulated since the late eleventh century.[26] One of the advantages to be gained from the opening up of lands was that they were freed from the payment of tithes. In 1132 the White Monks obtained a papal concession that they did not need to pay tithes on any land which they cultivated themselves. So prized was this tax concession that others sought it too, and in the thirteenth century the abbot of Cîteaux complained that certain English nunneries were wrongfully claiming Cistercian status in order to obtain the privilege.[27] It can well be imagined that exemption was a cause of conflict between abbeys and parish churches, and the cartularies of many religious houses contain copies of agreements under which the monks made a token payment for tithes. In 1215 the Fourth Lateran Council addressed the general problem and restricted exemption to those lands acquired before the Council and those which had been brought into cultivation by the monks, 'new land' (*novalia*).

All over England Cistercian houses were associated to a greater or lesser degree with the clearance of forest, the drainage of marsh and the conversion of waste and scrub lands. In the Fens, Sawtry, Swineshead and Revesby were especially active, and in Yorkshire the monks of Meaux drained and banked the lands on their granges in the low-lying valley of the Humber. Wales was also an area which by the late twelfth century was becoming more intensively farmed. Two Cistercian granges, one belonging to Neath and the other to Tintern, were known as the 'grange of the assart', indicating that they were situated on lands which had been newly brought into use. Further evidence for assarting, particularly in woodland areas, comes from the royal pipe rolls, the accounts of the sheriffs of each shire which show the money owed to the king each year. Among other things they note any unlicensed activity; and on forty occasions between 1155 and 1212 Cistercian houses were fined either for wasting (felling trees) or assarting in the royal forests without permission. Some abbeys in Wales as in England fell foul of royal authority: in 1282 Tintern was fined for clearing 200 acres of royal forest without licence.[28]

Other natural resources

Revenue and resources also came to religious houses through the donation of assets and commodities which could be used or sold for cash. They obtained fisheries along rivers and coasts, which supplied them with a vital element in the monastic diet.[29] The Welsh Cistercians enjoyed access to a variety of fish: herrings from their fisheries on Cardigan Bay, eels and trout from the Teifi pools, and salmon from the Teifi and the Wye, from where Tintern supplied its daughter house of Kingswood in Gloucestershire.[30] Stixwould Priory obtained the right to take fish from the rivers Witham and Humber at points thirty-five miles from the house.[31] Saltpans yielded salt for preserving food; quarries provided stone for building; woodland offered valuable pasture for pigs as well as timber for building and furnishing the conventual church, for constructing houses and sheepfolds, for hedging and fencing, and for fuel. Peat was another important source of fuel, and many houses were in receipt of the grant of turbaries. Some religious houses obtained important mineral rights and materials, such as iron ore and charcoal for smelting. The Cistercians of Byland and Rievaulx produced pig-iron in their smithies in the West Riding of Yorkshire. In the thirteenth century Margam Abbey received the right to mine coal, lead and iron, though the evidence for their actually doing so is sparse. Similarly the degree of involvement of the monks of Monmouth, Tintern and Grace Dieu in the iron industry of the Forest of Dean is difficult to judge.[32] Tintern had two forges here, one as early as 1141, and one forge at least was in operation in 1267, when the abbey was apparently smelting without licence. The White

Monks of the Scottish abbeys of Newbattle and Culross were pioneer coal-miners.[33]

Manors and manorial rights

Land was an especially valuable asset when it was conveyed to a religious house with existing rights and jurisdiction. The basic rural unit of settlement in England was the village, but in terms of organization in much of the country it was not the village that was important so much as the manor. A manor (Latin *manerium*) was not just a piece of land: it was a complex institution, the origins of which are still being investigated by archaeologists and historians. A manor could be co-terminous with a village; on the other hand, a manor might comprise several villages, or a village several manors. There was a variety of patterns. In practical terms a manor comprised land held in demesne by a lord, that is, worked directly on his behalf, and land held by the lord's tenants. The tenants owed service to the lord on the demesne for a certain number of days a year, and rent for their share of the tenanted land, either in money or in kind. A survey of Peterborough's manors made between 1125 and 1128 indicates that each demesne manor provided a 'farm' of cash or grain, or both; the total received was £382 5s. 4d., of which £284 13s. 4d. came from money rents and £97 12s. from grain.[34] The transfer of a manor to a religious house, therefore, provided a major economic asset. Because possession of a manor involved financial gain through the work of others it was rejected as a source of revenue by the early Cistercians. It is therefore the Black Monks who are most readily associated with the administration of their lands through manors, particularly in the South and midlands, which in contrast to the North had been heavily manorialized for centuries. Benedictine houses so became important lords of the manor, enjoying the possession not just of agricultural assets and labour, but also of jurisdictional privileges.

The possession of manors was not, however, limited to the Benedictines. The regular canons, as might be expected given the diversity in the size, location and nature of their houses, enjoyed a wide variety of economic assets. Some, like Christchurch, Oseney and Waltham, owned many manors.[35] Although the site of remote Llanthony Prima associated it with Cistercian rather than Benedictine practice, the priory's Herefordshire estates were organized through a traditional manorial structure, with the canons being in receipt of the labour services of the peasantry, rent and the profits of manorial courts.[36] As in other areas Cistercian rigour began to break down by the later twelfth and thirteenth centuries. When King John founded a Cistercian house his endowment included the manor of Faringdon, and when the monks moved to

Beaulieu in 1204 they retained the manor with all its appurtenant rights.[37] It was not just new foundations which succumbed to the temptation to hold manorial rights. In 1230 the monks of Margam took over the vill of Bonvilston, which, although not described as a manor, was in fact a similar settlement with a complex of rights and jurisdiction.[38] Indeed, the transfer of labour services to the Welsh Cistercians may have come much sooner, and it has been argued that the granges of Strata Florida were superimposed upon a semi-manorialized Celtic organization of just such rights and dues.[39]

The manorial system can be seen in the twelfth century at its most comprehensive in the survey of Templar lands in England, compiled around 1185.[40] The famous Inquest lists all the properties acquired by the Knights Templar in the seventy-five years or so since their introduction into Britain: these sometimes comprised a few acres in a village, and sometimes an entire manor. It clearly indicates, too, the money and labour services due to the Knights as landlords and lords of the manor. A later example of services owed by monastic tenants can be drawn from the records of Westminster Abbey, which give us a detailed picture of the annual dues of a customary tenant on the abbey manor of Teddington (Middlesex). A tenant had to perform three works each week during harvest and three each fortnight for the rest of the year. If he owned a plough he was to plough and harrow three acres for seeding and two for fallow. He mowed the demesne meadow together with the other tenants, for which he got his dinner and 6d. for ale. He was further responsible for finding two men for three boon-works during harvest, who received allowances of food and ale. His renders in kind comprised fifteen sheaves of rye, barley and oats, and a hen at Christmas (shared between two tenants), a bushel of grain at Whitsuntide, and five eggs at Easter. Finally, as money rent he paid 2s. yearly and 1d. per animal for the right of pannage, that is, for pasturing his pigs.[41]

Mills

Mills too provided a valuable source of income.[42] When a religious house came into possession of a mill it could use it for its own purposes; on the other hand it might also exercise the right of multure, that is, charge villagers to have their corn ground there. The Cistercians, in rejecting any such forms of revenue, allowed their houses to have mills only for domestic use. In time, however, they came to accept the grant of mills for use by other than their own communities. As early as 1157 the general chapter reminded the order of the ban on the acceptance of mills, but only a year later Woburn Abbey accepted one from the king. Bordesley, Thame and Warden were among other Cistercian houses which violated the rule.[43] The value to a community of the possession of a mill is demonstrated by a story, told by Jocelin of Brakelond, of how the abbot of Bury reacted when he heard that Herbert the dean had built a wind-mill near one controlled by the abbey:

he boiled with fury and could hardly eat or speak. The following day, after Mass, he told the sacrist to get his carpenters there without delay to demolish it and store the timber in a secure place. On receiving news of this, the dean came to say that he was quite within his rights to act as he had on his freehold land, and that no one ought to be denied the use of the wind. He maintained that he had intended to grind only his own grain there and no one else's, so as not to be regarded as having caused loss to neighbouring mills.

The abbot was not convinced:

What on earth do you think you are doing? It is certainly not without loss to my mills, as you contend, because the townspeople will flock to your mill to grind their grain as they please . . . Go away. Before you get home you will hear what is going to become of your mill.

The abbot succeeded in terrifying the dean so much that he himself demolished the mill before the sacrist's men could get there.[44]

Town property and monastic boroughs

Some of the revenue of monasteries and nunneries derived from the possession of property and other economic assets in towns. Occasionally this was in the form of cash income, like the 40s. annual rent from the revenues of Roxburgh granted by King David of Scotland to Kelso Abbey. More often, however, tenements were granted to the religious, who then either retained the property for their own use, or leased it to tenants. Sometimes monasteries located at a distance from a major urban centre found it convenient to retain property in towns such as London and York for their own use, in order to provide accommodation for monastic officials on business there. It was common, however, for urban property to be leased to tenants, who paid rent either in kind – such as the annual render of a buck, a pound of cumin, a pair of white gloves, and a rose received by Shrewsbury Abbey from some of its tenants – or in money; Matthew Paris tells how John of Hertford, who became abbot of St Albans in 1235, acquired property in London, and then 'constructed some noble new houses there and raised the rent'.[45] Several Augustinian houses, notably those which were themselves located in or near towns, obtained urban property. Southwark had a foothold in London early in the twelfth century, and by 1291 apparently held forty-seven properties there; while the London tenements of Holy Trinity, Aldgate, accounted for around 60 per cent of the priory's income from temporalities.[46] Two other Augustinian houses, Oseney Abbey and Barnwell Priory, became the largest landowners in medieval Oxford and Cambridge respectively.

In Scotland, by 1296, twenty-four or so religious houses came to possess property in around forty burghs.[47] Often these properties were of major importance in a monastery's economy; the second largest estate of Lindores (Tironensian), for example, was the burgh at Newburgh which the monks created and developed.[48] The strongest monastic presence, however, was in the important burgh of Berwick, on the river Tweed, which formed the border between England and Scotland. Here fifteen Scottish houses held tenements, of which Melrose with ten and Kelso with nine were the most prominent.[49] The fiscal nature of their interests in town property is indicated by the frequency with which it was rented out: only three houses, Melrose, Newbattle and Arbroath, seem to have retained one property for their own use, and a fourth house, Coupar Angus, did so until some time between 1212 and 1240. It is for these very houses that we also have evidence of involvement in trade, and their desire to retain use of their Berwick property rather than to view it simply as a source of income was undoubtedly dictated by the importance of Berwick as a commercial centre.

It was probably because of their growing involvement with trade that the Cistercians, who at first avoided urban areas, increasingly came to own town property. By 1300 seventeen Cistercian monasteries had houses in London. Abbeys in Yorkshire and Lincolnshire concentrated on acquisitions in York, Boston and Lincoln, while the Welsh houses turned to Bristol (where Margam was the most important Welsh monastic landowner), and Cardiff and Chester. An urban toe-hold was also important for those who wished to buy and sell at local markets. By 1225 Strata Marcella had three shops in the market place at Shrewsbury. The monks of Melrose obtained land in Boston on which to build houses, and when these were complete they agreed to share them during fair time with the monks of their daughter house of Holm Cultram.[50] Stixwould Priory obtained land in Lincoln with a landing stage on the river Witham three miles from the city, and also in Boston, where with one property the nuns obtained the right of free entry and exit for themselves, their servants, horses, wagons and carts, during the annual fair.[51] Privileges within urban areas were also important, and by 1200 Whitland, Neath, Llantarnam and Tintern were all free from toll in Bristol, a concession which had been enjoyed by Margam since 1183 at the latest.[52]

Thirty towns in England and Wales, known as monastic boroughs, were totally under the control of a religious house. Twenty-five were controlled by the Benedictines and five by the Augustinians. They included Bury St Edmunds (where the abbey's administration is chronicled in Jocelin's account of Abbot Samson), Burton-on-Trent, Evesham, Tavistock, Winchcombe and St Albans, and among the post-Conquest foundations, Shrewsbury, Durham, Whitby, Selby and Battle, where the borough grew up around the Conqueror's abbey and provided the services which the community needed.[53] The monastic boroughs produced revenue from the fines and amercements collected in the abbey's court, rents and rates, and tolls from market and mill. Bury is undoubtedly the best-documented monastic borough. After the division of the revenues of abbot and convent, the borough became the property of the abbey, and thus it was the sacrist rather than the abbot who was lord of the borough.[54] When this development first occurred is not certain, and the first reference to the sacrist as lord of the borough appears to date from 1145–54. Thereafter he was responsible for the appointment of the bailiffs, overseeing the administration of justice and supervising the gaol and its keeper. Within these boroughs the monastery was an important factor in urban growth. Under Abbot Baldwin (1065–97) five new streets and a new market place were constructed at Bury. Matthew Paris tells us that Abbot Leofstan of St Albans (d. 1064 or 1066) made a number of improvements in the town, including building bridges and improving the road to London, following the tradition of one of his predecessors, Wulfsig (fl. c. 968), who laid out the market place and provided building material for settlers.[55]

The relationship between monastery and borough was seldom free from strain, and underlying tensions sometimes broke into open resistance, as tenants tried to shake off an abbey's authority. Indeed, the existence of monastic boroughs was the single greatest cause of violence in which religious houses became involved. At Bury the townspeople started to look for ways to assert their independence from the abbey from the early thirteenth century: they sided with the sacrist's opponents in the convent during the election dispute which followed the death of Abbot Samson in 1211; and some of them supported the coming of the friars to the town, which, as we have seen, was bitterly opposed by the abbey.[56] Stimulated by national events, notably the baronial discontent of Simon de Montfort and his followers in the late 1250s, monastic boroughs began to aim at independence and self-government. The townspeople of Reading, for instance, demanded that their gild merchant be recognized by the abbey. At St Albans the townspeople registered their resentment by trying to break the abbey's monopoly on milling, and set their sights on the establishment of a commune. In 1264 the setting up of a gild of youths in Bury St Edmunds led to a violent attack on the abbey and its monks, during which the sacrist and cellarer were excluded from the town. Discontent in monastic boroughs was to become a feature of the later Middle Ages. The monks did not enjoy their rights and privileges unopposed or unchallenged.

Markets and fairs

A privilege granted by benefactors which was often associated with urban property was permission to hold a market or fair, or to impose a toll on the passage of goods brought for sale; these were valuable concessions. Some of the earliest annual fairs in England are mentioned in the eleventh century in connection with religious houses. From the late eleventh century the monks of Shrewsbury held an annual fair there for three days from 31 July. Nearly two hundred years later the burgesses of the town issued a charter which reaffirmed this right to the abbey, and which makes clear how valuable the grant of a fair could be: during the three days no shops within the town were open for the sale of any commodity except wine and ale. The town's own trade might suffer, but no one was to be prevented from attending the fair. The fair was supervised by the abbey servants, who took for the house all its profits. The great fair at Shrewsbury was not the only one controlled by the monks: in 1256 King Henry III granted them the right to hold a weekly market at Baschurch, and an annual fair there lasting four days from 31 October, and a weekly market at Betton in Hales, with an annual fair of four days, beginning on 20 September.[57] Income from markets and fairs was not allowed to the Cistercians, but here, as in many other areas of the White Monk economy, early restrictions faded by the late twelfth century. The first and only recorded twelfth-century Cistercian fair was that at Hoo, granted to Boxley Abbey in 1189/90; but four markets and six fairs were obtained by other houses between 1200 and 1250, and twenty markets and the same number of fairs between 1250 and 1300.[58]

Spiritualia

All the sources of revenue so far discussed were classed as *temporalia*. A second category of assets were termed *spiritualia*, that is, they derived from ecclesiastical sources, notably churches and tithes. We have noted how a considerable number of patrons, particularly those of Augustinian houses, transferred parish churches to the ownership of religious houses. As the place where men and women worshipped, and where they received the Christian sacraments, the parish church was part of the ecclesiastical organization of the country, which was itself becoming clarified and defined in the course of the eleventh and twelfth centuries.[59] What concerns us here is the parish church as a source of revenue. The degree of monastic involvement could vary. A religious house could exercise the right to choose a rector and present him to the bishop for institution; this was known as the right of patronage, or advowson. The monastery or nunnery, as patron, was normally in receipt of a pension from the church, and also enjoyed the advantage of influence in the parish. The house could, if it so decided, go one step further and act as corporate rector. It would then be obliged to appoint one of its own members who was a priest to conduct services. Financially this brought great advantage, for the house would be entitled to take all the revenues of the church: the glebe land, the offerings of the parishioners, the tithes (a tenth of the produce of land which was paid to the parish church), and other dues such as mortuary fees (payment for burial). In these cases the monastery was said to have appropriated the church. Finally a religious house which appropriated a church but could not provide a priest as rector from its own ranks might appoint a vicar, to whom a proportion of the revenues would be paid, or a stipendiary priest. Though there are instances of the ordination of vicarages in the early to mid twelfth century, they are not common, and it was only after the Fourth Lateran Council of 1215 that the system became widespread.

Because of the lack of definition in the wording of many charters, which simply record the grant of a church, *ecclesia*, it is not always easy to discover what monasteries and nunneries did with the churches which they were granted, or what the donors intended. In the early twelfth century appropriation is not always easy to detect, because it is possible that informal appropriations, that is, those not recorded in writing, took place.[60] It is not until about the end of the twelfth century that charters begin to be more specific and distinguish between the grant of a church and the patronage or advowson, that is, the right of presentation. In addition, in time it became normal practice for licence for appropriation to be sought and obtained (usually on the grounds of the poverty of a house) from the diocesan bishop or from the pope, and it is from among episcopal, and to a lesser extent, papal records that most of our evidence for appropriations derives. Religious houses all over Britain came into the possession of appropriated churches or ones from which, as patron, they drew a pension. Among the Benedictines St Albans enjoyed the tithes of sixteen churches and presented to four more.[61] Westminster Abbey claimed pensions in nineteen churches in the diocese of London by 1167 and in 1189 received licence to appropriate any of them. In 1291 the income from Westminster's *spiritualia* amounted to £273, 77 per cent of which came from appropriated rectories. The total annual value of the abbey was £1,294.[62] As a New Year present one year Jocelin of Brakelond decided to compile, for presentation to Abbot Samson, a list of churches in which the abbot or convent had rights and the rents which could be expected when they were farmed out, and he was able to name over sixty-five.[63] Durham's Scottish cell of Coldingham received no fewer than eighteen parish churches on the border; the Scottish Cluniac abbey of Crossraguel depended heavily on the possession of parish churches and teinds (tithes) for its income, and the other Ayrshire monastery of Kilwinning (Tironensian) had sixteen appropriated churches.[64]

The Augustinian canons, being a clerical order, were particularly favoured with the gift of churches.[65] Although the 1291 taxation of Pope Nicholas is a source which has to be treated with great caution, which undoubtedly left much unrecorded, it is of interest as indicating that 40 per cent of Augustinian revenue derived from *spiritualia*. Even if this figure is inaccurate, it still suggests that churches were a significant economic asset. Appropriation in the twelfth century appears to have been reasonably common, and it increased in the thirteenth. The 1291 taxation shows 325 churches appropriated to 120 houses of Black Canons. The *Liber Antiquus* of Bishop Hugh de Welles of Lincoln, dated to c. 1220, gives evidence of vicarages in 126 benefices belonging to the Augustinians in the diocese of Lincoln. Some monasteries derived revenue from churches located at a distance from the house. Llanthony Prima, for instance, enjoyed the appropriated income from fourteen Irish churches, which combined with the proceeds from nine in the diocese of Hereford to form a substantial asset.[66] The Premonstratensians were at first willing to accept churches only when they could be used as the basis for a new abbey. This ruling soon became a dead-letter, however, and one example of a British Premonstratensian house with extensive interests in parishes is provided by Talley, which had a stake in nine churches and sixteen chapels by 1271.[67]

The Cistercian ban on the acquisition of churches and tithes did not outlast their first twenty years in Britain. In a notorious case (1147) the monks of Barnoldswick (Kirkstall) destroyed the parish church which they claimed interfered with their own worship, an action upheld by the Cistercian archbishop of York and the Cistercian pope. They then proceeded to obtain possession of the patronage of the parochial chapels of the church which were themselves raised to the status of parish churches.[68] There was no such restriction on the acceptance of churches by the Savigniacs, although at least one abbot, Roger of Byland, followed Cistercian practice in refusing the offer of churches. When the union with Cîteaux took place in 1147 the Savigniacs were allowed to retain the churches and tithes in their control, and indeed accepted new ones. It has been argued that the union led to laxity, and was thus a source of decline and weakness among the Cistercians.[69] Certainly appropriations became more common after mid-century, and the order as a whole did not

scruple to accept from King Richard the grant of the Yorkshire church of
Scarborough, whose revenues were intended to offset some of the costs
of the general chapter.[70]

Expenditure and consumption

The economic assets acquired by religious houses provided them with
many of the basic necessities of life. They also generated cash, either from
rents or services or from the sale of surplus produce. It is appropriate,
therefore, before considering how the monastic economy was managed,
to look briefly at why cash was required: what constituted the main items
of expenditure in religious houses? First, items of food and drink which
were not produced on the monastic lands were to be purchased. These
might be staple items or more luxurious fare, such as Gascon wine and
spices from the East, bought, perhaps, for the entertainment of important
guests at the abbot's or abbess's table. The head of a religious house, as we
have seen, often invited members of important local families to dine, and
was an established part of the social scene. The church and claustral
buildings needed wax candles for lighting, and the kitchen and warming
house fuel for cooking and heating. Each of the monastic officials required
money to discharge his or her obligations: the almoner, for instance, to
feed and clothe the poor, or to provide a few pence in charity; the
kitchener for implements and cooking utensils; the sacrist for equipment
for the church, cloth and plate for the altar, and vessels and vestments
for liturgical use; the monk or nun in charge of the scriptorium for
skins for parchment and the equipment required for their preparation.
Some of these goods, to be sure, could be crafted in the monastic
workshops; some expenses, too, could be met by special donations
or by utilizing the talents of the monks. Not all houses were as lucky as
Bury, however, where the rebuilding of the almonry in stone was
partly financed by 'Walter the physician, the almoner', who 'gave
a large donation of money that he had made from his medical
practice'.[71]

  Regular expenditure included the payment of servants and hired
labour, both at a religious house itself and on its outlying farms, granges
and manors, where shepherds, woodsmen and workers in the fields would
all be required. The numbers would have swelled at certain times of the
year, as at harvest. At the monastery the abbot or abbess sometimes had
need of extra staff. Of Abbot Samson of Bury Jocelin records that 'if at any
time, responding to the request of some important person or friend, he
employed any page-boys or harpists or anyone of that kind in his
household, he wisely got rid of such unnecessary extras as soon as an

opportunity arose of travelling abroad or going on a journey'.[72] Guests evidently did not only require food and drink at the abbot's table, but expected entertainment as well; and not all the abbots were as prudent as Samson in trying to minimize expenditure.

Finally, a monastery or nunnery could be involved from time to time in two major pieces of expenditure: in the purchase of lands, which we shall look at shortly, and in building. Clearly, the latter activity and its associated expenditure fluctuated; at times, sustained rebuilding campaigns were a severe drain on monastic resources, which were called on to provide materials – wood, stone, lead and glass – as well as to pay the workforce.[73] But there was also more regular building and repair work to be financed, in the claustral buildings and the monastic workshops, farms, granges, mills, sheepfolds and cattle sheds. This could consume no little money, and Abbot John of Hertford expended over £100 in repairing the mills belonging to St Albans Abbey.[74] Monastic account rolls – such as the particularly good example from the Cistercian abbey of Beaulieu from the year 1269/70 – illustrate the nature of monastic expenditure, great and small, usual and extraordinary. The 18d. spent that year on the abbey manor of Great Faringdon 'in guarding the roads in the times of fairs and market, lest anyone avoid the payment of tolls' may have been a regular item of expenditure; and the annual stipend of the steward (53s. 4d.), bailiff (13s. 4d.), reeve (26s. 6d.) and catchpole (9s. 8½d.) certainly would have been. But it was surely not every year that the abbey's keeper of the pleas spent 67s. 6d. on gifts to persons 'hastening several pieces of business' through the courts, or 15s. 5d. 'for two chests bought for the safekeeping of charters'. The total expenses of the keeper of the pleas was just one penny-farthing less than his receipts: such balance between monastic income and expenditure was not always easy to achieve.[75]

THE MANAGEMENT OF ECONOMIC RESOURCES

The administration of manors

A religious house which had been granted a manor could do one of two things. First, it could retain the manor in demesne, and cultivate it itself. In such circumstances the manor was usually placed under the administration of a lay reeve or bailiff, who was responsible for arranging for the foodstuff produced on the demesne, and rents in money and kind, to be conveyed to the abbey or priory. Alternatively, the manor could be leased or farmed out to a tenant. After the Conquest a number of tenancies were created to help the monastery fulfil its obligations of military service.[76] On these and other tenancies a lease stipulated the length of time the land was to be held by the tenant, the services due and the amount of rent to be paid. Such an arrangement had the advantage of releasing the house from the responsibility of administering the land and of yielding a regular, though fixed, cash income. In the first part of the twelfth century leasing out of Benedictine estates was common with respect to both urban property and rural manors. The York abbey of St Mary's for example, leased many of its properties in the city and its rural holdings to tenants for a mixture of services and cash rents. In 1176 all of Peterborough's manors appear to have been leased out.[77] More than thirty manors of Westminster (one-third of those mentioned in Domesday Book) were farmed out in the late twelfth century.[78]

During the twelfth century, however, the disadvantages of this system became apparent. Prices were rising, but income from fixed rents remained stable, and tenant rather than landlord benefited from the sale of surplus food at market. From around 1150 monastic landlords began to attempt to take back into their own direct exploitation lands which had been rented out at a fixed charge. Leases which expired were not renewed; and on occasion a religious house went to law to regain possession of its estates. This was not always an easy task because of the length of time which had elapsed since the creation of a tenancy. The abbey of Bury St Edmunds hoped, on the death of Adam of Cockfield around 1198, to repossess three manors which the family had held for rent. However, after going to law the monks failed to dislodge Adam's heirs, because it was judged that he and his father and grandfather had held the manors in fee farm for over one hundred years. The monks were unable to resume the manors as demesne and had to be satisfied with an annual rent.[79] At Peterborough a move towards direct management of manors and estates can be seen under Abbot Benedict (1177–93), and among the first lands to be reclaimed as demesne was Biggin Grange, the large manor created from forest assart. The vacancy account of 1210 shows that by that date all the abbey manors had been brought back into direct exploitation.[80] The process of reclamation of the abbot's manors at Bury began under Samson (1182–1211), and the pages of Jocelin's chronicle allow us to see an energetic abbot at work on his manors.[81] The writer's only regret was that Samson was not as solicitous over the manors belonging to the convent. Elsewhere the process of reclaiming manors was slow. Westminster's manor of Deerhurst, given by Edward the Confessor and farmed in fee between 1138 and 1157, was not repossessed until purchased back in 1299. The manor of Hampstead, originally granted by King Æthelred and fee farmed in the twelfth century, was redeemed between 1246 and 1258.[82]

The taking back of lands into demesne and a move towards direct farming led to a revolution in estate management which is discernible both in the ways in which financial affairs were managed at the abbey or priory and externally, on its manors. As we have seen, in the post-Conquest period and into the twelfth century there developed in Benedictine houses a system of administration through obedientiaries: monks were given a particular area of responsibility, and received and expended revenues for that purpose. Thus the revenues of Tavistock's appropriated church of Milton Abbot were assigned to the sacrist and the almoner. The Essex manor of Paglesham was granted in the early twelfth century to the almoner of Westminster for alms and pittances.[83] Each obedientiary appointed his own bailiff on his manors, and received the income himself. This led in many cases to inefficiency and waste, examples of which at Bury are chronicled by Jocelin of Brakelond. One dispute occurred in 1197 when the abbot ordered the prior to pay the cellarer an additional sum of £50 per annum to supplement his income, which the cellarer thought inadequate. The cellarer still failed to end the year 'in the black', and the abbot turned to his monks for advice on how to deal with the large debt which had accumulated:

Many cloister monks were glad to hear these words and half-smiled to themselves, saying in private that what the abbot had said was correct. The prior put the blame on the cellarer, and the cellarer blamed the guest-master. Each man made excuses for himself.[84]

And so the monks sought a solution to the financial problems of the abbey, which had arisen largely from the decentralization of its finances. Even very small houses, such as Brecon with only eight monks, had a prior, sub-prior, cellarer, chamberlain, sacrist and almoner, all in receipt of their own income.[85] The disadvantages of the obedientiary system, then, were a lack of central policy for economic management and the consequent danger of waste, inefficiency and abuse.

What we see in the thirteenth century, in the wake of a movement to high farming, is accordingly the development of a central system for managing the economy. Canterbury was early in the field of improved financial management. A central treasury emerged at Christ Church from the 1160s, and a regular audit from 1225.[86] A parallel development was the redefinition of the relationship of the administration of manors to the central economy. This is also well documented at Christ Church, Canterbury, where the major revolution in estate management was the work of Prior Henry of Eastry (1285–1331).[87] The most important priory estates had long been grouped into four custodies, east Kent, the Weald and Romney Marsh, Essex, and the counties of the Thames valley, over each of which was placed a warden, who had a supervisory role; much

power for deciding policy on individual manors and in financial matters
was left to the local serjeants and reeves. Under Henry of Eastry the
wardens were exclusively monk-wardens, and their administrative and
financial powers were greatly increased. They appointed and supervised
bailiffs or reeves for each of the manors, and presented their accounts at
the priory. The system was not without its dangers, for although the
monk-wardens were supposed to be resident at the priory, they might
easily stay on the manors and slip into the lack of discipline associated with
non-residence; they were, however, more accountable. The manorial
accounts submitted by the monk-wardens were audited at the priory by a
group of senior monks who ran the central treasury, and decided general
policy with regard to the estates. The prior acted in consultation with
both the monk-wardens whose manors he toured and the senior monks.
During his long period of office Henry of Eastry turned the priory deficit
into a healthy profit.

Similar developments took place at other Benedictine houses. From the
late thirteenth-century account rolls of Peterborough Abbey we begin to
get a clearer picture of how its estates were run. Two monk-wardens
were, as at Canterbury, responsible for the management of the estates,
although they were associated with a lay steward. The abbey manors were
grouped into three areas (the Soke of Peterborough, Northamptonshire,
and Lincolnshire) each under a lay bailiff who organized both the labour
services of customary tenants and also the stipendiary labour which
became necessary: cowmen, shepherds and ploughmen and so on. Biggin
Grange in the early fourteenth century employed twenty-five full-time
and three part-time workers who cost the abbey over £50 per annum.[88]
Elsewhere there was variation on this general method according to the
size of the house, the location of its estates and whether they lay in a
compact area or were scattered. Some houses employed a single lay
steward of the estates, who travelled around the monastic property and
reported direct to the cellarer. Late thirteenth-century Oseney, an
Augustinian house which organized its estates through manors, divided its
lands into bailiwicks which were administered by a number of officials
who presented their individual accounts at the abbey.[89] Despite local
variations it is clear that the most important developments in the
exploitation of monastic estates in the thirteenth century, that is, in the era
of high farming, were the establishment of a common treasury and
committees of audit, which replaced the decentralized obedientiary
system. These developments encouraged more concentrated and efficient
farming, as they allowed manors to specialize in the production of
commodities, and for livestock to be moved from one manor to
another.[90]

The Cistercians and the grange economy

Right from the outset the Cistercians avoided the dangers associated with the decentralization of administration through obedientiaries by entrusting financial power to a single cellarer.[91] But the differences in economic practice were more fundamental than that, for the White Monks aimed to operate outside the existing manorial system and deliberately rejected the kind of labour services on which the Benedictines relied. They therefore did not administer their estates through manors, but evolved a system of farming through granges. Their distinctive grange economy came to be emulated by other groups and orders, who acquired lands on the fringes of settlement, notably the Premonstratensians and Gilbertines, but also the Augustinians and, in some instances, the Benedictines. When a Cistercian house acquired substantial holdings in a district, a grange, or farm, was established from which the surrounding arable was farmed and the pasture lands controlled. In order that monastic discipline should not be undermined, Cistercian regulations stipulated that granges were to be no more than a day's journey from the mother house; thus the lay brethren who supervised the grange were able to return to the mother house for the offices on the greater festivals. This ruling supposed that estates would not be too far distant, but gradually the acquisition by some abbeys of far-flung property meant that it was ignored. Byland abbey, for instance, created an important grange at Bleatarn, over sixty miles from the abbey across the Pennines in Westmorland.[92] The dispersal of granges was swift. Fountains Abbey, founded in 1132, established its first grange at Aldburgh in 1145/6; Meaux created seven granges in its first twenty years; and by the close of the twelfth century the eight Yorkshire houses between them controlled seventy-four granges.[93] The first task in the creation of a grange was to acquire and consolidate land. Where the monks were operating within an existing pattern of settlement, some depopulation took place, with the peasants being resettled or absorbed into the community as lay brethren. This took place at Meaux's home grange (North Grange), Pipewell's West Grange, at Byland and at Barnoldswick (Kirkstall). In the interests of economy and efficiency, efforts were made, through gift and purchase, to consolidate land holdings within the area of a grange. The activities of successive abbots of Meaux, which have been described as 'calculated and empirical', are well documented in the abbey chronicle. It took a mere twelve years, from 1160 to 1172, to consolidate Moor Grange; and in the face of opposition from interested parties, other landowners were expelled from areas of the East Riding which came to be covered by a network of granges.[94]

Each grange was provided with a set of buildings which would have varied according to the nature of the terrain and dominant form of agriculture. Some monastic chroniclers noted when grange buildings were built. The fourth abbot of Meaux was said to have 'constructed very many buildings in granges';[95] and Abbot Richard Dunham of Louth Park (1227–46) built in his abbey's granges 'halls and chambers, dormitories and dining-rooms for guests, and barns, cowhouses and sheepfolds'.[96] The buildings of the grange were substantial, although archaeological investigation as well as documentary research has modified the earlier thesis that granges were 'mini-abbeys'.[97] Some grange buildings, like Cawston Grange of Pipewell Abbey, were indeed conceived on a lavish scale, but generally the essential buildings comprised living quarters for the lay brethren with dormitory, kitchen and bakehouse, a chapel or more modest oratory, a granary, threshing barn, and pens for the animals. Some granges had sheds for the storage of wool; however, the most important building would have been the barn, where grain was stored before transport to abbey or market. The fine thirteenth-century barn of Beaulieu Abbey at Great Coxwell (Berkshire), which served as the focus of the Faringdon estates, survives to show how large and imposing the grange barn could be. The buildings were often enclosed, and varied in extent. Neath's grange at Monknash was at the centre of over a thousand acres of arable, and comprised an enclosure of over one mile square, surrounded by earthen banks; the grange buildings included a granary over 200 feet long, a dovecot and three mills.[98]

Some granges were predominantly arable; others, although a minority, like Strata Florida's Cwmystwyth grange, were largely pastoral. Most, however, operated a mixed economy, like another Strata Florida grange, Mefenydd, where oats were grown below the 250-metre contour and sheep farmed above it.[99] Some had more specialized activities. At North Grange of Meaux there was a tile-kiln, and tanners and smiths who, between 1235 and 1249, were transferred to the abbey and to Wawne Grange.[100] Granges were staffed by lay brethren, one of whom, in overall charge, was known as the granger. The extent of Cistercian lands meant that there was no way that they could be cultivated 'by the labour of their own hands'. In practice, even an abbey with a large number of lay brethren could not have staffed its granges entirely from among their ranks, and on most granges the *conversi* would have numbered only a handful who supervised peasant workers. Non-manorial lands carried with them no customary labour, and the Cistercian statutes eschewed gifts of serfs and villeins. Nevertheless the White Monks did, on occasion, accept grants of villagers and their families and services. This was not sufficient to provide either permanent or seasonal labour for the harvest, and the monks had to rely on hired workers. The Cistercians were therefore dependent on local labour, possibly in some cases (as at Thorpe Underwood Grange of Fountains Abbey) provided by those who had been dispossessed of their land. Archaeological evidence suggests that the Cistercians settled peasant labourers on the edges of their remoter granges where there was no labour to hand. The earthworks of Cayton Grange of Fountains Abbey and at Braithwaite (Jervaulx) are suggestive of two settlements, the grange enclosure and houses for peasant cultivators and hired labourers. Croo Grange (Meaux) shows surviving earthworks to the west of the grange buildings which probably represent peasant accommodation.[101] This is the reverse of the view of the White Monks as depopulators; 'resettlement' rather than 'depopulation' might better describe their activities here.[102]

As the monastic expansion of lands continued unchecked in the twelfth century there was a real danger of overlap of interests. The Cistercians themselves had early decided that granges of different houses should not lie within two leagues of each other. In 1164 they reached a similar agreement with the Gilbertines: no house of either order was to have a grange or sheepfold within two English leagues of each other. Many nunneries had granges, particularly those which styled themselves Cistercian. Stixwould, for instance, operated a grange economy: the nuns controlled eight granges where they carried on a mixed farming, the production of cereal crops and the rearing of sheep.[103] The Yorkshire nunnery of Swine received a grant of pasture in Spaldington for the grazing of cows, sheep, mares and foals, with twelve acres of land on which to construct a grange.[104] Even the Black Monks came to have properties which approximated to the Cistercian grange, especially in areas newly cleared. The monks of Peterborough received a confirmation in 1189 of an assart of 400 acres near Oundle, which they called at first the 'New Place', and later La Biggin or Biggin Grange; it was to become one of the largest of the abbey manors.[105] The Benedictines of Crowland established granges on the Lincolnshire lands which they had brought into cultivation.[106] By 1301 the Benedictine nuns of Yedingham had a grange at Sinnington which had been built around the grant of the church and odd parcels of land; and the nuns and canons of Sempringham consolidated estates at Woodgrange (Bulby) out of a total of eighteen grants.[107] And so we could multiply examples of houses of all orders which emulated the Cistercian grange economy, the classic element of which was the consolidation of estates, free from all customary service and farmed directly using wage labour supervised by a few lay brethren or (in non-Cistercian houses) monks.

As the thirteenth century wore on, the grange economy changed. From being a 'demesne farm, directed by lay brethren and worked by a dependent peasantry'[108] granges came to be leased. Until 1208 the general chapter insisted on upholding the original prohibition of the leasing of granges to lay people; in that year, however, it allowed houses to rent out their distant lands. The response to this relaxation evidently caused concern, for in 1214 and again in 1215 the original ban was renewed. However, pressure was increasing for permission to take lands out of direct production, and in 1220 this was given: the general chapter allowed abbeys to rent their granges and other lands for a term of years if they were considered by senior monks to be 'less useful' to the house. The White Monks were, accordingly, considering steps which were entirely the reverse of the economic trend among Benedictine houses: the general chapter permitted the leasing of lands which were being farmed directly at the time when the Black Monks were trying hard to bring back rented lands into demesne.[109] It is not entirely clear why the Cistercians should have turned to the leasing of lands in the early thirteenth century when they could have hoped to benefit from the same kind of economic advantages – a labour glut, low wages and high prices paid for produce – which had brought many Benedictine houses to direct exploitation of their estates. It may be that a clue lies in the general chapter's ruling of 1208 allowing *distant* lands to be leased. Was it perhaps a desire to preserve monastic discipline, indeed adhere to the ruling that granges should not be more than a day's journey from the abbey, that made them consider taking dispersed estates out of direct farming? And was it, perhaps, the difficulties, which some houses evidently encountered, in controlling and supervising the lay brothers which reinforced the wisdom of this course of action? Or was it that, when abbeys needed ready money, it was easier and quicker, if, in the area of high farming, in the long run less profitable, to lease for cash than farm land directly? Certainly it seems unlikely, in the early thirteenth century, that abbeys were simply unable to staff and work the demesne. British Cistercian houses seem not to have taken advantage of the general chapter's ruling in great numbers before the late thirteenth century. Meaux Abbey started to rent out its granges in 1286. The grange economy of Furness was apparently intact in 1292 but began to break up shortly afterwards. Fountains Abbey probably held all its granges in direct production in the late thirteenth century, but like many northern houses it suffered particular financial problems because of the damage its estates sustained during the Scottish wars, and it was for this reason that the monks sought permission in 1336 to lease three of the abbey granges to lay persons. By 1363 fifteen out of twenty-three granges of Fountains were leased to tenants. It was therefore in the fourteenth century, rather than the thirteenth, that the greatest changes took place in the Cistercian economy, and that granges came to be leased in any numbers. The process was accelerated, indeed partly caused, by the decline of the class of lay brothers. Even before the Black Death decimated the population and led to a shortage of labour, the numbers of *conversi* had dropped, as would-be recruits sought employment in the secular market rather than in the service of a religious house.[110] As I have argued earlier, there is evidence of discontent among the lay brethren by the late twelfth century; and it was thus a combination of labour problems, economic pressure and social unrest which led to a widespread practice of leasing and to the break-up of grange estates.

Religious houses as traders and exporters
Under the more intensive direct farming method with its improved techniques, food was grown to provide surplus for sale in the markets of Britain and abroad. Corn from monastic lands was sold in the markets of London; the houses of Kent exported grain to Flanders; Glastonbury sent cheeses for sale in Southampton and Winchester.[111] The most important commodity in which the religious houses traded, however, was wool. For generations before the coming of the White Monks the English Benedictines had kept flocks of sheep and surplus wool must have been sold, but there is little evidence for widespread or organized trade. The contribution of the Cistercians to the production of wool was highly significant, and under their management sheep and wool became the principal cash-crop of the monasteries of Britain. Contemporaries noticed this, and in 1193 the historian William of Newburgh remarked that wool was 'the chief part of their substance'. The Cistercians settled for the most part in areas which were outside the manorial economy, and came into possession of vast tracts of upland and moor suitable for the keeping of flocks: in Northumbria, Yorkshire, the Welsh hills and Scottish uplands, and in the Cotswolds. Based on their granges, a relatively small force of lay brethren could organize the keeping of large flocks. At appropriate locations within the grange the monks constructed *bercariae*, sheepfolds. The well-documented abbey of Meaux had, in the 1280s, 2,000 sheep at Sutton Grange accommodated in eight *bercariae*. Part of the importance of the Cistercians lay, therefore, in the ubiquity of their sheep pastures and the size of their flocks. But there was more to it than this, and in many aspects of sheep farming the Cistercians were innovators. Whereas the Benedictines sold mixed fleeces, the Cistercians graded them and sold wool of varying quality. They also paid attention to problems of breeding, nutrition and disease. They became entrepreneurs, and far from relying on their own wool, their lay brethren bought up the stock of small producers to supplement their own yield. As early as 1157 the general chapter forbade such purchase of wool for resale, but the prohibition

appears to have been ignored. The crop was also boosted by tithes, and wool from these three sources meant that the Cistercians became the most important monastic wool producers in Britain.

It became the practice for merchants both native and foreign, or their agents, to visit and inspect the flocks of sheep on Cistercian estates. They were then able to assess the potential of the wool and offer a price for the year's yield. After shearing, the wool was taken to a central wool house for cleaning, sorting and packing. Meaux's wool house was at nearby Wawne Grange; Beaulieu had a collecting point some three miles from the abbey; while the nuns of the Benedictine priory of Arden, who possibly did not have a facility of their own, used the wool shed of Byland Abbey. On at least one occasion Dundrennan Abbey stored its wool at a grange of Holm Cultram.[112] It is clear from contracts which have survived from the thirteenth century that some houses (such as Fountains, Rievaulx, Meaux and Vaudey) were expected to prepare the wool at the abbey; other contracts specify that the merchants were to send in their own men. A contract of 1275, for instance, stated that Darnhall Abbey was to supply twelve sacks of *collecta* as good as that supplied by the monks of Dore: this wool was to be dressed at Hereford by a man sent by the merchant for whom the abbey was to find board and lodging for as long as the work took.[113] After dressing and packing the wool was delivered, generally at the expense of the vending abbey, to a sea port for export to the continent. Those houses which had secured urban property would have found it useful in the context of both storage of wool and the accommodation of officials.

It will be clear from this description that Cistercian wool was bought in advance after the merchant's agent had inspected the wool 'on the sheep'. It was but a small step from this to agreeing to a sale further in advance. A house would pledge its wool for a number of years to a purchaser, for an agreed price. This could be to the advantage of the monastery, but there are many instances in which it backfired, and the monks or canons were obliged to compensate the purchaser when the yield had been poor. Monastic chroniclers were quick to note when disease such as murrain decimated their flocks. In the year 1269/70 the monks of Beaulieu lost over half their lambs and 16 per cent of their adult sheep through disease.[114] These problems were exacerbated when the wool yield had already been bought and paid for. The practice of pledging wool in advance was an understandable but unfortunate one. Its dangers were recognized by the general chapter, which in 1181 made an attempt to limit advance sales to one year. This was, however, unsuccessful. The earliest British instances of the practice of selling in advance appear to relate to sales to local dealers. In 1194–5 Martin son of Edric paid £5 to the Crown for a quick judgement in his claim against the nuns of Swine for six sacks and four stone of good wool and four sacks of other wool, as well as ten marks, which may well have been sold to him in advance.[115] The practice is more commonly recorded in connection with overseas trade. In response to a government enquiry of 1275 the abbey of Meaux said that it had sold its wool for the next two years to the Scotti merchants of Piacenza, who had paid an advance of 400 marks, but for the ten years after that the wool was pledged to the Cerchi of Florence, who had paid an earnest of 1,600 marks.[116]

The Cistercians probably supplied wool to English weavers in towns such as Lincoln and Stamford, but the evidence is stronger for their export to continental markets. Various pieces of evidence help us to identify those houses most prominent in wool export, and the importance of this activity for their economy. The movement of abbey goods for sale was aided by freedom from the payment of tolls. The monks of Rievaulx Abbey, for instance, enjoyed freedom of movement for themselves and their goods, as early as 1133. King David I of Scotland granted similar liberties to May, Cambuskenneth, Dryburgh, Dunfermline, St Andrews and all the Cistercian houses; later kings confirmed these privileges.[117] These may initially have been intended to cover local movement to market, but came to apply to the wider trading activities of the monks; many grants date from the second half of the twelfth and the thirteenth century, when such activities increased. By the late twelfth century many houses had secured tax concessions abroad – in the 1180s, for instance, the count of Flanders granted the monks of Melrose freedom from tolls there – and there are references to twelve houses, among them Beaulieu, Boxley and Buildwas, owning their own ocean-going vessels.[118] From the thirteenth century comes evidence which ties these concessions more definitely to the wool trade. Royal licences were issued to trade abroad; and in 1224–5 fifteen Cistercian abbeys received permission to export wool.[119]

Other evidence comes from lists of wool-exporting religious houses compiled by foreign merchant houses. One, deriving from Flanders, has been dated not later than the 1260s.[120] It lists some 102 abbeys, priories and hospitals in Britain with wool available for sale overseas. No amount is given, but the list supplies, for half the houses, the price which their wool would command. Top of the list was the Welsh house of Neath, whose wool was valued at £50. Many of the houses had their wool valued at between £30 and £40, and the price given for the wool of Byland Abbey (£38) actually accords with what the monks received for wool sales in 1259. A later document (which has been dated to the years between 1281 and 1296), the *Pratica della Mercatura* of the Italian merchant

Francesco Balducci Pegolotti, lists some sixty-five British houses supplying Flemish and Italian merchants.[121] Although its evidence has to be treated with extreme caution as regards the actual amount of wool available for export and its value, Pegolotti's list is a useful indicator of those houses which were active in the wool trade. Most of the houses concerned (85 per cent) were Cistercian, with several Premonstratensian and Gilbertine ones; and the greatest producer appears to have been Fountains Abbey, with seventy-six sacks available for export. The biggest producer among the non-Gilbertine nunneries was Stixwould, which had fifteen sacks for sale; from these and other figures it has been estimated that the flocks of the nunnery may have numbered 1,500 sheep yielding seven or eight sacks of wool, and that almost as much again for export derived from *collecta*.[122] Pegolotti's list demonstrates the importance in wool production of north Yorkshire, the midlands and the Cotswolds, and shows that the Lincolnshire and Yorkshire houses were close rivals.

The production and export of wool was crucial to the well-being, even the survival, of many Cistercian houses. They, and to a lesser extent the Gilbertines and Premonstratensians, were so noted as wool producers that in 1193 one year's wool clip was confiscated from each of their houses as their contribution towards Richard I's ransom. Wool could be a source of wealth and of cash income with which to finance capital expenditure, such as building. It could also make the Cistercians a source of revenue for others: King John managed to mulct 24,000 marks from the Cistercians during the Interdict (1206–13), his financial exactions causing some houses temporarily to disband. However, a close dependence on one crop had obvious drawbacks, and the scab epidemic of the 1270s and 1280s brought several Cistercian houses to the brink of bankruptcy.[123] The Cistercians were pioneers in the large-scale production of wool and its export overseas, but their pre-eminence did not last. By 1300 their share in the production of the national wool crop was probably about one-sixth, less than it had been a century before.[124] Not only were the White Monks facing rivals from among the older monastic orders, but flocks on the pastures of the secular aristocracy had come to be as numerous as their own.

The land market and the money market

There were many occasions on which even the wealthiest and best-endowed religious houses failed to balance their income with their expenditure, borrowed money, and ended up in debt. Sometimes this was the result of mismanagement or incompetence. Abbot Hugh of Bury (1157–80) was no manager, and seeing the financial situation growing daily more desperate, he sought refuge and consolation in a single remedy: that of borrowing money, to maintain at least the dignity of his household. In the last eight years of his life, sums of £100 or £200 were regularly added to the debt every Easter and Michaelmas. The bonds were always renewed, and further loans were taken out to pay the growing interest.

The problem spread:

from the top downwards, from the ruler to the ruled, so that before long each obedientiary had his own seal and pledged himself in debt as he chose, to both Jews and Christians. Silk copes, gold vessels, and other church ornaments were often pawned without the consent of the convent.[125]

Sometimes income was simply not sufficient to meet extraordinary needs, and perhaps the most obvious of these was building. At a time when the Cistercian economic ethic was at its purest, in the 1130s and 1140s, when the monks worked their own lands through the grange in order to live 'by the labour of their own hands', they were beginning to indulge in massive and costly building programmes. Money was necessary to pay for both material and skilled and unskilled labour. As the decades wore on, cash needed to be generated for other purposes, to develop overseas trade and to buy land to consolidate granges. Members of all orders came to make a contribution to the land market, and instances of purchase of estates could be found from all major houses. They bought in order to build up estates; and they sold or leased in order to shed distant and not easily exploited lands. One instance will suffice: between 1222 and 1307 Westminster Abbey bought six major and many minor properties. Capital had become available through more efficient management and direct farming to make possible this participation in the market.[126]

Monastic involvement in the money market can be seen in other ways. During the period 1159–71 the Cistercian abbeys of Louth Park and Roche had borrowed money from the financier and merchant William Cade of St Omer, and were in his debt to the tune of 70 marks, and 22 pounds of wool and 2,200 fleeces respectively.[127] When Aaron the Jewish money-lender of Lincoln died in 1186, nine Cistercian houses were recorded as being in his debt, and three years later the king pardoned them a total debt of 6,400 marks for a cash payment of 1,000 marks. The chief debtor was Rievaulx, and it has been suggested that this abbey and others (Newminster, Kirkstead, Louth Park, Revesby, Rufford, Kirkstall, Roche and Biddlesden) were perhaps acting together to borrow money from the Jews.[128] This practice may illustrate houses borrowing money to finance their building, but there may be another reason, and it is worth while returning for a few moments to the Yorkshire house of Meaux for a glimpse of the involvement of the monks in the world of finance.

William Fossard, a benefactor of Meaux, persuaded Abbot Philip to accept land in Wharram le Street in return for discharging his debts of over 1,800 marks to the Jews. The abbot was a little alarmed at the prospect, but agreed when Aaron of Lincoln offered to forgo 500 marks if the abbey took on the debt. Tempted by Wharram, and two other parcels of land which were offered as pledges, Philip agreed to pay back Fossard's debt at a rate of 40 marks a year. Unfortunately for him, Aaron died shortly afterwards and the Crown called in his debts. When the 500 marks which had been remitted were demanded from Fossard, he explained that the abbey had sole responsibility for the entire debt. Eventually, after a long and costly court case, the abbot proved his point. What this incident shows us is a Cistercian abbey venturing far beyond primitive economic ideals into the world of lending and borrowing. The acquisition of Wharram was far from being a straightforward purchase of land but a conscious decision by Abbot Philip, albeit against his better judgement, to enter into the money-market.[129] Meaux was not alone in this, and there are other instances of monastic houses taking over the debts of the laity.[130] Monastic borrowing from the Jews was therefore linked to the acquisition of encumbered estates.[131]

We have already met religious houses as securers of loans from their patrons.[132] In other instances they appear to have acted as a kind of private bank, where money could be held in relative security.[133] Of all the monastic orders who made a contribution to international finance, however, that of the Knights Templar is perhaps the most remarkable. The estates of the knights in the West were exploited solely for the cash which they could generate, and the major part of this income was destined for the upkeep of the order in the East. From early on, then, the knights developed a system of collecting, storing and transporting large sums of cash. They became known as international bankers and financiers and were used by many outside the order. Their houses were used as a kind of safe-deposit; it was in the London Temple, for instance, that King John stored the Crown jewels in 1204–5. The knights became money-lenders; in England they advanced loans to King John and to his son Henry III. They were also a part of the system of national taxation, as money raised in taxes was collected at the Temple before being transferred to the Exchequer. The knights' contribution to international finance was innovative and important.[134]

But what, finally, was the significance of the monastic contribution to that economic activity with which they were most frequently engaged, agriculture? To find an assessment which applies across the board is difficult. One conclusion might be that with an important exception, that of the Cistercian grange, the monastic orders introduced no innovations: in terms of the way in which they were managed there was little difference between ecclesiastical estates and those of the great lay lords. Change, notably the return to high farming, might be documented earlier on ecclesiastical estates than their lay counterparts, but both were subject to the same economic fluctuations of prices and wages. However, such a conclusion undoubtedly underplays the part of the religious orders in economic developments of the period. Members of all orders made a contribution to the opening up of marginal lands, and in the creation of granges and the attempt to consolidate demesne farming the White Monks were pioneers. 'A new scientific agriculture began with the Cistercians and their imitators, and it is to their initiative that we owe, among other things, the first establishment of many of those farms on the hills and on the flood-plains of our rivers that have survived intact as units to this day.'[135] Colin Platt here rightly emphasizes the monastic contribution to the development of the British landscape. The twelfth- and thirteenth-century economy of Britain owed a great deal to the religious orders, not least because they were large farming corporations, and economic forces of the thirteenth century favoured those landowners who were engaged in agriculture on a large scale.

12

ON THE BRINK OF CHANGE

·

The subject of this study has been the monastic and religious orders in Britain, but it may be useful to conclude by re-emphasizing that Britain was not isolated from trends in western Christendom as a whole. The period to which this work is devoted saw many changes in the concept and practice of the monastic life of Europe. Intellectual developments, social and economic change and notions of ecclesiastical reform all contributed to an explosion of new types of religious practice which were manifest in a proliferation of religious houses for both men and women. As the twelfth century dawned and developed, the pursuit of a religious vocation was no longer limited to a choice between the solitary existence of a hermit and the largely aristocratic ambience of a monastery or nunnery following the Rule of St Benedict, perhaps with the addition of customs derived from one of the centres of reform, like Cluny or Fleury. Monasticism now embraced a much wider range of ideals and practices which had fused the eremitical spirit of primitive monasticism with the concept of community – for monasticism is, perhaps above all, about community. With the friars came yet more novelty, the realization that life according to a religious vow and rule need not be lived within the confines of the cloister but could be evangelical, not contemplative, outward-, not inward-looking.

Britain played a full role in these general European trends, eventually producing a native order which, although it did not spread beyond the shores of Britain, yet made a distinctive contribution to the development of opportunities for women to live the religious life. Fashioned by an Englishman, the Gilbertine Order was a product of European thought and influence, and owed a great deal to contemporary European practice. There was also much cultural interchange. If monastic life in Britain was affected by the importation to Canterbury of an Italian archbishop from Normandy, by Norman abbots who arrived in the wake of conquest, and by Bernard, abbot of Clairvaux, there was commerce in the other direction. An Englishman, Stephen Harding, was instrumental in the development of the constitution of Cîteaux; St Bernard's secretary, William, was an Englishman who entered the religious life in Burgundy, and who then returned to England at the head of the mission, Bernard's 'army', which planted Cistercian monasticism in the North. Another example was the native of Yorkshire, Henry Murdac, who became abbot of Vauclair before returning home to become abbot of Fountains, and then archbishop of York. The Cistercian Order provides the most obvious example of a monastic organization which stretched across Europe, and whose institutions, notably the general chapter, and desire to achieve uniformity of practice raised it to a supra-national level not altogether attained by other groups until the coming of the friars. Yet it is salutary to remember that in the Europe of the eleventh to the thirteenth century ideas, as well as people, could travel, and that religious aspirations and identity were not bounded by political borders. King Henry I's nephew, Henry of Blois, became a monk of Cluny, and from there was appointed to be bishop of Winchester; the king's own patronage of Cluny (and that of the bishop's brother, King Stephen) may have owed much to the presence, in the Burgundian abbey, of Henry of Blois. Bishops like Alexander of Lincoln and Malachy of Armagh helped to bring the customs of Arrouaise to Britain. Pope Innocent III could contemplate making a Gilbertine foundation in Rome. The religious of all orders brought their lawsuits and appeals to the papal curia in Rome. The friars travelled across Europe, bringing the message of salvation to the growing urban populations. And those most exotic of monastic adventurers, the Knights Hospitaller and Templar, accepted property in the West to aid military adventure in the East.

At the close of our period, monastic Britain was dotted with religious houses, great and small, which had benefited in varying degrees from the religious emotion stirred by the intellectual climate of the previous three centuries: from the spiritual aspirations of those who sought admission into their communities; from the endowments of those who saw in religious houses a way to obtain vicarious intercession for their sins, general or specific, or more temporal returns for their generosity. By 1300 the impulse which led to the proliferation of monastic houses was in many ways spent, and religious houses could no longer count on streams of recruits on the one hand, and seemingly endless endowments on the other. In other ways, too, the monastic world was on the brink of change.

First, let us consider why the number of recruits to religious houses should have waned. The monastic life was the answer to those who saw the way to salvation within a community. In a religious house notions of 'self' had to be abandoned, sacrificed to the endless routine of prayer, work and contemplation. What the friars in the early thirteenth century had begun successfully to tap – and to appeal to – was individuality. Not only did they draw away recruits from the traditional monastic orders, but their message was also that a good, religious life could be lived in the ordinary, everyday world of the town and the market place. Professor Lawrence has compellingly contrasted the pull of monasticism for country people, those who lived by the seasons and whose life was dominated by the routine of the agricultural year and by the memory of traditions, with the aspirations of the new townsmen and women, cut off from their roots, divorced from rural tradition, relying on themselves to prosper in the labour market or in the mercantile world. To the latter, monasticism in its traditional form had less appeal.[1] We have seen how enthusiastically women responded to the informal religious groups, such as the Beguines, which grew up in the towns and trading communities of Flanders and the Low Countries from the late twelfth and early thirteenth centuries; they fulfilled a need which traditional monasticism apparently failed to answer. The rise of the concept of the individual was matched by falling numbers of postulants in monastic houses. Evidence from a number of houses, both in Britain and on the continent, shows that recruitment declined during the later Middle Ages. Although the larger and more prestigious abbeys probably experienced little difficulty in maintaining numbers, the monastic population on the eve of the Dissolution had shrunk from the size it enjoyed in the heyday of the twelfth century.[2]

It was not just the number of entrants into the religious life that contracted in the later Middle Ages: the monastery or nunnery was a less-favoured target for endowment by the lay man or woman. The desire for a more individualistic manifestation of piety may also help to explain the waning of benefactions to religious houses. The patron, that is, the descendant of the founder of a monastery and nunnery, always occupied a special place in the intercessions of the house, and many continued to make grants in addition to fulfilling their roles as advocates of the religious. We have seen how other benefactors, by obtaining rights of confraternity, could also claim mention in the prayers of the monks, canons or nuns. But a monastic house, in its long history, would have promised to intercede for dozens, if not hundreds, of named men and women who had offered their support in one way or another. From the thirteenth century there emerged a new target for a man or woman's generosity which offered a more individual form of intercessory prayer. This was the chantry. A donor now made an endowment which yielded money to pay a chaplain to pray specifically for his or her soul. The chantry therefore offered a more personal form of commemoration than inclusion on a roll of the many men and women for whom a religious house prayed. Together these factors led in some cases to a crisis of recruitment and income. Abbeys could no longer afford to open their gates to all – as Rievaulx apparently did under Ailred (1147–67), and Cluny under its great abbots Odo (926–44), Odilo (994–1049) and Hugh (1049–1109). Entry now had to be more carefully controlled, and the registers of bishops and archbishops contain occasional warnings to houses not to admit recruits without permission – an indication of the need to balance carefully the intake of novices with the resources of the house.[3] The decline in the number of recruits in the monastic houses of Britain is accordingly not to be explained solely in terms of the failure of the spiritual appeal of the monastic life, but also as the result of attempts to keep religious communities to a size which could realistically be maintained.[4]

The change in religious or spiritual psychology was not the only factor to affect the fortunes of the religious houses of Britain. Political developments, such as war, had a major impact. We noted in chapter 10 how the Welsh wars of Edward I and the loss of Welsh independence in the years 1282–4 brought religious houses, some of which had been centres of Welsh cultural identity, under the heel of an alien king, and turned them into agents of his political domination. The Scottish abbeys were soon to experience devastation in the wars of the last years of the thirteenth and the early fourteenth century: the Augustinian community of Scone was sacked in 1296 after Edward I had taken away the Stone of Destiny, on which the Scottish kings were crowned; some houses, like Melrose, Kelso and Dryburgh, were burnt to the ground both by the armies of Edward I and later in the fourteenth century; others suffered economic hardship from which they found it difficult to recover. In the same period, monasteries in the North of England suffered from Scottish raids and the billeting on them of English troops. The French wars of the late thirteenth century led to the seizure of the property of the alien priories, founded in the wake of the Norman Conquest, and early in the fourteenth century came their final separation from their continental mother houses. Political developments in the Holy Land had repercussions in the West: the fall of Acre in 1291 and subsequent disillusionment with the crusading ethos undermined the morale and reputation of the military orders. In contrast to the Hospitallers, who founded a new headquarters when they captured the island of Rhodes in 1308, the Templars never recovered a *raison d'être*, and this made them vulnerable to the attacks of those who envied their successful financial operations and their wealth. There was little opposition to their suppression, at first in France by Philip IV (1307) and then in England by Edward II. The property donated by the faithful in the West for the relief of the Holy Land and the protection of pilgrims went in part to the Knights Hospitaller, but much of it went to swell the coffers of the kings of France and England.

More momentous and far-reaching than the effects of political developments were the consequences of economic change. In the period we have been considering the religious houses of Britain were, for the most part, able to enjoy the benefits of a general economic boom. Those with shrewd financial managers as abbots, priors or obedientiaries were able to bring leased property back into direct farming, and to enjoy more fully the profits of the land. Labour was plentiful and cheap, ensuring that the class of lay brothers would be buoyant and that there would be no shortage of servants or peasant labour. In the fourteenth century the circumstances were to change drastically, especially with the onset of successive outbreaks of plague. Some religious houses lost a high proportion of their inhabitants to plague – smaller houses disappeared altogether – and many suffered economic devastation. The climate was now one of economic contraction. As the supply of labour dried up, wages rose and labour came to be at a premium. Those who, in the labour glut of the twelfth and thirteenth centuries, had sought employment within religious houses now benefited from the increased opportunities and prosperity offered by the labour market. The class of lay brothers, already on the wane, now disappeared. A rethinking of the economic basis of many monastic houses had to be sought. In more ways than one, the history of the religious orders in Britain in the later Middle Ages presents us with a very different picture from that in the period discussed in this volume: an age of spectacular economic growth apparently followed by steady consolidation. It is a tribute to the strong foundations laid by the religious orders in the eleventh, twelfth and thirteenth centuries that most of the institutions founded within that period survived until the Dissolution, and thus enjoyed a continuous history for a further two and a half centuries.

GLOSSARY

advocate	lay protector of a religious house
advowson	right to present a clerk to a vacant ecclesiastical benefice
alien priory	religious house dependent on a continental monastery
ambulatory	passage or walkway around the east end of a church
anchorite/anchoress	one living the solitary life
apostolic life	*see **vita apostolica***
appropriation	transfer of the endowments and income of a parish church to a religious house, in return for the provision of pastoral care
apse	semi-circular eastern end of a church
asceticism	severe self-denial undertaken for spiritual reasons
assart	piece of land cleared for cultivation
benefice	ecclesiastical living
canons regular/secular	*see **regular/secular canons***
cartulary	volume containing copies of charters, deeds and other legal documents giving title to property
cellarer/cellaress	official in a religious house with responsibility for provisions
cenobitism	the monastic life lived in a community (cf. **eremiticism**)
chancel	eastern arm of a church containing the main altar
chapter	(1) as prescribed in the Rule of St Benedict, the daily meeting of a community, which took place in the **chapter house**, for the reading of a chapter of the Rule, confession of faults and imposition of penance etc. (2) body of clergy or monks/regular canons serving a cathedral church

clas	in Wales, a church staffed by secular canons (*claswyr*), who provided pastoral care for the church and its dependent chapels
claustral prior/ess	*see* **prior/ess**
confraternity	agreement reached between religious houses, or a house and a lay person, for the sharing of spiritual benefits
conversus	(1) adult convert to the religious life (cf. oblate) (2) lay brother (in the Cistercian, Gilbertine and other 'new' orders)
corrody	pension, in the form of lodging at a religious house, or an allowance of food, clothing etc., granted to a lay person
Culdee	in Scotland, either a hermit or a member of a collegiate-type establishment
demesne	land kept in the possession of, and worked on behalf of, the landlord, and not leased to tenants
dowry	a gift of land or an entrance fee offered to a religious house (especially a nunnery) with a new entrant
enclosure	the ceremony by which an enclosed one, anchorite or anchoress, is immured in a cell
eremiticism	the religious life as lived by hermits, individually or in groups (cf. **cenobitism**)
general chapter	annual meeting of the heads of all houses of an order (Cistercian etc.)
grange	farm estate, worked by hired labour and supervised by lay brethren; a system of farming, created by the Cistercians and followed by others, which existed outside the manorial system
honour	the lands held by a tenant-in-chief of the Crown, which comprised a complex of rights and duties
horarium	the monastic timetable
knight's fee	unit of land held for military service
lavatorium	trough with running water where the monks washed their hands before meals
lectio divina	'sacred reading'; reading of the Scriptures and works of the Christian Fathers, for which St Benedict allotted portions of the day
liturgy	public, as opposed to private, prayer
mendicant orders	general description of the orders of friars, indicating that they lived by begging
minster church	mother church at the centre of a large parish with a number of dependent chapels
novice/noviciate	member of a religious house who has not yet taken final vows; the period spent as a novice

obedientiary	monk, canon or nun to whom has been assigned particular administrative responsibilities
oblate	child placed by parents in a religious house with a view to taking vows when he/she reached the required age; the practice was rejected by the Cistercians and gradually died out
Opus Dei	literally, the 'Work of God'; the performance of the liturgy, the daily round of services in the monastic church
ordinary	the bishop of a diocese
patron	founder of a religious house, his/her heir, or the person to whom his/her estates passed; the patron had responsibility for protection of the interests of a religious house in secular affairs
pittance	small dishes of food and drink allowed to members of a community on special occasions, for example, on the anniversary of a founder
postulant	one seeking admission to a religious community
prior/ess	(1) head of a house of lesser status than an abbey (2) in an abbey, the second-in-command of the abbot/abbess; sometimes called the claustral prior/ess
rector	incumbent of a parish in receipt of all its income, responsible for the pastoral care of parishioners
regular canons	communities of clergy living under a monastic rule, especially the Rule of St Augustine
reredorter	building containing the monastic latrines
sacrist	monastic official responsible for the upkeep of the fabric of the church and the altars
secular canons	communities of clergy, for instance, those serving a cathedral chapter, who do not live under a monastic rule, and may be allowed to hold private property
simony	the sin of buying an ecclesiastical office or benefice
spiritualia	church property (churches, glebe (church land), tithes, burial dues etc.) from which income is derived (cf. ***temporalia***)
temporalia	possessions such as land, rent, mills etc., from which revenue is derived (cf. ***spiritualia***)
tenant-in-chief	one who holds lands directly of the king
tithe	a tenth part of produce, given to the church
vicar	incumbent of a parish church which has been appropriated to a religious corporation; the religious house receives all the income, and gives a portion of it to the vicar in return for his undertaking pastoral duties
vita apostolica	the apostolic life; the life of the apostles and early church in Jerusalem

—— • ——

NOTES

—— • ——

1 Before the Normans

1 The daily routine laid down by Benedict is discussed below, chapter 8.
2 See, for instance, the catalogue of the exhibition at the British Museum in 1991–2, *The making of England: Anglo-Saxon art and culture AD 600–900*, edited by Leslie Webster and Janet Backhouse (British Museum, 1991); on the contribution of the church in Northumbria see especially pp. 108–56. On later Anglo-Saxon art, see the similar catalogue for the 1984–5 exhibition, *The golden age of Anglo-Saxon art 966–1066*, edited by Janet Backhouse, D. H. Turner and Leslie Webster (British Museum, 1984).
3 Asser's Life of King Alfred, in Simon Keynes and Michael Lapidge (transl.), *Alfred the Great* (Harmondsworth, 1983), pp. 103, 107.
4 On nunneries in Anglo-Saxon England see Barbara Yorke, '"Sisters under the skin"? Anglo-Saxon nuns and nunneries in southern England', *Reading Medieval Studies* 15 (1989), 95–117.
5 The *Regularis Concordia* has been edited by T. Symons for Nelsons Medieval Classics (London, 1953). For essays on this and other aspects of the tenth-century revival see D. Parsons (ed.), *Tenth-century studies* (London, 1975).
6 For Anglo-Saxon influence on the *Regularis Concordia* see Antonia Gransden, 'Traditionalism and continuity during the last century of Anglo-Saxon monasticism', *Journal of Ecclesiastical History* 40 (1989), 159–207, especially 164–80.
7 The Danelaw was that area of eastern England ceded by King Alfred to the Danish invaders and settlers and gradually won back by his successors.
8 For a general discussion of monasteries and nunneries in this period, see Frank Barlow, *The English church 1000–1066*, 2nd edn (London, 1979), pp. 311–38.

9 Nicholas Brooks, *The early history of the church of Canterbury: Christ Church from 597–1066* (Leicester 1984), pp. 255–7; Gransden, 'Traditionalism and continuity', 173.

10 Cnut's foundation of Bury and St Benet's is accepted by David Knowles, *The monastic order in England*, 2nd edn (Cambridge 1966), p. 70, but questioned by Gransden, 'Traditionalism and continuity', 185–6. Gransden treats as more likely Cnut's foundation of a nunnery.

11 For the distribution of monastic houses in England in 1066 see Barlow, *English church 1000–1066*, pp. 312–13 and the map in David Hill, *An atlas of Anglo-Saxon England* (London 1981, repr. 1989), p. 153. Unless otherwise stated, all references to the dates of foundation of religious houses are taken from David Knowles and R. N. Hadock (eds.), *Medieval religious houses: England and Wales*, 2nd edn (London, 1971), and Ian B. Cowan and David E. Easson (eds.), *Medieval religious houses: Scotland*, 2nd edn (London, 1976). Details of the dates of the heads of houses are taken from David Knowles, C. N. L. Brooke and V. London (eds.), *The heads of religious houses: England and Wales 940–1216* (Cambridge, 1972).

12 On this theme see R. H. C. Davis, 'Bede after Bede', in C. Harper-Bill, C. J. Holdsworth and J. L. Nelson (eds.), *Studies in medieval history presented to R. Allen Brown* (Woodbridge, 1989), pp. 103–16.

13 Barlow, *English church 1000–1066*, p. 315.

14 William of Malmesbury, *Gesta Regum Anglorum*, in David C. Douglas and George W. Greenaway (eds.), *English historical documents*, vol. 2 (London, 1953), pp. 290–1.

15 On the estimated size of monastic communities see D. H. Farmer, 'The progress of the monastic revival', in Parsons (ed.), *Tenth-century studies*, pp. 10–19 (see pp. 16–17).

16 M. A. Meyer, 'Patronage of West-Saxon royal nunneries in late Anglo-Saxon England', *Revue Bénédictine* 91 (1981), 332–58.

17 Frank Barlow, *Edward the Confessor* (London, 1970), pp. 232–3.

18 But see below, pp. 30, 96 for Norman benefactors of St Albans and Shaftesbury in the post-Conquest period.

19 These figures are taken from Knowles, *Monastic order*, pp. 702–3, where a full list of values is given.

20 Edmund King, *Peterborough Abbey 1086–1310: a study in the land market* (Cambridge, 1973), pp. 6–18; see also *The Anglo-Saxon Chronicle*, translated in *English historical documents*, vol. 2, under the years 1052 and 1066; now cited as *ASC* followed by the year under which an entry occurs.

21 Edward Miller, *The abbey and bishopric of Ely* (Cambridge, 1951, repr. 1969), pp. 16–35.

22 J. Ambrose Raftis, *The estates of Ramsey Abbey: a study in economic growth and organization*, Pontifical Institute of Mediaeval Studies, Studies and Texts 3 (Toronto, 1957), pp. 1–21

23 Sandra Raban, *The estates of Thorney and Crowland* (Cambridge, 1977), pp. 8–15.

24 Barbara Harvey, *Westminster Abbey and its estates in the middle ages* (Oxford, 1977), pp. 24–7.

25 On this theme see also Gransden, 'Traditionalism and continuity', 186–9.
26 Miller, *Ely*, pp. 36–43.
27 For examples of this type of lease see Raban, *Thorney and Crowland*, pp. 19–20 and 23–4, and Raftis, *Ramsey Abbey*, pp. 18–19.
28 Emma Mason, *St Wulfstan of Worcester, c. 1008–1095* (Oxford, 1990), pp. 16–19.
29 Knowles, *Monastic order*, p. 81 and note 4; Barlow, *English church 1000–1066*, p. 325.
30 Raftis, *Ramsey Abbey*, pp. 10–12.
31 H. R. Loyn, *The governance of Anglo-Saxon England 500–1087* (London, 1984), pp. 107–8.
32 Ibid., p. 108.
33 *ASC* 1066; see also Knowles, Brooke and London, *Heads of religious houses*, pp. 31, 40, 42, 60, 74.
34 For a recent treatment, see Mason, *Wulfstan*.
35 Barlow, *English church 1000–1066*, pp. 182, 220–1.
36 M. McC. Gatch, 'The office in late Anglo-Saxon monasticism', in Michael Lapidge and Helmut Gneuss (eds.), *Learning and literature in Anglo-Saxon England* (Cambridge, 1985), pp. 341–62.
37 On daily occupations within a religious house, see below (chapter 8).
38 On Christ Church as 'one of the pre-eminent centres of English manuscript illumination' see Brooks, *Canterbury*, pp. 273–5. On manuscript production generally, see also Backhouse, Turner and Webster, *The golden age of Anglo-Saxon art 966–1066*, especially pp. 46–87.
39 On metalwork, ivories and stone sculpture of the period, see ibid., pp. 88–138.
40 Mason, *Wulfstan*, pp. 34–8, 41 and 52–3.
41 Barlow, *English church 1000–1066*, p. 337.
42 Gransden, 'Traditionalism and continuity', 198.
43 On Ælfric, see, for example, Stanley B. Greenfield and Daniel G. Calder, *A new critical history of Old English literature* (New York and London, 1986), pp. 75–88.
44 Thomas H. Bestul, 'St Anselm, the monastic community at Canterbury, and devotional writing in late Anglo-Saxon England', *Anselm Studies* 1 (1983), 185–98.
45 Gransden ('Traditionalism and continuity', 191–8) describes the Anglo-Saxon Chronicle as 'high quality narrative prose', especially the annals covering the years 983–1044, composed at Abingdon in the 1040s and sent from there to Canterbury.
46 See below, chapters 2 and 7.
47 Glyn Coppack, *Abbeys and priories* (London, English Heritage, 1990), pp. 35–8.
48 Frank Barlow (ed. and transl.), *The life of King Edward who lies at Westminster*, Nelsons Medieval Texts (London, 1962), pp. 46–8, 97–8.
49 On the cultural contacts between England and the continent in this period,

see Barlow, *English church 1000–1066*, pp. 10–23, especially pp. 20–1 for the examples cited here.

50 Knowles, *Monastic order*, p. 83.

51 For the distribution of Anglo-Saxon minster churches see Hill, *Atlas of Anglo-Saxon England*, p. 153, and for the conversion of a number of them into Augustinian houses, see below, chapter 3.

52 F. G. Cowley, *The monastic order in south Wales, 1066–1349* (Cardiff, 1977), pp. 1–8. See also Huw Pryce, 'Pastoral care in early medieval Wales', in John Blair and Richard Sharpe (eds.), *Pastoral care before the parish* (Leicester, 1992), pp. 41–62, especially pp. 49–55, for a discussion of the use and significance of the words *monasterium* and *clas*.

53 On Scottish monasticism in this period see the essay by Alan Macquarrie, 'Early Christian religious houses in Scotland: foundation and function', in Blair and Sharpe (eds.), *Pastoral care before the parish*, pp. 110–33.

54 On these see below, chapter 3.

2 The coming of the Normans

1 *ASC* 1066.

2 Florence of Worcester, *History of the kings of England*, transl. J. Stephenson, facsimile reprint (Felinfach, Lampeter: Llanerch Press, n.d.), p. 137.

3 Knowles, *Monastic order*, pp. 105–6, suggests that Abbot Wulfketel was one of the bishops and abbots associated with the revolt, but does not explain why ten years should have elapsed before his removal by William.

4 See Emma Mason, 'Change and continuity in eleventh-century Mercia: the experience of St Wulfstan of Worcester', in *Anglo-Norman Studies VIII: Proceedings of the Battle Conference 1985* (Woodbridge, 1986), pp. 154–76; see especially pp. 158–9 for Æthelwig.

5 D. Knowles (transl.), *The monastic constitutions of Lanfranc* (Nelsons Medieval Classics, London, 1951); on the architectural implications see below, pp. 39, 42.

6 *ASC* 1083.

7 Florence of Worcester, p. 144.

8 See Knowles, *Monastic order*, pp. 118–19.

9 However, David Rollason, *Saints and relics in Anglo-Saxon England* (Oxford, 1989), pp. 227–8, suggests that the revisions of the calendar might have taken place at an earlier date.

10 See especially the important article by Susan Ridyard, '*Condigna Veneratio*: post-conquest attitudes to the saints of the Anglo-Saxons', in *Anglo-Norman Studies IX: Proceedings of the Battle Conference 1986* (Woodbridge, 1987), pp. 179–206; also Rollason, *Saints and relics*, pp. 228–39.

11 Knowles, *Monastic order*, pp. 115–16.

12 Marjorie Chibnall, *Anglo-Norman England 1066–1166* (Oxford, 1986), p. 24.

13 H. P. R. Finberg, *Tavistock Abbey: a study in the social and economic history of Devon* (Cambridge, 1951, repr. Newton Abbot, 1969), pp. 8–10; King, *Peterborough Abbey*, p. 19.

14 John Gillingham, 'The introduction of knight service into England', in *Proceedings of the Battle Conference on Anglo-Norman Studies* IV *1981* (Woodbridge, 1982), pp. 53–64 and 181–7.

15 Chibnall, *Anglo-Norman England*, pp. 28–30.

16 Knowles, *Monastic order*, pp. 607–16.

17 *ASC* 1070.

18 Chibnall, *Anglo-Norman England*, p. 30.

19 Brian Golding, 'Wealth and artistic patronage at twelfth-century St Albans', in Sarah Macready and F. H. Thompson (eds.), *Art and patronage in the English Romanesque* (London, Society of Antiquaries occasional papers, n.s., VIII (1986)), pp. 112–13.

20 See Marjorie Morgan, *The English lands of the abbey of Bec* (Oxford, 1946).

21 Knowles, *Monastic order*, p. 136. Knowles gave no references to support this statement, but it was probably based on the evidence of late medieval visitation returns. See, for instance, A. Hamilton Thompson (ed.), *Visitations of religious houses in the diocese of Lincoln*, vol. I (1420–36) and vols. II–III (1436–49) (London: Canterbury and York Society vols. 17, 24, 33, 1915, 1919, 1927, repr. 1969).

22 On Battle see J. N. Hare, 'The buildings of Battle Abbey: a preliminary survey', in *Proceedings of the Battle Conference on Anglo-Norman Studies* III *1980* (Woodbridge, 1981), pp. 78–95 and 212–13, and, for the association with Tours, Trevor Rowley, *The Norman Heritage 1066–1200* (London, 1983), pp. 121–2. See also E. M. Hallam, 'Monasteries as "war memorials": Battle Abbey and La Victoire', *Studies in Church History* 20 (Oxford, 1983), pp. 47–57.

23 On Selby see R. B. Dobson, 'The first Norman abbey in northern England', *Ampleforth Journal* 74 (1969), 161–76.

24 The possibility can be suggested that Selby's abbots were intended to function in the North as Wulfstan of Worcester and Æthelwig of Evesham did on the Welsh border.

25 See L. G. D. Baker, 'The desert in the North', *Northern History* 5 (1970), 1–11.

26 Knowles, *Monastic order*, p. 162; Davis, 'Bede after Bede', p. 106.

27 See Cowley, *Monastic order in south Wales*, pp. 9–17, for the historical sources for these dependencies. The transition from cell to conventual priory is often very difficult to document.

28 David Walker, *Medieval Wales* (Cambridge Medieval Textbooks, Cambridge, 1990), p. 68.

29 For the equation between the 'reform' of the *clasau* and the spoliation of their property, see R. R. Davies, *The age of conquest: Wales 1063–1415* (Oxford, 1991), pp. 181–2.

30 Glanmor Williams, 'Kidwelly Priory', in Heather James (ed.), *Sir Gâr: Studies in Carmarthenshire History* (Carmarthen, 1991), pp. 189–204.

31 On the Culdees see above, chapter 1.

32 G. W. S. Barrow, *The kingdom of the Scots* (London, 1973), pp. 165–9 and *Kingship and Unity: Scotland 1000–1306* (London, 1981), pp. 77–8; Derek

Baker, '"A nursery of saints": St Margaret of Scotland reconsidered', in Derek Baker (ed.), *Medieval Women*, Studies in Church History Subsidia 1 (Oxford, 1978), pp. 119–41.

33 On Margaret and Lanfranc, see Margaret Gibson, *Lanfranc of Bec* (Oxford, 1978), pp. 126–9.

34 On this question see D. J. A. Matthew, *The Norman monasteries and their English possessions* (Oxford, 1962), pp. 25–8; see also David Bates, 'Normandy and England after 1066', *English Historical Review* 104: 413 (1989), 851–80, especially 869.

35 See above, p. 23.

36 Brian Golding, 'The coming of the Cluniacs', in *Proceedings of the Battle Conference on Anglo-Norman Studies III 1980* (Woodbridge, 1981), p. 66, suggests that three-quarters of Norman monasteries were influenced by Cluny.

37 On this episode see F. Barlow, 'William I's relations with Cluny', *Journal of Ecclesiastical History* 32 (1981), 131–41, repr. in *The Norman Conquest and Beyond* (London, 1983), pp. 245–56, and H. E. J. Cowdrey, 'William I's relations with Cluny further reconsidered', in Judith Loades (ed.), *Monastic Studies*, 1 (Bangor, 1990), pp. 75–85.

38 Christopher Brooke assisted by Gillian Keir, *London 800–1216: the shaping of a city* (London, 1975), pp. 312–14.

39 See Golding, 'Coming of the Cluniacs', pp. 65–77 and 208–12.

40 Barrow, *Kingdom of the Scots*, pp. 185–6. During the reign of Alexander III (1249–85/6), relations between May and Reading were severed, and the Scottish house was associated to St Andrews.

41 Jocelin of Brakelond, *Chronicle of the Abbey of Bury St Edmunds*, translated by Diana Greenway and Jane Sayers (Oxford, 1989), p. 110.

42 Noreen Hunt, *Cluny under Saint Hugh 1049–1109* (London, 1967), p. 3. The earliest surviving English visitations are from 1262: G. F. Duckett, *Visitations of English Cluniac foundations* (London, 1890).

43 William of Malmesbury, *Deeds of the kings of the English*, in *English Historical Documents*, vol. II, p. 291. On the Norman impact on church architecture, see Rowley, *Norman heritage*, pp. 132–43.

44 On the activities of Abbot Paul at St Albans, see Christopher Brooke, 'St Albans, the great abbey', in Robert Runcie (ed.), *Cathedral and City: St Albans ancient and modern* (London, 1977), pp. 44–53.

45 On Worcester, see Richard Gem, 'Bishop Wulfstan II and the Romanesque cathedral church of Worcester', in Glenys Popper (ed.), *Medieval Art and Architecture at Worcester Cathedral*, The British Archaeological Association Conference Transactions for the year 1975 (1978), pp. 15–37.

46 Christopher Wilson, 'Abbot Serlo's church at Gloucester (1089–1100): its place in Romanesque architecture', in T. A. Heslop and V. A. Sekules (eds.), *Medieval Art and Architecture at Gloucester and Tewkesbury*, The British Archaeological Association Conference Transactions for the year 1981 (1985), pp. 52–83.

47 Mason, *Wulfstan*, p. 202.

48 See below, chapter 7.
49 Arnold William Klukas, 'The architectural implications of the *Decreta Lanfranci*', *Anglo-Norman Studies* VI: *Proceedings of the Battle Conference 1983* (Woodbridge, 1984), pp. 136–71.

3 The regular canons

1 For the texts and history of the Rule, see George Lawless (ed.), *Augustine of Hippo and his monastic rule* (Oxford, 1987).
2 On this see two articles by Ludo Milis, 'Ermites et chanoines réguliers au XIIᵉ siècle', *Cahiers de Civilisation Médiévale* 22, pt 85 (1979), 39–80, and 'L'Evolution de l'érémitisme au canonicat régulier dans la première moitié du douzième siècle: transition ou trahison', in *Istituzioni monastiche et istituzioni canonicali in occidente (1123–1215)*, Miscellanea del centro di studi medioevali IX (Milan, 1980), 223–38.
3 There are many treatments of the papal reform movement of the mid to late eleventh century; for a recent discussion see Colin Morris, *The papal monarchy: the western church from 1050–1250* (Oxford, 1989), pp. 79–108. On the regular canons, see ibid., pp. 74–8.
4 On the Augustinians in England and Wales see J. C. Dickinson, *The origins of the Austin canons and their introduction into England* (London, 1950), and David M. Robinson, *The geography of Augustinian settlement in medieval England and Wales*, British Archaeological Reports, British series 80 (2 vols., Oxford, 1980).
5 Dickinson, *Austin canons*, pp. 104–5, links the adoption of the Rule to the increase in numbers at the hospital.
6 Huntingdon deserves mention as a house from which a number of other eminent ones – Barnwell, Hexham, Bolton and Merton – derived.
7 This description is indebted to Brooke and Keir, *London*, pp. 314–25; see also Jeremy Haslam, 'Parishes, churches, wards and gates in eastern London', in J. Blair (ed.), *Minsters and parish churches: the local church in transition 950–1200*, Oxford University Committee for Archaeology, monograph no. 17 (Oxford, 1988), pp. 35–43, where it is suggested (p. 36) that Holy Trinity took over the rights and jurisdiction of an earlier church.
8 It was also on the advice of Anselm and the king that the first small Augustinian priory had been founded at Little Dunmow (Essex) in 1106.
9 On minster churches, see John Blair, 'Secular minster churches in Domesday Book', in Peter Sawyer (ed.), *Domesday Book: a reassessment* (London, 1985), pp. 104–42, and the essays in Blair, *Minsters and parish churches*.
10 Michael Franklin, 'The bishops of Winchester and the monastic revolution', in *Anglo-Norman Studies* xii: *Proceedings of the Battle Conference 1989* (Woodbridge, 1990), pp. 47–65.
11 On St Frideswide's, see John Blair (ed.), *Saint Frideswide's monastery at Oxford, Archaeological and Architectural Studies* (Oxford: Oxfordshire Architectural and Historical Society, 1990), pp. 226–8.

12 Cowley, *Monastic order in south Wales*, pp. 32–3. On later Welsh foundations associated with Celtic sites, see below, pp. 60–1.

13 Blair has calculated that altogether eighteen out of forty-three Augustinian houses founded before 1135 may have had their origin in earlier foundations; see 'Secular minster churches in Domesday Book', p. 138.

14 D. Nicholl, *Thurstan, archbishop of York 1114–1140* (York, 1964), pp. 127–39.

15 On the grant of parish churches to the religious orders see below, chapter 11.

16 See Robinson, *Geography of Augustinian settlement*, pp. 172–7.

17 For a discussion of the performance of parochial work by members of the religious orders generally see Marjorie Chibnall 'Monks and pastoral work: a problem in Anglo-Norman history', *Journal of Ecclesiastical History* 18 (1967), 165–72.

18 See, for example, Christopher Harper-Bill, 'The struggle for benefices in twelfth-century East Anglia', in *Anglo-Norman Studies XI: Proceedings of the Battle Conference 1988* (Woodbridge, 1989), pp. 113–32, where it is argued that the transfer of benefices into monastic hands created 'a new form of proprietary church' (p. 132).

19 Brooke and Keir, *London*, pp. 325–8.

20 J. Patrick Greene, *Norton Priory: the archaeology of a medieval religious house* (Cambridge, 1989), pp. 1–3. The Runcorn community was transferred to Norton in 1134.

21 Jane Herbert, 'The transformation of hermitages into Augustinian priories in twelfth-century England', in *Monks, hermits and the ascetic tradition*, Studies in Church History 22 (Oxford, 1985), pp. 131–45. On this theme in a wider geographical context see Milis, 'Ermites et chanoines', and 'L'Evolution de l'érémitisme au canonicat régulier'.

22 See especially Cowley, *Monastic order in south Wales*, pp. 30–2.

23 W. E. Wightman, *The Lacy family in England and Normandy, 1066–1194* (Oxford, 1966), pp. 67–8; T. N. Burrows, 'The foundation of Nostell Priory', *Yorkshire Archaeological Journal* 53 (1981), 31–5.

24 Royal foundations were Carlisle, Cirencester, Dunstable, St Denys by Southampton, and Wellow.

25 On this see D. Postles, 'The foundation of Oseney Abbey', *Bulletin of the Institute of Historical Research* 53 (1980), 242–4. Oseney was founded by a *curialis* who had married Edith Forne, a former mistress of Henry I; the cartulary of the house suggests that it was at her instigation that the monastery was established.

26 J. C. Dickinson, 'The origins of the cathedral of Carlisle', *Transactions of the Cumberland and Westmorland Antiquarian and Archaeological Society*, n.s., 45 (1946), 134–43.

27 Dickinson, *Austin canons*, pp. 80–1, 86–7 and 173; L. Milis, *L'Ordre des chanoines réguliers d'Arrouaise* (Bruges, 1969).

28 For example, Bourne (Lincolnshire), Dorchester (Oxfordshire), Hartland (Devon), Haughmond and Lilleshall (Shropshire) and Missenden (Buckinghamshire).

29 Dickinson ('Origins of the cathedral of Carlisle', 142) notes the influence of

Malachy. On Alexander, see A. G. Dyson, 'The monastic patronage of Bishop Alexander of Lincoln', *Journal of Ecclesiastical History* 26 (1975), 10–14.

30 For an English nunnery affiliated to Arrouaise, see below, pp. 100–1.

31 See especially Barrow, *Kingdom of the Scots*, pp. 170–2 and 177–84.

32 J. Wilson, 'The foundation of the Austin priories of Nostell and Scone', *Scottish Historical Review* 7 (1910), 141–59.

33 G. W. S. Barrow, 'The cathedral chapter of St Andrew's and the Culdees in the twelfth and thirteenth centuries', *Journal of Ecclesiastical History* 3 (1952), 23–39, and *Kingdom of the Scots*, pp. 212–32.

34 A phrase used by Christopher Brooke; see his 'King David I of Scotland as a connoisseur of the religious orders', in C. E. Viola (ed.), *Mediaevalia Christiana, xie–xiie siècles: hommage à Raymonde Foreville* (Paris, 1989), pp. 320–34.

35 On the attraction of the Augustinians for this class of society, see R. W. Southern 'King Henry I', in *Medieval humanism and other studies* (Oxford, 1970), pp. 206–33, especially p. 214, and *Western society and the church in the middle ages* (Harmondsworth, 1970), pp. 241–50. For the composition of the class of royal *curiales*, see now Judith A. Green, *The government of England under Henry I* (Cambridge, 1986), pp. 134–93.

36 On this theme see Caroline Walker Bynum, 'The spirituality of regular canons in the twelfth century', in *Jesus as mother: studies in the spirituality of the high middle ages* (Berkeley, Los Angeles and London, 1982), pp. 22–58, and Christopher N. L. Brooke, 'Monk and canon: some patterns in the religious life of the twelfth century', in *Monks, hermits and the ascetic tradition*, pp. 109–29.

37 R. W. Southern, *Western society and the church in the Middle Ages* (Harmondsworth, 1970), pp. 240–50.

38 Robinson, *Geography of Augustinian settlement*, pp. 29–30.

39 On the Cornish collegiate churches after 1066 and their land holdings in Domesday Book, see Lynette Olsen, *Early monasteries in Cornwall* (Woodbridge, 1989), pp. 86–97.

40 G. Constable and B. Smith (eds. and transls.), *Libellus de Diversis Ordinibus et Professionibus qui sunt in Aecclesia* (Oxford, 1972), p. 57.

41 H. M. Colvin, *The White Canons in England* (Oxford, 1951), pp. 33–6.

42 For the suggestion that Soulseat was originally intended to be a Cistercian house, see J. G. Scott, 'The origins of Dundrennan and Soulseat Abbeys', *Transactions of the Dumfriesshire and Galloway Natural History and Antiquarian Society* 63 (1988), 35–44.

43 Other small Premonstratensian houses in Scotland were Tongland, Fearn and Holywood, deriving respectively from Cockersand, Whithorn and Soulseat.

44 Cowley, *Monastic order in south Wales*, pp. 35–7.

45 Davies, *Age of conquest*, p. 195.

46 See below, chapter 8.

47 Davies, *Age of conquest*, pp. 195–6; see also C. N. Johns, 'The Celtic monasteries of north Wales', *Caernarvonshire Historical Society Transactions* 21 (1960), 14–43, and 'Postscript to "The Celtic monasteries of north Wales"',

Caernarvonshire Historical Society Transactions 23 (1962), 129–31, and T. Jones
Pierce, 'Bardsey – a study in monastic origins', *Caernarvonshire Historical
Society Transactions* 24 (1963), 60–77.

48 The thirteenth-century Scottish expansion continued to be marked by the
take-over of sites of ancient religious significance, especially at Abernethy
(Perth), which could traditionally trace its foundation back to King Nechtan
of the Picts, c. 600.

49 Cowley, *Monastic order in south Wales*, pp. 33–5.

50 Bynum, 'Spirituality of regular canons', pp. 22–58.

4 The new monastic orders of the twelfth century

1 Among the many works on this theme, see Norman F. Cantor, 'The crisis of
western monasticism 1050–1130', *American Historical Review* 66 (1960/1),
47–67; J. Leclercq, 'The monastic crisis of the eleventh and twelfth centuries',
translated from 'La Crise du monachisme aux xie et xiie siècles', in Noreen
Hunt (ed.), *Cluniac monasticism in the central middle ages* (London, 1971),
pp. 217–37; John Van Engen, 'The "Crisis of Cenobitism" reconsidered:
Benedictine monasticism in the years 1050–1150', *Speculum* 61 (1986),
269–304; Lester K. Little, *Religious poverty and the profit economy in medieval
Europe* (London, 1978), pp. 61–9.

2 On the importance of the eremitical element see Milis, 'Ermites et
chanoines', 39–80; Giles Constable, 'Eremitical forms of monastic life', in
Istituzioni monastiche e istituzioni canonicali in occidente (1123–1215), Miscellanea
del centro di studi medioevali ix (Milan, 1980), 239–64; Henrietta Leyser,
Hermits and the new monasticism (London, 1984). See also Morris, *Papal
monarchy*, pp. 68–74.

3 The secondary literature on the Cistercians is vast; useful works to consult are
R. A. Donkin, *A check-list of printed works relating to the Cistercian Order as a
whole and to the houses of the British Isles in particular* (Rochefort, 1969) and
Louis J. Lekai, *The Cistercians: ideals and reality* (Kent, OH, 1977).

4 On Cistercian sites see below, chapter 7.

5 The development of Cistercian thought can be charted through the early
statutes; these are published in P. Guignard (ed.), *Les Monuments primitifs de la
règle cistercienne* (Dijon, 1878), and in J. de la Croix Bouton and J. B. van
Damme, *Les Plus Anciens Textes de Cîteaux: Commentaria Cisterciensis, Studia
et Documenta*, ii (Achel, 1974). A translation into English by Bede K. Lackner
appears in Lekai, *The Cistercians: ideals and reality*, pp. 442–66. Their
originality and date have been the subject of debate over the last thirty or
forty years: for commentary and dating problems, see David Knowles, 'The
primitive documents of the Cistercian order', in *Great historical enterprises:
problems in monastic history* (London, 1963), pp. 197–222, and C. Waddell,
'The *Exordium Cistercii* and the *Summa Cartae Caritatis*', in J. R. Sommerfeldt
(ed.), *Cistercian ideals and reality* (Kalamazoo, Michigan, 1978), pp. 30–61,
especially pp. 30–6.

6 Among the English Tironensian houses was Hamble (Hampshire),

established by William Giffard, bishop of Winchester, founder of the Cistercian abbey of Waverley; see below, p. 69.

7 A point made by R. R. Davies, *Domination and conquest: the experience of Ireland, Scotland and Wales, 1100–1300* (Cambridge, 1990), p. 17.

8 On Lindores, see K. J. Stringer, *Earl David of Huntingdon 1152–1219: a study in Anglo-Scottish history* (Edinburgh, 1985), pp. 92–101.

9 Cowley, *Monastic order in south Wales*, pp. 19–20.

10 For a discussion of the Savigniac houses in England see Knowles, *Monastic order*, pp. 227–8, 249–52, and Bennett D. Hill, *English Cistercian monasteries and their patrons in the twelfth century* (Urbana, 1968), pp. 80–115.

11 These were Neath (1130), Basingwerk (1131), Quarr (1132), Combermere (1133), Rushen (1134), Buildwas, Stratford Langthorne and Swineshead (1135), Buckfast (1136), Calder (1134), which moved to Byland (1138), Coggeshall (1140), Calder II (1142/3) and Jervaulx (1145). See Janet Burton and Roger Stalley, 'Tables of Cistercian affiliations', in Christopher Norton and David Park (eds.), *Cistercian art and architecture in the British Isles* (Cambridge, 1986, repr. 1988), p. 400; six further houses of the line of Savigny were added after the merger with Cîteaux in 1147.

12 See Janet Burton, 'The abbeys of Byland and Jervaulx, and the problems of the English Savigniacs, 1134–1156', in Judith Loades (ed.), *Monastic Studies*, II (Bangor, 1991), pp. 119–31.

13 F. M. Powicke (ed. and transl.), *The life of Ailred of Rievaulx by Walter Daniel*, Nelsons Medieval Classics (London, 1950), p. 35; on effects on the Cistercians of the addition of the monks of the congregation of Savigny, see Hill, *English Cistercian monasteries*, pp. 104–15.

14 On the Cistercian expansion, see Janet Burton, 'The foundation of the British Cistercian houses', in Norton and Park (eds.), *Cistercian art and architecture*, pp. 24–39, and on affiliations, ibid., pp. 394–401.

15 Bruno Scott James (transl.), *The letters of St Bernard of Clairvaux* (London, 1953), pp. 141–2, modified translation.

16 For this episode, and the difficulties surrounding some of the sources, see Nicholl, *Thurstan, archbishop of York*, pp. 151–91; D. Bethell, 'The foundation of Fountains Abbey and the state of St Mary's, York, in 1132', *Journal of Ecclesiastical History* 17 (1966), 11–27; D. Baker, 'The foundation of Fountains Abbey', *Northern History* 4 (1969), 29–43.

17 On this theme see Christopher Brooke, 'St Bernard, the patrons and monastic planning', in Norton and Park (eds.), *Cistercian art and architecture*, pp. 11–23. On motives for monastic foundations generally see below, chapter 10.

18 David Crouch, *The Beaumont twins* (Cambridge, 1986), pp. 198–201.

19 One exception was Saddell Abbey, a daughter house of the Irish monastery of Mellifont. On the date of foundation of Dundrennan see Scott, 'The origins of Dundrennan and Soulseat Abbeys', 35–44; see also K. J. Stringer, 'Galloway and the abbeys of Rievaulx and Dundrennan', *Transactions of the Dumfriesshire and Galloway Natural History and Antiquarian Society* 55 (1980), 174–7.

20 Walter Map, *De Nugis Curialum: Courtiers' Trifles*, edited and translated by M. R. James, revised by C. N. L. Brooke and R. A. B. Mynors, Oxford Medieval Texts (Oxford, 1983), p. 93. For modern comment see R. A. Donkin, 'Settlement and depopulation on Cistercian estates during the twelfth and thirteenth centuries, especially in Yorkshire', *Bulletin of the Institute of Historical Research* 33 (1960), 141–65.

21 Peter Fergusson, *Architecture of solitude: Cistercian abbeys in twelfth-century England* (Princeton, NJ, 1984), p. 18.

22 Powicke (ed.), *Life of Ailred of Rievaulx*, pp. 36–7.

23 E. King, 'Mountsorrel and its region in King Stephen's reign', *Huntingdon Library Quarterly* 44 (1980), 1–10, especially 2–6; Crouch, *Beaumont twins*, pp. 198–9.

24 Burton, 'The foundation of the British Cistercian houses', p. 28; Crouch, *Beaumont twins*, pp. 80–2.

25 For what follows, see K. Stringer, 'A Cistercian archive: the earliest charters of Sawtry Abbey', *Journal of the Society of Archivists* 6 (1980), 325–34.

26 Walter Map, *Courtiers' Trifles*, p. 93.

27 On Beaulieu, see Frederick Hockey, *Beaulieu: King John's Abbey* ([Beaulieu], 1976).

28 See below, chapter 10. The history of the Cistercian Order in Wales has been comprehensively treated by David H. Williams, *The Welsh Cistercians* (2 vols., Caldey Island, Tenby, 1984), and, on aspects of geography, see his *Atlas of Cistercian lands in Wales* (Cardiff, 1990). The divide between the 'Welsh' and 'Anglo-Norman' Cistercian houses should not be overstated: see Davies, *Age of conquest*, pp. 196–201.

29 Gerald of Wales, *The journey through Wales and the description of Wales*, translated by Lewis Thorpe (Harmondsworth, 1978), p. 106.

30 On the Cistercian attitude to the Rule of St Benedict, see M. Basil Pennington, 'Towards discerning the spirit and aims of the founders of the order of Cîteaux', in M. Basil Pennington (ed.), *The Cistercian Spirit: a symposium in memory of Thomas Merton* (Shannon, Ireland, 1969), pp. 1–26; and Louis J. Lekai, 'The Rule and the early Cistercians', *Cistercian Studies* 5 (1970), 243–51.

31 David Knowles, 'The case of St William of York', *Cambridge Historical Journal* 5 (1936), 162–77 and 212–14, reprinted in *The Historian and Character* (Cambridge, 1963), pp. 76–97. See also Derek Baker, '*Viri religiosi* and the York election dispute', in *Councils and assemblies*, Studies in Church History 7 (Oxford, 1971), pp. 87–100.

32 Quoted by Henrietta Leyser in 'Hugh the Carthusian', in Henry Mayr-Harting (ed.), *St Hugh of Lincoln* (Oxford, 1987), p. 6.

33 Adam of Eynsham, *Magna Vita Sancti Hugonis*, edited and translated by D. Douie and D. H. Farmer (2 vols., London, 1961–2, repr. Oxford, 1985). The foundation of Witham is described in I, pp. 46–63, especially pp. 60–3.

34 Karl J. Leyser, 'The Angevin kings and the holy man', in Mayr-Harting, *St Hugh of Lincoln*, pp. 49–73.

35 On spirituality at Witham in the fifteenth century, see Roger Lovatt, 'The

library of John Blacman and Carthusian spirituality', *Journal of Ecclesiastical History* 43 (1992), 195–230.

36 Later foundations were London (1371), Hull (1377), Coventry (1381), Axholme (1397–8) and Mount Grace (1398).

37 The most recent treatment is Alan Forey, *The military orders from the twelfth to the early fourteenth centuries* (London, 1992). For a brief introduction see C. H. Lawrence, *Medieval monasticism: forms of religious life in western Europe in the Middle Ages* (2nd edn, London, 1989), pp. 206–15.

38 H. de Curzon, *La Règle du Temple* (Paris, 1886); recently translated as *The rule of the Templars* by J. M. Upton-Ward (Woodbridge, 1992).

39 The phrase comes from the work written by St Bernard, 'De Laude Novae Militiae', 'In praise of the New Knighthood', printed in J. Leclercq, C. H. Talbot and H. Rochais (eds.), *S. Bernardi Opera* III (Rome, 1963), pp. 207–39.

40 For a general treatment, see T. W. Parker, *The Knights Templars in England* (Tucson, 1963).

41 On the Hospitallers in Britain, see J. Riley Smith, *The Knights of St John in Jerusalem and Cyprus c. 1050–1310* (London, 1967), and W. Rees, *History of the order of St John in Wales and on the Welsh border* (Cardiff, 1947).

42 See the examples discussed in Emma Mason, 'Fact and fiction in the English crusading tradition: the earls of Warwick in the twelfth century', *Journal of Medieval History* 14 (1988), 81–95, and Janet E. Burton, 'The Knights Templar in Yorkshire in the twelfth century: a reassessment', *Northern History* 27 (1991), 26–40. On patrons and their motives, and on the acquisition of estates in the West by the knights, see Forey, *Military orders*, pp. 98–132.

43 For the part played by the religious orders in land clearance, see below, pp. 237–9.

5 Women and the religious life

1 Sharon K. Elkins, *Holy women of twelfth-century England* (Chapel Hill, NC, 1988); Sally Thompson, *Women religious: the founding of English nunneries after the Norman Conquest* (Oxford, 1991).

2 For some of the problems associated with the dating of monastic foundations see V. H. Galbraith, 'Monastic foundation charters of the eleventh and twelfth centuries', *Cambridge Historical Journal* 4 (1934), 205–22 and 296–8; on female houses see particularly Sally P. Thompson, 'Why English nunneries had no history. A study of the problems of English nunneries founded after the Conquest', in John A. Nichols and Lillian T. Shank (eds.), *Medieval religious women*, I, *Distant Echoes* (Kalamazoo, MI: Cistercian Studies publications, 1984), pp. 131–49.

3 These were Llanllŷr (before 1197), Llanllugan and Usk (both founded before 1236). Llansanffraid in Elfael was established between 1170 and 1174, but apparently did not survive the scandal of the elopement of one of its nuns with the abbot of Strata Marcella: Cowley, *Monastic order in south Wales*, pp. 37–8.

4 D. E. Easson, 'The nunneries of medieval Scotland', *Scottish Ecclesiological Society Transactions* 13 (2) (1940–1), 22–38.

5 On the nunneries of late Anglo-Saxon England see above, chapter 1. At least one nunnery was founded between the revival and the Conquest: this was Chatteris, established between 1006 and 1016. Two further Anglo-Saxon nunneries, Polesworth, and Minster in Sheppey, were refounded in the twelfth century.

6 For the imagery of marriage in the ceremony of consecration of nuns, see Penelope D. Johnson, *Equal in monastic profession: religious women in medieval France* (Chicago and London, 1991), p. 63.

7 See Kathleen Cooke, 'Donors and daughters: Shaftesbury Abbey's benefactors, endowments and nuns, c. 1086–1130', in *Anglo-Norman Studies XII: Proceedings of the Battle Conference 1989* (Woodbridge, 1990), pp. 29–45.

8 Walter Fröhlich (ed. and transl.), *The letters of Saint Anselm of Canterbury* (Kalamazoo, MI, 1990), pp. 43–4.

9 For an account of Eve, see Elkins, *Holy women*, pp. 21–7.

10 For the lives of saints as a source for Anglo-Saxon nunneries, see Susan Millinger, 'Humility and power: Anglo-Saxon nuns in Anglo-Norman hagiography', in Nichols and Shank (eds.), *Distant Echoes*, pp. 115–29. As the author points out, these lives are more valuable as evidence of eleventh-century ideas of female sanctity than the reality of tenth- and eleventh-century English convent life.

11 C. H. Talbot (ed.), *The life of Christina of Markyate, a twelfth-century recluse* (1959, repr. with corrections, Oxford, 1987); see also C. J. Holdsworth, 'Christina of Markyate', in Baker (ed.), *Medieval Women*, pp. 185–204; Thompson, *Women religious*, pp. 16–24.

12 See above, chapters 2, 3 and 4, passim.

13 See, for instance, the discussion of the terms 'hermit' and 'anchorite/ anchoress' in A. K. Warren, *Anchorites and their patrons in medieval England* (California, 1985).

14 H. Mayr-Harting, 'Functions of a twelfth-century recluse', *History* 60 (1975), 337–52.

15 See, for instance, Janet E. Burton, 'The eremitical tradition and the development of post-Conquest religious life in northern England', in *Eternal values in medieval life*, ed. Nicole Crossley-Holland (Lampeter, 1991), 18–39.

16 On this theme see Thompson, *Women religious*, pp. 16–37.

17 Emma Mason (ed.), *Westminster Abbey charters 1066–c. 1214* (London: London Record Society, 1988), nos. 249–50.

18 Martin Biddle, 'Alban and the Anglo-Saxon church', in Runcie (ed.), *Cathedral and city*, p. 31.

19 Thompson, *Women religious*, pp. 23–4.

20 Ibid., p. 64; Elkins, *Holy women*, pp. 48–50.

21 For this and other examples, see Thompson, *Women religious*, pp. 27–31.

22 See especially E. J. Dobson, *The origins of Ancrene Wisse* (Oxford, 1976); see also Thompson, *Women religious*, pp. 31–5 and bibliographical references there cited.

23 On this theme, see Ann K. Warren, 'The nun as anchoress. England 1100–1500', in Nichols and Shank (eds.), *Distant Echoes*, pp. 197–212, and Patricia J. F. Rosof, 'The anchoress in the twelfth and thirteenth centuries', in L. T. Shank and John A. Nichols (eds.), *Medieval religious women*, II, *Peaceweavers* (Kalamazoo, MI: Cistercian Studies Publications, 1987), pp. 123–44.

24 Thompson, *Women religious*, p. 177.

25 W. Dugdale, *Monasticon Anglicanum*, rev. edn, ed. J. Caley, H. Ellis and B. Bandinel (6 vols. in 8, London, 1817–30, repr. 1846) (henceforth cited as *Mon. Angl.*), v, p. 508.

26 Elkins, *Holy women*, p. 14.

27 David M. Smith (ed.), *English Episcopal Acta I: Lincoln 1067–1185* (London, British Academy 1980), no. 33.

28 Thompson, *Women religious*, p. 169.

29 On the establishment of the Yorkshire houses, see Janet E. Burton, *The Yorkshire nunneries in the twelfth and thirteenth centuries*, Borthwick Paper no. 56 (York, 1979), pp. 5–11.

30 Easson, 'Nunneries of medieval Scotland', 22–3.

31 Elkins, *Holy women*, pp. 13–18; Thompson, *Women religious*, pp. 191–210.

32 Burton, *Yorkshire nunneries*, pp. 6 and 12; R. B. Dobson and Sara Donaghey, *The history of Clementhorpe Nunnery* (York: York Archaeological Trust, 1984), pp. 9–11; Thompson, *Women religious*, pp. 193–5.

33 One Gilbertine priory, Haverholme, owed its foundation to a bishop; see below, p. 98.

34 Burton, *Yorkshire nunneries*, pp. 17–27; Thompson, *Women religious*, p. 163.

35 Ibid., p. 131.

36 Other royal foundations for women were Amesbury (see below, pp. 97–8) and the small house of Burnham founded in 1266 by Richard, earl of Cornwall and king of the Romans.

37 Burton, *Yorkshire nunneries*, p. 7.

38 Ibid., p. 20.

39 For a general discussion of the problem see J. H. Lynch, *Simoniacal entry into religious life from 1000 to 1260* (Columbus, OH, 1976); see also below, pp. 174–5, 219–21.

40 See Thompson, *Women religious*, p. 181 and pp. 176–82 for examples.

41 Cooke, 'Donors and daughters', pp. 29–45.

42 Burton, *Yorkshire nunneries*, pp. 19–23.

43 J. Smith, 'Robert of Arbrissel: *Procurator mulierum*', in Baker (ed.), *Medieval women*, pp. 175–84; P. S. Gold, 'Male/female co-operation: the example of Fontevrault', in Nichols and Shank (eds.), *Distant echoes*, pp. 151–68; Thompson, *Women religious*, pp. 113–21.

44 On the question of the status of men at Fontevrault see Thompson, *Women religious*, pp. 117–18. There is a contrast with the Gilbertines here, for after the death of the founder and first master, St Gilbert, authority over the order passed to another man.

45 For this and other English foundations (there were none in Wales or

Scotland), see M. Chibnall, 'L'Ordre de Fontevraud en Angleterre au xiie siècle', *Cahiers de Civilisation Médiévale* 29 (1986), 41–7; on Kintbury see also Crouch, *Beaumont twins*, pp. 203–4.

46 A point made by Thompson, *Women religious*, pp. 121–32.

47 However, on suggestions of continued links with the continent see Chibnall, 'L'Ordre de Fontevraud', 45.

48 Thompson, *Women religious*, p. 228. On the Gilbertines see Rose Graham, *St Gilbert of Sempringham and the Gilbertines* (London, 1901) and the forthcoming study by Dr Brian Golding.

49 Smith, *Lincoln Acta*, no. 37.

50 Thompson, *Women religious*, p. 74 and note 129; Brian Golding, 'St Bernard and St Gilbert', in B. Ward (ed.), *The influence of St Bernard: Anglican essays with an introduction by Jean Leclercq* (Oxford, 1976), pp. 42–52, especially p. 46.

51 Malachy did not arrive at Cîteaux until October 1148 and died shortly afterwards; Golding, 'St Bernard and St Gilbert', pp. 47–8; see also Sharon K. Elkins, 'The emergence of a Gilbertine identity', in Nichols and Shank (eds.), *Distant Echoes*, pp. 169–82.

52 For a discussion of the physical layout of Gilbertine double houses, and the chain of command within the order, see below, pp. 149, 172, 182–3.

53 See Golding's forthcoming study.

54 Thompson, *Women religious*, pp. 75–6.

55 A point made by Gold, 'Male/female co-operation', p. 162.

56 Thompson, *Women religious*, pp. 140–5.

57 See above, chapter 3, p. 54.

58 Elkins, *Holy women*, p. 121; Thompson, *Women religious*, pp. 150–5.

59 Sally Thompson, 'The problem of the Cistercian nuns in the twelfth and early thirteenth centuries', in Baker (ed.), *Medieval women*, pp. 227–52.

60 Williams, *Welsh Cistercians*, I, p. 11.

61 Burton, *Yorkshire nunneries*, p. 46, note 13.

62 Ibid.; C. V. Graves, 'The organization of an English Cistercian nunnery in Lincolnshire', *Cîteaux* 33 (1982), 333–50, especially 335–6.

63 Thompson, *Women religious*, p. 105.

64 Elkins, *Holy women*, pp. 84–8; John A. Nichols, 'The internal organization of English Cistercian nunneries', *Cîteaux* 30 (1979), 23–40, especially 28–30.

65 Burton, *Yorkshire nunneries*, pp. 30–1.

66 Graves, 'English Cistercian nunnery in Lincolnshire', 337–8.

67 See Burton, *Yorkshire nunneries*, p. 35 for male administrators at Yedingham, Moxby and Wilberfoss.

68 Elkins, *Holy women*, pp. 93–4. Thompson suggests that the 'order' might have been dictated by that of the chaplains or male administrators appointed to nunneries, and that this might account for the change in the affiliation of certain houses: *Women religious*, p. 214.

69 For a general discussion of these factors, see Brenda M. Bolton, '*Mulieres sanctae*', in *Sanctity and secularity: the church and the world*, Studies in Church History 10 (Oxford, 1973), pp. 77–95; Johnson, *Equal in monastic profession*, pp. 257–60.

70 See above, pp. 100–1.

71 Burton, *Yorkshire nunneries*, p. 8; there are indications that the two establishments were, even thirty years later, regarded as a single institution.

72 Thompson, *Women religious*, pp. 156–7.

73 For the episode, see Giles Constable, 'Aelred of Rievaulx and the nun of Watton: an episode in the early history of the Gilbertine order', in Baker (ed.), *Medieval women*, pp. 205–26. See also R. Foreville and Gillian Keir (eds.), *The Book of St Gilbert*, Oxford Medieval Texts (Oxford, 1987), pp. liv–lv.

74 Walter Map, *Courtiers' Trifles*, p. 117.

75 David Knowles, 'The revolt of the lay brothers of Sempringham', *English Historical Review*, 50 (1935), 465–87; Foreville and Keir, *Book of St Gilbert*, pp. lv–lxii; Elkins, *Holy Women*, pp. 111–17.

76 Foreville and Keir, *Book of St Gilbert*, pp. 145, 147, 149–53.

77 Bolton, '*Mulieres sanctae*', pp. 77–95; Caroline Walker Bynum, *Holy feast and holy fast: the religious significance of food to medieval women* (Berkeley and London, 1987), pp. 14–23.

78 See Rosalind B. Brooke and Christopher N. L. Brooke, 'St Clare', in Baker (ed.), *Medieval women*, pp. 275–87.

79 See Bolton, '*Mulieres sanctae*', and Bynum, *Holy feast*, p. 16, where it is suggested that women did not turn to less traditional forms of religious life because they felt that the church was failing to meet their needs but because they were responding to a way of life which better expressed basic female interests: the emphasis on affective piety and the humanity of Christ, antagonism to clerical authority, and penitential asceticism. The Beguines gave a religious significance to the ordinary female life within society.

80 On anchoresses, see Warren, *Anchorites and their patrons in medieval England*.

6 The mendicant orders

1 A number of lesser orders reached Britain also: the Crutched Friars, the Friars of the Sack, who were suppressed in 1274, and the Trinitarians or Red Friars (who were particularly popular in Scotland).

2 On some of these groups, see Rosalind B. Brooke, *The coming of the friars* (London, 1975), pp. 40–74; Lester K. Little, *Religious poverty and the profit economy in medieval Europe* (London, 1978), pp. 113–45; Brenda Bolton, *The medieval reformation* (London, 1983), pp. 55–66.

3 The *Regula Secunda* is translated in Brooke, *The coming of the friars*, pp. 120–5. It is also called *Bullata* because the final version was enshrined in the papal bull *Solet Annuere*.

4 Translated in Brooke, *The coming of the friars*, pp. 117–19.

5 On the fourteenth-century schism between the Conventual and Spiritual or Observant Franciscans see, for instance, John Moorman, *A history of the Franciscan order* (Oxford, 1968), pp. 188–204, 369–83 and 441–56. The Observants were the reforming group in the order, who wished to see strict observance of the rule.

6 On the Cathars see, for instance, Little, *Religious poverty*, pp. 134–45.

7 The most comprehensive survey of the Black Friars in England is William A. Hinnebusch, *The early English Friars Preacher* (Rome, 1951).

8 On the Oxford friary, which moved in 1236 to a location outside the south gate of the town, see ibid., pp. 1–19.

9 On the London friary see ibid., pp. 20–55.

10 A. G. Little (ed.), *Fratris Thomae Vulgo Dicti de Eccleston, Tractatus de Adventu Fratrum Minorum in Angliam*, 1st English edn (Manchester, 1951); translated as *The coming of the Franciscans, Thomas of Eccleston, De adventu fratrum minorum in Angliam*, by Leo Sherley-Price (London, 1964); quotations are taken from, and reference made to, this translation.

11 These were York, Berwick, Boston, Bristol, Cambridge, Kings Lynn, Lincoln, London, Newcastle, Northampton, Norwich, Oxford, Stamford and Winchester: see Susan Reynolds, *An introduction to the history of English medieval towns* (Oxford, 1977), pp. 51, 63; Barrie Dobson, 'Mendicant ideal and practice in medieval York', in P. V. Addyman and V. E. Black (eds.), *Archaeological papers from York presented to M. W. Barley* (York, 1984), pp. 109–22 (pp. 111–12).

12 Eccleston, *The coming of the Franciscans*, p. 80.

13 Lawrence Butler, 'The houses of the mendicant orders in Britain: recent archaeological work', in Addyman and Black (eds.), *Archaeological papers from York*, pp. 123–36 (p. 128).

14 For a full list, see Keith J. Egan, 'Medieval Carmelite houses: England and Wales', *Carmelus* 16 (1969), 142–226 and 'Medieval Carmelite houses: Scotland', *Carmelus* 19 (1972), 107–12.

15 F. Roth, *The English Austin Friars 1249–1538*, I, *History* (New York, 1966), pp. 19-32.

16 David Knowles, *The religious orders in England*, 1 (Cambridge, 1948, repr. 1974), p. 201.

17 Roth, *The English Austin Friars*, p. 259.

18 Ibid., p. 320.

19 Eccleston, *The coming of the Franciscans*, p. 11.

20 Ibid., pp. 17–18.

21 Ibid., p. 7.

22 Cowley, *Monastic order in south Wales*, pp. 135–6.

23 A. G. Little, *Studies in English Franciscan history* (Manchester, 1917), pp. 68–72, gives examples which include, for the Minors, 80 in London and 23 in Winchester (1243) and 26 in Chichester (1253). When discussing the numbers in priories of the mendicant orders it should be remembered that their population was not likely to be complete, as a number of friars could have been preaching or studying away.

24 This acreage would have included both the site of the house and the surrounding garden, orchard or arable.

25 Eccleston, *The coming of the Franciscans*, pp. 15–18.

26 See Egan, 'Medieval Carmelite houses: England and Wales', 144–225 (passim) for such grants to the White Friars.

27 R. C. Easterling, 'The friars in Wales', *Archaeologia Cambrensis*, 6th series, 14 (1914), 323–56 (334).

28 Little, *Religious poverty*, p. 204. See also Hinnebusch, *Early English Friars Preacher*, p. 505, for a summary of royal grants to the Dominicans in the thirteenth century.

29 For royal patronage of the London Preachers see Hinnebusch, *Early English Friars Preacher*, pp. 33–40.

30 Egan, 'Medieval Carmelite houses: England and Wales', 207–9.

31 C. L. Kingsford, *The Grey Friars of London* (Aberdeen, 1915, repr. Ridgewood, NJ, 1965), pp. 70–1; see pp. 70–144 for a full list of monuments, derived from the register of the friary.

32 Hinnebusch, *Early English Friars Preacher*, p. 44.

33 See below, pp. 126–8.

34 D. M. Palliser, *The Reformation in York 1534–1553*, Borthwick Paper no. 40 (York, 1971), p. 2; Dobson, 'Mendicant ideal and practice', pp. 116–17. R. W. Southern, *Western society and the church in the middle ages* (Harmondsworth, 1970), p. 288, notes that 'in the last half of the fourteenth century one third of the wills of the citizens of Oxford contain bequests to the Franciscans; and . . . a high proportion of these wills contain bequests to other friars as well'. He further suggests that the friars were more suited than members of the monastic orders to benefit from the testamentary benefactions of the humblest in society, since they could make good use of small monetary gifts.

35 Little, *Studies in English Franciscan history*, pp. 35–6.

36 Ibid., pp. 37, 39.

37 Hinnebusch, *Early English Friars Preacher*, pp. 30–1.

38 John R. H. Moorman, *The Grey Friars in Cambridge, 1225–1538* (Cambridge, 1952), p. 246; Easterling, 'The friars in Wales', 335; Hinnebusch, *Early English Friars Preacher*, p. 73.

39 For these developments see Little, *Studies in English Franciscan history*, pp. 27–35.

40 C. H. Talbot, 'Cîteaux and Scarborough', *Studia Monastica* 2 (1960), 95–158.

41 Little, *Studies in English Franciscan history*, pp. 96–9.

42 Extracts from the Dominican constitutions are translated in Brooke, *The coming of the friars*, pp. 189–200. For a comprehensive treatment of the government of the order see W. Hinnebusch, *The history of the Dominican order*, 1 (New York, 1965).

43 The standard work on the constitutional development of the Franciscans is R. Brooke, *Early Franciscan government, Elias to Bonaventura* (Cambridge, 1959).

44 London, Oxford, Cambridge, York, Salisbury and Worcester, possibly Bristol, and Newcastle (which included Scotland). The Austin province was divided into four limits: Oxford, Cambridge, London and York.

45 Hinnebusch, *History of the Dominican order*, p. 184. On visitation circuits and the provincial chapter see Hinnebusch, *Early English Friars Preacher*, pp. 210–14.

46 Eccleston, *The coming of the Franciscans*, pp. 32–3.

47 Ibid., p. 77.

48 Brooke, *The coming of the friars*, p. 160.
49 Ibid., p. 122. The *Regula Bullata* is here quoting the beginning of chapter 48 of the Rule of St Benedict.
50 Brooke, *The coming of the friars*, p. 124.
51 The need for informed preaching led naturally to the greater provision of education; on this see below, chapter 9.
52 On *exempla* see below, pp. 206–7.
53 Little, *Religious poverty*, p. 186.
54 Quoted in Michael Prestwich, *English politics in the thirteenth century* (London, 1990), p. 70.
55 See Knowles, *Religious orders*, I, pp. 182–3.
56 See, for example, D. Owen, *Church and society in medieval Lincolnshire* (Lincoln, 1981), pp. 89–91.
57 Hinnebusch, *Early English Friars Preacher*, pp. 6–8
58 Roth, *English Austin friars*, pp. 250–1.
59 Quoted in Brooke, *The coming of the friars*, pp. 214–15.
60 Little, *Studies in English Franciscan history*, p. 134.
61 Hinnebusch, *Early English Friars Preacher*, p. 437.
62 Eccleston, *The coming of the Franciscans*, p. 59.
63 For Dominican participation in public life, see Hinnebusch, *Early English Friars Preacher*, pp. 458–91.
64 Eccleston, *The coming of the Franciscans*, p. 17.
65 Ibid., p. 17.
66 Ibid., pp. 4, 33
67 Southern, *Western society and the church*, p. 288.
68 Dobson, 'Mendicant ideal and practice', p. 110.

7 The physical setting: monastic buildings and the monastic plan

1 On this theme, see Lawrence Butler, 'Medieval urban religious houses', *Council for British Archaeology Research Report* 61 (1987), 167–76.
2 This information is drawn from M. W. Thompson, 'Associated monasteries and castles in the Middle Ages: a tentative list', *Archaeological Journal* 143 (1986), 305–21.
3 A useful table of Cistercian legislation related to sites, buildings, architecture and artistic activity of all kinds is to be found in Norton and Park (eds.), *Cistercian art and architecture*, pp. 315–93. For some comments on rural sites of houses of diverse orders, see Lawrence Butler, 'The archaeology of rural monasteries in England and Wales', in Roberta Gilchrist and Harold Mytum (eds.), *The archaeology of rural monasteries in England and Wales*, BAR British series 203 (Oxford, 1989), pp. 1–27.
4 See also the cases of Revesby, Woburn, Kirkstall and Combe, cited in Fergusson, *Architecture of solitude*, p. 9. For a general discussion see R. A. Donkin, *The Cistercians: studies in the geography of medieval England and Wales*, Pontifical Institute of Mediaeval Studies, Studies and Texts 38 (Toronto, 1978), pp. 37–44.

5 Barrow, *Kingdom of the Scots*, p. 204.

6 See Egan, 'Medieval Carmelite houses: England and Wales', under Boston, Barnham Norton, Cambridge, Hull, Newcastle, Oxford and York.

7 A point made by Donkin, *The Cistercians: studies in the geography of medieval England and Wales*, p. 31; for a general discussion of Cistercian site changes see ibid., pp. 31–6 and 179–80.

8 Hockey, *Beaulieu*, p. 15. Hockey suggests that the site at Faringdon might also have been too close for comfort (twelve miles) to the Benedictine abbey of Abingdon.

9 Robinson, *Geography of Augustinian settlement*, pp. 79–81.

10 See, for instance, Greene, *Norton Priory*, pp. 2–3.

11 Donkin, *The Cistercians: studies in the geography of medieval England and Wales*, p. 33; Robinson, *Geography of Augustinian settlement*, pp. 82–3.

12 Donkin, *The Cistercians: studies in the geography of medieval England and Wales*, p. 35.

13 Quoted in Williams, *Welsh Cistercians*, I, pp. 18–19.

14 For the sites of the abbey and details of the negotiations for the final transfer, see Rhŷs W. Hays, *The history of the abbey of Aberconway 1186–1537* (Cardiff, 1963), pp. 4–6 and 61–77.

15 Fergusson, *Architecture of solitude*, pp. 24–5.

16 Greene, *Norton Priory*, pp. 73–9.

17 R. Gilyard-Beer and Glyn Coppack, 'Excavations at Fountains Abbey, North Yorkshire, 1979–80; the early development of the monastery', *Archaeologia* 108 (1986), 147–88, especially 151–4 and 174–5.

18 See Coppack, *Abbeys and priories*, pp. 66–9, for a general discussion and the specific example of a small Benedictine priory, Sandwell.

19 On Anglo-Saxon monastic churches, see ibid., pp. 32–8.

20 The details in the following discussion derive mainly from R. Gilyard-Beer, *Abbeys* (London: HMSO, 1959, repr. with amendments, 1968), Coppack, *Abbeys and priories*, and for Scotland, Stewart Cruden, *Scottish abbeys* (Edinburgh: HMSO, 1960). See also C. P. S. Platt, *The abbeys and priories of medieval England* (London, 1984). Useful gazetteers are provided by Anthony New, *A guide to the abbeys of England and Wales* (London, 1985), and *A guide to the abbeys of Scotland with priories and collegiate churches* (London, 1988).

21 On wall paintings in the *capellae ante portas* at Kirkstead, Tilty, Coggeshall, Croxden, Hailes and Merevale, see David Park, 'Cistercian wall painting and panel painting', in Norton and Park (eds.), *Cistercian art and architecture*, pp. 181–27, especially pp. 190, 195–6, 205 and 220–3.

22 Brooke, 'St Albans: the great abbey', p. 55, suggests that the great screens at St Albans belong to the fourteenth and fifteenth centuries, when there was increased emphasis on the privacy of the monks, and that in earlier days the screens dividing the laity in the nave, the monks in the choir and the shrine of St Alban in the east end would not have been so high and obtrusive.

23 On burials in monastic churches, and their effect on the layout of the eastern ends, see Coppack, *Abbeys and priories*, pp. 58–60, citing the case of Bordesley.

24 On primitive Cistercian churches see J. O. Schaefer, 'The earliest churches of the Cistercian order', in M. P. Lillich (ed.), *Studies in Cistercian art and architecture*, I (Kalamazoo, MI, 1982), pp. 1–12, Fergusson, *Architecture of solitude*, pp. 23–9, and Richard Halsey, 'The earliest architecture of the Cistercians in England', in Norton and Park (eds.), *Cistercian art and architecture*, pp. 65–85.

25 Coppack, *Abbeys and priories*, p. 45.

26 See above, chapter 6, pp. 126–8; see also Butler, 'Houses of the mendicant orders in Britain', pp. 123–36, especially 129–31, and A. R. Martin, *Franciscan architecture in England* (Manchester, 1937).

27 See the example of the richly decorated processional doorway, now repositioned, at Norton: Greene, *Norton Priory*, pp. 94–105.

28 On the development of this distinctively Cistercian feature, see Nicola Coldstream, 'Cistercian architecture from Beaulieu to the Dissolution', in Norton and Park (eds.), *Cistercian art and architecture*, p. 142.

29 On developments in Cistercian churches see Fergusson, *Architecture of solitude*, pp. 54–100; Coldstream, 'Cistercian architecture from Beaulieu to the Dissolution', pp. 139–59, and Christopher Wilson, 'The Cistercians as "missionaries of Gothic" in northern England', also in Norton and Park (eds.), *Cistercian art and architecture*, pp. 86–116.

30 See the essay by Peter Draper, 'Architecture and liturgy', in *Age of chivalry: art in Plantagenet England 1200–1400* (catalogue to the 1987 London exhibition), pp. 83–91, and on Becket's tomb, catalogue entry 17, p. 207.

31 There has been no general agreement as to the date of the nave at Rievaulx; 'soon after the 1131 foundation', 1135 × 1140 and 'about 1145' have all been suggested (Halsey, 'Earliest architecture of the Cistercians in England', in Norton and Park (eds.), *Cistercian art and architecture*, p. 77 and note 59). Professor Fergusson, who is currently working on a monograph on the architecture of Rievaulx, tells me that he now considers the nave to date from the mid 1140s.

32 On this theme, see Wilson, 'Cistercians as "missionaries of Gothic"', in Norton and Park (eds.), *Cistercian art and architecture*, pp. 86–116.

33 Gilyard-Beer and Coppack, 'Excavations at Fountains Abbey', 151.

34 For a general discussion, see Coppack, *Abbeys and priories*, pp. 61–80.

35 On these activities, see below, pp. 164–5.

36 The chapter house was often also the burial place of superiors; see Coppack, *Abbeys and priories*, p. 72.

37 Particularly noteworthy eastern ranges are to be seen at Valle Crucis, where it survives to first-floor level, and Dryburgh, the most extensive one among the Scottish houses (Cruden, *Scottish Abbeys*, pp. 82–4). On plumbing and sanitation, see Coppack, *Abbeys and priories*, pp. 81–99.

38 For what follows see the stimulating discussion by Peter Fergusson, 'The twelfth-century refectories at Rievaulx and Byland Abbeys', in Norton and Park (eds.), *Cistercian art and architecture*, pp. 160–80.

39 Later the trend swung back, and there is evidence at Croxden, Whalley and (surviving intact) Cleeve that the refectory was built or rebuilt on an

east–west line: Butler and Given-Wilson, *Medieval monasteries of Great Britain*, p. 387. On the significance of the location of some refectories on the upper floors, see Fergusson, 'The twelfth-century refectories', pp. 173–7, and Coppack, *Abbeys and priories*, p. 74.

40 See, for example, the Cluniac priory of Monk Bretton, discussed by Coppack, *Abbeys and priories*, pp. 75–6.

41 Hinnebusch, *Early English Friars Preacher*, p. 169.

42 Coppack, *Abbeys and priories*, pp. 100–28; see also the remarks by Stephen Moorhouse in 'Monastic estates: their composition and development', in Gilchrist and Mytum (eds.), *Archaeology of rural monasteries*, pp. 39–43. For a particular example, see also Glyn Coppack, 'Thornholme Priory: the development of a monastic outer court', in the same collection, pp. 185–222.

43 Butler and Given-Wilson, *Medieval monasteries of Great Britain*, pp. 402–7.

44 See above, chapter 5. On some of the problems of sites of female houses see Roberta Gilchrist, 'The archaeology of medieval English nunneries: a research design', in Gilchrist and Mytum (eds.), *Archaeology of rural monasteries*, pp. 251–60.

45 Gilyard-Beer, *Abbeys*, fig. 30; Coppack, *Abbeys and priories*, pp. 38–9 (the church) and pp. 66–8 (nunnery buildings).

46 See W. H. St John Hope, 'The Gilbertine priory of Watton, in the East Riding of Yorkshire', *Archaeological Journal* 58 (1901), 1–34. See also below, p. 151.

47 Foreville and Keir, *Book of St Gilbert*, p. 145.

48 Burton, *Yorkshire nunneries*, p. 31.

49 Powicke (ed.), *Life of Ailred of Rievaulx*, p. 74.

50 See Fergusson, *Architecture of solitude*, pp. 165–72, for the involvement of monks in the planning of religious houses, particularly in the period before c. 1160, and for a discussion of the 'degree and nature of the work done by those inside and outside the monastery'; also Nicola Coldstream, *Medieval craftsmen: masons and sculptors* (London: British Museum, 1991).

51 See Richard Morris, *Cathedrals and abbeys of England and Wales* (London, 1979), p. 67.

52 Greene, *Norton Priory*, p. 89.

53 J. T. Fowler (ed.), *The coucher book of Selby Abbey*, Yorkshire Archaeological Society Record Series 10 (1891 for 1890), p. 23.

54 Morris, *Cathedrals and abbeys of England and Wales*, p. 217.

55 Brooke, 'St Albans: the great abbey', pp. 50–1; Morris, *Cathedrals and abbeys of England and Wales*, p. 93; Williams, *Welsh Cistercians*, I, p. 137.

56 Greene, *Norton Priory*, p. 62.

57 Morris, *Cathedrals and abbeys of England and Wales*, p. 93.

58 Donkin, *The Cistercians: studies in the geography of medieval England and Wales*, pp. 127–8.

59 For these figures, see Morris, *Cathedrals and abbeys of England and Wales*, p. 216.

60 Una Rees (ed.), *The cartulary of Shrewsbury Abbey*, 2 vols. (Aberystwyth, 1975), no. 382.

61 Williams, *Welsh Cistercians*, I, p. 133.

62 'The Foundation of Kirkstall Abbey', translated by E. K. Clark, in *Miscellanea*,

Thoresby Society IV (Leeds, 1895), pp. 179–80. For other Cistercian founders with an alleged interest in building, see Fergusson, *Architecture of solitude*, pp. 143 (Sallay) and 150 (Thame).

63 Elizabeth M. Hallam, 'Henry II as a founder of monasteries', *Journal of Ecclesiastical History* 28 (1977), 113–32 (117–18).

64 Hockey, *Beaulieu*, p. 22.

65 The appearance of a monograph devoted to Norton Priory is therefore much to be welcomed: see Greene, *Norton Priory*.

66 St Bernard, *An apology to Abbot William*, translated by Michael Casey, with an introduction by Jean Leclercq, in *The Works of St Bernard of Clairvaux*, I, *Treatises*, Cistercian Father Series 1 (Shannon, 1970), pp. 3–69, especially pp. 63–6.

67 The following section owes much to Christopher Holdsworth, 'The chronology and character of early Cistercian legislation on art and architecture', in Norton and Park (eds.), *Cistercian art and architecture*, pp. 40–55. See the tabulated Cistercian legislation relating to artistic and architectural activity in ibid., pp. 318–93.

68 Ibid., pp. 338, 340.

69 Fergusson, *Architecture of solitude*, pp. 38–9 and 169; Gilyard-Beer and Coppack, 'Excavations at Fountains Abbey', 174.

70 Halsey, 'Earliest architecture of the Cistercians in England', in Norton and Park (eds.), *Cistercian art and architecture*, pp. 77–82.

71 Williams, *Welsh Cistercians*, I, pp. 135–6.

72 Wilson, 'Cistercians as "missionaries of Gothic"', p. 108.

73 Ibid., pp. 86–116, and Fergusson, *Architecture of solitude*, pp. 54–68, who discuss the importance of Roche, Furness and Byland, and also the Herefordshire house of Abbey Dore.

74 Coldstream, 'Cistercian architecture from Beaulieu to the Dissolution', pp. 139–59, especially pp. 156–7.

75 Ibid., p. 142.

76 Ibid., p. 156.

77 David Knowles, *The religious orders in England*, III (Cambridge, 1971), pp. 352–3.

78 Park, 'Cistercian wall painting', in Norton and Park (eds.), *Cistercian art and architecture*, pp. 181–210.

79 Christopher Norton, 'Early Cistercian tile pavements', in Norton and Park (eds.), *Cistercian art and architecture*, pp. 228–55.

80 Richard Marks, 'Cistercian window glass in England and Wales', in Norton and Park (eds.), *Cistercian art and architecture*, pp. 211–27.

81 Richard Vaughan (ed.), *Chronicles of Matthew Paris: monastic life in the thirteenth century* (Gloucester, 1986), p. 50.

8 Inside a religious house: daily life and the chain of command

1 On the routine of the monk's life according to the rule see Lawrence, *Medieval monasticism*, pp. 31–9, and on the overwhelming preponderance of the liturgy in everyday life at Cluny, ibid., pp. 100–1.

2 The liturgical offices are underlined in this chart. For discussions of the monastic timetable, see Knowles, *Monastic order*, pp. 448–56 and 714–15, Knowles, *The monastic constitutions of Lanfranc*, pp. xiv–xviii and xxxv–xxxvii, and Lawrence, *Medieval monasticism*, pp. 111-21.

3 For liturgical practice generally in the late Anglo-Saxon period, see M. McC. Gatch, 'The office in late Anglo-Saxon monasticism', in Michael Lapidge and Helmut Gneuss (eds.), *Learning and literature in Anglo-Saxon England: studies presented to Peter Clemoes on the occasion of his sixty-fifth birthday* (Cambridge, 1985), pp. 341–62, and for that of eleventh-century Worcester, see Mason, *Wulfstan*, pp. 203–6. See also C. E. Hohler, 'Some service books of the later Saxon church', in Parsons (ed.), *Tenth-century studies*, pp. 69–83 and 217–27.

4 Knowles, *The monastic constitutions of Lanfranc*, pp. 1–149.

5 Margaret Gibson, *Lanfranc of Bec* (Oxford, 1978), pp. 173–4; Klukas, 'The architectural implications of the *Decreta Lanfranci*', p. 142; from Worcester Bishop Wulfstan sent a monk named Nicholas to Canterbury to train in the observances there: Mason, *Wulfstan*, pp. 116–17.

6 Mason, *Westminster Abbey charters*, no. 345. On pittances see below, pp. 166–7.

7 Vaughan (ed.), *Chronicles of Matthew Paris*, pp. 50–1.

8 Knowles, *Monastic order*, pp. 510–14.

9 Knowles, *Religious orders*, I, pp. 280–5.

10 See below, chapter 10, pp. 216–17.

11 See above, chapter 1, p. 20.

12 Mason, *Wulfstan*, pp. 197–200.

13 The list also includes a number of Augustinian houses: Janet E. Burton, 'A confraternity list from St Mary's Abbey, York', *Revue Bénédictine* 89 (1979), 325–33. For confraternity agreements among Norman houses, some of which extended to English monasteries and nunneries, see Marjorie Chibnall, *The world of Orderic Vitalis* (Oxford, 1984), pp. 67–9.

14 See D. F. L. Chadd, 'Liturgy and liturgical music: the limits of uniformity', in Norton and Park (eds.), *Cistercian art and architecture*, pp. 299–314, and the regulations relating to liturgical vestments and vessels and bells, ibid., pp. 318–93 (passim).

15 See the comments of Nigel Wireker, quoted in Dickinson, *Austin canons*, p. 178.

16 See, for instance, Lawrence, *Medieval monasticism*, pp. 34–7, and Jean Leclercq, *The love of learning and the desire for God: a study of monastic culture* (New York, Fordham University Press, 1961, repr. 1982), especially pp. 72–5; on literary activities see below, chapter 9.

17 Capitula xv, translated in Lekai, *The Cistercians: ideals and reality*, p. 449; see also Christopher J. Holdsworth, 'The blessings of work: the Cistercian view', in *Sanctity and secularity, the church and the world*, Studies in Church History 10 (Oxford, 1973), pp. 59–76.

18 Mason, *Westminster Abbey charters*, no. 248A.

19 See below, pp. 172–3.

20 Robert of Bridlington, *The Bridlington Dialogue: an exposition of the Rule of St*

Augustine for the life of the clergy, translated and edited by a religious of C.S.M.V. (London, 1960), p. 154; Dickinson, *Austin canons*, pp. 193-4.

21 Knowles, *The monastic constitutions of Lanfranc*, pp. 5, 29–30, 53–4, 78.

22 Vaughan (ed.), *Chronicles of Matthew Paris*, p. 37.

23 From the *Soliloquium de Instructione Animae*, quoted in James Bulloch, *Adam of Dryburgh* (London, 1958), p. 41.

24 On diet, see Knowles, *Monastic order*, pp. 456–65, and for the thirteenth century, Knowles, *Religious orders*, I, pp. 280–3. See also Hinnebusch, *Early English Friars Preacher*, pp. 246–9.

25 Powicke (ed.), *Life of Ailred of Rievaulx*, pp. lxxii–lxxv.

26 Dickinson, *Austin canons*, pp. 181–3.

27 Knowles, *The monastic constitutions of Lanfranc*, pp. 119–20; on visitations, see below, pp. 183–6.

28 Jocelin of Brakelond, *Chronicle of the abbey of Bury St Edmunds*, translated by Diana Greenway and Jane Sayers (Oxford, 1989), p. 14.

29 See, for example, the comments of Jocelin of Brakelond on Abbot Hugh of Bury St Edmunds, ibid., p. 3.

30 See above, chapter 1, for instances of royal intervention in elections.

31 On the role of lay patrons in elections, see below, chapter 10, pp. 212–14.

32 Jocelin of Brakelond, *Chronicle of the abbey of Bury St Edmunds*, pp. 15–22.

33 For these, see Knowles, *Monastic order*, pp. 402–3; for a general discussion of elections, see ibid., pp. 395–401.

34 See R. M. Thomson (ed. and transl.), *The chronicle of the election of Hugh, abbot of Bury St Edmunds and later bishop of Ely* (Oxford, 1974).

35 Cowan and Easson (eds.), *Medieval religious houses: Scotland*, p. 18.

36 Frank Barlow, *William Rufus* (London, 1983), p. 329; C. N. L. Brooke, 'Princes and kings as patrons of monasteries, Normandy and England', in *Il Monachesimo e la riforma ecclesiastica (1049–1122)* (Milan, 1977), pp. 125–44.

37 On the abbot's accommodation see above, chapter 7, p. 144.

38 See Mason, *Westminster Abbey charters*, pp. 15–18; Barbara Harvey, *Westminster Abbey and its estates in the middle ages* (Oxford, 1977), pp. 85–91.

39 Graves, 'English Cistercian nunnery in Lincolnshire', 333–50, Latin text given on p. 347. See also Nichols, 'The internal organization of English Cistercian nunneries', 23–40.

40 Rosalind Hill, 'Bishop Sutton and the institution of heads of religious houses in the diocese of Lincoln', *English Historical Review* 58 (1943), 201–9.

41 Nichols, 'The internal organization of English Cistercian nunneries', 28–30.

42 Easson, 'Nunneries of medieval Scotland', 23.

43 Thompson, *Women religious*, p. 214.

44 Thompson, 'Double monasteries and the male element in nunneries', pp. 151–6.

45 See Golding's forthcoming study.

46 Barlow, *English church 1000–1066*, pp. 327–9.

47 Knowles, *The monastic constitutions of Lanfranc*, p. 76.

48 Gerald of Wales, *Journey through Wales*, pp. 126–8. Elsewhere Gerald praises the charity of the White Monks, which he contrasts favourably with the

Cluniacs, who 'will . . . suffer the poor to collapse in heaps outside their very gates and die of hunger for want of Christian charity' (p. 106).

49 For the numbers at Christ Church, Canterbury, see R. A. L. Smith, *Canterbury Cathedral Priory: a study in monastic administration* (Cambridge, 1943, repr. 1969), pp. 3–4, 205.

50 On the monastic population, see J. C. Russell, 'The clerical population of medieval England', *Traditio* 2 (1944), 177–212; Knowles and Hadcock (eds.), *Medieval religious houses: England and Wales*, pp. 488–95. On numbers in priories of the mendicant orders, see above, p. 118.

51 Lawrence, *Medieval monasticism*, p. 181.

52 Cluny had come under severe criticism for relaxing the one-year noviciate, and this was another feature of primitive monasticism which the White Monks sought to restore. On the noviciate among the friars, see Hinnebusch, *History of the Dominican order*, I, pp. 290–9, especially 295–6.

53 Powicke (ed.), *Life of Ailred of Rievaulx*, pp. 2–18, especially p. 18.

54 Marsha L. Dutton, 'The conversion and vocation of Aelred of Rievaulx: a historical hypothesis', in Daniel Williams (ed.), *England in the twelfth century. Proceedings of the 1988 Harlaxton symposium* (Woodbridge, 1990), pp. 31–49.

55 On the question of monastic recruitment see J. H. Lynch, 'Monastic recruitment in the eleventh and twelfth centuries: some social and economic considerations', *American Benedictine Review* 26 (1975), 425–47, which takes examples from France, and, for a later period, G. Mark Dilsworth, 'The social origins of Scottish medieval monks', *Records of the Scottish Church History Society* 20 (3) (1980), 197–209.

56 On Waldef, see Powicke (ed.), *Life of Ailred of Rievaulx*, pp. lxxi–lxxv and Derek Baker, 'Legend and reality: the case of Waldef of Melrose', in *Church, society and politics*, Studies in Church History 12 (Oxford, 1975), pp. 59–82.

57 Cowley, *Monastic order in south Wales*, pp. 40–52; Gerald of Wales, *Journey through Wales*, p. 81.

58 Cowley, *Monastic order in south Wales*, p. 42.

59 Williams, *Welsh Cistercians*, I, pp. 147–63.

60 Thomson (ed.), *Chronicle of the election of abbot Hugh*, p. xlii.

61 See, for example, Dobson and Donaghey, *Clementhorpe Nunnery*, pp. 12–16.

62 Mason, *Westminster Abbey charters*, nos. 402–3.

63 Rees, *Shrewsbury cartulary*, nos. 276, 402b.

64 Jocelin of Brakelond, *Chronicle of the abbey of Bury St Edmunds*, pp. 7, 15, 35–6.

65 Rees, *Shrewsbury cartulary*, no. 402b. For a general discussion of all these kinds of lay people, see David H. Williams, 'Layfolk within Cistercian precincts', in Judith Loades (ed.), *Monastic Studies*, II (Bangor, 1991), pp. 87–117.

66 Cowley, *Monastic order in south Wales*, pp. 113–16; Williams, *Welsh Cistercians*, I, pp. 187–9.

67 Cowan and Easson have pointed out that the Scottish houses make occasional appearances in the records of the general chapter until 1282, when there is a hiatus in the record of their relationship with Cîteaux: *Medieval religious houses: Scotland*, p. 8.

68 Burton, 'The abbeys of Byland and Jervaulx', p. 125.

69 Knowles, *Monastic order*, pp. 637–9; Hill, *English Cistercian monasteries*, pp. 152–3.

70 Cowley, *Monastic order in south Wales*, pp. 113–16, 127–30.

71 Ibid., pp. 128–30.

72 Hill, *English Cistercian monasteries*, p. 115.

73 Cowley, *Monastic order in south Wales*, pp. 119–21.

74 Knowles, *Monastic order*, pp. 657–8; for problems with the *conversi* generally see Lekai, *The Cistercians: ideals and reality*, pp. 341–4.

75 Powicke (ed.), *Life of Ailred of Rievaulx*, p. 45.

76 Elkins, *Holy women*, pp. 134–8. On chapters and visitations among the mendicants, see above, pp. 122–4.

77 On these chapters see Knowles, *Religious orders*, I, pp. 9–27.

78 The southern province included Wales.

79 H. E. Salter (ed.), *Chapters of the Augustinian canons*, Canterbury and York Society 29 (London, 1922, repr. 1969).

80 Ibid., pp. 35–7 and 43–5.

81 On the struggle by some of these houses to establish their exemption, see Knowles, *Monastic order*, pp. 579–91. The most frequently recorded visitations in the twelfth century are those of papal legates: for injunctions from an early thirteenth-century visitation of St Mary's York, see C. R. Cheney, 'The papal legate (John of Ferentino) and English monasteries', *English Historical Review* 46 (1931), 443–52.

82 On the bishops as agents of reform after 1215, see Marion Gibbs and Jane Lang, *Bishops and reform 1215–1272* (Oxford, 1934), especially pp. 94–179. For a general treatment of the subject of visitation, see C. R. Cheney, *Episcopal visitation of monasteries in the thirteenth century* (Manchester, 1931; 2nd edn, 1983).

83 This also accounts for the infrequency of metropolitan visitations, the visitation by an archbishop of his entire province. Few had the energy of Archbishop Pecham, who between 1280 and 1284 covered most of southern England and Wales. For an example of his findings, see Cowley, *Monastic order in south Wales*, pp. 101–8; see also Decima L. Douie, *Archbishop Pecham* (Oxford, 1952), pp. 257–68.

84 Details given in the following section are derived from W. Brown (ed.), *The register of William Wickwane, lord archbishop of York, 1279–1285*, Surtees Society 114 (Durham, 1907).

85 Gerald of Wales, *Journey through Wales*, p. 107.

86 However, he used the words 'Cluniac' (*Cluniacensis*) and 'Black Monk' (*niger monachus*) synonymously: see Knowles, *Monastic order*, p. 719.

9 Learning and literary activities

1 *The Rule of St Benedict*, chapter 48, p. 113; on the procedure laid down by Lanfranc, see Knowles (ed.), *Monastic constitutions of Lanfranc*, p. 19.

2 These included the Scriptures, the Conferences and Institutes of John

Cassian, the lives of the Fathers, and the Rule of St Basil: *The Rule of St Benedict*, chapter 73, p. 161.

3 See Leclercq, *The love of learning and the desire for God*, passim.

4 C. J. Holdsworth, 'John of Ford and English Cistercian writing, 1167–1214', *Transactions of the Royal Historical Society*, 5th series, 11 (1961), 117–36, especially 122–3.

5 One exception is Clemence of Barking, author of a French version of the life of Edward the Confessor: Elkins, *Holy women*, p. 149.

6 See above, chapter 1, pp. 15–16.

7 Crouch, *Beaumont twins*, p. 7.

8 Knowles, *Monastic order*, p. 497.

9 These details are derived from R. W. Hunt, 'English learning in the late twelfth century', *Transactions of the Royal Historical Society*, 4th series, 19 (1936), 19–42; also Jocelin of Brakelond, *Chronicle of the abbey of Bury St Edmunds*, p. 31.

10 See, for instance, the case cited by the prior of Canons Ashby, quoted in Hunt, 'English learning', 28–9.

11 See M. W. Sheehan, 'The religious orders 1220–1370', in J. I. Catto (ed.), *The history of the university of Oxford*, 1, *The early Oxford Schools* (Oxford, 1984, repr. with corrections, 1986), pp. 198–208.

12 David Postles, 'The learning of Austin canons: the case of Oseney Abbey', *Nottingham Medieval Studies* 29 (1985), 32–43.

13 Colvin, *White Canons in England*, p. 320.

14 Sheehan, 'The religious orders', in Catto (ed.), *The history of the university of Oxford*, 1, pp. 218–19; Lekai, *The Cistercians: ideals and reality*, pp. 236–40.

15 Knowles, *Religious orders*, 1, pp. 25–7, and *Religious orders*, 11, pp. 19–20; Sheehan, 'The religious orders', in Catto (ed.), *The history of the university of Oxford*, 1, pp. 212–18.

16 Cowley, *Monastic order in south Wales*, p. 143; Hunt, 'English learning', 28.

17 Knowles, *Monastic order*, p. 523.

18 W. Farrer (ed.), *Early Yorkshire charters*, 11 (Edinburgh, 1915), no. 898; Golding, 'Wealth and artistic patronage', p. 112.

19 Edward Hutton, *The Franciscans in England 1224–1538* (London, 1926), p. 128.

20 C. R. Cheney, 'English Cistercian libraries: the first century', in *Medieval texts and studies* (Oxford, 1973), pp. 328–45 (p. 344).

21 Cowley, *Monastic order in south Wales*, p. 74.

22 See, for instance, the Premonstratensian statute on lending and borrowing: Colvin, *White Canons in England*, p. 319.

23 For examples, see Knowles, *Monastic order*, pp. 520–1 and *Religious orders*, 1, pp. 299–304.

24 Cowley, *Monastic order in south Wales*, pp. 156–7.

25 Ibid., p. 159.

26 Sheehan, 'The religious orders', in Catto (ed.), *The history of the university of Oxford*, 1, pp. 208–10 (p. 209).

27 K. W. Humphreys (ed.), *The friars' libraries*, Corpus of British medieval library

catalogues (London, the British Library and the British Academy, 1990). The York catalogue is of a fourteenth-century date (1372).

28 N. R. Ker, *Medieval libraries of Great Britain*, 2nd edn (London, Royal Historical Society, 1964), p. xi.

29 Cheney, 'English Cistercian libraries', p. 344; Jennifer M. Sheppard, 'The twelfth-century library and scriptorium at Buildwas: assessing the evidence', in Daniel Williams (ed.), *England in the twelfth century: Proceedings of the 1988 Harlaxton symposium* (Woodbridge, 1990), pp. 193–204. There are very few surviving books from Gilbertine or Premonstratensian houses.

30 Knowles, *Monastic order*, pp. 525–7. A single volume could contain a number of separate works.

31 Cheney, 'English Cistercian libraries', pp. 341–5; see also the forthcoming volume on Cistercian libraries in the Corpus of British medieval library catalogues, British Library.

32 Cheney, 'English Cistercian libraries', pp. 344–5.

33 The following discussion is indebted to A. Gransden, *Historical writing in England c. 550 to c. 1307* (London, 1974).

34 On this theme see R. W. Southern, 'Aspects of the European tradition of historical writing: 4: the sense of the past', *Transactions of the Royal Historical Society*, 5th series, 23 (1973), 243–63. See also Gransden, 'Traditionalism and continuity', 198–207.

35 Quoted Southern, 'Aspects of the European tradition of historical writing', 249–50; Gransden 'Traditionalism and continuity', 199–200.

36 Gransden, *Historical writing*, pp. 114–23 and pp. 148–51. Two other works were composed at Durham, though whether by a monk is not certain. These are *De Obsessione Dunelmi* (*Concerning the siege of Durham*) and *De injusta Vexatione Willelmi Episcopi* (*Concerning the unjust tribulation of Bishop William*); both grew out of controversy, and therefore merge into an attempt to write living history.

37 Ibid., pp. 76–7.

38 Ridyard, '*Condigna veneratio*', pp. 179–206.

39 Gransden, *Historical writing*, pp. 125–7; Ridyard, '*Condigna veneratio*', pp. 187–9.

40 Cowley, *Monastic order in south Wales*, pp. 160–2.

41 For compilations of the mid twelfth century, linked to the need to prove title to land in the wake of the anarchy of the reign of King Stephen, see Gransden, *Historical writing*, pp. 269–86.

42 On the Canterbury writers see ibid., pp. 129–42 (Eadmer), 253–60 (Gervase), 296–308 (lives of Becket).

43 Gransden, *Historical writing*, pp. 381–5.

44 Burton, 'The abbeys of Byland and Jervaulx', pp. 119–31.

45 L. G. D. Baker, 'The genesis of English Cistercian chronicles: the foundation history of Fountains Abbey', I and II, *Analecta Sacri Ordinis Cisterciensis* 25 (1969), 14–41 and 31 (1976 for 1975), 179–212.

46 Gransden, *Historical writing*, p. 143.

47 Martin Brett, 'John of Worcester and his contemporaries', in R. H. C. Davis

and J. M. Wallace-Hadrill (eds.), *The writing of history in the middle ages: essays presented to R. W. Southern* (Oxford, 1981), pp. 101–26.

48 Peter Hunter Blair, 'Some observations on the *Historia Regum* attributed to Symeon of Durham', in Kenneth Jackson et al. (eds.), *Celt and Saxon: Studies in the early British border* (Cambridge, 1964), pp. 63–118.

49 Gransden, *Historical writing*, pp. 318–45.

50 See, for instance, Martin Brett, 'The annals of Bermondsey, Southwark and Merton', in David Abulafia, Michael Franklin and Miri Rubin (eds.), *Church and city 1000–1500* (Cambridge, 1992), pp. 279–310.

51 Cowley, *Monastic order in south Wales*, pp. 146–56. The one Scottish contribution derives from Melrose: *The chronicle of Melrose Abbey*, facsimile, with an introduction by A. O. and M. O. Anderson (London, 1936).

52 On these see Gransden, *Historical writing*, pp. 212–18.

53 On William see ibid., pp. 166–85; Rodney Thomson, *William of Malmesbury* (Woodbridge), 1987.

54 Southern, 'Aspects of the European tradition of historical writing', 253.

55 On another distinguished historian, the Augustinian William of Newburgh, see Gransden, *Historical writing*, pp. 263–8.

56 Golding, 'Wealth and artistic patronage', pp. 107–17.

57 Gransden, *Historical writing*, p. 359; on his works see ibid., pp. 356–79.

58 The contribution of the mendicants to historical writing in Britain was small, and surviving works are limited to Thomas of Eccleston's chronicle (see above, chapter 6), the Lanercost chronicle, written by a north-country Franciscan, and the annals of Nicholas Trivet (Trevet), a London Dominican. On these see Gransden, *Historical writing*, pp. 487–507.

59 Ibid., pp. 170, 358.

60 For a useful survey of biblical study in Norman monasteries of the eleventh and twelfth centuries, see Chibnall, *The world of Orderic Vitalis*, pp. 89–99.

61 G. R. Evans, *Old arts and new theology* (Oxford, 1980), pp. 8–56, especially p. 13.

62 Holdsworth, 'John of Ford', 121–4. Gilbert probably resigned as abbot of Swineshead; described as former abbot, he died at L'Arivour in 1172.

63 Ibid., 124–36.

64 Cowley, *Monastic order in south Wales*, pp. 151–2; Sheehan, 'The religious orders', in Catto (ed.), *The history of the university of Oxford*, I, p. 210.

65 Postles, 'The learning of Austin canons', 33–4.

66 Hunt, 'English learning', 25–6; R. W. Southern, 'From schools to university', in Catto (ed.), *The history of the university of Oxford*, I, pp. 22–5.

67 J. I. Catto, 'Theology and theologians 1220–1320', in Catto (ed.), *The history of the university of Oxford*, I, p. 471.

68 Evans, *Old arts and new theology*, pp. 91–136.

69 On the Franciscans at Oxford, see A. G. Little, *Franciscan papers, lists, and documents* (Manchester, 1943), pp. 55–71; on Grosseteste's influence see especially pp. 58–61, and R. W. Southern, *Robert Grosseteste* (Oxford, 1986).

70 C. H. Lawrence, 'The university in church and state', in Catto (ed.), *The*

history of the university of Oxford, I, pp. 100–1; Catto, 'Theology and theologians', ibid., pp. 481–6.

71 B. Smalley, 'Robert Bacon and the early Dominican school at Oxford', *Transactions of the Royal Historical Society*, 4th series, 30 (1948), 1–19; Catto, 'Theology and theologians', in Catto (ed.), *The history of the university of Oxford*, I, p. 480.

72 Ibid., p. 490.

73 Little, *Studies in English Franciscan history*, pp. 193–221, and *Franciscan papers, lists, and documents*, pp. 72–121; Hinnebusch, *Early English Friars Preacher*, pp. 357–419; Catto, 'Theology and theologians', in Catto (ed.), *The history of the university of Oxford*, I, pp. 488–96. Catto points out that there is little evidence for the nature of theological study at Oxford between 1265 and 1280 (p. 496).

74 On the controversy, and the attitude of the English Dominicans to Aquinas, see Hinnebusch, *Early English Friars Preacher*, pp. 342–56.

75 Catto, 'Theology and theologians', in Catto (ed.), *The history of the university of Oxford*, I, pp. 497–8.

76 Ibid., p. 500.

77 Little, *Studies in English Franciscan History*, pp. 136–9.

78 Derek Pearsall, *Old English and Middle English Poetry* (London, 1977), pp. 94–100.

79 Ibid., p. 94; Glanmor Williams, *The Welsh church from Conquest to Reformation* (Cardiff, 1962), pp. 21–2, 27–9.

80 Powicke (ed.), *Life of Ailred of Rievaulx*, pp. 26–7.

81 Holdsworth, 'John of Ford', 130.

82 Cowley, *Monastic order in south Wales*, pp. 153–6.

83 Colvin, *White Canons in England*, pp. 324–6; Knowles, *Monastic order*, p. 384; James Bulloch, *Adam of Dryburgh* (London, 1958).

84 Dickinson, *Austin canons*, pp. 66, 183–7, 218–20 and 235–6.

85 Sheehan, 'The religious orders', in Catto (ed.), *The history of the university of Oxford*, I, pp. 217–21.

10 Religious houses and the wider community: founders, patrons and benefactors

1 This paragraph is indebted to a recent challenging work, Ludo J. R. Milis, *Angelic monks and earthly men: monasticism and its meaning to medieval society* (Woodbridge, 1992); see especially pp. 8–23 and 87–91.

2 Thompson, *Women religious*, p. 182; Cowley, *Monastic order in south Wales*, p. 194.

3 See above, chapter 2, pp. 26–8.

4 Hill, *English Cistercian monasteries*, pp. 58–9, cites, *inter alia*, the pipe roll of 1158/9 showing Pipewell Abbey owing 25s. to the Exchequer for scutage on lands held of the earl of Warwick, and the *Cartae Baronum* of 1166 giving evidence that three of sixty knights' fees of the honour of Derby were held by Cistercian houses. For a recent discussion of free alms tenure, see

Benjamin Thompson, 'From "alms" to "spiritual services", the function and status of monastic property in medieval England', in Judith Loades (ed.), *Monastic Studies*, II (Bangor, 1991), pp. 227–61.

5 Susan Wood, *English monasteries and their patrons in the thirteenth century* (Oxford, 1955), pp. 17–21, discusses a handful of cases when the patronage appears to have been separate from the advowson, but notes that these are exceptional. Wood's work remains the most comprehensive treatment of the subject of monastic patronage in England.

6 For this and other examples see Colvin, *White Canons in England*, pp. 302–3.

7 See below, pp. 229–31.

8 On this class of founders, see Christopher Harper-Bill, 'The piety of the Anglo-Norman knightly class', in *Proceedings of the Battle Conference on Anglo-Norman Studies*, II (Woodbridge, 1979), pp. 63–77.

9 Wood, *English monasteries and their patrons*, p. 57.

10 See also the assertions of the Clare family of their right to appoint the priors of dependencies of Bec: Morgan, *English lands of the abbey of Bec*, p. 29.

11 Vaughan, *Chronicles of Matthew Paris*, pp. 19–22.

12 R. M. T. Hill (ed.), *The rolls and register of Bishop Oliver Sutton, 1280–1299*, I, Lincoln Record Society 39 (Lincoln, 1948), pp. 209–10.

13 C. Warren Hollister, 'St Anselm on lay investiture', in *Anglo-Norman Studies X: Proceedings of the Battle Conference 1987* (Woodbridge, 1988), pp. 145–58, especially pp. 148–9; see also Christopher Brooke, 'Princes and kings as patrons of monasteries, Normandy and England', in *Il monachesimo e la riforma ecclesiastica (1049–1122)*, Miscellanea del centro di studi medieovali 6 (Milan, 1971), pp. 125–52.

14 Morgan, *English lands of the abbey of Bec*, p. 29.

15 Wood, *English monasteries and their patrons*, p. 82.

16 Thompson, *Women religious*, p. 185.

17 Cowley, *Monastic order in south Wales*, p. 201.

18 Dugdale, *Mon Ang*, V, p. 572.

19 Colvin, *White Canons in England*, pp. 162–3, 304–6.

20 For a further example from Egglestone from whom a benefactor received canons to celebrate in the chapel of his castle, see ibid., p. 271.

21 Ibid., pp. 257–9.

22 Williams, *Welsh Cistercians*, I, p. 42.

23 Harper-Bill, 'The piety of the Anglo-Norman knightly class', p. 70.

24 Colvin, *White Canons in England*, pp. 72, note 6, 106, 152. On the practice generally, see L. Gougaud, 'Deathbed clothing with the religious habit', in *Devotional and ascetic practices in the Middle Ages* (London, 1927), pp. 131–45.

25 Williams, *Welsh Cistercians*, I, p. 183.

26 K. J. Stringer, 'The early lords of Lauderdale, Dryburgh Abbey and St Andrew's Priory at Northampton', in K. J. Stringer (ed.), *Essays on the nobility of medieval Scotland* (Edinburgh, 1985), pp. 44–71 (p. 46).

27 Joan Wardrop, *Fountains Abbey and its benefactors 1132–1300* (Kalamazoo, MI, 1987), p. 251; Williams, *Welsh Cistercians*, I, p. 183.

28 W. Farrer (ed.), *Early Yorkshire Charters*, II (Edinburgh, 1915), no. 1138.

29 On this theme see two essays by Brian Golding, 'Burials and benefactions: an aspect of monastic patronage in thirteenth-century England', in W. M. Ormrod (ed.), *England in the thirteenth century: proceedings of the 1984 Harlaxton symposium* (Woodbridge, 1986), pp. 64–75, and 'Anglo-Norman knightly burials', in C. Harper-Bill and R. Harvey (eds.), *The ideals and practice of medieval knighthood* (Woodbridge, 1986), pp. 35–48. For the information which follows I am indebted to these two works.

30 Cowley, *Monastic order in south Wales*, p. 195.

31 Quoted in G. G. Coulton, *Scottish abbeys and social life* (Cambridge, 1933), p. 64.

32 Emma Mason, '*Timeo barones et dona ferentes*', in *Religious motivation: biographical and sociological problems for the church historian*, Studies in Church History 15 (Oxford, 1978), pp. 61–75 (pp. 72–3).

33 Golding, 'Anglo-Norman knightly burials', p. 43.

34 See the instances cited in chapter 5.

35 Thompson, *Women religious*, pp. 179–81.

36 Colvin, *White Canons in England*, p. 270.

37 Ibid., p. 304.

38 Mason, '*Timeo barones*', p. 65.

39 Burton, *Yorkshire nunneries*, p. 25.

40 Thompson, *Women religious*, p. 184.

41 D. Postles, '"*Patronus et advocatus noster*": Oseney Abbey and the Oilly family', *Historical Research* 60 (1987), 100–2.

42 For the benefactions and confirmations to Fountains Abbey by Roger and his sons, see D. E. Greenway (ed.), *Charters of the honour of Mowbray 1107–1191*, British Academy, Records of Social and Economic History, n.s., 1 (London, 1972), nos. 94–149.

43 Wood, *English monasteries and their patrons*, p. 118.

44 Ibid., p. 121.

45 David H. Williams, *Atlas of Cistercian lands in Wales* (Cardiff, 1990), p. 13.

46 M. T. Clanchy, *From memory to written record, England 1066–1307* (London, 1979), pp. 136–8.

47 J. C. Ward, 'Fashions in monastic endowment: the foundations of the Clare family, 1066–1314', *Journal of Ecclesiastical History* 32 (1981), 427–51 (p. 447); Gransden, *Historical writing*, pp. 416–17.

48 J. McNulty (ed.), *The chartulary of the Cistercian abbey of Sallay in Craven*, Yorkshire Archaeological Society Record Series 87, 90 (2 vols., Leeds, 1933–4), I, no. 615.

49 See above, chapter 7, pp. 134–5 and 153.

50 Stringer, 'The early lords of Lauderdale, Dryburgh Abbey and St Andrew's Priory at Northampton', pp. 44–71 (pp. 63–4).

51 Dugdale, *Mon. Angl.*, v, p. 569.

52 James W. Alexander, *Ranulf of Chester: a relic of the Conquest* (Athens, GA, 1983), p. 49.

53 Ibid., p. 50; Doris M. Stenton, *English justice between the Norman Conquest and the great charter 1066–1215* (London, 1965), pp. 148–53.

54 W. E. Wightman, *The Lacy family in England and Normandy 1066–1194* (Oxford, 1966), pp. 76–7.

55 For other instances of religious houses which suffered during the reign of Stephen, see Knowles, *Monastic order*, pp. 268–72.

56 This section relies heavily on Cowley, *Monastic order in south Wales*, pp. 209–16, and Williams, *Welsh Cistercians*, I, pp. 32–42.

57 For many aspects of the relationship of the abbey with those who endowed it, see the study by Joan Wardrop, *Fountains Abbey and its benefactors*.

58 Wood, *English monasteries and their patrons*, p. 18; Wardrop, *Fountains Abbey and its benefactors*, p. 239.

59 See Ward, 'Fashions in monastic endowment', 427–51; see also Harper-Bill, 'The piety of the Anglo-Norman knightly class', p. 67.

60 Burton, *Yorkshire nunneries*, p. 23.

61 Wood, *English monasteries and their patrons*, p. 23.

62 On this see Knowles, *Monastic order*, pp. 327–30.

63 Wood, *English monasteries and their patrons*, pp. 19–20.

64 For discussions of such activity see, for example, M. J. Franklin, 'The bishops of Winchester and the monastic revolution', in *Anglo-Norman Studies XII: Proceedings of the Battle Conference 1989* (Woodbridge, 1990), pp. 47–65, and Nicoll, *Thurstan, archbishop of York*, pp. 111–212.

65 Quoted in Wood, *English monasteries and their patrons*, p. 102.

66 Colvin, *White Canons in England*, p. 298.

67 Wardrop, *Fountains Abbey and its benefactors*, p. 238.

68 Knowles, *Monastic order*, p. 631.

69 Wood, *English monasteries and their patrons*, pp. 48–50.

70 Franklin, 'The bishops of Winchester and the monastic revolution', p. 51; G. V. Scammell, *Hugh du Puiset* (Cambridge, 1956), pp. 128–36.

71 For this and the revival of the scheme by Archbishop Hubert Walter, see Knowles, *Monastic order*, pp. 316–22.

72 On this theme see especially Thompson, 'From "alms" to "spiritual services"', especially pp. 250–61.

11 The monastic economy

1 On this, see 'Spiritualia', pp. 245–8 below.

2 Little, *Studies in English Franciscan history*, pp. 19–20, points out that the amount of land in the vicinity of Franciscan priories recorded in Dissolution accounts varies from 43 acres, the largest amount, at Babwell, to 3–4 acres (one of the smallest) in urban Shrewsbury. For a rare mendicant cartulary, see Christopher Harper-Bill (ed.), *The cartulary of the Augustinian friars of Clare*, Suffolk Records Society, Suffolk Charters XI (Woodbridge, 1991). The discussion in this chapter is therefore limited to houses of monks, canons and nuns.

3 *Taxatio Ecclesiastica Angliae et Walliae . . . P Nicholai IV* (London, Record Commission, 1802); for comment see R. Graham, 'The taxation of Pope

Nicholas IV', *English Historical Review* 23 (1908), 434–54, reprinted in *English ecclesiastical studies* (London, 1929), pp. 271–301.

4 Cowley, *Monastic order in south Wales*, pp. 274–5; I have given the figures to the nearest pound.

5 Burton, *Yorkshire nunneries*, pp. 11–17 and 45; Thompson, *Women religious*, pp. 211, 215.

6 The valuations of the Scottish houses are given in Cowan and Easson (eds.), *Medieval religious houses: Scotland*.

7 For example, the Augustinian houses of Cirencester and Letheringham (Robinson, *Geography of Augustinian settlement*, p. 279) and the Tironensian abbey of Lindores (K. J. Stringer, *Earl David of Huntingdon 1152–1219: a study in Anglo-Scottish history* (Edinburgh, 1985), p. 97). For a general treatment of the build-up of estates by religious houses see Stephen Moorhouse, 'Monastic estates: their composition and development', in Gilchrist and Mytum (eds.), *Archaeology of rural monasteries*, pp. 29–81.

8 The fullest recent treatment is Sandra Raban, *Mortmain legislation and the English church 1279–1500* (Cambridge, 1982).

9 The earliest set of manorial accounts is the Winchester pipe roll of 1209.

10 Robinson, *Geography of Augustinian settlement*, p. 274.

11 I. Kershaw, *Bolton Priory, the economy of a northern monastery, 1286–1325* (Oxford, 1973), pp. 71–8 and 161–8; Rose Graham, 'The finance of Malton Priory 1244–1257', in *English ecclesiastical studies* (London, 1929), pp. 247–70, especially pp. 258–9.

12 E. G. Bowen, 'The monastic economy of the Cistercians at Strata Florida', *Ceredigion* 1 (1950), 34–7.

13 Cowley, *Monastic order in south Wales*, p. 82.

14 Ibid., p. 83; Williams, *Welsh Cistercians*, II, pp. 304–5.

15 Donkin, *The Cistercians: studies in the geography of medieval England and Wales*, pp. 68–9. On vaccaries, bercaries and stud-farms in general see Moorhouse, 'Monastic estates', pp. 44–50.

16 King, *Peterborough Abbey*, p. 154.

17 Knowles, *Religious orders*, I, p. 72; Hockey, *Beaulieu*, p. 65.

18 Donkin, *The Cistercians: studies in the geography of medieval England and Wales*, p. 107; for a list of houses associated with assarts see R. A. Donkin, 'The English Cistercians and assarting, c. 1128–1350', *Analecta Sacri Ordinis Cisterciensis* 20 (1964), 49–75, appendix 1.

19 King, *Peterborough Abbey*, pp. 70–87.

20 Knowles, *Religious orders*, I, pp. 44–5. For activities at other Benedictine houses see, for example, Raban, *Thorney and Crowland*, pp. 51–7; D. Owen, *Church and society in medieval Lincolnshire*, History of Lincolnshire 5 (Lincoln, 1981), p. 57; Raftis, *Ramsey Abbey*, pp. 72–6.

21 Robinson, *Geography of Augustinian settlement*, pp. 285–90.

22 Donkin, *The Cistercians: studies in the geography of medieval England and Wales*, pp. 103–34; see also his 'The English Cistercians and assarting', 49–75.

23 On the depopulation which took place at some sites to ensure the monks that solitude and independence they desired, see above, chapter 7, p. 132.

24 Donkin, *The Cistercians: studies in the geography of medieval England and Wales*, p. 112.
25 The value of the waste land recorded in the North in Domesday Book was due to factors such as the damage created during the harrying of the North by the army of the Conqueror.
26 Colin Platt, *The monastic grange in medieval England* (London, 1969), pp. 92–3.
27 Thompson, *Women religious*, p. 105.
28 Williams, *Welsh Cistercians*, II, pp. 271–2.
29 See C. K. Currie, 'The role of fishponds in the monastic economy', in Gilchrist and Mytum (eds.), *Archaeology of rural monasteries*, pp. 147–72.
30 Williams, *Welsh Cistercians*, II, pp. 320–6.
31 Graves, 'Stixwould in the market place', p. 227.
32 Cowley, *Monastic order in south Wales*, p. 54; Williams, *Welsh Cistercians*, II, pp. 326–30.
33 Hugh Talbot, *The Cistercian abbeys of Scotland* (London, 1939), pp. 29, 58.
34 King, *Peterborough Abbey*, pp. 140–6.
35 Robinson, *Geography of Augustinian settlement*, p. 275.
36 Cowley, *Monastic order in south Wales*, p. 66.
37 Hockey, *Beaulieu*, p. 14; see also S. F. Hockey (ed.), *The account book of Beaulieu Abbey*, Camden Society, 4th series 16 (London, 1975), pp. 11–13.
38 Cowley, *Monastic order in south Wales*, p. 90.
39 Williams, *Atlas of Cistercian lands in Wales*, p. 23; T. Jones Pierce, 'Strata Florida Abbey', *Ceredigion* 1 (1950), 18–33.
40 B. A. Lees (ed.), *The records of the Templars in England in the twelfth century*, British Academy, Records of Social and Economic History, IX (1935), pp. 1–135.
41 Harvey, *Westminster Abbey*, pp. 220–3.
42 On the importance of mills generally see Moorhouse, 'Monastic estates', in Gilchrist and Mytum (eds.), *Archaeology of rural monasteries*, pp. 52–5, and C. J. Bond, 'Water management in the rural monastery', in the same collection, pp. 83–111, especially pp. 102–4.
43 Hill, *English Cistercian monasteries*, p. 73.
44 See Jocelin of Brakelond, *Chronicle of the abbey of Bury St Edmunds*, pp. 53–4.
45 Vaughan, *Chronicles of Matthew Paris*, p. 78.
46 Robinson, *Geography of Augustinian settlement*, p. 274.
47 Wendy B. Stevenson, 'The monastic presence in Scottish burghs in the twelfth and thirteenth centuries', *Scottish Historical Review* 60 (2), no. 170 (1981), 97–118.
48 Stringer, *Earl David*, p. 97.
49 Wendy B. Stevenson, 'The monastic presence: Berwick in the twelfth and thirteenth centuries', in Michael Lynch, Michael Spearman and Geoffrey Stell (eds.), *The Scottish medieval town* (Edinburgh, 1988), pp. 99–115.
50 Ibid., p. 110.
51 Graves, 'Stixwould in the market place', pp. 227–8.

52 Details of town property and privileges of the Welsh Cistercian houses are given in the individual inventories in Williams, *Atlas of Cistercian lands in Wales*, and in Williams, *Welsh Cistercians*, II, pp. 312–15.

53 Selby and Battle were two of a handful of post-Conquest monasteries which outgrew their rural origins by the cultivation of a settlement outside their precincts: Lawrence Butler, 'Archaeology of rural monasteries', in Gilchrist and Mytum (eds.), *Archaeology of rural monasteries*, p. 1.

54 On the administration of Bury, see Knowles, *Monastic order*, p. 446, and especially, M. D. Lobel, *The borough of Bury St Edmunds* (Oxford, 1935), pp. 16–117.

55 Reynolds, *An introduction to the history of English medieval towns*, p. 41.

56 On relations between the town and abbey see Lobel, *The borough of Bury St Edmunds*, pp. 118–70; more generally, see Knowles, *Religious orders*, I, pp. 263–9.

57 Rees, *Shrewsbury cartulary*, nos. 52, 276, 386.

58 Donkin, *The Cistercians: studies in the geography of medieval England and Wales*, p. 154.

59 On the involvement of regular canons with parish churches, see above, chapter 3.

60 A point made by Harper-Bill, 'The struggle for benefices in twelfth-century East Anglia', p. 118.

61 Butler and Given-Wilson, *Medieval monasteries of Great Britain*, p. 81.

62 Harvey, *Westminster Abbey*, pp. 45–55. On the abbey and its churches see further Emma Mason, 'Westminster Abbey and its parish churches', in Loades (ed.), *Monastic Studies*, II, pp. 43–65.

63 Jocelin of Brakelond, *Chronicle of the abbey of Bury St Edmunds*, pp. 56–8; for two other Benedictine abbeys with appropriated churches, see Raban, *Thorney and Crowland*, pp. 80–7.

64 Anthony Goodman, 'Religion and warfare in the Anglo-Scottish marches', in Robert Barlett and Angus MacKay (eds.), *Medieval frontier societies* (Oxford, 1989), p. 247; Ian B. Cowan, *Ayrshire Abbeys, Crossraguel and Kilwinning*, Ayrshire Collections, vol. 14, no. 7 (Kilmarnock, 1986), p. 269.

65 For the following discussion see Robinson, *Geography of Augustinian settlement*, pp. 110–272.

66 Cowley, *Monastic order in south Wales*, pp. 176–7.

67 Ibid., p. 68.

68 Janet E. Burton, 'Monasteries and parish churches in eleventh- and twelfth-century Yorkshire', *Northern History* 23 (1987), 41.

69 Hill, *English Cistercian monasteries*, pp. 109–15.

70 Talbot, 'Cîteaux and Scarborough', 95–158; on the general chapter see above, pp. 66, 180–2.

71 Jocelin of Brakelond, *Chronicle of the abbey of Bury St Edmunds*, p. 85.

72 Ibid., pp. 38–9.

73 On the costs of building, see above, chapter 7, pp. 152–3.

74 Vaughan, *Chronicles of Matthew Paris*, pp. 78–9.

75 Hockey (ed.), *Account book of Beaulieu Abbey*, pp. 84–7 and 256–7.

76 See, for example, on Westminster's enfeoffment for knight service, Harvey, *Westminster Abbey*, pp. 74–7.

77 King, *Peterborough Abbey*, pp. 140–6.

78 Harvey, *Westminster Abbey*, p. 77.

79 Jocelin of Brakelond, *Chronicle of the abbey of Bury St Edmunds*, pp. 108–10. On similar difficulties at Ramsey see Raftis, *Ramsey Abbey*, pp. 103–10; on the resumption of demesne at Thorney and Crowland, see Raban, *Thorney and Crowland*, pp. 61–79.

80 King, *Peterborough Abbey*, p. 145.

81 Jocelin of Brakelond, *Chronicle of the abbey of Bury St Edmunds*, p. 26. The division between the abbot's and convent's manors had taken place at Bury in the early twelfth century.

82 Harvey, *Westminster Abbey*, pp. 344, 352.

83 Finberg, *Tavistock Abbey*, pp. 20–1; Harvey, *Westminster Abbey*, p. 343.

84 Jocelin of Brakelond, *Chronicle of the abbey of Bury St Edmunds*, p. 78.

85 Cowley, *Monastic order in south Wales*, p. 61.

86 R. A. L. Smith, *Canterbury Cathedral Priory: a study in monastic administration* (Cambridge, 1943, repr. 1969), pp. 14–28; Knowles, *Religious orders*, I, pp. 49–54.

87 Smith, *Canterbury Cathedral Priory*, pp. 100–12; Knowles, *Religious orders*, I, pp. 49–54.

88 King, *Peterborough Abbey*, pp. 163–4.

89 Robinson, *Geography of Augustinian settlement*, p. 293.

90 Knowles, *Religious orders*, I, pp. 32–63.

91 The internal practices in some Cistercian houses did, however, develop from this centralized system. Tintern had sub-cellarers by 1293; Kingswood had a treasurer in 1240 and Abbey Dore one in 1245.

92 Janet Burton, 'Charters of Byland Abbey relating to the grange of Bleatarn, Westmorland', *Transactions of the Cumberland and Westmorland Antiquarian and Archaeological Society* 79 (1979), 29–50.

93 Donkin, *The Cistercians: studies in the geography of medieval England and Wales*, pp. 45, 51–67 and 'The Cistercian grange in England in the 12th and 13th centuries', *Studia Monastica* 6 (1964), 95–144. The fullest treatment of the grange is Platt, *The monastic grange*.

94 Platt, *The monastic grange*, pp. 219–20.

95 Donkin, *The Cistercians: studies in the geography of medieval England and Wales*, p. 55.

96 Owen, *Church and society in medieval Lincolnshire*, p. 64.

97 Platt, *The monastic grange*, pp. 16–48.

98 Williams, *Welsh Cistercians*, II, p. 239; *Atlas of Cistercian lands in Wales*, pp. 32 and 132 (plate 49).

99 Williams, *Welsh Cistercians*, II, pp. 293–6.

100 Platt, *The monastic grange*, pp. 224–5.

101 Ibid., pp. 88–90, 191–2, 196–7, 199.

102 Ibid., p. 93.

103 Graves, 'Stixwould in the market place', pp. 224–5.

104 Burton, *Yorkshire nunneries*, pp. 13–14.

105 King, *Peterborough Abbey*, pp. 81–2.

106 Owen, *Church and society in medieval Lincolnshire*, p. 57.

107 Platt, *The monastic grange*, pp. 233, 245; Owen, *Church and society in medieval Lincolnshire*, p. 58.

108 Platt, *The monastic grange*, p. 94.

109 The transformation of the Cistercian grange in the late medieval period is discussed ibid., pp. 94–117, and by James S. Donnelly, 'Changes in the grange economy of English and Welsh Cistercian abbeys, 1300–1540', *Traditio* 10 (1954), 399–458.

110 Donnelly (ibid., 451–8) argues that the number of *conversi* on the eve of the Black Death was surprisingly high.

111 Butler and Given-Wilson, *Medieval monasteries of Great Britain*, p. 84; Knowles, *Religious orders*, I, pp. 32–8.

112 Donkin, *The Cistercians: studies in the geography of medieval England and Wales*, pp. 99, 138n.

113 T. H. Lloyd, *The English wool trade in the Middle Ages* (Cambridge, 1977), p. 296.

114 Donkin, *The Cistercians: studies in the geography of medieval England and Wales*, pp. 92–3.

115 There is also evidence of this practice among the Black Monks. In 1198 William Elyas paid 20 marks to secure his claim to 7,000 fleeces from the Benedictine abbot of York: Lloyd, *English wool trade*, pp. 288–9.

116 See ibid., p. 39, for this and other examples.

117 Stevenson, 'The monastic presence: Berwick in the twelfth and thirteenth centuries', p. 108.

118 Ibid., p. 109; Donkin, *The Cistercians: studies in the geography of medieval England and Wales*, pp. 192–3.

119 Lloyd, *English wool trade*, p. 17.

120 Ibid., p. 290.

121 Donkin, *The Cistercians: studies in the geography of medieval England and Wales*, p. 100; Francesco Balducci Pegolotti, *La Pratica della Mercatura*, edited by A. Evans, Medieval Academy of America, xxiv (Cambridge, MA, 1936).

122 Graves, 'Stixwould in the market place', pp. 225–6.

123 Lloyd, *English wool trade*, p. 290.

124 Knowles, *Religious orders*, I, pp. 70–1.

125 Jocelin of Brakelond, *Chronicle of the abbey of Bury St Edmunds*, pp. 3–4.

126 Harvey, *Westminster Abbey*, pp. 65 and 164–98.

127 H. Jenkinson, 'William Cade: a financier of the twelfth century', *English Historical Review* 28 (1913), 209–27, especially 221.

128 H. G. Richardson, *The English Jewry under Angevin kings* (London, 1960), pp. 90–1.

129 The case is discussed ibid., pp. 89–90.

130 Ibid., pp. 83–108. For Gilbertine involvement see Graham, 'Finance of Malton Priory', pp. 256–7.

131 For an example of the borrowing activities of a Benedictine house, Christ

Church, Canterbury, both from Jews and from Italian bankers, see Smith, *Canterbury Cathedral Priory*, pp. 17–18.

132 See above, chapter 10, p. 222.

133 For some examples see Williams, *Atlas of Cistercian lands in Wales*, p. 13.

134 D. M. Metcalf, 'The Templars as bankers and monetary transfers between West and East in the twelfth century', in P. W. Edbury and D. M. Metcalf (eds.), *Coinage in the Latin East*, BAR International Series 77 (1980), pp. 1–17.

135 Platt, *The monastic grange*, p. 13.

12 On the brink of change

1 Lawrence, *Medieval monasticism*, pp. 281–2.

2 One estimate would put the number of those in religious orders c. 1300 at 17,000–18,000, and c. 1500 at around 12,000. The decline in the monastic population should not, therefore, be exaggerated.

3 See above, chapter 8, pp. 174–5, 185.

4 A point made by Christopher Dyer, *Standards of living in the later middle ages*, Cambridge Medieval Textbooks (Cambridge, 1989), p. 98.

SELECT BIBLIOGRAPHY

The following reading list is of necessity selective; for instance, not all printed sources referred to in the text, such as cartularies of individual houses, are cited here, since full bibliographical details are given in the notes. I have divided the bibliography into sections roughly corresponding to the chapters, with the addition of a section of general works (i), and works devoted to the history of individual Benedictine houses (iv). There is unavoidable overlap between many works, and I have placed books and articles under the section I have deemed most appropriate, and cross-referenced where necessary.

(i) General works

PRIMARY SOURCES

The basic text in the history of monasticism is *The Rule of St Benedict*, and a convenient edition and translation is that of J. McCann (London, 1972). Rules and constitutions of different orders and congregations are given in the sections following. A medieval view of how these groups differed is provided by the account of a canon of Liège, edited and translated by Giles Constable and B. Smith as *Libellus de Diversis Ordinibus et Professionibus qui sunt in Aecclesia*, Oxford Medieval Texts (Oxford, 1972). Other contemporary perceptions and comments on the monastic orders are provided by Gerald of Wales, in *The journey through Wales and the description of Wales*, translated by Lewis Thorpe (Harmondsworth, 1978), and Walter Map, *De Nugis Curialium: Courtiers' trifles*, edited and translated by M. R. James, revised by C. N. L. Brooke and R. A. B. Mynors, Oxford Medieval Texts (Oxford, 1983).

SECONDARY WORKS

Good general introductions to European monasticism are David Knowles, *Christian monasticism* (London, 1969); Christopher Brooke, *The monastic world 1000–1300* (London, 1974); and, more recently, C. H. Lawrence, *Medieval monasticism: forms of religious life in western Europe in the Middle Ages*, 2nd edn (London, 1989). Useful sections are also to be found in R. W. Southern, *Western society and the church in the middle ages* (Harmondsworth, 1970). A recent stimulating discussion is to be found in Ludo J. R. Milis, *Angelic monks and earthly men: monasticism and its meaning to medieval society* (Woodbridge, 1992).

The classic account of monasticism in England and Wales in this period remains David Knowles, *The monastic order in England: a history of its development from the times of St Dunstan to the fourth Lateran Council, 940–1216*, 2nd edn (Cambridge, 1963, repr. 1966) and *The religious orders in England*, 1 (Cambridge, 1948, repr. 1974). Details of the dates of foundation and dissolution of religious houses, together with brief historical notes, are found in two works: David Knowles and R. N. Hadcock (eds.), *Medieval religious houses: England and Wales*, 2nd edn (London, 1971), and Ian B. Cowan and David E. Easson (eds.), *Medieval religious houses: Scotland*, 2nd edn (London, 1976). The dates of office of heads of monasteries in England and Wales can be found in David Knowles, C. N. L. Brooke and V. London (eds.), *The heads of religious houses: England and Wales 940–1216* (Cambridge, 1972). A volume covering the period from 1216 is in preparation under the editorship of David M. Smith and V. London. A particular problem of chronology is dealt with in V. H. Galbraith in his article 'Monastic foundation charters of the eleventh and twelfth centuries', *Cambridge Historical Journal* 4 (1934), 205–22, 296–8. Alison Binns investigates patterns of dedication in *Dedication of monastic houses in England and Wales, 1066–1216* (Woodbridge, 1989). Details of surviving cartularies from British monastic houses are to be found in G. R. C. Davis, *Medieval cartularies of Great Britain. A short catalogue* (London, 1958). Welsh medieval monasticism has found its historian in F. G. Cowley, whose book *The monastic order in south Wales 1066–1349* (Cardiff, 1977) deals with all the monastic orders but does not treat the friars. There is no comparable general history of Scottish monasticism, but the reader will find useful discussion in G. W. S. Barrow, *The kingdom of the Scots* (London, 1973), chapters 5 and 6. A gazetteer of selected monastic sites, with introduction, is provided by Lionel Butler and Chris Given-Wilson, *Medieval monasteries of Great Britain* (London, 1979). Fashions in monastic building are also the main theme of C. P. S. Platt, *The abbeys and priories of medieval England* (London, 1984); see also Roy Midmer, *English medieval monasteries (1066–1540): a summary* (London, 1979). For those interested in individual houses or regions of England, the *Victoria county histories* (London, 1900–, in progress) should be consulted.

(ii) Monasticism before the Normans

PRIMARY SOURCES

The basic text for the study of monasticism in the late Anglo-Saxon period is the *Regularis Concordia*. This has been edited, with facing-page translation, by T. Symons, Nelsons Medieval Classics (London, 1953).

SECONDARY WORKS

Barlow, Frank, *The English church 1000–1066*, 2nd edn (London, 1979).

Bestul, Thomas H.: *see* section xi.

Brooks, Nicholas, *The early history of the church of Canterbury: Christ Church from 597–1066* (Leicester, 1984).

Fisher, D. J. V., 'The anti-monastic reaction in the reign of Edward the Martyr', *Cambridge Historical Journal* 10 (1952), 254–70.

Gatch, McC. M., 'The office in late Anglo-Saxon monasticism', in Michael Lapidge and Helmut Gneuss (eds.), *Learning and literature in Anglo-Saxon England: studies presented to Peter Clemoes on the occasion of his sixty-fifth birthday* (Cambridge, 1985), pp. 341–62.

Gransden, Antonia, 'Traditionalism and continuity during the last century of Anglo-Saxon monasticism', *Journal of Ecclesiastical History* 40 (1989), 159–207.

Macquarrie, Alan, 'Early Christian religious houses in Scotland: foundation and function', in John Blair and Richard Sharpe (eds.), *Pastoral care before the parish* (Leicester, 1992), pp. 110–33.

Mason, Emma, *St Wulfstan of Worcester, c. 1008–1095* (Oxford, 1990).

Parsons, David (ed.), *Tenth-century studies* (London, 1975).

Pryce, Huw, 'Pastoral care in early medieval Wales', in Blair and Sharpe (eds.), *Pastoral care before the parish*, pp. 41–62.

For individual houses *see below*, section iv, and on nunneries *see* section vii.

(iii) After the Normans

PRIMARY SOURCES

The statutes of Lanfranc for Christ Church, Canterbury, which were adopted by other Benedictine houses, are edited and translated by David Knowles as *The Monastic constitutions of Lanfranc*, Nelsons Medieval Classics (London, 1951).

SECONDARY WORKS

European developments in this period, particularly the contribution of Cluny, are discussed in: J. Evans, *Monastic life at Cluny, 910–1157* (Oxford, 1931); Noreen Hunt, *Cluny under St Hugh, 1049–1109* (London, 1967); and in Noreen Hunt (ed.), *Cluniac monasticism in the central middle ages* (London, 1971). There are also useful essays in Rose Graham, *English ecclesiastical studies* (London, 1929). On Norman monasticism see David Bates, *Normandy before 1066* (London, 1982), chapter 5, and Marjorie Chibnall, *The world of Orderic Vitalis* (Oxford, 1984).

Ayton, A. and Davis, V., 'Ecclesiastical wealth in England in 1086', in *The church and wealth*, Studies in Church History 24 (Oxford, 1987), pp. 47–60.

Baker, L. G. D., 'The desert in the North', *Northern History* 5 (1970), 1-11.

Barlow, Frank, 'William I's relations with Cluny', *Journal of Ecclesiastical History* 32 (1981), 131–41, repr. in Frank Barlow, *The Norman Conquest and beyond* (London, 1983), pp. 245–56.

Burton, Janet E., 'A confraternity list from St Mary's Abbey, York', *Revue Bénédictine* 89 (1979), 325–33.

Chew, Helena M., *The English ecclesiastical tenants in chief and knight service* (London, 1932).

Chibnall, Marjorie, *Anglo-Norman England 1066–1166* (Oxford, 1986).

Cowdrey, H. E. J., 'William I's relations with Cluny further reconsidered', in Judith Loades (ed.), *Monastic Studies*, I (Bangor, 1990), 75–85.

Dawtry, Anne, 'The Benedictine revival in the North: the last bulwark of Anglo-Saxon monasticism', in *Religion and national identity*, Studies in Church History 18 (Oxford, 1982), pp. 87–98.

Fernie, Eric: *see* section ix.

Franklin, M. J., 'The secular college as a focus of Anglo-Norman piety: St Augustine's, Daventry', in John Blair (ed.), *Minsters and parish churches: the local church in transition 950–1200*, Oxford University Committee for Archaeology, monograph no. 17 (Oxford, 1988), pp. 97–104.

Gibson, Margaret, *Lanfranc of Bec* (Oxford, 1978).

Gillingham, John, 'The introduction of knight service into England', in *Proceedings of the Battle Conference on Anglo-Norman Studies IV 1981* (Woodbridge, 1982), pp. 53–64, 181–7.

Golding, Brian, 'The Coming of the Cluniacs', in *Proceedings of the Battle Conference on Anglo-Norman Studies III 1980* (Woodbridge, 1981), pp. 65–77, 208–12.

Gransden, Antonia, 'Baldwin, abbot of Bury St Edmunds 1065–1097', in *Proceedings of the Battle Conference on Anglo-Norman Studies IV 1981* (Woodbridge, 1982), pp. 65–76 and 187–95.

Hallam, Elizabeth M.: *see* section xii.

Hare, J. N.: *see* section ix.

Klukas, Arnold William: *see* section ix.

Mason, Emma, 'Change and continuity in eleventh-century Mercia: the experience of St Wulfstan of Worcester', in *Anglo-Norman Studies VIII: Proceedings of the Battle Conference 1985* (Woodbridge, 1986), pp. 154–76.

Matthew, D. J. A., *The Norman monasteries and their English possessions* (Oxford, 1962).

Morgan, Marjorie, *The English lands of the abbey of Bec* (Oxford, 1946).

Ridyard, Susan, '*Condigna Veneratio*: post-conquest attitudes to the saints of the Anglo-Saxons', in *Anglo-Norman Studies IX: Proceedings of the Battle Conference 1986* (Woodbridge, 1987), pp. 179–206.

Ruud, Marylou, 'Monks and the world: the case of Gundulf of Rochester', in *Anglo-Norman Studies XI: Proceedings of the Battle Conference 1988* (Woodbridge, 1989), pp. 245–60.

Smith, R. A. L., 'The place of Gundulf in the Anglo-Norman church', *English Historical Review* 58 (1943), 257–72.

Wilson, Christopher: *see* section ix.

(iv) Benedictine houses (studies covering a long period)

Finberg, H. P. R., *Tavistock Abbey: a study in the social and economic history of Devon* (Cambridge, 1951, repr. Newton Abbot, 1969).

Harvey, Barbara, *Westminster Abbey and its estates in the middle ages* (Oxford, 1977).

King, Edmund, *Peterborough Abbey 1086–1310: a study in the land market* (Cambridge, 1973).

Miller, Edward, *The abbey and bishopric of Ely* (Cambridge, 1951, repr. 1969).

Raban, Sandra, *The estates of Thorney and Crowland* (Cambridge, 1977).

Raftis, J. Ambrose, *The estates of Ramsey Abbey: a study in economic growth and organization*, Pontifical Institute of Mediaeval Studies, Studies and Texts 3 (Toronto, 1957).

Runcie, Robert (ed.), *Cathedral and city: St Albans ancient and modern* (London, 1977).

Smith, R. A. L., *Canterbury Cathedral Priory: a study in monastic administration* (Cambridge, 1943, repr. 1969).

(v) The regular canons and their precursors

PRIMARY SOURCES

A discussion of the problems concerning the text of the Rule of St Augustine together with an edition of the Latin text and an English translation, is provided by George Lawless (ed.), *Augustine of Hippo and his monastic rule* (Oxford, 1987). Another translation with commentary is that by Tarsicius J. van Bavel, translated by Raymond Canning (London, 1984).

SECONDARY WORKS

Various general aspects of the emergence of the regular canons are discussed in: Caroline Walker Bynum, 'The spirituality of regular canons in the twelfth century', in *Jesus as mother: studies in the spirituality of the high middle ages* (Berkeley, Los Angeles and London, 1982), pp. 22–58. This is a stimulating investigation of the existence of a canonical theology or identity. The connection with the eremitical movement is pursued in two articles by Ludo Milis, 'Ermites et chanoines réguliers au xiiᵉ siècle', *Cahiers de Civilisation Médiévale* 22, pt. 85 (1979), 39–80, and 'L'Evolution de l'érémitisme au canonicat régulier dans la première moitié du douzième siècle: transition ou trahison', in *Istituzioni monastiche e istituzioni canonicali in occidente (1123–1215)*, Miscellanea del centro di studi medioevali ix (Milan, 1980), pp. 223–38. The history of a group of houses affiliated to a French abbey which formed an order in its own right is described by the same author in *L'Ordre des chanoines réguliers d'Arrouaise* (Bruges, 1969).

The canons in Britain

Baker, Derek: *see* section xii.

Barrow, G. W. S., 'The cathedral chapter of St Andrew's and the Culdees in the twelfth and thirteenth centuries', *Journal of Ecclesiastical History* 3 (1952), 23–39.

Blair, John, 'Secular minster churches in Domesday Book', in Peter Sawyer (ed.), *Domesday Book: a reassessment* (London, 1985), pp. 104–42.

Blair, John (ed.), *Minsters and parish churches: the local church in transition 950–1200*,

Oxford University Committee for Archaeology, monograph no. 17 (Oxford, 1988).

Saint Frideswide's monastery at Oxford, Archaeological and Architectural Studies (Oxford: Oxfordshire Architectural and Historical Society, 1990).

Brooke, Christopher N. L., 'Monk and canon: some patterns in the religious life of the twelfth century', in *Monks, hermits and the ascetic tradition*, Studies in Church History 22 (Oxford, 1985), pp. 109–29.

Burrows, T. N., 'The foundation of Nostell Priory', *Yorkshire Archaeological Journal* 53 (1981), 31–5.

Colvin, H. M., *The White Canons in England* (Oxford, 1951).

Dickinson, J. C., 'English regular canons and the continent in the twelfth century', *Transactions of the Royal Historical Society*, 5th series, 1 (1951), 71–89.

The origins of the Austin canons and their introduction into England (London, 1950).

'The origins of the cathedral of Carlisle', *Transactions of the Cumberland and Westmorland Antiquarian and Archaeological Society*, n.s., 45 (1946), 134–43.

Greene, J. Patrick: *see* section ix.

Herbert, Jane, 'The transformation of hermitages into Augustinian priories in twelfth-century England', in *Monks, hermits and the ascetic tradition*, Studies in Church History 22 (Oxford, 1985), pp. 131–45.

Johns, C. N., 'The Celtic monasteries of north Wales', *Caernarvonshire Historical Society Transactions* 21 (1960), 14–43, and 'Postscript to "The Celtic monasteries of north Wales"', *Caernarvonshire Historical Society Transactions*, 23 (1962), 129–31.

Kershaw, I.: *see* section xiii.

Pierce, T. Jones, 'Bardsey – a study in monastic origins', *Caernarvonshire Historical Society Transactions* 24 (1963), 60–77.

Postles, David, 'The foundation of Oseney Abbey', *Bulletin of the Institute of Historical Research* 53 (1980), 242–4; *see also* sections xi and xii.

Robinson, David M., *The geography of Augustinian settlement in medieval England and Wales*, British Archaeological Reports, British series 80 (2 vols., Oxford, 1980).

Scott, J. G., 'The origins of Dundrennan and Soulseat Abbeys', *Transactions of the Dumfriesshire and Galloway Natural History and Antiquarian Society* 63 (1988), 35–44.

Thompson, A. Hamilton, *History and architectural description of the priory of St Mary, Bolton in Wharfedale*, Thoresby Society vol. 30 (Leeds, 1928, for 1924).

Wilson, J., 'The foundation of the Austin priories of Nostell and Scone', *Scottish Historical Review* 7 (1910), 141–59.

(vi) The new orders of the twelfth century

PRIMARY SOURCES

The earliest documents of the Cistercian Order have been printed a number of times: P. Guignard (ed.), *Les Monuments primitifs de la règle cistercienne* (Dijon, 1878); J. de la Croix Bouton and J. B. van Damme, *Les Plus Anciens Textes de Cîteaux: Commentaria Cisterciensis, Studia et Documenta*, II (Achel, 1974); a convenient translation by Bede K. Lackner appears in Louis J. Lekai, *The Cistercians: ideals and reality* (Kent, OH, 1977), pp. 442–66. The controversy surrounding the dating of the early documents is explained by David Knowles in 'The primitive documents of the Cistercian order', in *Great historical enterprises: problems in monastic history* (London, 1963), pp. 197–222. The statutes of the order are printed in J. M. Canivez, *Statuta capitulorum generalium ordinis Cisterciensis ab anno 1116 ad annum 1786* (8 vols., Louvain, 1933–41).

No early rules have survived from Tiron and Savigny, but for that of the Grande Chartreuse and the Carthusian Order see *Guiges I coutumes de Chartreuse* (Paris, 1984). The rule of the Temple was edited by H. de Curzon, *La Règle du Temple* (Paris, 1886); de Curzon's text has been translated by J. M. Upton-Ward, as *The rule of the Templars* (Woodbridge, 1992). For the Knights Hospitaller, see E. J. King, *The rule, statutes and customs of the Hospitallers, 1099–1310* (London, 1933), and K. V. Sinclair (ed.), *The Hospitallers' 'Riwle' (Miracula et Regula Hospitalis sancti Johannis Jerosolimitani)*, Anglo-Norman Text Society XLII (London, 1984).

Light is also shed on aspects of the history of the new orders in Britain by biographies. The most famous of these are Walter Daniel, *The life of Ailred of Rievaulx*, edited and translated by F. M. Powicke, Nelsons Medieval Classics (London, 1950), and Adam of Eynsham, *Magna Vita Sancti Hugonis*, edited and translated by D. Douie and D. H. Farmer (2 vols., London, 1961–2, repr. Oxford, 1985). The life of St Waldef by Jocelin of Furness lacks a modern edition.

SECONDARY WORKS

There are many works on the European background to the emergence of the new orders, and only a selection is given here. The crisis of monasticism is discussed in Norman F. Cantor, 'The crisis of western monasticism 1050–1130', *American Historical Review* 66 (1960/1), 47–67; J. Leclercq, 'The monastic crisis of the eleventh and twelfth centuries', translated from 'La Crise du monachisme aux XIe et XIIe siècles', in Noreen Hunt (ed.), *Cluniac monasticism in the central middle ages* (London, 1971), pp. 217–37; and John Van Engen, 'The "Crisis of Cenobitism" reconsidered: Benedictine monasticism in the years 1050–1150', *Speculum* 61 (1986), 269–304. The eremitical element is the subject of: Giles Constable, 'Eremitical forms of monastic life', in *Istituzioni monastiche e istituzioni canonicali in occidente (1123–1215)*, Miscellanea del centro di studi medioevali IX (Milan, 1980), pp. 239–64, and Henrietta Leyser, *Hermits and the new monasticism* (London, 1984). An excellent account of the economic and social background out of which the new orders sprang is Lester K. Little, *Religious poverty and the profit economy in medieval Europe* (London, 1978).

The Cistercian Order has attracted most attention. Readers interested in the history of the order as a whole should consult the works of Louis J. Lekai, *The White Monks* (Okauchee, WI, 1953), translated and revised as *Les Moines Blancs* (Paris, 1957). A more recent work is the same author's *The Cistercians: ideals and reality* (Kent, OH, 1977), which contains a comprehensive bibliography. The series Cistercian Studies, published from Kalamazoo, Michigan, contains many useful titles, including M. Basil Pennington (ed.), *The Cistercian Spirit: a symposium in memory of Thomas Merton* (Shannon, Ireland, 1969), Bede K. Lackner, *The eleventh-*

century background of Cîteaux (1972), and J. R. Sommerfeldt, *Cistercian ideals and reality* (1978).

On Savigny, see Mary Suydam, 'Origins of the Savigniac order: Savigny's role within twelfth-century monastic reform', *Revue Bénédictine* 86 (1976), 94–108. The most recent treatment of the Hospitallers and Templars is Alan Forey, *The military orders from the twelfth to the early fourteenth centuries* (London, 1992). See also J. Riley Smith, *The Knights of St John in Jerusalem and Cyprus c. 1050–1310* (London, 1967).

The new orders in Britain
Baker, Derek, 'Legend and reality: the case of Waldef of Melrose', in *Church, society and politics*, Studies in Church History 12 (Oxford, 1975), pp. 59–82 (a discussion of the life by Jocelin of Furness).
  'The foundation of Fountains Abbey', *Northern History* 4 (1969), 29–43.
  '"The surest road to Heaven": ascetic spiritualities in English post-Conquest religious life', in *Sanctity and secularity: the church and the world*, Studies in Church History 10 (Oxford, 1973), pp. 45–57; *see also* section xii.
Bethell, D., 'The foundation of Fountains Abbey and the state of St Mary's, York, in 1132', *Journal of Ecclesiastical History* 17 (1966), 11–27.
Brooke, Christopher: *see* section ix.
Burton, Janet, 'The abbeys of Byland and Jervaulx, and the problems of the English Savigniacs, 1134–1156', in Judith Loades (ed.), *Monastic Studies*, II (Bangor, 1991), pp. 119–31.
  'The foundation of the British Cistercian houses', in Christopher Norton and David Park (eds.), *Cistercian art and architecture in the British Isles* (Cambridge, 1986, repr. 1988), pp. 24–39.
  'The Knights Templar in Yorkshire in the twelfth century: a reassessment', *Northern History* 27 (1991), 26–40.
Chadd, D. F. L.: *see* section x.
Cheney, C. R.: *see* section xi.
Coldstream, Nicola: *see* section ix.
Donkin, R. A., *A check-list of printed works relating to the Cistercian Order as a whole and to the houses of the British Isles in particular* (Rochefort, 1969). (*See also* the articles by Donkin on various aspects of Cistercian economy, cited in section xiii.)
Dutton, Marsha L.: *see* section x.
Fergusson, Peter: *see* section ix.
Gilyard-Beer, R. and Glyn Coppack: *see* section ix.
Graham, Rose, 'The order of Grandmont and its houses in England', in *English Ecclesiastical Studies* (London, 1929), pp. 209–46.
Hays, Rhŷs W., *The history of the abbey of Aberconway, 1186–1537* (Cardiff, 1963).
Hill, Bennett D., *English Cistercian monasteries and their patrons in the twelfth century* (Urbana, 1968).
Hockey, S. F., *Beaulieu: King John's Abbey* ([Beaulieu], 1976).
  Quarr Abbey and its lands 1132–1631 (Leicester, 1970).
Holdsworth, Christopher, 'The Cistercians in Devon', in Christopher Harper-

Bill, Christopher J. Holdsworth and Janet L. Nelson (eds.), *Studies in medieval history presented to R. Allen Brown* (Woodbridge, 1989), pp. 179–91; *see also* sections ix, x and xi.

Knowles, David, 'The case of St William of York', *Cambridge Historical Journal* 5 (1936), 162–77 and 212–14, reprinted in *The Historian and Character* (Cambridge, 1963), pp. 76–97.

Mason, Emma, 'Fact and fiction in the English crusading tradition: the earls of Warwick in the twelfth century', *Journal of Medieval History* 14 (1988), 81–95.

Mayr-Harting, H., 'Functions of a twelfth-century recluse', *History* 60 (1975), 337–52.

Mayr-Harting, Henry (ed.), *St Hugh of Lincoln* (Oxford, 1987).

Norton, Christopher and David Park: *see* section ix.

Parker, T. W., *The Knights Templars in England* (Tucson, 1963).

Rees, W., *History of the order of St John in Wales and on the Welsh border* (Cardiff, 1947).

Schaefer, J. O.: *see* section ix.

Scott, J. G.: *see* section v.

Squire, Aelred, *Aelred of Rievaulx: a study* (London, 1969).

Stringer, K., 'A Cistercian archive: the earliest charters of Sawtry Abbey', *Journal of the Society of Archivists* 6 (1980), 325–34.

Talbot, C. H., 'Cîteaux and Scarborough', *Studia Monastica* 2 (1960), 95–158.

Talbot, Hugh, *The Cistercian abbeys of Scotland* (London, 1939).

Thompson, M., *The Carthusian Order in England* (London, 1930).

Wardrop, Joan: *see* section xii.

Williams, David H., *The Welsh Cistercians* (2 vols., Caldey Island, Tenby, 1984). (*See also* the many articles by the same author listed in the printed works (p. viii) of vol. 1.)

Wilson, Christopher: *see* section ix.

For the economic activities of the new orders, particularly the Cistercians, *see below*, section xiii.

(vii) Women in the religious life

PRIMARY SOURCES

Foreville, R. and Gillian Keir (eds.), *The Book of St Gilbert*, Oxford Medieval Texts (Oxford, 1987).

Talbot, C. H. (ed.), *The life of Christina of Markyate, a twelfth-century recluse* (1959, repr. with corrections, Oxford, 1987).

SECONDARY WORKS

Various issues relating to the female religious vocation in the Middle Ages are discussed in the following: Brenda M. Bolton, '*Mulieres sanctae*', in *Sanctity and secularity: the church and the world*, Studies in Church History 10 (Oxford, 1973), pp. 77–95; Caroline Walker Bynum, *Holy feast and holy fast: the religious significance of food to medieval women* (Berkeley and London, 1987). There are two useful collections of essays on British and European themes: John A. Nichols and Lillian

T. Shank (eds.), *Medieval religious women*, I, *Distant Echoes* (Kalamazoo, MI: Cistercian Studies publications, 1984), and L. T. Shank and John A Nichols (eds.), *Medieval religious women*, II, *Peaceweavers* (Kalamazoo, MI: Cistercian Studies publications, 1987).

The issue of Cistercian nuns is discussed in Sister M. Connor, 'The first Cistercian nuns and renewal today', *Cistercian Studies* 5 (1970), 131–68, and by Sally Thompson, 'The problem of the Cistercian nuns in the twelfth and early thirteenth centuries', in Baker (ed.), *Medieval women*, pp. 227–52 (see below). Women within the Premonstratensian order are the subject of A. Erens, 'Les Sœurs dans l'ordre de Prémontré', *Analecta Premonstratensia* 5 (1929), 5–26. For Robert of Arbrissel see Jacqueline Smith, 'Robert of Arbrissel: *Procurator mulierum*', in Baker (ed.), *Medieval women*, pp. 175–84; and the roles of men and women at Fontevrault are treated by P. S. Gold, in 'Male/female co-operation: the example of Fontevrault', in Nichols and Shank (eds.), *Distant echoes*, pp. 151–68; see also P. S. Gold, *The lady and the virgin: image, attitude and experience in twelfth-century France* (Chicago, 1985). The anchoritic tradition is investigated in Patricia J. F. Rosof, 'The anchoress in the twelfth and thirteenth centuries', in Shank and Nichols (eds.), *Peaceweavers*, pp. 123–44, and Jane T. Schulenburg, 'Strict active enclosure and its effects on the female monastic experience, ca. 500–1100', in Nichols and Shank (eds.), *Distant Echoes*, pp. 51–86.

Religious women in Britain

Baker, Derek (ed.), *Medieval Women*, Studies in Church History Subsidia 1 (Oxford, 1978).

Bourdillon, A. F. C., *The order of Minoresses in England* (Manchester, 1926).

Burton, Janet E., *The Yorkshire nunneries in the twelfth and thirteenth centuries*, Borthwick Paper no. 56 (York, 1979).

Chettle, H. E., 'The English houses of the order of Fontevraud', *Downside Review* 60 (1942), 33–55.

Chibnall, Marjorie, 'L'Ordre de Fontevraud en Angleterre au xiie siècle', *Cahiers de Civilisation Médiévale* 29 (1986), 41–7.

Constable, Giles, 'Aelred of Rievaulx and the nun of Watton: an episode in the early history of the Gilbertine order', in Baker (ed.), *Medieval women*, pp. 205–26.

Cooke, Kathleen, 'Donors and daughters: Shaftesbury Abbey's benefactors, endowments and nuns, c. 1086–1130', in *Anglo-Norman Studies XII: Proceedings of the Battle Conference 1989* (Woodbridge, 1990), pp. 29–45.

Dobson, E. J., *The origins of Ancrene Wisse* (Oxford, 1976).

Dobson, R. B. and Sara Donaghey, *The history of Clementhorpe Nunnery* (York: York Archaeological Trust, 1984).

Easson, D. E., 'The nunneries of medieval Scotland', *Scottish Ecclesiological Society Transactions* 13 (2) (1940–1), 22–38.

Elkins, Sharon K., *Holy women of twelfth-century England* (Chapel Hill, NC, 1988).

  'The emergence of a Gilbertine identity', in Nichols and Shank (eds.), *Distant Echoes*, pp. 169–82.

Foreville, Raymonde, 'La Crise de l'ordre de Sempringham au xiie siècle: nouvelle approche du dossier des frères lais', in *Anglo-Norman Studies VI: Proceedings of the Battle Conference 1983* (Woodbridge, 1984), pp. 39–57.

Gilchrist, Roberta: *see* section ix.

Godfrey, J., 'The double monastery in early English history', *Ampleforth Journal* 79 (1974), 19–32.

Golding, Brian, 'Hermits, monks and women in twelfth-century France and England: the experience of Obazine and Sempringham', in Judith Loades (ed.), *Monastic Studies*, 1 (Bangor, 1990), pp. 127–45.

'St Bernard and St Gilbert', in B. Ward (ed.), *The influence of St Bernard: Anglican essays with an introduction by Jean Leclercq* (Oxford, 1976), pp. 42–52.

'The distortion of a dream: transformations and mutations of the rule of St Gilbert', *Word and Spirit* 11 (1989), 60–78.

Graham, Rose, *St Gilbert of Sempringham and the Gilbertines* (London, 1901); *see also* section xiii.

Graves, C. V., 'English Cistercian nuns in Lincolnshire', *Speculum* 54 (1979), 492–9.

'The organization of an English Cistercian nunnery in Lincolnshire', *Cîteaux* 33 (1982), 333–50; *see also* section xiii.

Hicks, Michael, 'The English Minoresses and their early benefactors, 1281–1367', in Loades (ed.), *Monastic Studies*, 1, pp. 158–70.

Holdsworth, C. J., 'Christina of Markyate', in Baker (ed.), *Medieval Women*, pp. 185–204.

Hope, W. H. St John: *see* section ix.

Knowles, David, 'The revolt of the lay brothers of Sempringham', *English Historical Review* 50 (1935), 465–87.

Meyer, M. A., 'Patronage of West-Saxon royal nunneries in late Anglo-Saxon England', *Revue Bénédictine* 91 (1981), 332–58.

'Women in the tenth-century monastic reform', *Revue Bénédictine* 87 (1977), 34–61.

Millinger, Susan, 'Humility and power: Anglo-Saxon nuns in Anglo-Norman hagiography', in Nichols and Shank (eds.), *Distant Echoes*, pp. 115–29.

Nichols, John A., 'The internal organization of English Cistercian nunneries', *Cîteaux* 30 (1979), 23–40.

Power, Eileen, *Medieval English nunneries c. 1275–1535* (Cambridge, 1922).

Thompson, A. Hamilton, 'Double monasteries and the male element in nunneries', in *The ministry of women. A report by a committee appointed by his grace the lord archbishop of Canterbury* (London, 1919), pp. 145–64.

Thompson, Sally P., 'Why English nunneries had no history. A study of the problems of English nunneries founded after the Conquest', in Nichols and Shank (eds.), *Distant Echoes*, pp. 131–49.

Women religious: the founding of English nunneries after the Norman Conquest (Oxford, 1991).

Warren, A. K., *Anchorites and their patrons in medieval England* (California, 1985).

'The nun as anchoress. England 1100–1500', in Nichols and Shank (eds.), *Distant Echoes*, pp. 197–212.

Williams, D. H., 'Cistercian nunneries in medieval Wales', *Cîteaux, Commentarii Cistercienses* 26 (1975), 155–74.

Yorke, Barbara, '"Sisters under the skin"?: Anglo-Saxon nuns and nunneries in southern England', *Reading Medieval Studies* 15 (1989), 95–117.

(viii) The mendicant orders

PRIMARY SOURCES

The major source for the coming of the friars to Britain is the history of Brother Thomas of Eccleston. This is available in a Latin edition by A. G. Little, *Fratris Thomae Vulgo Dicti de Eccleston, Tractatus de Adventu Fratrum Minorum in Angliam*, 1st English edn (Manchester, 1951); and it has been translated as *The coming of the Franciscans, Thomas of Eccleston, De adventu fratrum minorum in Angliam*, by Leo Sherley-Price (London, 1964).

SECONDARY WORKS

The history and constitutions of the Dominicans and Franciscans are treated in a number of works. See especially: Rosalind B. Brooke, *Early Franciscan government, Elias to Bonaventura* (Cambridge, 1959); John Moorman, *A history of the Franciscan order* (Oxford, 1968); R. F. Bennett, *The early Dominicans* (Cambridge, 1937); William A. Hinnebusch, *The history of the Dominican order* (2 vols., New York, 1965), and *The Dominicans: a short history* (New York, 1975).

The friars in Britain

Brooke, Rosalind, B., *The coming of the friars* (London, 1975).

Cotton, Charles, *The Grey Friars of Canterbury* (Manchester, 1924, repr. Ridgewood, NJ, 1965).

Dobson, Barrie, 'Mendicant ideal and practice in medieval York', in Addyman and Black (eds.), *Archaeological papers from York* (*see* section ix), pp. 109–22.

Easterling, R. C., 'The friars in Wales', *Archaeologia Cambrensis*, 6th series, 14 (1914), 323–56.

Egan, Keith J., 'Medieval Carmelite houses: England and Wales', *Carmelus* 16 (1969), 142–226.

'Medieval Carmelite houses: Scotland', *Carmelus* 19 (1972), 107–12.

Hinnebusch, William A., *The early English Friars Preacher* (Rome, 1951).

Humphreys, K. W.: *see* section xi.

Hutton, Edward, *The Franciscans in England 1224–1538* (London, 1926).

Kingsford, C. L., *The Grey Friars of London* (Aberdeen, 1915, repr. Ridgewood, NJ, 1965).

Little, A. G., *Franciscan papers, lists, and documents* (Manchester, 1943).

Studies in English Franciscan history (Manchester, 1917).

The Grey Friars of Oxford (Oxford, Oxford Historical Society, 1892).

Martin, A. R.: *see* section ix.

Moorman, John R. H., *The Franciscans in England* (Oxford, 1974).

The Grey Friars in Cambridge, 1225–1538 (Cambridge, 1952).

Roth, F., *The English Austin Friars 1249–1538* (2 vols., New York, 1961–6).

Smalley, B.: *see* section xi.

For works on aspects of the scholarship of the friars, *see* section xi.

(ix) Architecture and the monastic plan

Addyman, P. V. and V. E. Black (eds.), *Archaeological papers from York presented to M. W. Barley* (York, 1984).

Anderson, Freda, 'St Pancras Priory, Lewes: its architectural development to 1200', in *Anglo-Norman Studies XI: Proceedings of the Battle Conference 1988* (Woodbridge, 1989), pp. 1–35.

Blair, John (ed.), *Saint Frideswide's monastery at Oxford: archaeological and architectural studies* (Oxford Architectural and Historical Society, 1990).

Brooke, Christopher, 'St Bernard, the patrons and monastic planning', in Christopher Norton and David Park (eds.), *Cistercian art and architecture in the British Isles* (Cambridge, 1986, repr. 1988), pp. 11–23.

Butler, Lawrence, 'Medieval urban religious houses', *Council for British Archaeology Research Report* 61 (1987), 167–76.

'The houses of the mendicant orders in Britain: recent archaeological work', in Addyman and Black (eds.), *Archaeological papers from York*, pp. 123–36.

Coldstream, Nicola, 'Cistercian architecture from Beaulieu to the Dissolution', in Norton and Park (eds.), *Cistercian art and architecture*, pp. 139–59.

Medieval craftsmen: masons and sculptors (London: British Museum, 1991).

Coppack, Glyn, *Abbeys and priories* (London: English Heritage, 1990).

Cruden, Stewart, *Scottish abbeys* (Edinburgh: HMSO, 1960).

Fergusson, Peter, *Architecture of solitude: Cistercian abbeys in twelfth-century England* (Princeton, NJ, 1984).

'The twelfth-century refectories at Rievaulx and Byland Abbeys', in Norton and Park (eds.), *Cistercian art and architecture*, pp. 160–80.

Fernie, Eric, 'The effect of the Conquest on Norman architectural patronage', in *Anglo-Norman Studies IX: Proceedings of the Battle Conference 1986* (Woodbridge, 1987), pp. 71–85.

Gem, Richard, 'Bishop Wulfstan II and the Romanesque cathedral church of Worcester', in Glenys Popper (ed.), *Medieval art and architecture at Worcester Cathedral*, The British Archaeological Association Conference Transactions for the year 1975 (1978), pp. 15–37.

Gilchrist, Roberta, 'Community and self: perceptions and use of space in medieval monasteries', *Scottish Archaeological Review* 6 (1989), 55–64.

Gilchrist, Roberta and Harold Mytum (eds.), *The archaeology of rural monasteries in England and Wales*, BAR British Series 203 (Oxford, 1989).

Gilyard-Beer, R., *Abbeys* (London: HMSO, 1959, repr. with amendments, 1968).

Gilyard-Beer, R. and Glyn Coppack, 'Excavations at Fountains Abbey, north Yorkshire, 1979–80; the early development of the monastery', *Archaeologia* 108 (1986), 147–88.

Greene, J. Patrick, *Norton Priory: the archaeology of a medieval religious house* (Cambridge, 1989).

Hare, J. N., 'The buildings of Battle Abbey: a preliminary survey', in *Proceedings of the Battle Conference on Anglo-Norman Studies III 1980* (Woodbridge, 1981), pp. 78–95 and 212–13.

Holdsworth, Christopher, 'The chronology and character of early Cistercian legislation on art and architecture', in Norton and Park (eds.), *Cistercian art and architecture*, pp. 40–55.

Hope, W. H. St John, 'The Gilbertine priory of Watton, in the East Riding of Yorkshire', *Archaeological Journal* 58 (1901), 1–34.

Klukas, Arnold William, 'The architectural implications of the *Decreta Lanfranci*', in *Anglo-Norman Studies VI: Proceedings of the Battle Conference 1983* (Woodbridge, 1984), pp. 136–71.

Knowles, David, 'The monastic buildings of England', in *The historian and character* (Cambridge, 1963), pp. 179–212.

Martin, A. R., *Franciscan architecture in England* (Manchester, 1937).

Morris, Richard, *Cathedrals and abbeys of England and Wales* (London, 1979).

New, Anthony, *A guide to the abbeys of England and Wales* (London, 1985).

A guide to the abbeys of Scotland with priories and collegiate churches (London, 1988).

Norton, Christopher and David Park (eds.), *Cistercian art and architecture in the British Isles* (Cambridge, 1986, repr. 1988).

Platt, C. P. S., *The abbeys and priories of medieval England* (London, 1984).

Schaefer, J. O., 'The earliest churches of the Cistercian order', in M. P. Lillich (ed.), *Studies in Cistercian art and architecture*, 1 (Kalamazoo, MI, 1982), pp. 1–12.

Thompson, M. W., 'Associated monasteries and castles in the Middle Ages: a tentative list', *Archaeological Journal* 143 (1986), 305–21.

Wilson, Christopher, 'Abbot Serlo's church at Gloucester (1089–1100): its place in Romanesque architecture', in T. A. Heslop and V. A. Sekules (eds.), *Medieval art and architecture at Gloucester and Tewkesbury*, The British Archaeological Association Conference Transactions for the year 1981 (1985), pp. 52–83.

'The Cistercians as "missionaries of Gothic" in northern England', in Norton and Park (eds.), *Cistercian art and architecture*, pp. 86–116.

(x) Daily life, government and discipline

PRIMARY SOURCES

References to the constitutions of the various religious orders and groups are given in the appropriate sections above. Other governmental and constitutional aspects are covered in H. E. Salter (ed.), *Chapters of the Augustinian canons*, Canterbury and York Society 29 (London, 1922, repr. 1969); W. A. Pantin (ed.), *Chapters of the English Black Monks*, Camden series, 3rd series, 45, 47, 54 (London, 1931–7); G. F. Duckett, *Visitations and chapters of the order of Cluny* (Lewes, 1893), and *Visitations of English Cluniac foundations* (London, 1890).

For descriptions of life in a medieval monastery see Jocelin of Brakelond, *Chronicle of the abbey of Bury St Edmunds*, edited and translated by H. E. Butler, Nelsons Medieval Classics (London, 1949). There is a new translation by Diana

Greenway and Jane Sayers (Oxford, 1989). See also the extracts from Matthew Paris, monk of St Albans, in *Chronicles of Matthew Paris, monastic life in the thirteenth century*, edited and translated by Richard Vaughan (Gloucester, 1986).

SECONDARY WORKS
Aspects of the daily life of the religious orders are treated in many of the general works cited in section (i) above. The following books and articles are on specific topics of daily life, liturgy, administration, visitation, personnel etc.

Chadd, D. F. L., 'Liturgy and liturgical music: the limits of uniformity', in Norton and Park (eds.), *Cistercian art and architecture* (*see* section ix), pp. 299–314.

Cheney, C. R., *Episcopal visitation of monasteries in the thirteenth century* (Manchester, 1931; 2nd edn, 1983).

'The papal legate (John of Ferentino) and English monasteries', *English Historical Review* 46 (1931), 443–52.

Dutton, Marsha L., 'The conversion and vocation of Aelred of Rievaulx: a historical hypothesis', in Daniel Williams (ed.), *England in the twelfth century. Proceedings of the 1988 Harlaxton symposium* (Woodbridge, 1990), pp. 31–49.

Hill, Rosalind, 'Bishop Sutton and the institution of heads of religious houses in the diocese of Lincoln', *English Historical Review* 58 (1943), 201–9.

Holdsworth, Christopher J., 'The blessings of work: the Cistercian view', in *Sanctity and secularity, the church and the world*, Studies in Church History 10 (Oxford, 1973), pp. 59–76.

Lynch, J. H., 'Monastic recruitment in the eleventh and twelfth centuries: some social and economic considerations', *American Benedictine Review* 26 (1975), 425–47.

Simoniacal entry into religious life from 1000 to 1260: a social, economic and legal study (Columbus, OH, 1976).

Russell, J. C., 'The clerical population of medieval England', *Traditio* 2 (1944), 177–212.

Williams, David H., 'Layfolk within Cistercian precincts', in Judith Loades (ed.), *Monastic Studies*, II (Bangor, 1991), pp. 87–117.

(xi) Literary, artistic and intellectual activities

Baker, L. G. D., 'The genesis of English Cistercian chronicles: the foundation history of Fountains Abbey', I and II, *Analecta Sacri Ordinis Cisterciensis* 25 (1969), 14–41 and 31 (1976 for 1975), 179–212.

Bestul, Thomas H., 'St Anselm, the monastic community at Canterbury, and devotional writing in late Anglo-Saxon England', *Anselm Studies* 1 (1983), 185–98.

Brett, Martin, 'John of Worcester and his contemporaries', in R. H. C. Davis and J. M. Wallace-Hadrill (eds.), *The writing of history in the middle ages: essays presented to R. W. Southern* (Oxford, 1981), pp. 101–26.

Catto, J. I. (ed.), *The history of the University of Oxford*, I, *The early Oxford Schools* (Oxford, 1984, repr. with corrections, 1986).

Cheney, C. R., 'English Cistercian libraries: the first century', in *Medieval texts and studies* (Oxford, 1973), pp. 328–45.

Evans, G. R., *Old arts and new theology* (Oxford, 1980).

Golding, Brian, 'Wealth and artistic patronage at twelfth-century St Albans', in Sarah Macready and F. H. Thompson (eds.), *Art and patronage in the English Romanesque* (London, Society of Antiquaries occasional papers, n.s., VIII (1986)), pp. 107–17.

Gransden, A., *Historical writing in England c. 550 to c. 1307* (London, 1974).

Holdsworth, C. J., 'John of Ford and English Cistercian writing, 1167–1214', *Transactions of the Royal Historical Society*, 5th series, 11 (1961), 117–36.

Humphreys, K. W., *The book provisions of the friars* (London, 1964).

Humphreys, K. W. (ed.), *The friars' libraries*, Corpus of British medieval library catalogues (London, the British Library and the British Academy, 1990).

Hunt, R. W., 'English learning in the late twelfth century', *Transactions of the Royal Historical Society*, 4th series, 19 (1936), 19–42.

Hunter Blair, Peter, 'Some observations on the *Historia Regum* attributed to Symeon of Durham', in Kenneth Jackson et al. (eds.), *Celt and Saxon: Studies in the early British border* (Cambridge, 1964), pp. 63–118.

Ker, N. R., *Medieval libraries of Great Britain*, 2nd edn (London, Royal Historical Society, 1964).

Leclercq, Jean, *The love of learning and the desire for God: a study of monastic culture* (New York, Fordham University Press, 1961, repr. 1982).

McLachan, Elizabeth Parker, *The scriptorium of Bury St Edmunds in the twelfth century* (New York and London, 1986).

Postles, David, 'The learning of Austin canons: the case of Oseney Abbey', *Nottingham Medieval Studies* 29 (1985), 32–43.

Smalley, B., 'Robert Bacon and the early Dominican school at Oxford', *Transactions of the Royal Historical Society*, 4th series, 30 (1948), 1–19.

The Study of the Bible in the middle ages, 3rd edn (Oxford, 1983).

Southern, R. W., 'Aspects of the European tradition of historical writing: 4: the sense of the past', *Transactions of the Royal Historical Society*, 5th series, 23 (1973), 243–63.

Thomson, Rodney, *Manuscripts from St Albans Abbey, 1066–1235* (Woodbridge, 1992).

'The library of Bury St Edmunds abbey in the eleventh and twelfth centuries', *Speculum* 47 (1972), 617–45.

William of Malmesbury (Woodbridge, 1987).

Wormald, F. and C. E. Wright, *The English library before 1700* (London, 1958).

(xii) Religious houses and their patrons

Baker, Derek, 'Patronage in the early twelfth-century church: Walter Espec, Kirkham and Rievaulx', in B. Jaspert and R. Mohr (eds.), *Festschrift Winfried Zeller* (Marburg, 1975), pp. 92–100.

Barrow, G. W. S., 'Scottish rulers and the religious orders, 1070–1153', *Transactions of the Royal Historical Society*, 5th series, 3 (1953), 77–100.

Brooke, Christopher N. L., 'King David I of Scotland as a connoisseur of the religious orders', in C. E. Viola (ed.), *Mediaevalia Christiana XIe–XIIIe siècles. Hommage à Raymonde Foreville* (Paris, 1989), pp. 320–34.

'Princes and kings as patrons of monasteries, Normandy and England', in *Il monachesimo e la riforma ecclesiastica (1049–1122)*, Miscellanea del centro di studi medieovali 6 (Milan, 1971), pp. 125–52.

Coulton, G. G., *Scottish abbeys and social life* (Cambridge, 1933).

Dyson, A. G., 'The monastic patronage of Bishop Alexander of Lincoln', *Journal of Ecclesiastical History* 26 (1975), 1–24.

Franklin, Michael, 'The bishops of Winchester and the monastic revolution', in *Anglo-Norman Studies XII: Proceedings of the Battle Conference 1989* (Woodbridge, 1990), pp. 47–65.

Golding, Brian, 'Anglo-Norman knightly burials', in C. Harper-Bill and R. Harvey (eds.), *The ideals and practice of medieval knighthood* (Woodbridge, 1986), pp. 35–48.

'Burials and benefactions: an aspect of monastic patronage in thirteenth-century England', in W. M. Ormrod (ed.), *England in the thirteenth century: proceedings of the 1984 Harlaxton symposium* (Woodbridge, 1986), pp. 64–75.

Gougaud, L., 'Deathbed clothing with the religious habit', in *Devotional and ascetic practices in the Middle Ages* (London, 1927), pp. 131–45.

Hallam, Elizabeth M., 'Henry II as a founder of monasteries', *Journal of Ecclesiastical History* 28 (1977), 113–32.

'Monasteries as "war memorials": Battle Abbey and La Victoire', in *The church and war*, Studies in Church History 20 (Oxford, 1983), pp. 47–57.

Harper-Bill, Christopher, 'The piety of the Anglo-Norman knightly class', in *Proceedings of the Battle Conference on Anglo-Norman Studies*, II (Woodbridge, 1979), pp. 63–77 and 173–6.

Hockey, Frederick, 'The house of Redvers and its monastic foundations', in *Anglo-Norman Studies V: Proceedings of the Battle Conference 1982* (Woodbridge, 1983), pp. 146–52.

Hollister, C. Warren, 'St Anselm on lay investiture', in *Anglo-Norman Studies X: Proceedings of the Battle Conference 1987* (Woodbridge, 1988), pp. 145–58.

Mason, Emma, 'A truth universally acknowledged', in *The church in town and countryside*, Studies in Church History 16 (Oxford, 1979), pp. 171–86.

'*Pro statu et incolumnitate regni mei*: royal monastic patronage 1066–1154', in *Religion and national identity*, Studies in Church History 18 (Oxford, 1982), pp. 99–117.

'*Timeo barones et dona ferentes*', in *Religious motivation: biographical and sociological problems for the church historian*, Studies in Church History 15 (Oxford, 1978), pp. 61–75.

Mortimer, Richard, 'Religious and secular motives for some English monastic foundations', *Religious motivation: biographical and sociological problems for the church historian*, Studies in Church History 15 (Oxford, 1978), pp. 77–85.

Nicholl, D., *Thurstan, archbishop of York 1114–1140* (York, 1964).

Postles, D., '"*Patronus et advocatus noster*": Oseney Abbey and the Oilly family', *Historical Research* 60 (1987), 100–2.

Stringer, K. J., 'The early lords of Lauderdale, Dryburgh Abbey and St Andrew's Priory at Northampton', in K. J. Stringer (ed.), *Essays on the nobility of medieval Scotland* (Edinburgh, 1985), pp. 44–71.

Thompson, Benjamin, 'From "alms" to "spiritual services", the function and status of monastic property in medieval England', in Judith Loades (ed.), *Monastic Studies*, II (Bangor, 1991), pp. 227–61.

Walker, John, 'The motives of patrons of the order of St Lazarus in England in the twelfth and thirteenth centuries', in Judith Loades (ed.), *Monastic Studies*, I (Bangor, 1990), pp. 170–81.

Ward, J. C., 'Fashions in monastic endowment: the foundations of the Clare family, 1066–1314', *Journal of Ecclesiastical History* 32 (1981), 427–51.

Wardrop, Joan, *Fountains Abbey and its benefactors 1132–1300* (Kalamazoo, MI, 1987).

Williams, Glanmor, 'The church and monasticism in the age of conquest', in Trevor Herbert and Gareth Elwyn Jones (eds.), *Edward I and Wales* (Cardiff, 1988), pp. 97–122.

Wood, Susan, *English monasteries and their patrons in the thirteenth century* (Oxford, 1955).

(xiii) Economy and finance

The estates and economy of individual houses are discussed in works listed in earlier sections. See also:

Barley, M., 'Cistercian land clearances in Nottinghamshire: three deserted villages and their moated successor', *Nottingham Medieval Studies* I (1957), 75–89.

Bishop, T. A. M., 'Monastic granges in Yorkshire', *English Historical Review* 51 (1936), 193–214.

Bond, C. J., 'Water management in the rural monastery', in Gilchrist and Mytum (eds.), *Archaeology of rural monasteries* (*see* section ix), pp. 83–111.

Bowen, E. G., 'The monastic economy of the Cistercians at Strata Florida', *Ceredigion* I (1950), 34–7.

Burton, Janet E., 'Monasteries and parish churches in eleventh- and twelfth-century Yorkshire', *Northern History* 23 (1987), 39–50.

Chibnall, Marjorie, 'Monks and pastoral work: a problem in Anglo-Norman history', *Journal of Ecclesiastical History* 18 (1967), 165–72.

Constable, Giles, 'Monastic possession of churches and "spiritualia" in the Age of Reform', *Il monachesimo e la riforma ecclesiastica (1049–1122)* (Milan, 1971), pp. 304–31.

Monastic tithes from their origins to the twelfth century (Cambridge, 1964).

Currie, C. K., 'The role of fishponds in the monastic economy', in Gilchrist and Mytum (eds.), *Archaeology of rural monasteries*, pp. 147–72.

Donkin, R. A., 'Cattle on the estates of medieval Cistercian monasteries in England and Wales', *Economic History Review*, series 2, 15 (1962–3), 31–53.

'Settlement and depopulation on Cistercian estates during the twelfth and thirteenth centuries, especially in Yorkshire', *Bulletin of the Institute of Historical Research* 33 (1960), 141–65.

'The Cistercian grange in England in the 12th and 13th centuries', *Studia Monastica* 6 (1964), 95–144.

'The Cistercian settlement and English royal forests', *Cîteaux* 11 (1960), 117–32.

The Cistercians: studies in the geography of medieval England and Wales, Pontifical Institute of Mediaeval Studies, Studies and Texts 38 (Toronto, 1978).

'The English Cistercians and assarting, c. 1128–1350', *Analecta Sacri Ordinis Cisterciensis* 20 (1964), 49–75.

'The urban property of the Cistercians in medieval England', *Analecta Sacri Ordinis Cisterciensis* 15 (1959), 104–31.

Donnelly, James S., 'Changes in the grange economy of English and Welsh Cistercian abbeys, 1300–1540', *Traditio* 10 (1954), 399–458.

The decline of the medieval Cistercian laybrotherhood, Fordham University Studies, History Series 3 (Fordham, 1949).

Eckenrode, T. R., 'The English Cistercians and their sheep during the middle ages', *Cîteaux* 24 (1973), 250–66.

Graham, Rose, 'The finance of Malton Priory 1244–1257', in *English ecclesiastical studies* (London, 1929), pp. 247–70.

'The taxation of Pope Nicholas IV', *English Historical Review* 23 (1908), 434–54, reprinted in *English ecclesiastical studies*, pp. 271–301.

Graves, Coburn V., 'Stixwould in the market place', in Nichols and Shank (eds.), *Distant echoes* (*see* section vii), pp. 213–35.

'The economic activities of the Cistercians in medieval England (1128–1307)', *Analecta Sacri Ordinis Cisterciensis* 13 (1957), 30–60.

Harper-Bill, Christopher, 'Battle Abbey and its East Anglian churches', in Christopher Harper-Bill, Christopher J. Holdsworth and Janet L. Nelson (eds.), *Studies in medieval history presented to R. Allen Brown* (Woodbridge, 1989), pp. 159–72.

'The struggle for benefices in twelfth-century East Anglia', in *Anglo-Norman Studies XI: Proceedings of the Battle Conference 1988* (Woodbridge, 1989), pp. 113–32.

Jenkinson, H., 'William Cade: a financier of the twelfth century', *English Historical Review* 28 (1913), 209–27.

Kemp, Brian, 'Monastic possession of parish churches in England in the twelfth century', *Journal of Ecclesiastical History* 31 (1980), 133–60.

Kershaw, I., *Bolton Priory, the economy of a northern monastery, 1286–1325* (Oxford, 1973).

Lloyd, T. H., *The English wool trade in the Middle Ages* (Cambridge, 1977).

Lobel, M. D., *The borough of Bury St Edmunds* (Oxford, 1935).

Mason, Emma, 'Westminster Abbey and its parish churches', in Judith Loades (ed.), *Monastic Studies*, II (Bangor, 1991), pp. 43–65.

Moorhouse, Stephen, 'Monastic estates: their composition and development', in Gilchrist and Mytum (eds.), *Archaeology of rural monasteries*, pp. 29–81.

Owen, Dorothy, *Church and society in medieval Lincolnshire*, History of Lincolnshire 5 (Lincoln, 1981).

Pegolotti, Francesco Balducci, *La Pratica della Mercatura*, edited by A. Evans, Medieval Academy of America, xxiv (Cambridge, MA, 1936).

Pierce, T. Jones, 'Strata Florida Abbey', *Ceredigion* 1 (1950), 18–33.

Platt, Colin, *The monastic grange in medieval England* (London, 1969).

Power, Eileen, *The wool trade in English medieval history* (Oxford, 1941).

Raban, Sandra, *Mortmain legislation and the English church 1279–1500* (Cambridge, 1982).

Richardson, H. G., *The English Jewry under Angevin kings* (London, 1960).

Stevenson, Wendy B., 'The monastic presence: Berwick in the twelfth and thirteenth centuries', in Michael Lynch, Michael Spearman and Geoffrey Stell (eds.), *The Scottish medieval town* (Edinburgh, 1988), pp. 99–115.

'The monastic presence in Scottish burghs in the twelfth and thirteenth centuries', *Scottish Historical Review* 60 (2), no. 170 (1981), 97–118.

Taxatio Ecclesiastica Angliae et Walliae . . . P Nicholai IV (London, Record Commission, 1802).

Trenholme, N. M., *The English monastic boroughs* (Columbia, MS, 1927).

Williams, David H., *Atlas of Cistercian lands in Wales* (Cardiff, 1990).

INDEX

Canterbury, archbps of, 14, 230; *see also*
Ælfheah, Anselm, Augustine, Baldwin,
Becket, Boniface, Dunstan, Edmund of
Abingdon, Hubert Walter, John
Pecham, Lanfranc, Robert Kilwardby,
Robert of Jumièges, Robert
Winchelsey, Stephen Langton, Stigand,
Theodore of Tarsus, William of
Corbeil

Canterbury, Christ Church (Ben. cath.
pr.), 5, 7, 9, 14, 15, 16, 17, 23, 24–5, 27,
28, 35, 39, 42, 113, 138, 140, 141, 146,
162, 173, 174, 180, 190, 192, 193, 194,
195, 196, 197, 231, 251–2; chamberlain
of, 173; mks of, *see* Ælfwine, Eadmer,
Gervase, Robert of Hastings, Wido;
prior of, 24, *see also* Henry of Eastry

Canterbury, city council, 119

Canterbury, friars at: Dom. fr., 113, 120;
Franc. fr., 113, 119, 121

Canterbury, St Augustine's, originally St
Peter and St Paul (Ben. abb.), 1, 5, 9, 10,
13, 15, 24, 25, 39, 136, 184, 193; abt of,
see Hadrian

Canterbury, St Gregory's, hosp. and Aug.
pr., 45, 229

Canterbury, St Sepulchre, pr. n., 94

Cantipule family, 229

Caradoc, St, 61

Cardiff (Glam.), 243; Ben. pr., 34; Dom.
fr., 118; Franc. fr., 114

Cardigan (Cards.): Ben. pr., 211; constable
of the castle, 75

Cardigan Bay, 67, 239

Carew (Pembs.), lord of, 226

Carlisle (Cumb.): Aug. cath. pr., 29, 51–2,
53, 54; Dom. fr., 113; Franc. fr., 114

Carlisle, bp of, *see* Æthelwold

Carmarthen (Carms.): Aug. pr., 48, 61,
177, 192, 226, canon of, *see* Simon; Ben.
cell, 48; church of St Peter, 48; Franc.
fr., 114

Carmelite friars, 109, 111, 118; in Britain,
114–15; site changes, 133

Carolingian empire, 4

Carta Caritatis, 64, 65, 182, 218

Carta Caritatis Posterior, 182

Cartae Baronum (1166), 26

Carthusian Order, 63, 77, 80; in Britain,
80–1

Castle Acre (Norfolk), Cl. pr., 37, 134,
137, 138, 142

Cassiodorus, 200

castles, siting of monasteries near, 32, 33,
34, 69, 131–2, 133–4

Cathar heretics, 110

cathedrals, monastic, 14–15, 28–9, 51–2,
53, 60, 230–1

Catley (Lincs.), Gilb. pr., 99

Cawston (Warws.), grange of Pipewell
Abbey, 254

Cayton (Yorks., WR), grange of Fountains
Abbey, 255

cellarer of monastery, 173; of Brecon, 251;
of Bury, 244, 251; in Cistercian houses,
253

cells, monastic, 29–30

Cemais, lord of, 67, 226; *see also* Robert
fitz Martin

Cerchi, merchants, 259

Ceredigion, 33, 34, 75

Ceri and Maelienydd, prince of, 75

Cérisy (Ben. abb.), 22

Cerne (Dorset), Ben. abb., 4, 9, 16, 27; mk
of, *see* Ælfric

chamberlain, monastic, 173, 251

chapter, daily, 165–6, 172, 180

chapter, general: Carthusian, 80;
Cistercian, 65, 66, 69, 74, 98, 101, 122,
132, 135, 154, 155, 180–2, 183, 188, 191,
225, 256, 257, 265; of Cistercian nuns in
Spain and France, 101; Cluniac, 38;
Dominican, 112, 121, 123, 182; of order
of Fontevrault, 97; Franciscan, 113, 123,
182; Gilbertine, 182; Premonstratensian,
182, 217

chapter, provincial: Augustinian, 60, 183;
Benedictine, 183, 191, 222

chapter house, *see* buildings, monastic

Charnwood (Leics.), 73

Chepstow (Monm.): al. pr., 34; castle, 69

Chertsey (Surrey), Ben. abb., 5, 9, 163

Chester (Ches.), 243; Ben. abb., 29, 31, 34,
140, 198, 218, 223, 224, abt of, *see*
Robert of Hastings; Dom. fr., 113

Chester, constable of, 50; countess of, *see*
Lucy; earl of, 73, *see also* Ranulf

Chesterton (Cambs.), Carm. fr., 115

Chichester (Sussex), Franc. fr., 289 n. 23

Chichester, bp of, *see* Richard of Wyche

Chicksands (Beds.), Gilb. pr., 99

Cholsey (Berks.), Ben. abb., 4

Christchurch (Hants.), Aug. pr., prior of,
222, 240

Christian, bp of Candida Casa (Whithorn),
60

121–2; churches, 139; organization, 122–4; educational organization, 189–90; coming to Britain, 113–14; in Britain, 115, 118–22, 124, 126–30; opposition to, 122; at universities, 190, 203–6, 208; theological writings, 203–6; part in debate about teachings of Aquinas, 205–6

frankalmoin tenure, 211–12

Friars Minor, *see* Franciscan friars

friars' miscellanies, 206–7

Friars Preacher, *see* Dominican friars

Furness (Lancs.), Sav./Cist. abb., 67, 68, 69, 73, 146, 156, 181, 198, 256; abt of, 181

Galloway, lords of, 95; *see also* Fergus

Gant family, 219; *see also* Alice, Baldwin, Gilbert, Walter

Garendon (Leics.), Cist. abb., 71, 72, 73; abt of, 182, *see also* Reginald

Geoffrey, abt of St Albans, 89, 90, 91

Geoffrey d'Ainai, mk of Clairvaux, 155

Geoffrey de Clinton, 51

Gerald of Wales, 19, 76, 167, 173, 182, 186, 192

Germanus, St, 31

Gervase, abt of Arrouaise, 100

Gervase, abt of Louth Park, 188

Gervase, mk of Canterbury, 196

Ghent, Ben. abb., 3

Giffard, *see* Walter, William

Gilbert, sheriff, 47

Gilbert de Fresney, OP, 112

Gilbert de Gant, 217, 218, 224

Gilbert de Leya, 216

Gilbert fitz Richard de Clare, 33

Gilbert of Hoyland, abt of Swineshead, 201

Gilbert of Sempringham, 96, 98, 99, 100, 107, 108; life of, 98; *see also* Gilbertine Order

Gilbert Pecche, 214

Gilbertine Order, 45, 77, 85, 86, 87; foundation of, 98; organization of, 98–100, 103, 165, 172, 182–3; increased segregation in, 106–8; buildings, 148–9, 151

Glamorgan, bp of, 50

Glanville, *see* Ranulf, Roger

Glasgow, bp of, 52, *see also* John

Glastonbury (Somerset), Ben. abb., 3, 4, 9, 10, 13, 17, 24, 25, 27, 28, 141, 229, 234, 237, 257; abts of, *see* Æthelnoth, Dunstan, Thurstan

Glenluce (Wigtown.), Cist. abb., 156

Gloucester: Ben. abb., 34, 39, 162, 163, 198; Dom. fr., 119, 145; Franc. fr., 114, friar of, 124

Gloucester, earl of, 222, 227–8; *see also* Robert

Godeman, abt of Thorney, 16

Godfrey, abt of Malmesbury, 191

Godric, abt of Winchcombe, 22

Godstow (Oxon.), abb. n., 92, 93, 211; abbess of, *see* Edith

Godwin, hermit of Kilburn, 90

Godwin Gretsith, mason, 150

Godwine, earl of Kent, 14, 15

Gokewell (Lincs.), pr. n., 91

Goldcliff (Monm.), al. pr., 30, 34, 176, 211, 234

Goscelin, author of *Liber Confortatorius*, 89

Grace Dieu (Monm.), Cist. abb., 134, 135, 152, 226, 236, 239

Grande Chartreuse, La, 63, 77, 80; *see also* Carthusian Order

granges, monastic: Cistercian, 65, 76–7, 235, 238, 253–7, leasing of, 256–7; emulated by Benedictines, 255; by Gilbertines, 255; of nunneries, 255; buildings, 254

Great Coxwell (Berks.), barn, 254

Great Malvern (Worcs.), Ben. pr., 39, 164, 220

Gregorian reform movement, 44, 46, 49, 53

Gregory I (the Great), pope, 1

Gregory IX, pope, 38, 124, 128

Grenoble, 77

Grosseteste, *see* Robert

Grovebury (Beds.), Font. pr., 97

Gruffydd ap Llywelyn, 225, 226

Gruffydd ap Rhys, 217

guests in religious houses, 50, 179, 221, 229

Guildford (Surrey), Dom. fr., 120

Guisborough (Yorks., NR), Aug. pr., 48

Gundreda, mother of Roger de Mowbray, 68

Gundreda, wife of Roger de Glanville, 95

Gundulf, bp of Rochester, 94

Gunhild, nun of Kilburn, 90

Guyzance (Northumberland), Prem. n., 100

Gwern y Gof, grange of Cwmhir, 226

Gwynedd, princes of, 60–1; *see also* Llywelyn ap Iorwerth

Cambridge Medieval Textbooks

Other titles are in preparation